THE STAKES

THE STAKES

America at the
Point of No Return

MICHAEL ANTON

Regnery Publishing
WASHINGTON, D.C.

Regnery® is a registered trademark and its colophon is a trademark of Salem Communications Holding Corporation

ISBN: 978-1-68451-230-0
Library of Congress Control Number: 2020932587

First trade paperback edition published 2021

Published in the United States by
Regnery Publishing
A Division of Salem Media Group
Washington, D.C.
www.Regnery.com

Manufactured in the United States of America

10 9 8 7 6 5 4 3 2 1

Books are available in quantity for promotional or premium use. For information on discounts and terms, please visit our website: www.Regnery.com.

Sarò animoso in dire manifestamente quello che io intenderò di quelli e di questi tempi; acciocché gli animi de' giovani che questi mia scritti leggeranno, possino fuggire questi, e prepararsi ad imitar quegli, qualunque volta la fortuna ne dessi loro occasione.

Contents

Preface to the Paperback Edition

The Stakes was written between December 2019 and May 2020, then augmented in June as the effects of the spring and summer rioting and crime wave, plus the COVID-19 lockdowns and mask mandates, were just beginning to be felt. Since the book was published in an election year and intended to influence the outcome, a potential reader may reasonably ask, "Now that the election is over, why should I read this?"

The answer is that the recommendation to vote for Trump culminates from an analysis that is truer to America's present and future than it would have been had Trump remained president. The America of 2021 is the America of 2020, only more so, and the country will continue in this direction for the foreseeable future. The trends that Trump might have reversed, or at least slowed, are now barreling forward full speed ahead.

The Stakes is intended as a work of political science. It offers an analysis of the American regime: what it was designed to be and once was (Chapter 2), and what it now is. The book does not presuppose but attempts to show that the government of the founding fathers, of the Declaration and Constitution, of some two hundred years of continuous operation, is today but a memory. While formally still the law of the land, that regime has in practice been repealed and replaced. I describe our present regime in detail in Chapter 3.

Chapter 4 explains the nature and character of those who run it, for a lawless regime is defined above all by those who move the levers of power.

We are now somewhere in Chapter 6. The present regime and its ruling class have consolidated their power. They consider dissent to be threats to "national security" and are looking to wipe out all actual or perceived remaining pockets of opposition. They despise not merely the American founding but also the America of the frontier, of the King James Bible, of folkways and habits stretching back to the first years of the seventeenth century, and they treat those who cherish these things as enemies.

How long the ruling class can maintain their rule depends on their competence and the conformity of their regime to human nature. There are reasons to doubt on both scores, which are explored in the second half of Chapter 6.

When the present regime fails—which must be regarded as inevitable, since nothing human lasts forever—new possibilities will open up. Some of those possibilities are sketched in Chapter 7.

Chapter 8 presents a policy agenda for the Trump second term that will not take place. Yet its ideas could usefully inspire a positive agenda for the Right not just at the national level but, more important, at the state and local levels, where much more is possible for our side.

To know what to do, we must know where we are and what we face. *The Stakes* is intended to help clarify both, and I hope it becomes a useful tool in the coming struggle.

—Michael Anton
Rancho Bernardo, California
June 30, 2021

Introduction

In September 2016, I called that year's presidential contest "The Flight 93 Election." My thesis was simple: a Clinton victory would usher in an era of semi-permanent Democratic-leftist rule. I here add the qualifier "semi-" only to make the point that nothing human lasts forever. But I asserted and still believe that one-party rule of the USA—blue-state politics from coast to coast—could, once established, last a very long time and might end only with the country itself.

Since then, the question I'm most frequently asked is: Will 2020 be *another* "Flight 93 Election"? The tone is almost always one of weariness, a sense that the asker just wants politics to recede in importance, wants all this to be over and things to go back to "normal."

I wish I had a more encouraging answer. Yet nothing in the intervening time—certainly not the first half of 2020!—has shaken my confidence in that earlier judgment. The left has, if anything, become more aggressive, more vindictive, more leftist.

Therefore, not only will 2020 be another "Flight 93 Election," so will every election, until and unless one of two things happens. Either the left achieves the final victory it has long sought, and the only national elections that matter are Democratic primaries to determine who goes on to defeat—inevitably—a hopelessly outnumbered and ineffectual "opposition." Or the Republican Party—or some successor—leads a realignment along nationalist-populist lines that forces the left to moderate and accept the legitimacy of red-state/flyover/"deplorable" concerns. Then real politics—voting, ruling and being ruled in turn, compromise, acceptance of the other side's legitimacy—can return, and the "normal" that so many long for can reemerge.

This book is an effort to encourage the latter outcome. It is part "regime analysis"—an attempt to describe how America is really governed in 2020—and part exhortation: to calm down, to moderate, to reassert common bonds of American citizenship, and to restore the primacy of American principles. Call it "polemical political science."

If the writing at times seems fraught with urgency, that's because the times are urgent. The country appears to be careening toward something very bad. It's long past time to tap the brakes, take stock, and learn to live with one another. Every day that we don't, the likelihood of a bad outcome increases.

■ ■ ■

Never has a man been so fortunate in his friends.

The institutional and personal support I receive from Hillsdale College can't be exaggerated. The opportunity to work with so many longtime mentors and friends and to make so many new ones is literally a dream come true. Hillsdale president Larry P. Arnn in a sense "discovered" me, mentored me, kicked me out of the nest when he judged it was time, continued to guide and nurture my career, and then hired me again for the best job I've ever had. My gratitude to him and his family knows no bounds.

I also wish to thank my boss and longtime friend Matt Spalding, who is not only building Hillsdale's Washington, D.C., presence into a powerhouse, but who read the manuscript carefully and gave many excellent suggestions, all of which I followed. But don't blame him for any remaining misjudgments or mistakes.

My colleagues and friends Tom West and David Azerrad also read the book with care, saved me from many errors of commission and omission, and otherwise just helped make it better. More important than their comments, though, are the years of serious discussion we've shared about the weightiest matters.

Krystina Skurk, a Hillsdale graduate student, provided research assistance and fact-checking that went well above and beyond anything that could reasonably have been expected of anyone. Needless to say—but I'll say it anyway—all remaining errors are solely my responsibility.

I must also state—and not merely pro forma—that this text in no way represents any "official position" of the college but is only an expression of my own views.

The great Victor Davis Hanson—fellow native Californian and the hardest-working public intellectual in the known world—somehow managed to find the time to comment extensively on an early draft. The degree to which I acted on his suggestions is tantamount to plagiarism; I hope he does not mind.

It's clear in hindsight that the decisive event of my life (so far) was finding Claremont, half by accident, in 1994. For that I have to thank Deborah Stone Colloton, then a fellow student at St. John's College in Annapolis, who turned to me one day and declared: "You should be a Publius Fellow." "Great," I replied, "what's that?" Turns out it's a summer fellowship run by the Claremont Institute. Debbie ensured that I got it. Off I went, expecting to be in Claremont six weeks. I stayed three years. In a way, I never left.

My principal teacher and mentor was Charles Kesler, who has in the decades since become my friend and frequent editor. I may have disappointed Charles in leaving grad school early, but I can never thank him enough for all he taught me, and especially for the enormous amounts of time he spent with my fellow students and me, inside and outside the classroom.

The late Harry Neumann taught me more about modernity—especially Nietzsche, of whom he remains the greatest interpreter I have ever encountered—than I thought it was possible to know.

Other important teachers I never experienced in the classroom. It's impossible to quantify how much I learned from the great John Marini. Those who know his work will recognize in these pages his analysis of "modern rationality" and the administrative state. Chris Flannery has consistently encouraged me in every endeavor I've ever undertaken, no matter how far-fetched, and introduced me to a great deal of literature that he thought I should know and knew I would like. Doug Jeffrey—today another of my bosses at Hillsdale—first red-penciled my writing in 1994 with a ruthlessness I found upsetting then but have since come to appreciate. He still thinks I'm too wordy and go on too long, but imagine how much worse I would be without his influence! Others I've been fortunate to know and learn from include Angelo Codevilla, John Eastman, Ed Erler, Ken Masugi, the late Peter Schramm, and the late Michael Uhlmann.

The debts I owe to four Claremont Institute presidents—Larry Arnn, the late Tom Silver, Brian Kennedy, and now Ryan Williams—and to the institute itself can never be repaid. All I can say is that they trained me, and many others like me, to make public arguments that move politics. This book is an attempt to give them something of a return on their investment.

As if all that were not enough, I have Claremont to thank for my best friend, David DesRosiers, and my wife.

Throughout the drafting process, I was fortunate to be able to bounce ideas off of many friends, benefit from their insights, and improve from their criticisms. Among those not yet named are Ben Boychuk, Arthur Milikh, Matt Peterson, Nathan Pinkoski, Julie Ponzi, James Poulos, David Reaboi, Michael Ritger and the "goose group," and Kyle Shideler.

I gratefully acknowledge the late Larry Peterman, who took a callow undergraduate obsessed with the "Great Books" and first helped him understand what they really mean. The fruits of our careful readings of

Aristotle, Dante, and Machiavelli remain cherished possessions that I will carry for life.

In one sense, I have been writing this book in my head for twenty years. But in the more precise sense, I never would have written it at all had not Harry Crocker suggested I do so. I don't think he quite knew what he was getting into when we had that first conversation in September 2019; I certainly didn't know what I was getting into. To say that it's been an adventure would be an understatement.

It would feel wrong not to acknowledge my parents, who did more for me than any parents ever did for anyone, but who—especially my mother—I'm pretty sure will disapprove.

My debt to the late Harry V. Jaffa is explained elsewhere.

—**Michael Anton**
July 2020

CHAPTER ONE

Be Afraid, Very Afraid: California as Case Study of America's Possible Future

"California Is Booming; It's Also a Mess"

—New York Times *headline, December 29, 2019*

A hoary—but not therefore inaccurate—cliché holds that as goes California, so goes the nation. That is to say, social and political trends that first appear in the Golden State eventually—and inevitably—take hold throughout America. Examples include the rise of capital-P Progressivism—Hiram Johnson was elected the nation's first Progressive governor two years before Woodrow Wilson became president—the revolutions of the 1960s, and the tax revolt that in 1978 sparked California's Proposition 13 and two years later swept another California governor, Ronald Reagan, into the White House.

If the old cliché remains true, then the rest of the country should be afraid—very afraid. My parents' and grandparents' California—the California of my own youth—is long gone. That California was the greatest middle-class paradise in the history of mankind. Its promise—which it mostly delivered—was nothing less than the American dream writ large, but better: freer, wealthier, sunnier, happier, more advanced, more future-oriented.

In barely one generation, that California was swept away and transformed into a left-liberal one-party state, the most economically unequal and socially divided in the country, ostensibly run by a cadre of would-be Solons in Sacramento and in the courts, but really by oligarchic power concentrated in a handful of industries, above all Big Tech and Big Hollywood. The middle class—what's left of them—continue to flee high taxes, higher costs, cratering standards of living, declining services, deteriorating infrastructure, worsening quality of life, and an elite that openly despises them and pushes policies to despoil and dispossess them.

Despite California's myriad evident failures, its grandees—in and out of government—consider the state a rousing success and model for the rest of the country. As do their fellow elites in Washington, New York, college towns, and the other True-Blue strongholds of post-1960s America. Perhaps the purest exemplar of today's overclass, Mike Bloomberg—Harvard grad, Manhattanite, Wall-Streeter, billionaire, presidential aspirant, booster of open borders, open trade, and any and all measures that pound down wages—gleefully says that "California can serve as a great example for the rest of this country."

Hizzoner is hardly alone. With apologies to the Red Hot Chili Peppers, America's bicoastal oligarchs and tastemakers celebrate "Californication" as a heady brew of technological innovation, economic futurism, environmental consciousness, social enlightenment, and political progressivism. Or, as one Left-Coast booster put it, "gay marriage, medical marijuana, universal health care, immigrant sanctuary, 'living' minimum wage, bicycle-friendly streets, stricter environmental and consumer regulations."

According to the public presentation of this vision—the marketing brochure copy—the New California formula provides everything, with no downsides: economic growth and job security; equitable distribution of inherently scarce goods and environmental protection; fantastic innovation alongside regulation that protects against every contingency; endless energy without drilling or carbon emissions; social reengineering with no erosion of the habits necessary for a strong economy or stable society—all gain, no pain, all the time.

There's an underside to this vision, though: rising inequality and neo-feudalism, a yawning and widening gap between the wealth and political power of the haves and have-nots, demonization and persecution not merely of overt dissent but of passive refusal to celebrate the new order. These aspects the elites don't talk about but quietly also push. "California is booming"—but only for them. When they say they want the rest of the nation to look more like California, the state's dystopian, oppressive features are a big part—perhaps the biggest—of what they mean.

We shouldn't be surprised. It's the nature of an elite to work to augment, entrench, and perpetuate its privilege and power. The questions for the rest of us are: why should we go along, and how can we stop them?

PARADISE LOST

The lands that, since 1850, have encompassed the American state of California are perhaps the most coveted, prized, fertile, livable, productive, and strategically significant in the world. There may be more important choke points: for instance, Istanbul astride the Bosporus and Singapore on the Malacca Strait. New York and London may be more globally dominant in our increasingly financialized economy than San Francisco or Los Angeles. But acre-for-acre, even before a single soul sets foot on it, California is the richest, most temperate, resource-laden, and enviable place in the world.

Yet just as a block of flawless marble requires a sculptor to become a statue, California didn't build itself. The Americans who began trickling in after 1840, then flooding in after 1849, transformed that geographic raw material into what was, briefly, the most politically, socially, and economically successful society the West has ever known.

California's multitude of natural advantages, combined with the farsighted efforts of its leadership and the rock-solid virtues of its majority middle class, once added up to the nation's highest standard of living, incomes, educational attainment, health, and general well-being.

The public education system—at every level—was the envy of the world, and its strengths reverberated throughout the state. California schools churned out an extraordinary number of workers ready, willing, and able to man the economy at every level, from necessary and mundane brawn up to and including hard science and high tech. The schools' quality and price—free through high school, dirt cheap for post-secondary—encouraged family formation and high birthrates. And those schools, with the exception of certain corners of the most elite universities, inculcated a unifying ethos that gave Californians a common pride in their country and state along with a common sense of citizenship as both Californians and Americans.

California's infrastructure, too, was the envy of the world. Despite the natural fertility of the soil, California—except on the western slope of the Sierra Nevada, with its (typically) abundant snowpack runoff—lacks sufficient water to fulfill the land's potential. No matter. Americans provided what nature omitted via the greatest irrigation system built since the Roman aqueducts—and in scope, reach, and sophistication surpassing even those.

Too "spread out" to make widespread passenger rail practical, economic, or efficient, California instead built the nation's first and best network of highways and freeways, both to facilitate transportation within metro areas and to knit the state together. Already blessed with two of the world's finest natural harbors—the San Francisco and San Diego Bays—Californians built another from scratch and made Los Angeles–Long Beach into the world's busiest container port.

Think, also, of all the world-transforming industries that California either invented, pioneered, took over, or indispensably furthered—including railroads, oil, shipbuilding and navigation, automobiles, aerospace, motion pictures and television, nuclear physics, and (of course) computing. Add to these the state's excellence in ancient industries such as mining, timber, farming, ranching, and fishing, and you have what is arguably history's greatest combination and concentration of old and new.

Despite—or because of—all this world-beating success, California was for decades the country's "easiest" and most pleasant place to live. The vastness of the land and the (relative) sparseness of the population outside the state's (then) few concentrated urban centers made the cost of living on par with the national average. Combine that with above-average wages and well-above-average quality of life, and living and working in the state was actually a bargain. The weather alone—no humidity, very little rain, moderate temperatures, snow only if you seek it—attracted, and still keeps, millions. Then there are the plethora of natural marvels—beaches, forests, mountains, deserts, and nine national parks—to explore within a day's drive. Man-made amenities included first-rate infrastructure, efficient services funded by moderate taxes, and high standards of living.

Outside the state's few truly upper-class enclaves—Pacific Heights, Pebble Beach, Beverly Hills, La Jolla—virtually any man could earn a living and raise a family on one income almost anywhere. Every city, town, and county offered clean, functional housing for every income level, while shared services and infrastructure facilitated a level of social equality across the spectrum. Few even in the upper strata sent their kids to private schools. Beauty and weather aside (the coast is always more temperate than the hot valleys or the cold mountains), there was little difference in quality of life along the glamorous Pacific shoreline than in the vast interior.

It couldn't last. Mid-twentieth-century California was too good a deal, too much of a steal, for people not to come and grab their piece of the California Dream. Which millions did—mostly, at first, other Americans but eventually, and increasingly, foreigners from our South, followed by newcomers from literally everywhere.

Yet the transformation of California wasn't simply inevitable. It was pushed along by deliberate policy—often including a willful refusal to enforce certain laws, which is itself a policy. Nor did New

California just "happen"; it was created no less than the Old. We'll examine the "how" below. But first let's look at the features and contours of modern California.

CALIFORNIA TODAY: SELF-IMAGE

California's ruling class does an excellent job of presenting precisely—and only—the image of their state that they want you to see. Their self-image is perhaps best exemplified by the tourism ads the state beams and streams to the rest of the country. In these slickly produced spots, a succession of movie and TV stars, recording artists, famous athletes, politicians, and other luminaries take brief breaks from surfing, skiing, skydiving, sailing, climbing Half Dome, singing, acting, picking wine grapes, or some similarly upmarket and/or übermenschy activity to look directly into the camera and entice ordinary Americans to come spend their precious vacation dollars in California. The backdrop, too, is always glamorous: a beach, a movie set, a Napa winery, the Golden Gate Bridge, the Santa Monica Pier, Big Sur, the Avenue of the Giants, and the like.

This is not merely a matter of putting one's best foot forward; it's rather a state whose self-conception pretends that its less-than-glamorous parts simply don't exist. In those ads, freshly paved roads are crawling with hybrid and electric cars on their way to the coast—but look in vain for pickups traversing potholed gravel beds on their way to a Kern County oil field. Dinner plates are bursting with organic vegetables—but the Great Central Valley, 11 percent of the state by land area, where most of that food is grown? Out of sight. As are the various barrios, ghettos, trailer parks, tent cities, and people sleeping in their cars. All of those are integral to modern California, too, but California's grandees don't want you to notice—or know about—any of them.

In the real California, six big industries dominate: technology, entertainment, tourism, the ports (Chinese container ships don't unload themselves), agriculture, and government. California's image-makers prefer to focus on the first three, with limited nods to agriculture (cult Cabs and artisanal cheese, yes; Salinas Valley lettuce or Fresno County raisins, no) and government. Not, needless to say, the latter's competence, which is all but nonexistent, but its woker-than-thou "progressivism."

An out-of-state tourist, certainly, and a business traveler, mostly, will only ever see Haute California: the thin ribbon along the coast up to Marin, or maybe Mendocino (north of which the coast gets kind of redneck, or—as we Californians say—"Okie"), plus outposts in the interior such as Palm Springs and Lake Tahoe. Unless he's in the food or farm equipment business seeing clients or suppliers along Highway 99, or petitioning the government, the businessman will likely spend his time in the gleaming glass towers of downtown San Francisco or Los Angeles, perhaps along the Miracle Mile, or—more likely—in the low-key but hypermodern office parks of Sand Hill Road or the toy-stocked preschool playgrounds of tech firms in SoMa and Mountain View. A petitioner in Sacramento will see a junior imperial capital, glitzy and glossy despite its unglamorous location on the Valley floor, whose wealth—like that of all imperial capitals—derives from taxing and spending the productivity of the surrounding provinces. The tourist—unless she's on a budget, in which case she's a fool for coming to California at all—will see the state at its very, very best: the aforementioned natural amenities plus swanky resorts, opulent hotels, and elegant eateries.

Economically, culturally, socially, and even physically, Haute California looks, sounds and feels like The Future. Can anywhere else claim the world's highest-margin, highest-impact, life-revolutionizing industry? Or a globe-bestriding story-telling colossus that journalist John O'Sullivan, at a conference on the Paramount lot, once called "the Athens of a new Hellenistic world"? The state's newer buildings may be awful but—so modern! Richard Meier's ghastly Getty, high above Sepulveda Canyon, set the tone for nearly every major project since: from the Frank Gehry monstrosities that seem to dominate every streetscape to the Killer Robot from Outer Space (Helen Bernstein High School) that squares off across the Hollywood Freeway against Stasi Headquarters

West (Cathedral of Our Lady of the Angels), to the gulag-chic de Young Museum in Golden Gate Park that replaced the gracious original, to the flying-donut-that-just-touched-down-in-Cupertino where Tim Cook and his court rule with velvet-gloved intensity.

A crucial element of the California Dream in the twenty-first century is to marshal the Enlightened Future to confront, conquer, and crush the Benighted Past. Structurally, so far, the wrecking ball has been restrained. That first Getty, the picture-perfect copy of a Roman villa in Pacific Palisades; the Beaux Arts San Francisco, Pasadena, and Beverly Hills City Halls; the Corinthian California Palace of the Legion of Honor? They still stand but are—emphatically—remainders of the Eurocentric Past, reminders of how far into The Future the state has progressed.

One wonders, though, on what terms and for how long the Missions—the twenty-three Spanish-Catholic adobe church-settlements from which California grew—will be allowed to remain. They are historic, surely, and "Hispanic," sort of, but not in the way meant today: non-white and therefore Good. The Missions, and the mission of their founder—and true founder of California, Saint Junipero Serra—stand in stark contrast to the ethos of modern California. He and his fellow Franciscan friars were religious, ascetic, morally serious, and unapologetically ethno-nationalistic. No wonder, then, that at the time of this writing, statues of Father Serra (and of many others) are falling to woke mobs all over the state.

Yet in a way, the friars' missionary zeal lives on in modern California, which insists on sweeping aside—even attacking as evil—norms, standards, and traditions observed for millennia. So you've become used to distinguishing "male" from "female" using English pronouns that predate Chaucer? Here comes the California Wokerati—headquartered in Berkeley, Santa Cruz, Westwood, and the Castro, backed by Malibu and Menlo-Atherton money—to cancel you for being Literally Hitler. Such provocations are in part tests to see if you really belong. Those who can adapt, quickly and enthusiastically—who affirm the New Normal without a moment's hesitation—can stay. Those who can't or won't—well, that's what Idaho is for. California is reserved for the Elect.

For a certain kind of person—ashamed of where she's from, embarrassed by her background, her family, neighbors, co-workers and even friends—visiting or, better yet, moving to California can be a godsend. Finally, she is free of Babbittry, absolutism, colonialism, slavery, fascism, the Inquisition, plastic straws, MAGA hats, and other dreadful things people flee red states to get away from. Finally, the only opinions to breach her delicate ears will be the correct ones. Finally she can bathe in the purified, rarified air for which she was born.

But whether you share these sentiments or not, if all you know of California is Silicon Valley and Hollywood (not the physical Hollywood, which is a slum, but meta-Hollywood, the tony haunts on LA's West Side and along Ventura Boulevard where movies and streaming series are actually written and made), Rincon Hill and Century City, Montecito and Newport Beach, Disneyland and Squaw Valley, Coronado Island and the Ahwahnee Hotel, the French Laundry and Spago, then the state does, indeed, look pretty good.

It's certainly expensive. Leave aside housing prices for now; hotels alone cost per night what within a middle-aged person's lifetime used to cover a month's rent. Restaurants abound, many of them very good, some even spectacular—and spectacularly priced to boot. The shopping, too—at least in Union Square, Rodeo Drive, and Carmel—is world-class.

But be careful. Stray too far in the wrong direction from Union Square into the Tenderloin, or from a newly revitalized downtown LA into Skid Row, and you'll be kicking away trash, tripping over needles, stepping in poop, and fighting off thieves, drug addicts, and the mentally ill. Be careful with that, too: if you actually land a punch, even in self-defense, chances are you'll be prosecuted while your attacker will be hailed in the *Chronicle* or the *Times* as an innocent naïf victimized by the privileged patriarchy (i.e., you).

A VERY BRADY TRANSFORMATION

Perhaps the best lens through which to understand California, Then-Versus-Now, is *The Brady Bunch*, a sitcom that ran on broadcast television (remember that?) from 1969 to 1974. For those who need a refresher, the show depicted a middle-class family with six children (!) whose non-dufus dad (!!) provided, on one income (!!!), not just sustenance but also a spacious semi-suburban detached house, with front and back yards, in the City of Los Angeles (!!!!)—specifically, LA's San Fernando Valley, ground zero for middle-class bliss not just in California but in the entire postwar United States of America. And not just anywhere in that vast, rectangular plain but in Studio City, down at the Valley's good, southern edge, within spitting distance of the north slope of the Hollywood Hills. Oh, and all six of those kids attended clean, safe, orderly, and competent public schools in the Los Angeles Unified School District (LAUSD).

The crazy thing about the above summary is less how fantastic it sounds today but how plausible—true to life, even—it was then. Yes, in those days you really could live a comfortable middle-class life and raise a passel of kids on one income in California—and not just in some distant desert exurb like Lancaster or Central Valley farm town like Lodi, but in New Sodom itself.

Two decades after the series went off the air, Hollywood—even then out of ideas and mining old TV shows for "reboots"—turned its sights on *The Brady Bunch*. But the writers and producers all knew that recreating the prelapsarian innocence of the original couldn't possibly pass the laugh test in far-off 1995—they lived in the real LA, after all. A measure of ironic distance would be required.

The Brady Bunch Movie kidnaps the groovy, double-knit, bell-bottomed early-1970s Bradys and drops them into a contemporary California already in steep decline. The opening frames set up the joke: we see junkies, litter, graffiti, pawnshops, and tattoo parlors lining a decayed Hollywood Walk of Fame. Zoom down from an aerial shot onto LA's famous freeways and they're packed, bumper-to-bumper, in the middle of the day. To ram home the ubiquity of crime in the new, improved California, concertina wire is everywhere. One bumper sticker reads "Driver Carries Only $20—in AMMUNITION," a defiant nod to another common sign of that time, dashboard placards reading "No Radio"—which, translated, meant "Please Don't Bother Breaking My Window; There's Nothing in Here to Steal." A tracking shot shows the 101 North through the Cahuenga Pass to be an absolute wreck, in a state of semi-permanent, never-to-be-completed "repair." (A quarter century later, it still feels like it's paved with medieval cobblestone.) Amber Alerts announce an endless series of off-ramp closures along with the usual litany of Old California natural disasters—earthquakes, wildfires, killer bees, fruit-fly infestations—but one is more specifically tuned to the man-made plagues endemic to New California: "DRIVE-BY GANG WAR RIOT."

Similar contrasts are played for laughs throughout the film, as the naïve, throwback Bradys confront carjackers, gangbangers, and preda-tory immigrant scammers. The older kids' high school is overrun with disruptive punks, many of them ethnic minorities. (Needless to say, this movie could not get made today.)

The film's opening also makes clear that not everyone in New Cali-fornia is simply a parasite or a mark. Well-dressed screenwriters are shown tapping out dialogue on their laptops in trendy cafés while agents (or studio execs) pass by in an expensive convertible barking into brick-sized cell phones. The makers of this mostly forgotten comedy figured out long before the social scientists and politicians that California circa-1995 was already well on its way to becoming the most unequal state in the union and one of the most unequal societies in the world.

As for the Bradys' famous house—reportedly, after the White House, the second-most photographed residence in America—it sold in 2018 for $3.5 million. Granted, the buyer—home-renovation cable channel HGTV—paid a steep premium for the structure's fame. But the initial asking price, a more accurate measure of a similar home's worth, was $1.885 million—well out of reach for any family even remotely "middle-class," even on two incomes. And that's before mom and dad factor in the cost of private school, since these days handing your kids over to the LAUSD (assuming you can't get them into one of its few, intensely competitive "magnet" schools) is tantamount to child abuse. Private school tuition for six kids in the southern San Fernando Valley adds up to multiples of a mortgage that's already laughably unaffordable.

Welcome to New California, where services less than half as good cost more than twice as much; where half of what you pay for in taxes you'd be a fool to use and the other half is either worthless or a guided missile targeted right at your nose; where infrastructure and quality of life crash through the Valley floor while crime soars; where your daily commute time quadruples along with the price of gas; where "middle-class" homes cost $800 per square foot; where—if you're dumb enough to stay—you live far worse than your parents and pay multiples for the "privilege."

CALIFORNIA TODAY: REALITY

Not that the aforementioned glamour and glory, wealth and wellness aren't real. But they're only part of the story—the parts that Governor Gavin, Sergey, Larry, Mark, @Jack, and, down south, Ah-nold, Steven, and the rest of tout-Hollywood want you to see and think about to the exclusion of all else. Yet there are more things on the coast and in the valleys, dear reader, than are dreamt of in their California. Respectfully submitted for your perusal: some of the other relevant features of modern California, not all quite so groovy, but all interrelated and self-reinforcing.

Crowded

The first and fundamental fact to understand is that California today is seriously overpopulated. The official number is just under forty million, but the real figure is almost certainly higher, as the state has been America's primary locus of illegal immigration for at least fifty years and illegal aliens are by definition hard to count. No one really knows how many live in California, just as no one really knows how many are in the United States as a whole.

In terms of density, California ranks eleventh of the fifty states, denser than Illinois and even land-poor Hawaii. But this vastly understates the case, because California is really two states: the narrow (maximum fifty-mile wide, and in many places much narrower than that) coastal corridor and everywhere else. Two-thirds of the population cram themselves into the former, which is less than 15 percent of the state's land area. *That* California is the second-densest in the nation—behind New Jersey and ahead of tiny Rhode Island. Factor out the long stretch of nearly empty coast from Santa Barbara to Carmel, and Haute California is easily number one. All of the above also assumes that the official forty million population figure is accurate, which it almost certainly is not.

It's debatable whether the entire state's natural features could comfortably support—even with sufficient human engineering and ingenuity—a population of forty million or more. I have a native-born friend who insists that, with the right policies and infrastructure, California could easily sustain seventy-five million. Maybe. But that only begs the question: even if it were possible, would it be desirable? Would it be something the people already there would want—would choose for its own sake? This assumes, also, that all those extra people wouldn't do what the majority of all the other newcomers to California do: flock straight to the already jam-packed coast.

Whatever the answer, the simple fact is that California today absolutely does not have such an infrastructure, nor the policies necessary for sustaining such a large population at anything like California's formerly world-beating standard of living.

In 2000, former Republican senator Alan Simpson and Democratic Colorado governor Richard Lamm wrote:

> We both saw California in the 1950s, when it had 10 million people. It was paradise. But it soon grew to 20 million, is now

up to 34 million and is expected to have 50 million people by
the year 2010. We have yet to meet a Californian who wants
50 million neighbors.

For all we know, every Californian has that many right now. But
even at thirty-four million, the state was already a hard place to live.
Again, Simpson and Lamm:

> The entire western United States is under tremendous growth
> pressure, partly from Californians leaving California. The
> most common reasons for departing are too many people, too
> much congestion, too much traffic, a lowering of the quality
> of life. More people have left California since 1990 than actu-
> ally live in Wyoming. Is that a harbinger for the nation?

Overpopulation is the most transformative and harmful of California's vast menagerie of problems, not merely because of what it does in
and of itself, but how it compounds and exacerbates nearly all of the
state's other problems.

Costly

What effect does overpopulation have on housing prices? Suffice it
to say, not even the combined geniuses of the Stanford and Berkeley
Economics Departments have found a way to repeal the law of supply
and demand. More people crammed into the same space increases
demand; prices inevitably rise, especially as supply remains flat or grows
at a slower pace than population growth. Which, in California, it always
does, owing to the ruling class's unlimited appetite for more immigration
combined with punitive state and local regulation that—deliberately—
restricts building.

The median home price in California is now just north of $600,000—
well more than twice the national average and the highest in the Lower
Forty-Eight by far. And that figure is statewide—which is to say, it includes

California's dusty, dingy, depressed, old-and-extractive-economy backwaters. Factor out flyover-California and consider just the coastal enclaves where the celebrated "new economy" operates, and the figure is far, far higher. Then factor in the ratio of average family income to median home price. A financial planning rule of thumb is that your house shouldn't cost more than two and a half times your annual income. Well, in San Francisco, Silicon Valley, and Los Angeles, the median home price is ten times the local average yearly wage. Indeed, eight of the ten least affordable housing markets in the nation, and nine of the worst thirteen, are in California. Even in decidedly unhip, unglamorous Fresno—a city so far removed from haute America that, in the 1980s, Hollywood made an entire miniseries to spoof it—the ratio of median home price to income is 5.4, higher than Boston or Miami!

Can't afford to buy? Sorry, but you probably can't afford to rent, either—at least not a place in which you can outstretch your arms, or without lots of roommates, and not anywhere near your job (see commute times, below). Los Angeles rents alone rose 65 percent in the 2010s, almost twice the national average and twice the rate of income growth in the region. Don't even ask about Silicon Valley or San Francisco, the nation's first and third most expensive markets—Manhattan sneaks in between—where rents are almost double what they were a mere ten years ago, when they were already quite high.

Obviously, with upward of forty million people crammed into the state, folks must manage to live there somehow. The exact nature of that "how" depends on who one is, where one lives, how old one is, what one does, and where one came from. But examination reveals illuminating patterns.

A native son may have a few options. If he's an only child, or if his parents leave behind enough cash for him to buy out his siblings' share of the family homestead, he's got it made (assuming, as ever, that he's fool enough to want to stay). All he has to do is inherit, first, the house—which mom and dad no doubt bought decades prior, at a price-to-income ratio closer to 2:1—and, second, its Prop 13 assessment, which will guarantee, for life, that his property taxes will be a fraction of his neighbors'. Granted, this means he's stuck in place. Pop may have bought in 1970 in the very best part of Stockton, but that was a long time ago—well before that city suffered the nation's highest foreclosure rate following the housing bubble, before its government filed for the (then-) largest municipal bankruptcy in American history, before its crime rate soared to second highest in the state (behind always-edgy Oakland), and before its obesity and illiteracy rates rocketed to second and third worst in the nation, respectively.

All this is before you even ask what jobs are available, at what salaries. Hint: there's not a lot of app development going on in Stockton. The most common employer for native sons and daughters hanging on to California by their fingernails is the government, which pays better, on average, than all but the upper reaches of the private sector (though not nearly well enough to buy a house), offers terrific benefits, and from which you can't be fired.

For a woman, that typically means teacher. Depending on the demographics of her school, teaching can be a better or worse, safer or more hazardous way to make a living. "Rewarding," even, maybe—if she simply loves little kids, doesn't have high expectations, and teaches at a low enough grade that she's not responsible for ensuring that her charges leave her care having learned anything complicated. For a bright, well-educated, and ambitious young lady excited to teach the more advanced stuff to older kids going places and eager to learn, the dream is to crack into one of the state's handful of "super zips" that are coterminous with their own independent school district: Palo Alto, Piedmont, Los Gatos-Saratoga, San Marino, and the like.

But assuming she can even land such a job (the competition is fierce), where's she going to live? Ideally, she would inherit her house—and tax bill—not in Stockton or Barstow but in one of the aforementioned school districts. But that's like being born first son of a duke in a country with primogeniture. It does happen—there are dukes, after all—but there's no way to plan for that or make it happen. And you know from a pretty early age whether you are or aren't.

So assuming she's not born a peer, her options are: 1) Become a super-commuter and (for example) take an apartment in Gilroy—the sweet-smelling "Garlic Capital of the World"—fifty-plus miles south and east, to secure that job in Palo Alto. It'll be a ninety-minute trip each way, at best, and Gilroy isn't exactly a leafy, bourgeois Eden, but at least when she gets home, she can afford her own place. 2) Get a lot of roommates. Even with (say) four gals in a two-bedroom apartment, Palo Alto may still be out of reach, but Fremont, just across the Bay, isn't. Granted, living like a coed might eventually get old, and in terms of quality of life, crime, and other metrics, Fremont is barely a click above Gilroy, but it *is* on the Bay, not in the center of some hot, accursed farming valley, and that alone confers serious psychological benefit. 3) Marry a rich dude, or at least a successful functionary in the New-Blue Economy. This, at least, is partially within her control. And working in a place like Palo Alto means the supply of prospects will be plentiful; as the old saying goes, while the goods may be odd, her odds are good. From what I can observe of Blue America circa 2020, her biggest obstacle will be her own attitude. Are her twenties an extended adolescence, to be spent partying and swiping through Tinder hookups? Or are they for getting serious about finding a husband? But since this dilemma is hardly unique to modern California, let us lower the veil and move on.

One upside our young lady will have over her male peers is that, because immigrant inflow into California never seems to slake—and immigrants have lots of kids (especially relative to the native-born)—the state always needs a lot of teachers.

Not so for those jobs men tend to prefer. The gold standard is firefighter. The pay is great and—so long as you're not in the midst of battling one of the state's annual 50,000-acre infernos—the duties are manageable. But precisely because the livin' is so good, these slots are the hardest to land. Law enforcement jobs are far more numerous, but also significantly less remunerative and more unpleasant—and likely about to become much more so as California hits the accelerator on its

soft-on-crime crusade. That leaves a smattering of civil engineering possibilities and, for the short-sleeve dress-shirt set, the bureaucracy.

In terms of where to live, his options will be the same as hers, with
the seemingly optimistic difference that, since in today's America women
on average earn more than men, his matrimonial prospects ought to be
(economically) brighter. Except that, as demographic data consistently
shows, women don't want to marry men who earn less than they do. So
instead of getting together, our teacher and cop will super-commute
separately to their dingy one-bedrooms on opposite sides of Gilroy—she
to her cats, he to his dogs—and maybe pass one another occasionally in
a Safeway aisle, while, if an inheritance is coming, they wait for their
parents to die, at which point (jobs permitting) they can move to better
digs; or, if one isn't, shelter in place until it's time to retire and then bug
out to spend their pensions in a lower-cost, lower-tax state; but in either
case, dying alone, without (legitimate) progeny.

The adventurous of either sex can try their luck in the private sector.
This is dicey—high-risk, potentially high-reward, but nothing like the
surefire premium over government work that used to apply. The old trade-
off was: government jobs offer more security to compensate for less money.
The new paradigm for the private sector is winner-take-all—and low pay,
long hours, and shriveling benefits for everyone else. That's if you qualify
for benefits at all. California oligarchs laud the so-called "gig economy"
as a massive expansion of workers' flexibility and freedom when really the
purpose is to avoid paying benefits and skirt labor laws that only apply to
full-timers.

The real problem with going private, though, is that—apart from
agriculture, retail, and low-end services—that sector barely exists in
California outside the coastal corridor. Which means that anyone who
wants to take his chances has to live somewhere in or near one of the
most expensive housing markets and cost-of-living zones in the entire
world. Which, as noted, is not easy to do.

Whether their choice is public or private, pretty soon the few native sons
or daughters left in California—especially along the coast—whose roots go

back a generation or two will be only children whose parents or grandparents bought a house before Jobs and the Woz founded Apple—and then didn't sell out to enjoy opulent golden years in Boca. You see, in California, inheritances are dicey. It's not just siblings who complicate matters; so can mom and dad. The original California Dream was to do what the parents of Brian, Dennis, and Carl Wilson (a.k.a. the Beach Boys) did: leave behind a run-down rental in the snowy, rusting East or Midwest and move West into a detached house with two yards, buy your first car, and enjoy perpetual sunshine. Nobody does that anymore; who can afford to?

Today's California Dream is more like a societal reverse mortgage: realize in your mid-sixties that, hey, honey, it's not as big a problem as we feared that our 401(k) is a bit light. All we have to do is sell that San Jose tract house we bought for $62,500 in 1975, and the $1.625 million capital gain—combined with what little we *do* have in that 401(k), plus Social Security—will easily carry us to our eternal rest on the cruise line of our choice. Sorry, kiddo.

As for newcomers—the poor and decently paid alike—they out of necessity end up packed together like Monterey sardines. Illegal immigrants, who live mostly in barrios and farm towns, cram two or more large extended families into smallish houses built with only one nuclear family in mind. H-1B coder-drones earn enough to afford a quarter of a two-bedroom second-story walk-up with outdoor parking, if not in Palo Alto, then at least in Sunnyvale or San Carlos. Having no kids, no wife, no girlfriend, and no prospects helps.

But a house? Forget it—unless he happens to get, first, a green card and second, hired as employee #6 at a start-up that catches venture capital and tech media attention. If the firm goes public or, more likely, gets acquired by one of the big fish, then maybe—*maybe*—his equity slice will be enough for the down payment on one of those 1,700-square-foot 1960s ranch-style homes that dot the valley, which a rich-kid (Napa, Woodside, Russian Hill) friend of mine used to deride as "teacher housing." Which shows his age: no teacher has been able to afford one of those since before my buddy left middle school.

And still, there are more multimillion-dollar homes in California than syringes in the Tenderloin. The median price tops a mil in nearly 30 percent of the state's neighborhoods. Who owns those places and who's buying them? First and foremost, of course, the big winners of the tech lottery: those who build the latest multibillion-dollar photo-sharing app, the venture capitalists who fund them, and the college roommates and other grifters who luck into unearned equity stakes. It's not enough for any of these grandees to have just one California mansion; in addition to the spread in Los Altos Hills, which is just for weekdays, he must also have an Outer Broadway Edwardian for weekends and parties, a place in Pebble (or at any rate somewhere on the water) to unwind, plus one down south for the occasional change of pace.

Second are the other big winners in our financialized economy: bankers, hedgies, private equity mavens, and the like, most—but not all—from out of state. A few techies pick up a Manhattan pied-a-terre but other than that don't much care to spend their lucre outside California. East Coast moneymen, by contrast, prefer to have at least two Golden State crash pads, usually in resort areas—one for scuba and one for golf. Or something like that.

Third and perhaps most consequential are the foreigners: Russian oligarchs, Gulf oil sheikhs, subcontinental steel magnates, hereditary executives of Europe's giant multinationals, and above all Chinese kleptocrats. An estimated one in twelve California home purchases go to non-Americans, many of whom view California estates not as getaways but as safe places to park money, which they never or rarely visit. No matter; the effect on prices is the same: ever upward.

Lest ye think this applies only to mansions, know that foreign money is buying property up and down California (less so in the interior, of course)—all cash, sight unseen. A quarter of all home purchases in the state are now unfinanced. The best story I've yet heard is a 992-square-foot Old Palo Alto shoebox, purchased in 1970 for $35,000, selling in 2014 for $3 million to a Chinese techie with no plan to come to the States. Investment or bolt-hole?

Either way, even if an affluent Silicon Valley couple without Facebook options could manage to scrounge together 600 grand for a 20 percent down payment, *and* earn enough to meet the monthly nut on $2.4 million, *and* have enough left over to renovate or rebuild (no self-respecting tech couple can live in a 992-square-foot shoebox, even if it is in Old Palo Alto), how could they possibly expect a seller to put up with the paperwork and delays of a conventional mortgage when the broker on the phone has a client in Shanghai paying cash?

It's not just houses, either; foreigners are snapping up a wide range of properties and other assets all over the state. There's no end to the way in which foreign money makes California more expensive for Californians, and Americans.

Congested

Traffic may seem trivial—what's a little delay in exchange for living in utopia? But more traffic means less productivity, lower quality of life, and higher carbon emissions. Isn't the left supposed to care about that last one?

They claim to, but their solutions don't extend beyond the fanciful and impossible: ban cars, ban carbon, build high speed rail to nowhere. The practical result? Californians sit longer in traffic than any other people in the nation, suffer nightmare commute times, and spend a greater portion of their incomes on gas—the price of which averages one and a half to two times higher than anywhere else in America because of state-specific regulation.

Anecdotal but telling: When I was in graduate school in the mid-1990s, I frequently drove back and forth between campus, on the eastern edge of Los Angeles County, and my parents' home on the Central Coast. The trip—most of it through sparsely populated stretches of farmland—took exactly six hours without traffic, and there was never any traffic, even on weekdays. The same trip in the summer of 2019 took nine and a half—on a Sunday. Even I-5 through a completely empty stretch of the Western San Joaquin Valley was bumper-to-bumper, like the southbound

405—the world's busiest freeway—at 8:00 a.m. on a Monday morning. It had been a while since I'd made the trip, granted, but I'd never seen anything like *that* before. Estimated population of California, 1995: ~31.5 million. Minimum population of California today? Forty million, and likely higher than that.

Overcrowding increases traffic in the obvious way—more people, more cars, more trips, more congestion—but also in ways not so obvious. First, as seen, it drives up home prices and rents, forcing people to live farther and farther from where they work.

Second, it transforms once-recognizable neighborhoods into foreign enclaves, many monolingual (but not English!) and monocultural (but not American!). Denounce legacy Californians as bigots all you want— and the California Wokerati does, daily—but it's human nature to prefer to live among one's own, with some semblance of community or at least familiarity. It is never explained why it's A-OK—laudable, even—for Mexicans, Hondurans, Salvadorans, Guatemalans, Chinese, Hmong, Laotians, Bangladeshis, Punjabis, Bengalis, Pakistanis, Chechens, Armenians, Iraqis, Afghans, and Nigerians (the whole world is well-represented in California these days) to create their own exclusive enclaves but absolutely disgraceful for "Anglos" (typically a proxy for "white," but a more precise meaning might be "culturally American and speaks only English") to seek any like measure of affinity or commonality. You're just supposed to know the reason—and, I suppose, in modern, hectoring California, few are left who don't.

In any case, on top of not being able to afford living anywhere near one's job, people also move—far—in order to live where they understand the language and feel at home in the culture. One side effect is, again, longer commutes and more traffic.

Crumbling

Those commutes must be endured on roads that were once the marvel of the world but are now potholed, decaying shells of their former glory. The causes of that decay are interrelated. First and most simply, California freeways and highways are handling daily traffic loads about three times greater than their designed carrying capacity. Like anything in the physical world, they strain, crack, and erode with overstress and overuse.

Second, even as California opens its collective arms to an unlimited number of newcomers (at least so long as they're either foreign serfs or woke urbanites), it refuses all but token gestures toward expanding its infrastructure—especially roads, which are for cars, which burn fuel, which are therefore bad. In elite California opinion—often expounded from behind the wheel of a Tesla—roadbuilding is an evil, retrograde act. The solution is always something else: buses, hybrids, and electrics, maybe? But those require roads; try again!

OK, rail! But the state's topography isn't well-suited to rail. Its major population centers are separated by formidable natural barriers. There's a reason the Transcontinental Railroad terminated in Sacramento, not San Francisco: it was hard enough getting over the Sierras. Through the Delta and across the Bay? Even today, Amtrak only goes to Emeryville. San Francisco to LA? Mountains all the way down, which is why California's brain trust sited the "high speed rail" intended to connect those two cities—the celebrated "train to nowhere"—in the Central Valley, well away from either. At least it's flat!

As for Amtrak, if you think the Northeast Regional is bad—dank, slow, late, accident-prone—stay off the rails in California. The evocatively named "Coast Starlight" and "Pacific Surfliner" trains are even more decrepit and breakdown-plagued and, even when they're running, are frequently twelve hours or more behind schedule—after you've already boarded and can't get off. Regional and intracity systems are little better. BART is beset by system and equipment failures, to which it adds the charming additions of urine-soaked seats, high crime, and raving, mentally ill drug addicts. LA's subway could be worse—at least it's relatively new—but if you don't live along one of its few routes, well, too bad.

Which leaves: mixed developments! Live where you work! Walk or bike! The infeasibility of this, given the California real estate market, has, I think, been sufficiently explained.

Then there's the power situation. Even more than Haute California wants to be woke, it desperately wants to be "green." Hence for the same reason it won't build roads, it also won't consider expanding any energy source that can actually generate enough juice to charge more than a couple of iPhones. Yes to solar panels and switchgrass; no to oil, natural gas, coal, and—especially—nuclear.

Which is ironic, since carbon-free nuclear is by environmentalists' own metric the greenest of them all. California built three nuclear power plants at massive expense and has already shut down two of them, with the last expected to go permanently off-line in the mid-2020s. Needless to say, the state has not even tried to replace their generating capacity. Instead, it just imports power—produced, also needless to say, from coal, gas, and uranium—from other states, pushing ugly necessity out beyond California's sacred borders to red states whose troglodytic inhabitants don't mind pollution.

The rolling blackouts of the early 2000s felled one governor (Gray Davis). It remains to be seen what the economic and political effects of their return in the late 2010s and early 2020s might be. The causes are somewhat different, though overlapping: a combination of bad policy, decayed infrastructure, and private sector incompetence. That is, if you want to call the state-backed monopoly PG&E "private."

Whatever your conclusion on that score, California's obsession with "green" means that that state does its utmost to prevent maintenance and modernization of the electrical grid—power stations, transformers, transmission lines, and the like. This theologically driven shortsightedness already caused the worst wildfire in American history (which in 2018 destroyed an entire town—ironically named "Paradise"). To prevent a recurrence, the geniuses who run and regulate PG&E could think of only one solution: when the humidity's low and the winds high, turn off the lights in huge swaths of the state. Which they do, sometimes with a courteous six or even twelve hours' notice, at other times *just like that*, right in the middle of dinner. But never, it should go without saying, in San Francisco, Silicon Valley, or Downtown Sacramento—whose functionaries at the California Franchise Tax Board (the state equivalent of the IRS) well know where the butter for their bread is churned.

Incompetent

Modern California's theological refusal to consider building any-thing new (or at least anything new that's not utterly utopian and unre-alizable) in part serves as a mask for the uncomfortable fact that modern California is incapable of building anything new. Certainly not on time or on budget.

The state's most recent big project may prove to be its last. In 1989, an earthquake damaged the eastern span (there are two, separated by Yerba Buena Island) of the San Francisco–Oakland Bay Bridge. It was quickly repaired (that was then), but state engineers also concluded that the span would have to be replaced: another, larger earthquake could bring the whole thing down.

Initial estimate? $250 million. Originally scheduled opening? 2007. Actual cost? $6.5 billion (!), an overrun of 2,500 percent (!!). Actual opening day? Labor Day, 2013—a mere six years late. And the full story is even worse than that sounds. It took longer—five years—just to navi-gate the lawsuits, political bickering and regulatory hurdles for the new, partial bridge than it took—less than four—to site, plan, design, and build the whole thing in the 1930s. Even worse: the original bridge—both spans—cost one-sixth, in inflation-adjusted dollars, the price tag of the single new span. Worse still: the steel for the new span was made in China. The bolts are already rusting.

And this is the state that thought it could build a high-speed rail line from San Francisco to Los Angeles?

No wonder California has lost its appetite for building real, neces-sary structures and prefers instead to fantasize about space-age trains to nowhere. As historian and native Californian Victor Davis Hanson lamented of his birthplace and home, "[S]ocieties in decline fixate on impossible postmodern dreams as a way of disguising their inability to address premodern problems."

Filthy

There are very few premodern problems that modern California is capable of addressing—which is unfortunate, because it has a lot of them. Allow me, for a moment, to turn the narrative over to the great Tom Wolfe:

> In 1968, in San Francisco, I came across a curious footnote to the hippie movement. At the Haight-Ashbury Free Clinic there were doctors who were treating diseases no living doctor had ever encountered before, diseases that had disappeared so long ago they had never even picked up Latin names, diseases such as the mange, the grunge, the itch, the twitch, the thrush, the scroff, the rot. And how was it that they had now returned? It had to do with the fact that thousands of young men and women had migrated to San Francisco to live communally in what I think history will record as one of the most extraordinary religious fevers of all time.
>
> The hippies sought nothing less than to sweep aside all codes and restraints of the past and start out from zero. . . . Among the codes and restraints [they] swept aside—quite purposefully—were those that said that you shouldn't use other people's toothbrushes or sleep on other people's mattresses without changing the sheets or, as was more likely, without using any sheets at all, or that you and five other people shouldn't drink from the same bottle of Shasta or take tokes from the same cigarette. And now, in 1968, they were relearning . . . the laws of hygiene . . . by getting the mange, the grunge, the itch, the twitch, the thrush, the scroff, the rot.

Wolfe entitled the essay where this passage occurs "The Great Relearning," evoking the hopeful note that a lesson once relearned will not soon again be forgotten. Alas, poor California!

Less than a half-century later, the Golden State can only wish its biggest public health problems were the mange and the grunge. Instead, huge swaths of San Francisco and Los Angeles—two of the richest cities in the history of the world—contend with public urination and defecation at levels exceeding the worst slums of Calcutta. And which, combined with rampant rat infestations, give rise to diseases that definitely *do* have names, though not necessarily in Latin: cholera, hepatitis A, typhus, and the Bubonic Plague, or "Black Death," which killed a third of Europe in the fourteenth century.

The state and its local governments have proven powerless or unwilling to do anything about this. Some of that arises from (again) theological refusal. For example, the elected San Francisco County district attorney Chesa Boudin—biological son of two New Left terrorists, adopted son of two others—announced, several years into the city's ever-worsening "defecation crisis," that his office will not prosecute any "quality-of-life crimes," including public pooping.

But one does not get the sense that, even in the event of theological conversion, California could muster the wherewithal to clean up or demand that its residents use toilets. The will is just not there, and even if it were, the know-how—the civic muscle memory—to perform basic tasks such as sanitation has atrophied from sustained disuse. Legendary New York mayor Fiorello La Guardia famously said of municipal politics that "there's no Democratic or Republican way to pick up the garbage." In California, Republicans are irrelevant (and in SF and LA, nonexistent) and the Democrats either don't know how or don't care. An odd stance for a state that all but invented the modern environmental movement. But when upscale preferences collide with downscale bad habits, the latter always trump—at least until and unless they don't intrude too far into Haute California. So long as they don't, the "privileged" must never "punch down."

Who could have predicted, in the halcyon days of Governors Pat Brown and Ronald Reagan—when so much of the state's magnificent infrastructure was built and its reputation as paradise for the common man definitively established—that by 2020 you could replace the old joke about bears crapping in the woods with "Californians" and "streets" and not have to change the punch line? Yet headlines such as "Fecal Bacteria in California's Waterways Increases with Homeless Crisis" are enough to show that something fundamental has changed. You don't even have to read the article to know they aren't talking about fish.

Dangerous

As a tidal wave of crime engulfed America following various 1960s liberal "reforms," California never sank to *Taxi Driver*–levels of menace and depravity. Los Angeles was hit hard by the crack epidemic and ensuing turf wars of the late 1980s and early 1990s, and parts remain wracked by Central American gangs, but mostly the state has been spared the worst. That is, until recently.

One of the factors that long kept Californians (relatively) safe was the political class's bipartisan aggressiveness against crime. Democrat Gray Davis may have been the most anti-crime California governor ever—and that's saying something. Appointed police chiefs no less than elected sheriffs and district attorneys long shared a firm commitment to law and order.

Not anymore. Electoral pressures are softening mayors' attitudes toward policing. Soros money is electing left-wing, let-'em-go DAs all over the state. Via referenda, voters recently repealed some of the state's tougher laws and decriminalized theft under $950.

The results? Violent crime immediately spiked—by 12 percent between 2013 and 2017 alone—and is still going up. It's not just in the big cities, either. California's once-bucolic rural areas have seen crime surges as well. Victor Davis Hanson reports that his rural neighbors believe three-fourths of the crime in their communities goes unreported because residents assume, from experience, that the police won't even try to bring perps to justice or recover stolen goods.

Big-ticket criminal law still nominally applies to all (though it's worth noting that clearance rates for homicides in non-white communities—especially in Los Angeles County—are rock-bottom). But one wonders how long even that will last. Boudin, perhaps the most pro-criminal DA in the nation, favors babying the violent with so-called "restorative justice." After two young men assaulted an elderly man who was collecting cans to recycle, the SFPD did its job and arrested the assailants. The DA, though, declined to press charges. It's unclear what, exactly, "restorative justice" entails. It's easier to say what it's not: punishment or deterrence.

But property crime? California cops have all but given up. San Francisco now has the highest property crime rate in the nation. A friend tells of reporting—by phone; cops no longer visit crime scenes without dead bodies—a break-in to the SFPD. To his plaintive plea, "Do you think you're going to catch the guys?" the detective responded, "Do ya think we're gonna look?" Across the Bay in Berkeley, a food deliverer was caught on video stealing all the accumulated Christmas presents from the lobby of a building where she had just made a delivery. She was easily identified, but the Alameda County district attorney refused even to issue a citation; property crime in California is now effectively legal.

The situation would appear poised to get a lot worse before it gets better (if it ever does). On his second day in office, that new San Francisco DA fired his seven most-experienced prosecutors—because they were too good at their jobs. Which, as he has redefined, is no longer to convict criminals but to further "social justice." Similar stories can be told throughout the state, anywhere Bloomberg–Soros–Steyer money floods in to determine local elections, which is everywhere.

Since the real cops won't do anything—to be fair, in many cases not because they don't want to but because they've been ordered not to—people with means in the tonier parts of the state have started paying private security forces. Granted, there's not a whole lot rent-a-cops can do; they aren't sworn peace officers and so can't arrest anyone, and even if they could, the courts would just instantly turn the offenders back onto the streets anyway. Which is what they do when the real cops bring them criminals. But at least private security can keep a watchful eye and deter some of the worst mayhem.

Rapacious

Californians pay dearly for all this indifference and incompetence: the nation's highest income, sales, and gas taxes, and one of its highest overall state tax burdens. Only Prop 13—which limits property tax increases to prevent Sacramento's greed from driving people from their homes—saves the state from being number one.

The state also leads the nation in special "excise" taxes on disfavored products, especially cigarettes and gasoline. Smokers are, of course, a despised minority nationwide—didn't they vote for Trump?—but nearly everyone drives, even liberals. In California—despite its elites' fondest wishes—you have no choice. And the state takes pains to make you pay extra for the privilege. Nothing personal against you, just against the auto and oil industries, which California will find a way to get rid of any day now. That, and to fund all its very-expensive-yet-still-lousy services, the state really needs your money.

It wasn't always this way. Competent, growing, thriving mid-century California enjoyed a moderate tax burden—neither the nation's lowest nor highest but somewhere in the middle—and still managed to build most or all of the roads, airports, dams, canals, and power plants that Californians still (over)use today.

But as the state's ambitions soared, its "need" for cash soared right alongside. The middle and especially professional classes who remain pay half or more of their income in taxes, only to be called greedy for not being eager to pay more. The state already suffers from the highest out-migration rate of any in the nation, yet its political class can't stop working to make things worse. It's almost as if they're deliberately engineering policy to encourage undesirables—wrong-thinkers and the retrograde—to leave, the way Mayors James Michael Curley chased Yankees out of Boston and Coleman Young whites out of Detroit.

One might object that this can't possibly be the plan because even California's dullard leaders must know that, without a tax-paying middle and upper-middle class, the state will quickly go broke. But don't assume that they've thought things through or that—if they have—they prioritize fiscal sanity over tribal and class warfare.

As evidence that they don't, we may point to two growing movements. First is the push to restore the state's punishing inheritance tax, which—if successful—will drive scads of productive Californians and their children away.

The second, and potentially far more consequential, is the hunger to repeal Prop 13. The strategy is already obvious: first, repeal the limits for commercial property by denouncing them as a form of "corporate welfare" while disingenuously implying that the provisions protecting homes are sacrosanct. Then once the camel's nose is under the tent, wait for the next "budget emergency"—those happen a lot in California—and repeal the rest. As soon as it becomes clear that's a serious possibility, astute California homeowners will sell before their tenfold tax hike (temporarily) craters the value of their property. Those who miss the window will sell out of necessity, at whatever price they can get. Those "legacy" Californians discussed above, counting on inheriting a home and its Prop 13 assessment? They'll scoot—along with their incomes, assets, and skills. Within a few years, nobody born in—or who even remembers—the old, American California will be left.

Then what happens to all the houses? One strong possibility is that the California landscape will be even more dotted with foreign-owned properties that nobody but the landscapers ever visit—the same way that slender towers with one giant apartment per floor continue to proliferate in Manhattan and Miami. Not for anyone to live in, but so that shady foreigners can launder money and shield assets. The state government not only won't care, it will be delighted to replace native Californians—whom it denigrates as deadbeats—with owners who can actually afford the new-and-improved property tax bills.

But that solution only works for Haute California. What happens to all the "teacher housing" in the state's dry, dusty parts once the old occupants scoot? Are stoop-labor wages somehow going to climb high enough to make post–Prop 13 California property taxes affordable?

Finally, Californians and Californiaphiles alike love to brag that the state boasts the finest public university system in the world. Which, I suppose, it does, if one ignores quality of instruction and measures only by reputation and prestige (and, to be fair, the University of California system still does important work in the hard sciences). Supposedly that system exists to serve the citizens of the state: the parents who pay the taxes that subsidize the campuses, and their kids who might, in an alternate universe, grow up to become productive Californians. And on one level, that's true; in-state tuition is still about half what outsiders pay.

But the system gets around that by aggressively recruiting out-of-staters—and especially foreigners—who pay full freight. In the 2019–2020 academic year, twenty-seven thousand students from China alone were enrolled at the UC System. Every slot at Berkeley, UCLA, UCSD, or Irvine taken by a kid from Shenzhen or Mumbai is one that can't go to a kid from Fullerton or Fairfield. The president of the system, the regents, and the chancellors don't care; they'd rather have the money than serve their state.

Profligate

As fast as the state vacuums up money, it spends it even faster. The last state budget clocked in at $214 billion—well over four times what it was just thirty years ago, when the state's population was three-quarters what it is today. Inflation accounts for less than a third of the increase. Sacramento just loves shoveling money out the door: per capita spending has nearly tripled since 1990. From 2010 to 2020 alone, spending shot up 70 percent—ten times the rate of population growth over the same period.

In terms of per capita state debt and unfunded liabilities, California's state government currently ranks, respectively, third and second worst in the nation—not nearly as bad as New Jersey or Illinois, which are about as solvent as the USSR circa 1985, but broke is broke.

That doesn't stop Sacramento from spending or the voters from green-lighting more debt on trains to nowhere. Actually, in March 2020 Californians did, for the first time in twenty-six years, reject a bond initiative. Perhaps they've noticed how deep they are in the red?

Well, if they didn't know before, they know now. Governor Gavin Newsom—a suit so empty, a hot-air balloon has more substance—in mid-2020 announced that the state is facing a $54 billion one-year gap. Some red states are hurting, too—shutting down the economy for months will do that—but none that bad. That's because of California's ridiculous fiscal policy, which guarantees massive shortfalls every time there's an economic slowdown. The state budget relies overwhelmingly on income tax revenue—and overwhelmingly on a tiny number of the very highest earners. In 2017, an estimated fifteen thousand households—in a state whose population is supposed to be forty million—paid 46 percent of all state income tax. About once a decade, like clockwork—except that you never know the precise time the gong will strike—the American and/ or state economy goes into recession and state revenues crash. It's the silliest and most childish fiscal regime outside the Third World. And everyone knows it. And no one does anything about it.

Suffocating

In a sense, California remains a land where hope springs eternal. Despite being unable to perform such basic tasks as persuading people to relieve themselves into toilets, the state's political class still believes it can legislate or regulate away any and all problems. Hence California imposes the worst regulatory burden in the nation and is America's undisputed leader in pushing loads of business-killing policies at the behest of radical activists.

With a few exceptions, what California really hates is building things—development. The Apple spaceship in Cupertino is cool; and what's one more glass tower on Rincon Hill? But middle-class housing?

That's bad for the environment! (And might, you know, cause prices to go down, which would be bad for current owners.) Hence, anything that touches or might affect the environment is regulated to near-, and often actual, death. California is famous for blocking or stopping building projects in the name of insect species not hitherto known to biology. Some of this intransigence arises from genuine conviction—there are a lot of sincere environmentalists in the state—but much is driven by NIMBY (not in my backyard) or BANANA (build absolutely nothing anywhere near anyone) cynicism that manipulates the rules for private ends.

California's environmentalism is shot through with double standards. God forbid an oil or gas company disrupt the migratory path of a single California quail; executives will be besieged by state apparatchiks and lawyers, while their shareholders foot the enormous bill to "get back into compliance." But wind turbines can slaughter birds by the tens of thousands and . . . nothing. Wind is "green," you see.

California also goes out of its way to "protect" workers—of a certain type. Those in disfavored, old-economy industries are tied up like rodeo calves in a tangle of rules ostensibly written for their benefit. But one wonders how much such workers actually benefit when their employers are so overburdened by compliance costs that they can't afford to give raises, much less expand or hire anyone new. California has the highest workers' comp costs in the nation—nearly twice the national average—yet another factor pushing businesses, and the people who own and run them, out of the state. It's hard not to conclude that this, too, is deliberate. California's message to its boring legacy economy is the same as that for its boring legacy citizens: Just Leave.

Turn to the tech sector and suddenly California's regulatory behemoth becomes obsequiously employer-friendly. Google can fire James Damore for defending his (then-) employer's hiring practices, and the state will not lift a finger to help him or rebuke Google. Tech companies matter in ways that old boring stuff just doesn't. They either aren't targeted with regulation in the first place or, if they are, they lobby for, and get, exceptions and carve-outs. If that fails, the favored few just ignore the rules that might harm the bottom line, confident the state won't come after them. Because it never does.

That's barely the half of it, though. Beginning in the late nineteenth century and intensifying in the mid-1960s, elites inside and outside government—state and federal—have centralized authority in a "fourth branch," the executive branch's agencies and bureaucracies. Those institutions, the people in them, and their governing philosophy and methods have come to be known as "the administrative state." Administrative state rule is fundamentally anti-democratic and anti-constitutional, intended to be rule by "expert consensus." (We will have much more to say about this phenomenon in the following chapter.)

Nowhere in America is the process of administrative state consolidation more advanced than modern California. The state has a legislature, but one wonders why since nearly everything important is decided by unelected bureaucrats, boards, and commissions. (Actually, I do know why: to provide jobs for Democratic politicians.) There's nothing remotely small-d "democratic" about modern California, since statewide elections have only one outcome—the left always wins—and voting changes nothing.

So long as policy always continues to move in the correct, leftward direction—and it always does—elected officials are mostly content to enjoy the perks of office. The idea of serving constituents—that a citizen could go to his assemblywoman for help against a Coastal Commission trying to fine his family into bankruptcy for building a fence—is laughable, a fact which no one knows better than said assemblywoman.

The bureaucrats, though, are deadly earnest and defied at one's peril. Concepts such as the separation of powers and double jeopardy don't apply. Administrative state apparatchiks act as cops, prosecutors, and judges—all in the same action. They can come after you over anything, as often as they want for as long as they want. You can try your luck in the courts, but before you write your lawyer a retainer check, know well that in one-party California, the ruling class sticks together.

Prejudicial

In modern California, hypocrisy and double-standardism aren't merely part of the business climate; they're endemic to the whole society. Former Heritage Foundation scholar and *Washington Times* writer Sam Francis dubbed this system "anarcho-tyranny": complete freedom—even exemption from the gravest laws—for the favored, maximum vindictive enforcement against the pettiest infractions on the disfavored.

Just like regulations, only worse, civil and criminal laws are enforced spectacularly unequally. As long ago as 2002, Victor Davis Hanson—in his prophetic but unheeded book *Mexifornia*—observed that a great deal of California state law simply does not, as a practical matter, apply to immigrants, especially illegals. State officials long ago gave up trying to enforce the law evenly—bureaucrats in the belief that enforcement is unfair to the "disadvantaged," peace officers from the knowledge that there is no point. Illegals don't pay their fines or show up for court dates, and no one tries to see that they do.

But the native-born middle class? Try building an unpermitted addition to your house or evading the requirement to buy auto insurance; the state will crush you. By contrast, illegals on the road are never insured and never face any consequences. If you're struck by one and are naïve enough to call the California Highway Patrol in the belief that it will make a difference, you will, for your trouble, simply watch as the "motorist," uninsured and likely unlicensed, is handed a bench warrant that officer and offender alike know will never be honored. That's assuming the driver waits around for the cop to show—a foolish assumption.

This arrangement partly arises for Willie Sutton reasons: the state predatorily targets its middle class with fines because that's where the money is. It also knows that the middle class can be counted on to pay: both parties to the transaction are well aware of the punishment the state metes out to citizen-scofflaws.

The other motive for the double standard is ideological zeal, a fact that snaps into focus during California's not-infrequent eruptions of left-wing violence. When a conservative speaker tries to come to Berkeley, for instance, you can expect Antifa to show up in force and beat people—and the cops will either do nothing or make desultory arrests that the courts shrug off. After community college adjunct philosophy professor Eric Clanton walloped three people on the head with a five-pound iron bike lock, Alameda County let him go with probation. When Donald Trump campaigned in San Jose in the run-up to the 2016 California primary, his supporters were openly beaten by thugs, all while police stood by and watched.

In modern California, justice ain't blind; she has 20/20 vision—which she uses to tell the good guys from the bad and exempt the former and stick it to the latter. One could be forgiven for concluding that this, too, is part of an overarching strategy to convince the "wrong" Californians to move out.

Theocratic

What California cannot accomplish through regulation and two-track enforcement it attempts to impose via stultifying conformity, backed up by public humiliation and ostracism for those who don't fall in line. California may not be the birthplace of every silly and destructive leftist fad in the nation (Oberlin and its ilk deserve a little credit), but it's at least the origin of most. And the ones it doesn't invent, it quickly embraces with the zeal of Torquemada.

Use the "wrong" pronoun? (With apologies to Donald Trump), you're fired! Object to your eleven-year-old daughter's sharing a changing room with a fifty-five-year-old "woman" who realized just last month he'd always been a girl on the inside? Canceled!

The climate of opinion—at least in Haute California—amounts to medieval piety without God and with similar ferocity against heretics. Some California obsessions are merely trivial, and some possibly even helpful if pursued in a more moderate way. For instance, the world is not made better by plastic bags and is probably marginally improved by their absence. But California's jihad against the offending vessels, and especially against those who refuse to affirm the fullness of their evil, is well out of proportion to any actual harm.

In hindsight, California's last stand against street-sleepers was fought—and lost—more than two decades ago. In the early 1990s, a massive homeless encampment all but covered San Francisco's elegant Civic Center Plaza. Leftist mayor Art Agnos—the West Coast David Dinkins—refused, as a matter of high principle, to do anything about the fetid tent city just outside his office window. In 1993, just as Dinkins was swept out of New York City Hall by Rudy Giuliani, so too was the one-term Agnos given the boot in favor of police chief Frank Jordan, who vowed to clean up the town. San Franciscans, it appeared, had finally had enough. Jordan began the cleanup but then lost four years later to Willie Brown, longtime doyen of California politics. Brown—no conservative but a pragmatist if ever there was one—did his best to keep the city reasonably clean. But *après lui, le déluge.* San Francisco—and the rest of the state—has elected only dippy liberals since, none of whom have ever lifted a finger to do anything about homelessness.

Except, that is, overspend on "housing solutions" that solve nothing and that few "homeless" ever set foot in. By one estimate, a single such unit costs the government $700,000—$100,000 more than the state's median home price. A whole industry exists—a "homeless industrial complex"—ostensibly to "help the homeless" but really to pay their "service providers," salve consciences, and perpetuate the problem. Nobody knows how much the state spends on homelessness overall. One mystified and frustrated state legislator has called for an accounting; the bureaucracy said they'd get back to him in about eighteen months. We do know that the governor's last budget proposed spending $1 billion in direct relief, on top of another $1.75 billion for "affordable housing."

But nothing illustrates better California's pathological altruism than its wide-open arms for any and all illegal immigrants. This is the trend that contributes most to all the others: overpopulation, punishing costs, crumbling infrastructure, overwhelmed public services, rapacious taxation, and two-tiered law enforcement.

To be sure, the problem is as much federal as state. The feds are supposed to control the southern border and, until the inauguration of

Donald Trump, hadn't—by design—for nearly fifty years. But California goes out of its way to compound the problem, which it doesn't even consider a problem but a great boon. Whenever the feds try to enforce the law and protect the border—admittedly, not a frequent occurrence before Trump—California rises as one to "resist."

Californians weren't always so profligate with the precious right to live in the most bountiful spot on the entire planet. In 1994, 60 percent of the electorate—a landslide—voted for a ballot initiative denying welfare to illegal aliens. A federal judge quickly blocked the measure, and that was that.

Today, 55 percent of immigrants to California—legal and illegal—receive state benefits, compared with just 30 percent of natives. Victor Davis Hanson describes going to the grocery store near his Central Valley farm and being the only person there not paying with an electronic benefit transfer (welfare) card.

State law actually prohibits officials and agencies from distinguishing legal from illegal immigrants and mandates that welfare—along with driver's licenses and other benefits—be granted equally to both. California pioneered the concept of "sanctuary cities"—nullification zones where federal law is openly flouted—and then took it to the next level by making the entire state a "sanctuary state."

California is so pro–illegal immigrant that even its distaste for murder and hatred of guns can't overcome its reflexive love of the illicit interloper. After a five-time deportee and career criminal shot an innocent San Franciscan in the back and killed her, he was acquitted of all but one minor charge, which was later overturned on appeal. California collectively shrugged. When Donald Trump voiced objection, California's elites were finally roused to anger—at Trump.

Perhaps the ur-example of California's pathological altruism—its eagerness to reward any selfish insanity at its own citizens' expense, so long as the grifter isn't dismissible as "privileged"—is Nadya "Octomom" Suleman. The daughter of an immigrant of questionable legality (after his daughter's rise to fame, dad fled back to his native Iraq to dodge bullets and IEDs as a driver for the Iraqi military), Suleman was briefly married but quickly divorced before having a single child. Then she proceeded to have six—all while single, unemployed, and on welfare. But she had always wanted a "big family" and six was not, apparently, enough. So—again, underwritten by taxpayers—she underwent extensive fertility treatments and soon after gave birth to octuplets. Suleman later parlayed her celebrity into a porn film and was convicted of welfare fraud.

Officially, California will acknowledge no limits to immigration whatsoever. Taking California's leaders at their word, if a billion people were to arrive in the state tomorrow, they would insist that every single one has a fundamental right to stay—and collect welfare. And shoot innocent women in the back. And have octuplets as a single mom at taxpayer expense.

Partly to alleviate overcrowding in ERs, California recently extended free health insurance to illegal aliens between ages nineteen and twenty-five. In a state with such a massive illegal population, that amounts to around 100,000 people (the state's no-doubt low estimate). And it's estimated to cost "only" about $100 mil—all paid for by California's state-level restoration of the individual mandate, which forces taxpaying Californians to buy insurance in part to underwrite illegal immigrants. It would be foolish to assume California will stop there. It's the nature of such programs to expand; that's what they're designed to do.

The biggest stresses from illegal immigration fall on the public education system. Conservatives like to chide California for its "bad schools." On one level, they have a point. California in the Brady Bunch era, and well beyond, had the finest public schools in the nation. Now its school system ranks thirty-eighth out of fifty. Factor out the super-wealthy super zips, and they drop to near dead last.

The typical ed-reformer blames the education code and the teachers' union. No doubt there's something in those complaints. But the single biggest factor—which no one dares name—is demographic change. Specifically, demographic change fueled by poor people fleeing poor countries, whose parents' education stopped well before the equivalent of American high school and took place in classrooms much less functional than those in California's alleged "bad schools."

In fact, all things considered, California's public schools aren't that bad. They're actually pretty good at teaching non-native speakers English, something they were required to do by the passage of Proposition 227 in 1998, which banned the idiotic practice of "bilingual education." California's schools are, however, unequal to the Herculean task they've been assigned: to take poor, non-English-speaking, culturally diverse immigrants from all over the world and bring their achievement levels up to the native-born American mean just like that. No school system in the history of the world is "good" enough to do that.

As for bilingual education, that particularly destructive California fad helped ensure that a generation of immigrant kids entered adulthood not proficient in English and hence unequipped to compete in the California job market—that is, apart from picking crops, but farmers prefer to give those jobs to the newest wave of illegal immigrants, who will work for much less. Banning the practice and teaching kids English accomplished the opposite: it helped them compete and slowed (for a bit) the further fracturing of the state along ethnic and linguistic lines.

Naturally, since English immersion worked, it was intolerable to New California, which in 2016 repealed Prop 227, ensuring that a big chunk of the next generation will never learn English but instead end up stuck on the lower rungs of California's serf economy. The repeal also ensures that the state will become ever more fractured and distrustful.

All in the name of "justice" for sanctified out-groups. What's good for those already in California is not only never considered, but to ask is to reveal oneself a monster, the quintessential non-Californian. The essence of California-ism is to care—ostentatiously—about everyone but Californians.

Balkanized

Except there are no "Californians" anymore; the term denotes only residency. The state has no common culture or civic identity. It is rather a polyglot economic zone dotted with myriad little "communities" that at best don't care about or understand one another, in many cases can't even talk to each other, and at worst hate one another.

Some degree of this fractiousness is inevitable when you cram, cheek-by-jowl, into a capacious but by no means infinite space people from literally every race, nationality, ethnic group, culture, subculture, and religion in the world. But on top of that, a lot of those groups harbor decades and even centuries of enmity against one another stretching back to the old country—enmity which California has imported by choice and now must live with and attempt to manage. New enmities arise among groups formerly separated by oceans, forests, jungles, deserts, and mountain ranges suddenly living in the same town and discovering—lo!—they have nothing in common and don't much like each other.

California's theocrats insist that all this be celebrated as "diversity" as they ride UberBLACKs into gated sanctuaries. Meanwhile, politics in the state becomes ever more nakedly Leninist: Who? Whom? Who gets to do, and take, what? To, and from, whom?

Feudal

Californian-by-choice (one wonders "Why?" and "For how long?") Joel Kotkin has taken to referring to his adopted home's present and future as "high-tech feudalism." He's not wrong. Feudalism is the culminating feature of every trend thus far discussed.

The state is grotesquely unequal, with a tiny number of winners taking virtually all the spoils while a serf class of immigrants, legal and illegal, do much of the work beyond high-concept tech design and entertainment production, and nearly all of the grinding toil.

California now has the highest poverty rate in the nation. It also has, by some metrics, the highest income gap in the nation—but whichever study you look at, it's never out of the top five.

For all of California's self-congratulation about its new-age economy, over the last dozen years, its private sector generated five times more minimum-wage jobs than plum spots in Silicon Valley or Hollywood.

Kotkin reports that 86 percent of California jobs created over this period paid below the U.S. median income, with half paying less than $40,000. That is a salary that, even if you were able to save the entire sum for an entire year, amounts to the down payment on a house costing one-third the statewide median.

Actually, the binary population asserted above is a bit simplistic. In reality, there are seven classes of people in modern, hip California (not counting foreign and out-of-state oligarchs who at most drop in on their manors from time to time and who outrank almost everyone below):

- Dukes: overlords whose wealth derives from IPOs, under-taxed stock grants, and capital gains, who leave the so-called 1 percent in the dust and dwell in the most exclusive slices of the state's most exclusive zip codes.
- Earls: mere decamillionaires who seem rich by ordinary American standards but who can barely afford, on a million a year, their house in Seacliff or Pacific Palisades plus two private school tuitions, the right cars, and a home in Tahoe or, if you're old, Palm Desert.
- Knights: highly paid servants—lawyers, managers, mid-level bankers, support staff (public relations and investor relations above all)—who help the wheels turn but don't do anything that generates real profits. Knights share the same tastes as their overlords but have a much harder time paying for them and so struggle to afford neighborhoods and lifestyles they deem worthy of their status; many go broke in the attempt and end up leaving the state in shame.
- Burghers: if we were to apply Plato's "divided line" to contemporary California, we'd draw the first and fundamental division between the above three categories and these humble four, below. A California burgher earns in the low to lower-middle six figures, a sum that used to make one comfortably middle class or even upper-middle—and still does

in the American parts of America—but barely allows one to hang on in California. If a burgher owns a home, she either inherited it or super-commutes from a distant exurb; forget about saving for retirement, or for anything, really. This class is shrinking fast—in the private sector it's almost entirely gone—and Haute California has not even begun to think through what happens after the last teacher and fire-fighter move to Missouri or Montana after selling their house following the repeal of Prop 13.

- Indentured servants: H1-Bs and the like who serve the tech oligarchy; they're decently paid, though not nearly well enough for a middle-class standard of living anywhere near where they work. Everything they have, they owe to their lord, and they know it.

- Serfs: this category is mostly made up of recent immigrants from Mexico and (increasingly) Central America, who work the fields for a lot less than H1-Bs get for writing code. They live mostly in formerly middle-class, if not particularly elegant, Valley towns. There is a serf class in the coastal cities, too, who do all the menial labor, especially cooking and cleaning. The one advantage to being a serf is that you can actually afford to live within striking distance of the California you serve; the downside is that you live in very crowded conditions, often in dirty and dangerous parts of town. No one around speaks English, but for this class that's not a problem, since they don't either.

- But at least serfs work, something that can't be said for millions of other Californians and "homeless" from other states who come west for the sunshine, welfare, and—in some California cities today—government-provided drugs and booze. No joke, look it up. Sadly, this class also includes many of the serfs' children, who have no recollection of escaping grinding poverty in Oaxaca or San Salvador and finding California a promised land, but who instead compare their California lives to those in the classes above them, resent their lot, and seethe that it's the result of racism.

None of this—not one iota—is an accident. The Californiarati want things this way, like them this way. This societal structure preserves and augments the dukes' wealth and power, which is the arrangement's main purpose, while also providing a measure of influence to California's lecturing lords of leftism.

HOW DID THIS HAPPEN?

There were, fundamentally, four overlapping causes that turned California from ultimate middle-class paradise to woke, feudal dystopia in barely a generation.

First was (is) the vast influx of poor immigrants from Latin America that began in the 1970s and then exploded after President Reagan's 1986 amnesty. Which was supposed to be coupled with strict border and workplace enforcement, but Hollywood liberals, Central Valley land barons, and the burgeoning tech elite helped ensure those provisions were never enacted. After that, voters made one attempt to get control of the problem—the aforementioned Prop 187—but it was promptly shut down. The feds in turn insisted that only they had the power to secure the border and then (and ever since) steadfastly refused to do so. Which was exactly the outcome elite California wanted. The resulting mass arrivals tipped the political balance of the state irretrievably, causing a snowball effect. More immigration makes the state bluer—and the bluer it gets, the more pro-immigration, legal and illegal, it gets, culminating in California's declaring itself a "sanctuary state" with policies that effectively exempt illegal aliens from the laws.

Second is woke anti-assimilationism, the demonization of the "melt-ing pot" and its replacement with the "salad bowl" or (to borrow from David Dinkins) the "gorgeous mosaic." Assimilation stopped being encouraged, much less insisted upon, and instead came (and remains) under furious assault.

Third was the infusion of more than four trillion dollars (on paper, at least) into Silicon Valley and San Francisco that created the world's richest elite, who enjoy advocating psychologically pleasing bromides, certain that they can exempt themselves from the real-world ramifica-tions which fall only on distant others. Which—so far—has been entirely true. California can be a very traditional society for the very wealthy, who can—and do—wall themselves off from the dysfunction they cause, live in gated communities, and send their kids to private schools. Such families, of course, also all employ Hispanic help—gardeners, maids, cooks, nannies—and so have both pecuniary and conscience-salving reasons to advocate for illegal immigration: doing so is a public show of noblesse oblige that helps legitimize their privilege. This new wealth and the way its owners spend it thus only intensified the state's hard-left turn as elites voted for—and, more to the point, financed—ever-more radical politicians and ballot initiatives.

The most important consequence of that turn was to cleanse the state of its old middle class. The people who voted Republican in six straight presidential elections and for Republican governors six out of eight times were chased out by high taxes, costly homes, terrible schools, indifferent law enforcement, smothering red tape, lousy services, and broken infra-structure. Many in the coastal corridor were fortunate enough to own homes that appreciated spectacularly over their lifetimes, which they could sell and reap a windfall—and then live like kings in low-tax states while escaping California's vindictive utopianism, punishing taxes, and cratering quality of life for all but the very rich.

And it wasn't just the Republicans—though they were the first to see the writing on the wall—but also the old blue-collar Democrats, the ones who tugged their party in a more moderate direction. Until around the mid-2000s, almost the entire western half of San Francisco was populated by old-style, working-class, union Democrats. They would, to one another, refer to the precise neighborhood where they lived by parish—and could assume that everyone whom they told knew exactly where they meant. Those people are all gone, of course, which isn't surprising. What's perhaps a bit surprising is that no one in the city today even knows they were ever there. It's like these mostly Irish, Italian, and Polish Catholics who worked construction, on the docks, and in the police and fire departments never existed, were never part of the scene. In modern San Francisco's self-conception, there were the Native Americans who had the land stolen out from under them—then fast-forward to the hippies, the gays, the hipsters, the techies, and the oligarchs. American California isn't merely gone; it never was.

A NEW REGIME

Ultimately, what California is, or is in the process of becoming, or wants to be, is a new kind of regime. Who really rules is not entirely clear—which, I think, is the point. It's "democratic" in that people vote—but they always vote for the same things or for a series of interchangeable hacks who all believe and do the same things. Elections mean nothing in the sense that the real rulers can never lose. Voting simply provides the veneer of legitimacy.

Those real rulers are the monied oligarchs, plus the funds and companies they run. Entertainment moguls, always looking for opportunities to virtue-signal, and agriculture barons, who before every harvest salivate for a fresh tranche of serfs to underpay, play supporting roles. Big Leftism—concentrated in the media, the universities, nonprofits, and government—is the servant, the instrument of their power.

The implicit deal—which I've called the "San Francisco Compromise"—is that, first, the left does nothing that directly threatens oligarchic wealth or power. It can tax and spend all it wants, so long as those taxes are easily bearable—and, to the extent possible, legally avoidable—by dukes. So long as the other policies that increase oligarchic wealth are never questioned, it almost doesn't matter what California tax rates are; the dukes can afford them. The lefties also agree to use their considerable rhetorical power to whitewash and lionize the oligarchs.

For their part, the oligarchs take their cues from leftists on matters of passionate conviction that don't directly threaten said wealth or power. They also spend some of their lucre on lefty institutions and make-work jobs.

California's real rulers don't exercise their power in the manner of the oligarchs of old. They wield it indirectly, by controlling not just the politicians who can't win without their money but especially by controlling discourse. The real decisions are made in the communication between the oligarchs and the officeholders. And that "communication" is not necessarily—not even primarily—a Palo Alto grandee picking up the phone and calling Sacramento. (They have people for that.) It's more using their complete control of all avenues of information—from grammar schools all the way up to prestige and social media—to tell only one cramped, constrained "story."

All this is underwritten by the massive demographic change that ensures one-party rule in Sacramento and in the judiciary plus a lopsidedly leftist congressional delegation. Even today—after decades of middle-class exodus—millions of Californians still harbor red-state habits and political inclinations. But their preferences—like their votes—don't matter because such people are overwhelmingly outnumbered. Stay and pay, suffer and be ignored—or leave. Either way, you're not voting your way out of this. That's the message Haute California hurls at dwindling Red California.

The corporations and their leaders tell the government what to do and as much as possible exempt themselves from its mandates. Apple is based in Cupertino but does most of its manufacturing in China and, until recently, paid the bulk of its taxes in Ireland. But even the Emerald Isle's notoriously low corporate rates—Apple paid an effective tax rate in Ireland of 0.005 percent in 2014—designed to suck profits away from the countries where they're earned, got to be too much, and the company moved its legendary pile of cash to the Isle of Jersey, which levies no taxes at all. Sacramento not only doesn't try to stop that, it defers to Cupertino on every matter of importance. Who is the real sovereign?

We know why Apple's factories are in China—cheap labor—and the money is in Jersey, but why is the mothership still in Cupertino? Partly it's similar to the reason why, in Tom Wolfe's explanation, "many chief executive officers kept their headquarters in New York long after the last rational reason for doing so had vanished . . . because of the ineffable experience of being a CEO and having lunch five days a week in Manhattan!" Jersey has ocean views but no good restaurants. Tech oligarchs envy Chinese despotism and censorship but don't want to live there—wouldn't even if they were in charge.

But that isn't the whole story, nor even the most important part. It's telling that many Apple products are stamped with the phrase "Designed by Apple in California." In Apple's conception of itself, the company is located not in "the United States" or "America" but in "California." Apple makes this distinction for three reasons, which can easily be extended to the rest of the tech industry, and to all of Haute California. First, California oligarchs want to distance themselves from the notion that they are part of, or own allegiance to, any country at all. They are above such petty concerns, beyond—and in many ways more powerful than—the nation-state. It's here worth pausing to note the irony of Governor Gavin's self-congratulatory description of California as a "nation-state." California is not only in no respect a "nation"—a united people with a common lineage, language, and history—it has been deliberately reengineered to resemble a nation as little as possible. When Newsom and other California-boosters so describe their state, all they really mean is "big" and "rich."

Second, the oligarchs want to distance themselves from all that is held by elite and world opinion to be bad about America: racism, sexism, Bible-thumping, guns, and so on. Third, they wish to evoke California not as an American state but as an idea: the Golden State, the California Dream, paradise, the future.

But it's a very selective, exclusive paradise and future. Which is the fundamental reason why the lords still live there. Partly, of course, because the state's natural beauty is so profound that even the worst human mismanagement can barely scratch it. More fundamentally, Haute California has become like one of those clean, pristine space stations to which, in sci-fi movies, elites escape a ravaged earth. The only people you will see are people just like you—or properly deferential servants who work for you. Life in La Jolla, Montecito, Carmel, Palo Alto, Woodside, and Napa has never been better. If you have several million and don't mind the taxes—and the state has plenty who do, and don't—you can insulate yourself from toxic California and enjoy the weather, natural beauty, and pricey, world-class amenities.

On the flip side, subsidized poverty in California is heaven compared to penury in southern Mexico or Central America. As bad as California's crime, infrastructure, and dysfunction are by historic American standards, they're all still orders of magnitude better than prevailing conditions in parts south.

These two realities explain why no one much cares about high-speed rail boondoggles, dumping precious water out to sea in a drought, homeless encampments, poop on the sidewalks, or rural Central California's Wild West, where many laws are simply not enforced. High and low alike—the only demographics who matter—have it too good.

ESCAPE?

Disgruntled Californians at least have an escape hatch, somewhere else to go. Indeed, so many people are leaving California that the state is likely, for the first time in its history, to lose a congressional seat after the 2020 census—even with the continued influx of illegal immigrants. Though it's fair to ask whether other states should want any fleeing

Californians, given that they have the nasty habit of pushing, in their new homes, the very policies that spurred them to flee their old one.

At any rate, Americans don't have the luxury of fleeing a Californicated America. Where are we supposed to go?

Californians can also take for granted that the U.S. military, the Federal Reserve, and—until the events of spring and summer 2020 called these into question—federal cops and federal prisons will back them up and cover their mistakes. How well will any of these function when the entire country is as broke and broken as modern California?

For the last thirty years, at least, California has ridden a tech tailwind that has underwritten the state's spending orgy and crazed utopianism. California has literally bet the entire existence of its "new regime" on that wind continuing. Will it? If and when Californocracy subsumes the United States as a whole, is a new high-paying, high-profit, high-margin economic sector waiting in the wings to carry aloft the entire country?

Yet Californication is what the broader left wants for America. It's what I believe they were one election away from getting in 2016. They think so too. They desperately want another chance in 2020.

CHAPTER TWO

Torching the Parchment

Americans' self-conception—at least among those of us not convinced by the *New York Times*' "1619 Project" that the country is nothing but a giant slave plantation—is that America is the land of the free and the home of the brave, the land of opportunity. We are a classless society, a meritocracy in which everyone is free to rise as high as his talents will take him. Here in the United States of America, cherished rights such as freedom of speech and religion, the right to bear arms and to be secure in one's property, are enshrined in our laws and embedded in our societal DNA. We judge people by the content of their characters, not the color of their skin. Everyone is equal before the law, innocent until proven guilty, and justice is blind.

All this—and more—is (supposedly) guaranteed by the fundamental charters of our liberties, above all the Declaration of Independence and the United States Constitution: "the parchment."

Yet those of us who actually find this vision appealing and believe it (used) to be (mostly) true of our country also intuit that, noble and appealing as it may sound, much of it no longer quite holds. Something— many things, actually—have changed, and not all for the better.

WHAT OUR PARCHMENT SAYS

American civics education ain't what it used to be, but those of us over a certain age and/or who lucked into a good education understand the basics of how our government and society are supposed to work.

The Declaration of Independence famously declares that "all men are created equal." The men whom we used to refer to as our "Founding Fathers"—before that phrase was cast into outer darkness for its alleged "toxic masculinity"—meant by this that all human beings are equal in possessing equal natural rights, including but not limited to life, liberty, and the pursuit of happiness. Our founders well understood that human beings are manifestly not equal in talent, virtue, strength, and wisdom. Some people are simply better at certain things—including things that contribute to success in this world—than are others. In addition, some people are better than others at politics, at ruling and running things. These are facts of nature that man cannot change.

However, inequality of talent or virtue has no bearing on equality of rights. The greatest specimen of human virtue—say, George Washington—is not ordained by God or nature to rule other human beings without their consent. The American founders were hardly unaware of how novel this claim was at the time; they were after all breaking away from a monarchy-aristocracy with a distinct caste system that explicitly declared human beings to be unequal. Nearly every government on earth in their day operated the same way. Moreover, the ancient philosophers and historians whom the founders consulted for guidance either assert that inequality of rank is part of nature or else argue that, as a practical matter, some form of legally enforced conventional (as opposed to natural) inequality will always prevail in real-world politics.

Yet our founders rejected this as a basis for their new government. Why? The full answer is complex and involves a complete understanding of the fundamental ways the human situation changed in the West with the destruction of the ancient city, the advent of Christianity, the sundering of civil from religious law, the flowering of modernity, and the Reformation.

But the core reason is that our founders were seeking a new and stable basis for political legitimacy in the modern world. In the old understanding—the one the founders rejected—God Himself had chosen George III to rule Britons and Americans alike, every one of whom owed the king and his heirs perpetual allegiance. Few of the newly liberated colonists were eager to throw off one system of formal inequality only to establish another. Suggestions that Washington be crowned king were rejected with abhorrence by the general himself and most of his compatriots.

But the founders strongly felt the need to declare on what basis—on what claim to justice—they were establishing their new country. The Declaration says that "a decent respect to the opinion of mankind" requires the revolutionaries to explain and justify their actions. The founders were not content to simply say, "We threw off that government because we didn't like it; now we're implementing this one which we like better." They wanted to establish their new government on the basis of truth, of truths inherent in human nature. And they wanted the American people to believe those truths, to understand that the American Revolution had been just, and to be confident that their new government would fulfill the Revolution's promise.

If "all men are created equal," then every man is entitled by "the laws of nature and of nature's God" to some say in how he is governed. That input is actualized through representative institutions, which allow citizens to change the personnel and direction of the government through elections. The people, not any monarch, are sovereign; their will is properly channeled through said institutions and refined by deliberation among their representatives. The ultimate guarantees of government by consent, however, are the right of individuals to emigrate—if you really don't like it here no matter who's in charge, you're free to leave—and by the right of revolution, which is enshrined and explained in the Declaration itself.

According to the founders, a just and legitimate government is formed when a free people come together to secure their mutual defense and promote their mutual benefit; in other words, when they form a social compact. James Madison explains:

> All power in just and free Government is derived from Compact, that where the parties to the Compact are competent to make it, and where the Compact creates a *Government*, and arms it not only with a moral power but the physical means of executing it, it is immaterial by what name it is called. Its real character is to be decided by the Compact itself: by the nature and extent of the powers it specifies, and the obligations imposed on the parties to it.

Thus government's legitimate powers are derived from the free grant of a free people, who give up a portion of their natural rights—essentially, the right to "take the law into their own hands"—and consent to the government's use of coercive powers in order to secure the majority of their rights.

This task—securing rights—is the core function of government. It entails above all securing people's physical safety against foreign attack and domestic crime. At the most basic level, a government that does this effectively is legitimate, a real government. One that cannot is a government in name only—a failed, or fake, state.

Government also has a role in promoting the people's happiness and well-being. While it does not take the lead on these all-important considerations, a good government works to create and maintain conditions for private institutions—families, churches, civic associations, schools and universities, among others—to work toward the betterment of individuals and communities.

Our founders limited the American government's powers to fit the limited nature of its role. They also specifically enumerated those powers to make clear what the government may and may not legitimately do, and they devolved powers to the lowest possible level to preserve local control over local issues. Most day-to-day matters would be handled by townships and cities, or else states, with the federal government taking on only those tasks that the smaller jurisdictions could not do, at least not well, such as regulate foreign trade and provide for the common defense. At every level, the government's powers were separated into legislative, executive, and judicial functions to prevent the concentration of power—especially deadly power—in the same hands.

At any rate, that is what the parchment *says*. But James Madison himself—the "Father of the Constitution"—warned that mere "parchment barriers" would not be enough to secure Americans' liberties over the long term. Real, living men—jealous of their freedom, prudent and spirited enough to maintain it—would have to do the hard work. The system bequeathed to us by our founders requires maintenance.

OBJECTIONS TO THE PARCHMENT FROM THE RIGHT

Since this is a book of, by, and for the right, I must address what I anticipate will be substantial objections, even attacks, from that quarter. The controversies we're about to explore have dogged conservatism for three generations at least. I personally find them fascinating and enormously fun to debate.

But debate is not the aim of this section, much less victory. Quite the contrary: it is, to the extent possible, to oil the waters, to offer not merely an olive branch but the whole tree. I cheerfully admit, for instance, that others were right long before I was about the importance of and the need to rethink allegedly "conservative" positions on immigration, trade, and war. We therefore not only face the same enemies but also favor the same present solutions. If that's not the basis for at least a temporary alliance, I don't know what is. In this present crisis, we must all hang together, or most assuredly we shall all hang separately.

My aim for this section is threefold. First, to further illuminate our founders' understanding of America's founding principles—in particular, those features with direct relevance to the predicaments of the present age. Second, to show that those principles did not directly or inevitably lead to the contemporary evils we all perceive and oppose. And third, to argue that if we are to achieve something better than what we have now—whether that entails going back to a better version of ourselves or forward to whatever comes next—we will need to do so on the basis of a sound understanding of politics generally and of Americanism specifically, and can follow no better guides than our founders.

"Propositionism" and Its Discontents

Many will interpret my account of core American principles as "universalist," "propositionist," and even "neoconservative." "Propositionism" is the clever—and not altogether unfair or inaccurate—name that some use to attack the tendency of certain conservatives to say silly things like "America is an idea" or "America is a credal nation" (that is, if America is allowed to be called a nation at all), "Nationalism has no place here," and so on. Be at ease: I come not to praise this understanding but to bury it.

The word "proposition" presumably refers to Lincoln's description, in the first paragraph of the Gettysburg Address, of America as a nation "conceived in liberty and dedicated to the proposition that all men are created equal"—the last six words being, of course, a direct quote from the Declaration of Independence. Propositionism's critics typically make one of two arguments: either that the founders didn't believe in propositionism and later figures—Lincoln especially—pulled a fast one by reinterpreting America as propositionist; or that the founders did believe in propositionism but were mistaken. Let's examine these in turn.

The "Rights of Englishmen"

The claim that the founders were not really propositionist at all rests on the argument that they didn't intend their famous language— especially "all men are created equal"—the way it reads or how subsequent figures interpreted it. According to this understanding, later generations forgot or never learned the original context of those words. The seemingly universalist claims are actually very specific to time,

place, and people. The founders intended merely to assert the traditional "rights of Englishmen," not state a wholly new political philosophy based on universal equal natural rights. They were just sticking up
for their side, for their people.

Say what you will of this critique—I disagree with it, as I shall make
clear—but it's at least a pro-American, pro-founding critique. No one
makes this claim out of hatred or disdain for America or the founding.
They do so for precisely the opposite reason: to vindicate America and
the founders from what they judge to be mistaken understandings that
have reaped disastrous consequences, specifically the appeal to "equality" as an interminable engine of left-wing levelling.

And, indeed, there is some truth to these claims. The founders *were*
sticking up for their side, for their people. Yes, they declared a universal
basis for doing so, but they did not intend or expect their declaration to
revolutionize the world—nor were they under any illusion that it, or they,
had the power to do so. Our Revolution was fundamentally *for us*—We
the People, ourselves and our Posterity. The universalist claims made on
the Revolution's behalf were intended only to establish and explain the
legitimacy of America's new government, not as a call for world conquest
in the name of "democracy." Because the truths on which America was
founded are universal, America is—in the words of John Quincy
Adams—"the well-wisher to the freedom and independence of all" but
also "the champion and vindicator only of her own." If the universal
truth of human equality means that every nation in the world deserves
liberty, each will still have to achieve it on its own.

I understand and share frustration with neoconservative misuse of
the founding principles and the founders' words to press for democracy
wars around the world. That frustration does not, however, make the
truth any less universal. Nor does it even come close to suggesting that
the founders didn't mean what they said. Do a little digging through their
pamphlets, proclamations, state constitutions, speeches, sermons, notes
from political assemblies and conventions, and even their private letters,
and the meaning of their words becomes crystal clear. They all repeated

the same sentiments over and over in the same terms. For those wishing to take a guided tour, I recommend Thomas G. West's *The Political Theory of the American Founding*. Make sure to follow the footnotes to the original sources so you can see for yourself.

Nor does the "rights of Englishmen" claim fly even on its own terms. The plain meaning of the founders' words tells against it: they didn't say "all Englishmen are created equal." They also knew full well that all Englishmen were *not* considered equal. The founders were specifically rebelling against England and the English system—not to set up a mixed aristocracy-monarchy on the English model, but instead to establish a republic that explicitly rejected the rank orders inherent in the English system. The principle of equality was thus not grafted onto America later; properly understood, it was there from the beginning.

The final, serious objection to equality is the claim that it somehow requires or encourages open borders, or at least leaves one intellectually defenseless against arguments in favor of open borders. This is wrong. As we shall see, the founders' political philosophy is not only entirely compatible with immigration restriction; it in some sense *requires* it. For to maintain a citizenry "dedicated to the proposition," one cannot willy-nilly import anyone from anywhere: one must screen for those likely to be or to become themselves "dedicated to the proposition."

Civic Nationalism

"Civic nationalism," a more precise term for propositionism, is the idea that a shared commitment to common citizenship—typically including principles, ideals, goals, and a body of laws, above all a constitution—can be a sufficient basis for binding a people together even absent ties of kinship, ethnicity, language, religion, or tradition. Proponents of civic nationalism find the idea beautiful and noble. Critics call it naïve and contrary to human nature. Both have a point.

There is, indeed, something beautiful and noble about human beings coming together to work toward a shared goal, being able to look beyond differences—even important ones—to achieve great and good things together. This is almost the definition of a "high-trust" as opposed to a "low-trust" society, in which people will not cooperate with others outside their families, or perhaps a slightly wider but still constricted circle of kin and known fellow tribesmen. Low-trust societies tend to be poor and backward and to lack significant civilizational accomplishments or high standards of living.

Thus a society that is both multi-ethnic and centered around the nuclear family must have recourse to some other, non-kin-based glue to hold it together and elevate its levels of trust. In the United States, that glue is—at least in part—civic nationalism. Those who rightly warn that American immigration policy is making American society more low-trust should consider that a core element of our high-trust success is precisely Americans' historic ability to see past kinship and tribal ties and feel ourselves to be full members of the larger American nation.

Yet civic nationalism's critics make true and necessary arguments that its shallower proponents either ignore or have forgotten. To see this, it's necessary to examine to what extent the American founders were, and were not, civic nationalists.

The practical problem they faced was how to bind the American people together, how to forge a new common political identity after deliberately throwing off the only such identity Americans had ever known: subjects of the English Crown. Ethnicity or ancestry alone would not do; while America then was far more homogenous than it is today, it was also far from monolithic.

In *Federalist* No. 2, America's future first chief justice, John Jay, summarized the advantages of his new country:

> With equal pleasure I have as often taken notice that Providence has been pleased to give this one connected country to one united people—a people descended from the same ancestors, speaking the same language, professing the same religion, attached to the same principles of government, very similar in their manners and customs, and who, by their joint

counsels, arms, and efforts, fighting side by side throughout
a long and bloody war, have nobly established general liberty
and independence.

And yet—as Jay well knew—even then the situation was not quite
that simple. The American people were not *all* descended from the same
ancestors. Many had German or Irish ancestry, and the population
included a smattering of other ethnicities, too. Even among the British,
there were—in addition to the dominant English—also Scots, Scotch-
Irish, and Welshmen. Indeed, Britain itself was not ethnically homogenous but an amalgamation of four distinct peoples gathered together by
the political unification of four distinct kingdoms.

Could ties of ethnicity and history bind the Americans together?
Yes—in part. By the time of the Revolution, there had been American
colonies in what would become the United States for more than 150
years. Americans had lived together, struggled together, fought together,
and strived together for a century and a half. They had moreover mostly
governed themselves, at least at the local level, for the simple reason that
the English Crown was so far away. And, as Jay notes, by the Revolution's end the American people had just emerged victorious from a daring
war for independence, and few things bind a people together more tightly
than shared struggle—especially if they win.

But the founders also well knew that ethnicity can be ambiguous. It's
far easier to say what, or who, an Englishman is right now than how the
English (or any other ethnicity) came to be. When did the English become
English? After the collapse of Roman rule over Britain? The reign of Alfred
the Great? In the decades following the Norman Conquest? The English
are in fact themselves a melding of various peoples: ancient Britons, Celts,
and Romans, later mixed with medieval Saxons and Normans from the
Continent. All of them, and some others, came together over time to form
the English. But one cannot say exactly when or precisely how.

The American people, by contrast, had to be formed on the spot,
with the whole world—not least the Americans themselves—watching.

And, indeed, in its very first sentence the Declaration of Independence declares, for the first time, the people of the United States to be "one people" as distinct from "another" from whom they are separating, and also as distinct from the other "powers of the earth," all of which are entitled by "Nature and Nature's God" to a "separate and equal station" from one another.

Nor did the American people all "profess the same religion." The vast majority—but not all—were Christians, but even at the time of the Revolution some Americans were Jews. The vast majority of the Christians—but not all—were Protestants. Maryland had been explicitly founded as a Catholic sanctuary, while Rhode Island was launched with a grant of complete religious freedom and toleration. Among the Protestants were a multitude of sects which, to be sure, had more in common with one another than with adherents of other faiths, but which also sought freedom of worship. Indeed, one may say that the first and most fundamental founding principle of the United States, going back to the Pilgrims, was religious freedom.

Thus some basis for common American citizenship other than shared ethnicity or faith had to be found—not to replace either but to bolster, support, and extend them.

The founders did not intend civic nationalism to take the place of any greater sense of fellow feeling based on a common American identity. To the contrary, they well knew that a defining task of the young country would be to create such fellow feeling, to take the former colonists and meld them into a new nation, the "Americans." Mere fealty to principle or parchment—to abstractions—would not suffice. To truly become one people and survive—and thrive—as a nation, Americans would have to develop the same sense of inner kinship, loyalty, and sameness that defines the English or French or countless other peoples—but without the benefit of centuries or even millennia of proximity and shared experience whose beginnings are forgotten in the mists of time.

Civic nationalism also offers a formal acknowledgment that everyone part of the enterprise belongs—there are no second-class citizens and no

castes.* By contrast, an appeal to ethnicity or religion as the core foundation of citizenship would have raised questions without clear answers
and created more problems than it solved. If a true American is "English," then what about the Scottish and the Welsh? If central to being
"American" is British ancestry, then what about the country's then-
already sizable population of Germans and Irish? To address these and
similar complications, the founders sought a basis for common citizenship conducive to the development of a common American identity as
quickly as possible.

Let's also not forget the extent to which a book or books—writings—
can help form a disparate people into one. *The Iliad*, an epic about a
bloody, bitter intra-Greek war of annihilation, became the supreme unifying force for all Greeks throughout the Mediterranean. Dante, Petrarch,
and Machiavelli essentially created the Italian language that would eventually—with an assist from Verdi's "Va, pensiero"—unify the Italian penin-
sula for the first time since the fall of the Western Roman Empire.

Americans would have to wait until after formally winning independence to get our epics. But even before, we had the sermons and tracts
of the Great Awakening, Franklin's *Poor Richard's Almanack* and *Auto-
biography*, and the pamphlets of the Revolution. To these we soon added

---

* With the obvious exception of slaves, who were not understood at the time of the founding to be
members of the social compact. The leading founders were well aware that "all men are created equal"
is fundamentally incompatible with slavery. However, they judged that the urgencies of creating the
new country required compromises with slavery, which in any case they had no power to abolish at
that time. Had they made abolition their priority, not only would they have failed to achieve that
goal, but the new nation would not have been formed—the Southern colonies would have gone their
own way—and slavery might have survived longer than it eventually survived in the United States.
It is hardly an accident that slavery—the oldest human institution on earth after the family—was
abolished in North America "four score and seven years" after the American founders declared that
"all men are created equal." Another cost to not unifying—thoroughly explained in the early chapters
of the *Federalist Papers*—is that a divided patchwork of small, weak states would likely have quarreled
amongst themselves, making the North American continent violent and chaotic, or worse, an attractive playground for European adventurism. The former colonists, or many of them, might well have
found themselves once again under the thumb of some European empire, thus having fought the
Revolution for nothing.

Irving, Cooper, Hawthorne, Melville, Poe, Longfellow, Dickinson, Emerson, Thoreau, Whitman, and Twain. But America's greatest writings were then and still remain our great political charters—the parchment—and the documents that explain them: above all the *Federalist Papers* of Hamilton, Madison, and Jay, and the speeches of Clay, Webster, and Lincoln.

Limits of Civic Nationalism

Yet however necessary or noble civic nationalism may be in the right circumstances—however logical or elegant in theory—our founders understood that in the real world, it is subject to practical limits.

First, any social compact, and hence any political community, is inherently particular. There may be, at some level of abstraction, a "universal brotherhood of man." But down here on earth, human beings—with the help (or at the prompting) of climate, geography, and other natural elements—sort ourselves into tribes and nations. We always have and always will.

Most nations become nations over a long—and quite unplanned—process, the details of which historians spend entire careers trying to unearth without ever fully reconstructing. But the net result—that Nation A exists and is distinct from Nations B and C—is obvious to all, even if a full account of the origin of any is unavailable. In most such instances, the social compact exists but is implicit. There was no "signing ceremony." In a few rare cases—the American above all—the social compact is deliberately formed in full view of the world.

Either way, in any non-despotism, the social compact defines membership in the political community—in the nation. No one can simply declare himself "French" and become such solely on the basis of his declaration. One might, however, be accepted into the French nation by the French people—either via a process of assimilation to French culture and ideas, or legally, through a grant of French citizenship, or both. This process is always a two-way street. The full privileges of any social compact extend only to those who have consented to its terms and whose membership has been consented to by all other citizen-members.

The equal natural rights of all men do not demand or imply world government or open borders. On the contrary, a social compact without limits is impossible, a self-contradiction. A compact that applies indiscriminately to all is not a compact. As Gouverneur Morris, the man who actually wrote the U.S. Constitution—who set down on paper the Philadelphia Convention's conclusions—put it:

> As every society, from a great nation down to a club, has the right of declaring the conditions on which new members shall be admitted, there can be no room for complaint. As to those philosophical gentlemen, those citizens of the world as they call themselves, I do not wish to see any of them in our public councils. I would not trust them. The men who can shake off their attachments to their own country can never love any other. These attachments are the wholesome prejudices which uphold all governments.

Because mutual consent is an indispensable foundation of political legitimacy, membership in the political community must be invitation-only.

Second, equal natural rights do not demand a single regime type for all mankind. On the contrary, form must always fit matter. "Matter" is in this sense the actual country, the "facts on the ground": its people, their language, habits, talents, traditions, customs, and religion(s); the topography, resources, and climate; the geographical site and situation; and relations with neighbors and other world powers. "Form" is the regime or mode of government, and above all the principles informing that mode. There may be—as some philosophers assert—one form of government that is always and everywhere best. But those same philosophers quickly add that this best form is not always practicable or possible; it is suitable only for matter that is fit for it—capable of sustaining it—and only in those rare instances where and when circumstances permit.

While America's founding principles would seem to condemn monarchy as ipso facto illegitimate, that condemnation must be qualified. Strictly understood, monarchy violates the principle of natural human equality. And in most iterations, monarchy also violates the principle of government by consent, for the monarchical doctrine jus soli ("law of the soil"), which holds that the place of one's birth determines one's nationality, binds subjects to perpetual allegiance to the monarch and his heirs.

The founding principles would not, however, condemn out of hand other political arrangements but rather admit of regime plurality. There is, for instance, no reason why a constitutional monarchy with limited powers, or a parliamentary republic that fuses the legislative and executive functions, cannot be consistent with a natural right understanding of what makes government legitimate.

While the government our founders built takes its bearings from human nature, they well knew that this in itself does not mean that our particular regime—or even republicanism more broadly—can be successfully applied anywhere, to anyone. It is a perhaps sad but nonetheless intractable truth that not all peoples in all times and places are ready or able to assume the responsibilities of liberty or to secure their equal natural rights through republican government. Even we Americans were not inherently or immediately capable of creating or sustaining a republican regime. It took well over a century of quasi self-rule via colonial legislatures, plus the crucibles of the French and Indian War and the Revolutionary War, to make us ready for it. The great task before the founders of any government is thus to devise a form as consistent as possible with timeless truths about human nature yet also appropriate to the particular characteristics and circumstances of an actual people at a given time.

Third, while the incorporation of newcomers into the social compact is possible and even salutary in certain circumstances, great care must be taken in selecting whom to admit. Our founders knew that stability in any society requires a measure of commonality in customs, habits, and opinions. They thus prioritized assimilation and took pains to ensure that this country's society and institutions worked in concert to further that process. The founders also knew well that a high degree of commonality is doubly important in a republic, for republicanism is not possible where or when the people are so fractured that private, sectional, or group interests override agreement on the common good.

This is why the 1795 Naturalization Act specified that new Americans be "attached to the principles of the Constitution of the United States" and "well disposed to the good order and happiness of the same." It is hard to see how anyone who cares about the fate of liberty in this country could possibly object to that language. The overwhelming majority of Americans today reject with abhorrence, and have for decades, that same law's language limiting citizenship to "free white person[s]," but its inclusion at the time had more to do with the much larger problem of slavery than with immigration. Still, to select immigrants according to their "attachment to the principles of the Constitution of the United States" is so eminently sensible—so beneficial to domestic harmony and the continued thriving of republican government—that one wonders why we don't screen today's newcomers for those exact same sentiments!

Our founders also knew that the greater the distance—be it cultural, linguistic, historical, or religious—between native and immigrant, the more difficult assimilation is. There is no assimilative magic bullet that can take millions from anywhere and everywhere and instantly transform them into a different people.

Fourth, when it comes to admitting new members to the social compact, numbers are of the essence. The larger the influx, the more disruptive the process, the more difficult assimilation is, and the longer it takes. With numbers large enough, assimilative forces may simply be overwhelmed by sheer demographic weight.

A paramount consideration must be the capacity of the existing citizenry and its institutions and economy to absorb and assimilate newcomers. This capacity varies according to times and circumstances and is never unlimited. For civic nationalism to work, a republic that opens its doors to immigrants must choose carefully whom and how many to accept; it must insist on and facilitate assimilation; it must be able and willing to recognize its own limits in successfully assimilating newcomers; and it must protect its citizenry—and the stability of its society—accordingly.

For the founders, the purpose of civic nationalism was not to erase or replace ties of kinship and commonality but to create and augment them. Their goal was to meld together a population not necessarily descended from the same ancestors or professing exactly the same religion and to ensure that they all spoke the same language, were attached to the same principles of government, practiced their faiths freely and without sectarian strife, and were or would become similar in manners and customs. If the precise circumstances Jay described in *Federalist* No. 2 were never strictly true, the goal of all immigration and naturalization law should be to approximate as closely as possible that ideal.

That, in a nutshell, is "civic nationalism." Not "Anyone who yesterday disembarked at JFK or snuck across the border at Nogales is every bit as American—even more so—than a Daughter of the American Revolution."

I understand and share the frustration of those who mock that trite falsehood and deplore how it's used to rig elections, suppress wages, feed the welfare state, and strengthen the hand of leftist anti-Americanism.

But discarding the correct understanding of civic nationalism is not the answer. Civic nationalism properly understood was indispensable to the founding of the country: without it, we would not have united as a people or, over time, formed the American nation. Some might try to argue that, the formation of said nation being complete, we can dispense with civic nationalism today in favor of our common American identity. But this ignores the considerable extent to which that American identity was formed by civic nationalism—*is* civic nationalism—which remains at its core. Hence arguing that we ditch civic nationalism is tantamount to saying, "Let's dispense with our identity in order to strengthen our identity." The World War II movie cliché of an Army squad in which every soldier has an ethnically different last name, yet all still work and fight seamlessly as Americans, may be overused, but it precisely captures the success and strength of American civic nationalism.

There are some who would have European Americans "go back" to their roots—that is, to the specific roots of each individual's European ethnicity. But this is impossible, first, because after centuries of assimilation and intermarriage, very few European Americans are descended from any single ethnicity and so would have to appeal back to a jumble of competing and even contradictory traditions. Second, even those few who are long ago lost any direct connection to the Old World and its traditions but live and experience life simply as Americans. Even if old identities were strong enough—even if most of us weren't of widely mixed stock—recall that there are still real nations peopled by those old ethnicities. They won't accept us. To an Italian, an Italian American is an American, not an Italian. And so on across the board. We cannot but be who we are: Americans.

A possible exception might be if some new trial—as great or greater than the American Revolution—were to confront us. Should we, or some part of us, emerge from that trial to form a new nation, we might in the process form a new identity, the same way the original Americans did—indeed, in much the same way most of the world's nations have come to be. But, unless that trial were so great as to wipe out all memory of what came before, that new identity would inevitably be forced to rely on some form of civic nationalism. For if men were to remember their preceding Americanness—and prior to that, their Englishness or whatever—then unless each new state to emerge from the trial were to be reserved for only one narrowly construed ethnic group, men would have to unify along broader lines. And the value of unity would be the same as it was in the founding era: to achieve strength in numbers, to control territory and resources, to avoid petty squabbles and conflicts, to provide for the common defense, to keep meddling and hostile foreigners at bay.

But since such a trial is a thing hardly to be wished for, let us hasten to the next stage in the argument.

The American Founding as Universalist, Liberal, Levelling, Hyper-Rational, Anti-Religion, and/or Anti-Tradition

The claim that the founders got it wrong (as opposed to were misinterpreted) usually rests on some appeal to tradition or religion or both. In this telling, the universalism of "all men are created equal" acts as an irresistible solvent on all that came before: faith, kinship, community, folkways, customs, shared beliefs, and a common history. The phrase itself and all the other founding-era rhetoric is a mere epiphenomenon of the underlying true cause, which is modernity itself, or the Enlightenment, or liberalism, which in this understanding are all more or less the same thing. Specifically, it is alleged that the turn to reason as a basis for legitimacy, authority, and order undermined men's faith in every other source of guidance and eventually led to the present's rootlessness and hedonism, since in the final analysis reason is fit for calculating means but not for evaluating ends.

I do not want to seem dismissive here, because this criticism has some merit. Liberalism is absolutely a product of modernity, of which "the Enlightenment" was the public relations or propaganda arm. The root of "liberal" is the Latin liber—or "free"—and the goal of liberalism at its most extreme was to liberate mankind from many ancient constraints, including religion and tradition, which some of liberalism's progenitors believed were inherently irrational. There can be no question that liberalism—at least in its overtly leftist recent iteration—has done enormous damage to the country generally, and to tradition and religion specifically.

But critics of propositionism take this just complaint too far, first because the argument's logical end requires discarding many positive aspects of modernity, which few of us—including most of these critics—are prepared to do. Second, because the strict identification of the founding with liberalism is incorrect. To be sure, there are many respects in which the founders' thoughts, principles, and plans were liberal or drew on liberal ideas. It suffices to mention the separations of powers and of church and state, limited government, and guarantees of fundamental rights.

But we cannot conclude from this that the founders rejected religion, tradition, or community. Indeed, when we examine the Revolution and the founding, we see that one of the founders' primary motivations and goals was to secure the free exercise of religion and freedom of conscience. The Declaration itself cites God no fewer than four times: by name, as Creator, as judge, and as Divine Providence. Among the leaders of the Revolution were hundreds of ministers, preachers, and clergy, none of whom saw any contradiction between their faith and their support of the founding principles. In virtually every founding-era document—from the Declaration to the preambles of the state constitutions, from public speeches to private letters—one finds solemn praise for both the truth and necessity of religion.

Here are two representative quotes, the first from the Northwest Ordinance of 1787 (the law that governed the territories that would become Ohio, Indiana, Illinois, Michigan, Wisconsin, and part of Minnesota):

> Religion, morality, and knowledge, being necessary to good government and the happiness of mankind, schools and the means of education shall forever be encouraged.

The second is President John Adams to the Massachusetts Militia, October 11, 1798:

> We have no Government armed with Power capable of contending with human Passions unbridled by morality and Religion. Avarice, Ambition, Revenge or Gallantry, would break the strongest Cords of our Constitution as a Whale goes through a Net. Our Constitution was made only for a moral and religious People. It is wholly inadequate to the government of any other.

Hardly the actions and sentiments of a group of men hostile or indifferent to religion!

The founders' religious beliefs are often dismissed as deist—that is, faith in some sort of impersonal, inactive God—or else the founders themselves are condemned as outright atheists who masked their unbelief so as not to undermine piety among the people, which they considered a necessary support for republican virtue. There is some evidence for both claims, though much less than is often supposed and much less for the latter than for the former. Yet even if the latter case were true, it would at least suggest a certain respect for belief that cuts against the thesis that the founders were anti-religious hyper-rationalists.

In truth, leaving aside outliers such as Franklin and Jefferson—whose deism is hard to deny—the vast majority of the founders, along with the overwhelming majority of the American population at the time of the Revolution (and decades, if not centuries, thereafter), were orthodox believers who saw no contradiction between their faith and the principles of the Revolution or of their new government.

That doesn't mean they couldn't have been mistaken. But before we dismiss their reasoning, let's make sure we understand it. To the founding generation, it seemed reasonable that the God who revealed the Decalogue, preached the Sermon on the Mount, and created the natural world also endowed that world with natural moral principles that accord with His law. The alternative—moral commands with no basis in nature or that contradict nature—seemed to them irrational and implausible.

The founders' view of tradition or authority is more ambivalent and fell somewhere between complete disdain and unquestioning adherence. Men inclined to the latter would, of course, never consider revolting against a legitimate king, however tyrannically he might be acting in the moment. Indeed, determined adherence to authority rules out any appeal to a higher standard, or simply identifies that standard with one's tradition. Hence in this understanding, a legitimate king ipso facto cannot act tyrannically and there can be no such thing as an unjust law or illegitimate action by any long-established government. The founders rejected this view as irrational and slavish, as binding men to endure any treatment whatsoever so long as those inflicting it could claim traditional or authoritative status. In their view, unquestioning acceptance of authority was a recipe for perpetual tyranny, for the meek acceptance of any injustice.

But it goes too far to say that the founders rejected tradition out of hand in favor of pure rationalism. They understood human nature too well to attempt to sweep away all tradition in favor of cold reason. Certainly they sought to subject certain traditions with political import to rational analysis, lest tradition end up doing more harm than good. But they were too attuned to the complexities of human nature not to understand that man is far from a fully rational being: he has appetites and passions as well as his reason, which does not always govern the former. Moreover, the founders saw nothing fundamentally irrational about taking guidance from the past, from one's ancestors, from old books, from folkways—in short, from tradition. One may indeed say that as much as the Revolution was a tax revolt and an effort to protect religious liberty, it was also a defense of tradition—of our way, the by-then 150-year-old American way, which was being trampled by a far-off authority.

Furthermore, the founders saw no inherent contradiction between reason and tradition or between reason and religion (at least not at the level of daily life). Abraham Lincoln defined conservatism as "adherence to the old and tried, against the new and untried," a sentiment with which the founders would have fully agreed. Traditions become established not because they don't work or run counter to reality and human nature, but precisely because they *do* work, or at least don't undermine or contradict human nature.

This is not to say that all traditions are rational or good; such can't be taken for granted. Consider that the longer the soft tyranny under which we currently live goes on, the easier it will be for its rulers and beneficiaries to justify and defend its goals, institutions, and methods of operation as "traditional." Would any of us accept that claim? At least insofar as that would obligate us to affirm such a state as legitimate or just?

In the founders' view, those traditions that common sense tells us are operating contrary to the human good must be subjected to rational analysis. But most traditions—especially those that have stood the test of time and appear to be either beneficial, benign, or neutral—ought at least to be given the benefit of the doubt and never cast aside lightly.

Equality, Revisited

Those wishing to conclude that the founders' philosophy was false must establish why "all men are created equal" as the founders understood it must be false. As we have argued, their understanding of equality was historically momentous but also philosophically limited. It allows for—even insists upon—ample inequality of talent, wisdom, strength, and many other virtues and qualities. If this is false, then its opposite—inequality of natural rank, natural titles to rule coupled with natural status as fit-only-to-be-ruled—must be true.

I see no middle ground here. Either there exists a natural order of rank among men that distinguishes natural rulers from naturally ruled, or there doesn't. Noting the extraordinary differences of virtues and talents among men is not enough. Differences of degree are not necessarily differences in kind. And even if we could establish that in cases of the least- versus the best-endowed, differences of degree *were* differences in kind, we would still be left with the considerable problem that most people fall somewhere in the middle. Where's the line? Who is "above" and who "below"?

If nature *has* drawn such a line, she also declined to make it bright or even discernible to members of the very species to which it applies. She is not nearly so careless with the so-called "eusocial" animals, amongst which, within a given population group—for example, a colony or hive—ruler and ruled are clearly distinguished in ways insiders (members of the species themselves) and outsiders (predators, prey, and observers) alike all recognize. If among human beings there are in fact natural aristocrats and natural serfs, the fact that we can't tell one another apart at a glance—that most of us deny being the latter and deny others' claim to being the former—guarantees that any political order based on such an alleged distinction must be grounded in convention, not nature. It will hence be inherently unstable.

The problem is not that there are no individuals better able to rule than others. It is rather that this ability does not seem to be heritable, at least not in perpetuity. This is one reason why all hereditary aristocracies decay over time: the alleged "natural rulers" are likelier than not to be bad at their jobs. Another reason is that the "naturally ruled" tend not to accept their inferiority with resigned patience. Force is required to maintain order; and not merely the "monopoly of force" necessary to every regime, legitimate or otherwise, but the harsher, more ubiquitous kind characteristic of tyranny.

Nor is this consideration necessarily theoretical. In a crisis, people are likely to recognize a natural leader and follow his diktats—just as even democratic peoples often defer to superior talent. Indeed, one criterion by which to judge the soundness of this or that democracy is by how well and how often it manages to place naturally talented leaders, whatever their backgrounds, into political office. But democratic peoples still tend to insist on retaining the right to make the selections themselves and to change leaders.

If our present system were someday to give way and some group of former Americans were forced to reconstitute a functioning polity on their own, the leaders would be unwise to do so on the basis of an alleged natural or divine title to rule. I very much doubt that God will come down to anoint anyone a king or a duke. Absent such an endorsement, any assertion of one's own natural aristocratic superiority will be—and be seen as—nothing more than what the kids call "LARPing" ("live action role playing," or dress-up). It's hard to envision any former American accepting the assertion of his own permanent inferiority with good grace.

To the contrary, the claim itself would almost guarantee civil conflict and disunity. And to the extent that any did accept the claim, such would mark him as servile—not necessarily someone you want by your side in tough times. Lucius Junius Brutus, in galvanizing his cohorts to expel a Roman monarchy that had become tyrannical, made them swear an oath that "by sword, fire, and any means hence" they never again suffer a king to rule in Rome. Those are the kind of people you're going to want to have around.

This points us, finally, to the three fundamental reasons why the founders asserted that "all men are created equal." First, because— the way they understood and intended the phrase—they believed it to be true.

Second, it was to establish the legitimacy of their new government and of the Revolution itself. Political legitimacy is a tricky thing—intangible yet essential. A regime seen as illegitimate is unstable and unlikely to last—and unlikely to function well while it does. Its own people will not trust it even when it is acting for the common good, will not be inclined to give it the benefit of the doubt when its actions are questionable, and will be quick to disobey, undermine, or even assault it when its actions seem indefensible. Unfriendly foreign nations tend to see illegitimate regimes as easy targets, lacking sufficient support from their own people to defend their interests and allies to help out in times of need.

Political legitimacy has two foundations: justice and longevity. Obviously, a revolutionary regime cannot, in the beginning, rely on the latter. A claim to the former is its only option. To try to base that claim on an alleged right to rule by some part of the new polity was, for our founders, impossible and undesirable for all the reasons stated. The newly formed people, or most of them, simply would not have accepted such a claim. They would have deemed such a regime illegitimate from the start, proof that the Revolution had been a sham.

Nor would any of the Old World's monarchies or aristocracies have accepted a fresh American claim to royalty or nobility. Such claims— their own claims—they all well knew depended on the popular belief that their privileged status was part of some permanent, divinely ordained order, "the way things have always been." Obviously, such cannot be true—every human order has an origin. But when that origin is known and seen—when a man visibly crowns himself—that order is robbed of its necessary mystique. Napoleon and his family would learn this lesson the hard way a few short years later.

Which brings us to the founders' third and most important reason. A claim to legitimacy based on justice must have a standard of justice to which to appeal. The founders could not, as we have seen, appeal to divine right. Indeed, they could not seek political legitimacy in religion at all, beyond basic appeals to fundamental religious principles such as the Ten Commandments and Christ's moral teaching. The new United States was teeming with adherents to different Christian sects who did not see eye-to-eye on matters of doctrine or conscience. Trying to establish political legitimacy on a religious basis would, in those circumstances, have been a recipe for religious war—a calamity that many Americans, or their ancestors, had fled Europe to escape.

More fundamentally, Christianity severed the direct connection between religion and the civil law that had hitherto prevailed throughout the world in pagan antiquity and monotheistic Israel alike. This is the meaning of "render unto Caesar." In the Christian understanding, religion becomes a matter of faith, not law. The massive intellectual and political changes that all fit under the broad rubric of the "Enlightenment" rendered incredible any suggestion that written, civil law—the actual, enacted positive law (not to rule out biblical or religious guidance that informs the law)—is revealed directly from heaven. Which means that the law must be made by men and seen, known, and accepted to have been made by men. Which in turn means that the law may have, in the final analysis, only one of two possible bases. Either it is made according to the will of the lawmakers—that is, it simply institutionalizes their interests—or it is consciously crafted to reflect nature, natural justice, a standard that man does not will or create.

The former case is nothing more nor less than "might makes right." This the founders rejected out of hand, based on both their secular learning and religious belief. They judged that ancient doctrine to be both untrue and dangerous. The three criteria for political stability and long-term happiness within a society are justice, concord, and legitimacy. "Might makes right" undermines all three: it hastens the demise of any regime based thereon and makes life more turbulent, violent, and unpleasant while such a regime lasts.

The founders thus sought a true and rational basis for political legitimacy that neither contradicts nor offends anyone's faith and allows for the establishment of justice consistent with man's natural liberties, emphatically including freedom of conscience. In the final analysis, this is what "all men are created equal" *is*: a claim of natural justice, of natural right—a claim that good and bad, better and worse, good and evil, right and wrong, justice and injustice exist by nature, are knowable by man, and not only do not contradict the divinely established moral order but accord with it, indeed are part of it.

Those inclined to see nothing but airy-fairy abstractions in such a claim should pause to consider that every revolution—indeed every change from worse to better—justifies itself by some claim to a higher standard. Even if that standard is a "return" to lost superior practice, to mislaid justice, it still in turn depends on a judgment—which presupposes an evaluation—that what is past is truly superior to what is present.

Unless, that is, one wishes simply to assert that the past qua past is always superior to the present—an argument similar, perhaps identical, to the ancient identification of the good with the ancestral. But this quickly leads to a contradiction, for as soon as our defective present is changed for the better, it becomes the past—which by this understanding is also "better" simply by virtue of being the past. Nor is that the only problem. For if the past is always superior to the present, that means that in the American case the American past is superior to the American present—the very American past that those who condemn the present say they reject for being "propositionist," "liberal," and acid-bath rationalist!

In short, there must be a standard knowable to reason that exists outside of or transcends considerations of "tradition" or "one's own." This standard need not inherently contradict tradition or be anathema to one's own. But it is the only sound basis for evaluating and judging either of those, or for judging the present worse than the past, or for inspiring hope in a better future, or for planning and working toward that future. Everyone dissatisfied with the current regime and wishing for something better, something more just, implicitly appeals to some independent standard of justice, of right. Therefore, for them to condemn the founders for doing the same is both contradictory and hypocritical. Indeed, the American Revolution both intended and achieved exactly what today's regime dissenters claim to want: it replaced a tyranny with a just government. The Revolution was able to accomplish that only through rational appeals to knowledge of good and bad.

It's also ironic that many of those who most criticize the founders' alleged rationalism in the name of tradition, in the very act of rejecting the founders, reject *our* tradition—American tradition. For what is tradition but a way of doing things, this or that particular people's particular ways, developed and practiced over decades and centuries? To turn one's back on the American past, on the American way of doing things, way of thinking, way of life, all in the name of "tradition," is a massive self-contradiction. To what tradition are Americans supposed to appeal if not to our own?

All of which points to another, greater irony: many of those making these arguments consider themselves nationalists and state their criticisms allegedly on behalf of nationalism. Nationalism, naturally, requires a nation. In our case, which nation? If not the American nation, then which? The appeal to Europe faces the problems sketched above. But even if such a route were available, it would still seem impossible to be a nationalist who rejects his own nation.

As to the argument that the founders' rhetoric inevitably led to the present morass—how does the commonsense assertion that no man is by right born either a slave or a master inevitably cause democratic leveling? How does the equally commonsense observation that an idiot, dissipated, sixth-generation "aristocrat" is not naturally superior to, and cannot by right rule without consent, a talented and virtuous farmhand inevitably lead to "Harrison Bergeron"?

These questions become harder to answer when one considers that, when American society was (to say the least) more committed to the original understanding of equality than it is now, the country provided ample room for men of exemplary talent to excel. Meanwhile, America today—allegedly in the grip of democratic levelling brought on by "propositionsim"—is more unequal than ever. Indeed, what is 2020 America if not a regime based on de facto inequality, with a small elite lording it over an effectively disenfranchised citizenry? How is this a fault of the founders' understanding of the true principles of just government? The opposite would appear to be true: we got into this mess not by adhering to the founders' understanding but by discarding it.

Even if you think the founders, or my summary of their intentions, are wrong, isn't it at least obvious that what I sketched is infinitely superior to what we have now? Not that I'm suggesting we can get it all back any time soon; but as something to compare and contrast to current arrangements—as a standard that can be used to demonstrate the unfairness and injustice of the latter—is it not at least useful? What's closer to the government you'd like to see, to the utopia in your head: the founders' America or the America of 2020?

Bottom line: to get it back, we have to remember what it was—what it *is*. If it turns out that we can't get it back—if, despite our best efforts, America gives way to something else—the first and most fundamental divide will be between those who self-identify as American, and nothing else, and those who do not. The former will bring Americanism with us in our hearts as Aeneas carried his father on his back from the burning wreckage of Troy, on his way to plant the seed that would grow into the city of Rome.

"Concurrent Majoritarianism" and Group Rights

The schools of thought analyzed above, while influential today among certain intellectuals, have not actually exerted much of a real-world impact on American society or government. But one rightist critique of the founders definitely did: the attack mounted in defense of slavery.

That attack was both theoretical and practical. In the former sense, it was directed at the idea that "all men are created equal," which is obviously incompatible with slavery. The attack's most powerful proponent—Senator (and Vice President, Secretary of State, and many other offices besides) John C. Calhoun—called the central theoretical assertion of the Declaration of Independence "the most dangerous of all political error" and a "self-evident lie." His purpose was to rob that idea of any moral or philosophic power to undermine, or bolster opposition to, slavery.

Which points to the attack's practical purpose: when it was mounted, proponents of slavery sought to expand that institution into territories that would become new states, while their opponents sought to prevent slavery's spread. Ironically, the future leaders of the Confederacy agreed with Abraham Lincoln that barring the expansion of slavery into the territories would place that institution "in the course of ultimate extinction." They just disagreed about the desirability of that outcome! Slavery's supporters understood that if the effort to block slavery in the territories succeeded, their "peculiar institution" would die a slow death even if the federal government took no steps against it where it already existed. This is why, for instance, in the years before the Civil War, Southern statesmen were exploring the possibility of expanding southward into the slaveholding parts of Latin America and the Caribbean. They, or some of them, preferred a multicultural and polyglot slave country to a more unified free country, for the obvious reason that their status as elites was far more secure in the former.

Despite the South's smaller population and poorer economy, until the Civil War, Southern politicians managed to protect slavery even in the teeth of popular opposition—for instance, forcing the North and West to accept unpopular fugitive slave laws. But as the 1850s progressed, the South's leading men gradually recognized that anti-slavery forces had the votes to prevent slavery's expansion into the territories and thereby to prevent the creation of new slave states. This was important politically because the South could not outvote the North in the House of Representatives and so counted on a balanced Senate to preserve its political clout at the national level. If the number of slave states were fixed while free states continued to join the Union, then this last Southern check on Northern (and Western) political power would be lost.

Pro-slavery forces knew that their anti-slavery opponents were acting as a lawfully constituted majority within constitutional constraints. But they found the eventual, inevitable result intolerable. Their solution was to attack not just those constitutional constraints but majoritarianism simply, which eventually—and inevitably—required attacking the whole basis of the American political order.

Slavery's partisans tried out a number of arguments, the first being that the majority's wish to forbid slavery in the territories was not rightful. But they had a hard time explaining how keeping slavery out of a place where it had never existed—especially when that place itself only yesterday didn't exist as a political entity—violated anyone's rights. And since the territories were by definition federal—that is, the property of the entire nation—Southern statesmen also found it hard to explain why Northern and Western public opinion should have no say in how the territories would be governed.

Slaveholders next tried to argue that their property rights—which all but the most radical Northern abolitionists agreed were constitutionally protected in existing slave states—extended to *any* territory or state. This was essentially the finding of 1857's notorious *Dred Scott* decision, which, as Lincoln immediately grasped, erased the distinction between free and slave states by turning any of the former into one of the latter the instant a slaveholder crossed its border with one of his slaves. The nation as a whole did not, to say the least, accept this argument.

Which left the slave-holding South with only one option: reject even lawfully enacted majority will—even if it respects minority rights—as illegitimate insofar as it contravenes minority will. This in turn required rejecting the founders' understanding of rights, which was specifically and emphatically an idea of *individual* rights; that is, of rights which inhere in individual human beings precisely owing to their status as human beings. For the founders, a right is a moral claim that all individuals justly hold vis-à-vis all other individuals by virtue of all being born equally free and independent. In this understanding, the majority cannot rightfully vote to trample minority rights. For example, executing innocent citizens or expropriating their property can not be legitimized simply by a majority vote. But the majority *can* rightfully enact policies that a minority disagrees with, even abhors, so long as such policies do not infringe upon members of that minority's equal natural rights. Indeed, that's the whole point of republican or democratic politics: to make the government responsive to popular will, consistent with respect for minority rights.

Calhoun and his followers sought to do the opposite: to insulate policy—or at least one policy!—from popular will. Hence discarding majoritarianism was necessary to protect slavery, and discarding individual rights—already under attack as corrosive to public support for slavery—was required to dismiss majoritarianism.

But Calhoun also understood that once the baby of equal natural rights was thrown out with the bathwater of majoritarianism, his faction needed a new basis for political legitimacy. Thus he devised a new concept of rights, "concurrent majoritarianism," more simply understood as "group rights." Under this understanding, "rights" adhere not in individuals but in groups. Hence collections of persons as a class, based on some shared trait or self-identification, may rightly block majority will for any reason. Majority will is thus limited not by individual minority rights but by collective minority interest, by what a minority wants, even—especially—when it can't get it by following the parchment's normal processes.

Calhoun did not live to see the Confederacy. But the states that would form it took their momentous step under his tutelage, justifying their action with his doctrine. That action is sometimes defended on the ground that it was a reaction to Northern aggression and tyranny, no different than the American Revolution itself. After all, what was the latter if not "secession" from Britain?

The problem with this argument emerges from the very terms. The American revolutionaries did not claim to be merely "seceding" from Britain. They were mounting a revolution, overthrowing a government they boldly asserted to be tyrannical and illegitimate. The Declaration of Independence clearly and specifically asserts—twice—a natural right to revolution:

> whenever any Form of Government becomes destructive of these ends [of securing equal natural rights and government by consent,] it is the Right of the People to alter or to abolish it, and to institute new Government, laying its foundation on such principles and organizing its powers in such form, as to them shall seem most likely to effect their Safety and Happiness.

And:

> when a long train of abuses and usurpations, pursuing invariably the same Object evinces a design to reduce them under absolute Despotism, it is their right, it is their duty, to throw off such Government, and to provide new Guards for their future security.

A just revolution overthrows an unjust government and establishes a new one. We may thus say that all just revolutions are secessions, but not all secessions are just revolutions. The all-important question is the justice of the government being overthrown. As Lincoln explained in his first inaugural address, unanimity in any political community is impossible. Secession triggered by losing a fairly contested election is not only unjustified, it has no limiting principle: if secession is permitted, why not secession ad infinitum? There are thus only two logical end-points:

anarchy or despotism. Libertarian ideologue Murray N. Rothbard, in
his own inimitable way, agrees:

> Once one concedes that a single world government is not
> necessary, then where does one logically stop at the permis-
> sibility of separate states? If Canada and the United States can
> be separate nations without being denounced as in a state of
> impermissible "anarchy," why may not the South secede from
> the United States? New York State from the Union? New York
> City from the state? Why may not Manhattan secede? Each
> neighbourhood? Each block? Each house? Each person?

Every-man-a-government-unto-himself is literally Hobbes's "state
of nature," yet Rothbard appears to approve.

The founders were wiser. They replaced the Articles of Confederation with the Constitution in part because the former were too weak;
they exerted no binding power over the states and so were a government
in name only.

If the Southern states believed the North was acting as tyrannically against themselves as the British Crown had acted against the
thirteen colonies in 1776, they could have levelled that charge against
the North and asserted the right of revolution. They did not. Why
not? Because if the right of revolution is to exist, it must arise from
natural justice or natural right—from the existence of equal natural
rights that a slave state must perforce reject. This is why the South's
leading thinkers had to appeal instead to the anti-majoritarian concept of "group rights." Their support of slavery denied them recourse
to the natural right of revolution.

Calhoun's and his heirs' attempt to found a new basis for political
legitimacy was defeated, seemingly in speech by Abraham Lincoln, and
definitively on the battlefield in 1865. I say "seemingly" because, as we
shall see, it has proven surprisingly resilient.

South-Bashing?

I now must address the charge that, because I attribute a portion of our current malaise to antebellum Southern political doctrine, I am anti-South, a vessel for the vindictive spirits of Charles Sumner and Thaddeus Stevens.

Nothing could be further from the truth or my intent. I am, to be sure, pro-Union and an admirer of Lincoln. I'm glad the Union won the war—but wish that Lincoln had lived to implement his less harsh, more magnanimous vision for Reconstruction. I well understand that in today's America, the South is one of America's strongest redoubts of traditional conservatism and virtue. I oppose the removal of Confederate statues—especially by lawless mobs—contrary to local popular opinion and believe Lincoln would too, in the spirit of national reconciliation and cohesion.

Hence I do not intend a single word of the above as a blowtorch against the South. I'm just telling it like I see it. I certainly didn't mean the above as a purely academic exercise. To the contrary, my intent is eminently practical: to understand what came later, we must understand what came first. I hope, in what follows, to make clear why Calhoun's "concurrent majoritarianism" still very much matters. It's certainly true that Calhoun had no idea his concept would, beginning a century after his death, be used to justify such radical movements as Black Power, homosexual marriage, fourth-wave feminism, and puberty blockers for fourth-graders. But ideas have consequences. Sometimes those consequences are unforeseen.

Still, I know from experience of struggles past that, in the struggle ahead, there will be those who understand the gravity of the current crisis who nonetheless prefer relitigating old claims to fighting present battles. Some do so no doubt from the best of intentions, insisting that unless we understand the errors of the past, we are doomed to repeat them. I agree with that sentiment and differ only in believing that not all of what some consider errors were, in fact, errors.

Others go further and insist that the key to everything is to refight the Civil War until no one left alive denies that Lincoln was a tyrant and the father of all evil among us. I once asked such a person whether, with the militant left coming for both our throats, we could for the time being put aside such fratricide, turn our attentions against our common enemy, and then get back to killing one another over Lincoln after we win. He said no, it was much more important to kill me over Lincoln right now.

To those less committed to the Lost Cause, I say a few things. First, I agree with Lincoln's second inaugural address, which pointedly does not single out the South for blame for the war, or even for slavery. The whole nation had sinned, he insisted; he was right. Not only would it be factually incorrect and morally wrong for the North and West forever to despise the South while absolving themselves of all responsibility, it would also be deadly to the process of national reconciliation, which Lincoln sought above all things. As should we all.

Second, in the interminable rhetorical reenactment of the Civil War, some assert that tariffs were the war's true cause. It wasn't about slavery—that was just Northern grandstanding! Well, no; it was about slavery, specifically whether slavery would be allowed to expand westward. But even if one accepts that tariffs were the true cause, it is surely ironic that in today's South—home to much of President Trump's base—support for tariffs is strong, whereas the antebellum South was the epicenter of anti-tariff sentiment. Indeed, the economic policy preferences of today's Southern electorate share far more in common with Lincoln's protectionist economic nationalism than with Calhoun's free-trade absolutism!

Third, what are sanctuary cities and other efforts to flout federal law and popular will but revivals of "nullification"? In this sense, among Calhoun's most faithful adherents today are Gavin Newsom and Bill de Blasio.

Fourth and most important, consider the eerie parallels between what Lincoln denounced as "the Slave Power" and today's globalist oligarchy. Like the latter, the former was a trans-partisan movement that sought to protect its narrow economic, social, and regional interests. It never constituted anything close to a majority nationally, yet through various proxies and fellow travelers, it managed to achieve a near lock on certain levers of power to make effective checks on its power by majority will impossible.

Is not the similarity between slavery and mass immigration obvious? (Note to the hysterical that I said "similarity" and not "identicalness.") They both serve the same fundamental purpose: to provide cheap labor to squeeze working-class citizens and enrich a few. The fact that slaves are not free and immigrants are is, to be sure, a gigantic difference—for immigrant and slave alike. But what about the third man, William Graham Sumner's "forgotten man"—the man whose wages are undercut or whose job is entirely lost? In their effects on *him*, the two don't seem so very different after all.

A major source of opposition to the Slave Power arose from the Free Soil Movement: free men—American citizens—who wanted to earn decent livings without having to compete against the artificially low costs of slave labor. Does *that* sound familiar?

OBJECTIONS TO THE PARCHMENT FROM THE LEFT

But the real damage to America—and the real foundations of the current order—originated not on the right, but on the left, above all, formal Progressivism and 1960s Leftism. These two bodies of thought, conjoined with the idea of "group rights," together form the dominant intellectual-political-social paradigm of America's governing and opinion-making classes.**

Capital-P Progressivism

"Progressivism" has come to mean any movement or pattern of thought that looks back at the past as backward and benighted and

---

** I wrote about this paradigm at some length in my book *After the Flight 93 Election*. Since some of the topics discussed there are directly relevant here, some repetition proved impossible to avoid. However, not everything said there is repeated here or vice versa, so I point those interested to that earlier volume.

forward to the future as inevitably superior, more moral, more "diverse," "inclusive," "equitable," and "tolerant"—in short, more left-wing. When Barack Obama says this or that person or idea is "on the wrong side of history," this is what he means.

Originally, Progressivism—with a capital "P"—was an intellectual movement and later a political party. The movement arose from a new account of human nature and how the human good can be known.

Progressivism dismisses the natural rights philosophy of the founders in favor of one allegedly based on historical and scientific progress. According to this view, there is no fixed human nature; the human situation is always fundamentally changing as people become more knowledgeable and more capable. The thought and practice—especially the morality—of the present is always superior to that of the past, in part because of accumulated knowledge. We know more, therefore we know better. Progressivism takes its name from this alleged insight.

Progressivism further holds that present knowledge is superior to the thought of the past not only in quantity but in quality. Contemporary thought is sounder and more rigorous because it rests on empirical science and its methodology, in contrast to the inherent imprecision of philosophy, which never rises above the level of opinion. Progressivism insists that it can apply the methodology of the natural sciences to human things and come to conclusions superior to those of philosophy and equal in precision to those of natural science.

Progressivism's third major claim is that the American founders' political philosophy too narrowly defines rights in terms of things the government may not do—deprive a person of life, liberty, or property without due process of law, for instance. A fuller, truer conception affirms "positive" rights or liberties: obligations that people are owed. Under this conception, a well-lived life requires not merely the removal of unjustified constraints but the provision—by the government—of life-enriching goods. Of Franklin Roosevelt's four freedoms, the first two—freedom of speech and freedom of worship—are negative, while the latter two, freedom from want and freedom from fear, are positive.

On these bases, the original Progressives mounted a theoretical critique of core American principles and institutions. They condemned the machinery of American government, such as federalism and the separation of powers, as slow and cumbersome obstacles to progress. They rejected limited government as too narrow to effect what they saw as the necessary expansion of government's powers to cope with an increasingly complex world. They declared negative rights insufficient and insisted that government guarantee a host of new positive liberties. Above all, they dismissed the founding principles as time-bound and out-of-date, at best adequate for the simpler circumstances of the eighteenth century but insufficient to meet the challenges of the Progressives' own time and especially of later times.

Progressivism further asserts that progress in human understanding and the accumulation of knowledge so illuminate formerly obscure subjects that questions once deemed matters of legitimate disagreement, and therefore appropriately decided through political deliberation, become instead assertions that can be shown to be either correct or incorrect. As knowledge increases in volume and complexity, issues become understandable to fewer and fewer. And, as the universe of questions with known answers expands, the number of people capable of knowing those answers shrinks. Both dynamics work in tandem to reduce the number of issues properly left to political deliberation and to increase the number that should be decided and administered by trained experts: the scope of politics radically constricts. In Engels's famous formula, "[t]he government of persons is replaced by the administration of things." Except that Engels expected "the administration of things" to lead to the withering away of the state, whereas the wiser Progressives knew it would require a state larger and more powerful than any hitherto imagined.

Progressivism has a complicated relationship with democracy. The original Progressives welcomed greater voter involvement, worked to reduce the power of urban and state-level political machines that made a mockery of free and fair elections, and spearheaded the adoption of referendum processes in many states. But the rule of experts and rule by the people are fundamentally in tension. What if the people vote for something that experts—that "science"—have "proved" "incorrect?" Obviously, only the "correct" understanding of any issue should inform policy. "Error has no rights."

Over time, this tension was resolved in favor of expert consensus. Voters can be unwise, hidebound, prejudiced. Sometimes they fail to discern their own good and even vote for the opposite. Progressivism, by contrast, holds that it has discerned the people's true interest and redefines democracy as what the people *would* vote for if only they were smart enough to know their own good.

Under Progressivism, elites discern the spirit and imperatives of the age and then tell the people what they should want. Ur-Progressive Woodrow Wilson put it this way: Progressivism "seeks to substitute the person whom we call 'the man of the people' with the men of the schools, the trained, instructed, fitted men, the men who will study their duties and master the principles of their [bureaucratic] departments."

Progressives prefer, when possible, to correct voter mistakes through more voting. It's better if the "right" policy is endorsed by voters in some way; that helps ease public acceptance. Thus election outcomes that accord with expert judgment are welcomed as ratification of expert consensus. But there's no going back—not even through future elections. A Progressive policy, once enacted—*however* enacted—is sacrosanct. Voting is not done away with, exactly, but its effects are carefully circumscribed.

Sometimes, though, it's necessary to enact the correct policy by fiat—executive, administrative, or judicial—or to overturn majority will. When the voters have the temerity to reject expert consensus—say, in a referendum or by electing a true dissident—that's illegitimate. In such cases, Progressivism sees itself as justified in using every lever of power at its disposal to thwart backsliding. Typically this means blocking measures in the courts, but another effective method is sabotaging executive branch officials from the inside.

Progressivism's concrete manifestation—its enforcement arm—is the administrative state. From the dawn of the Progressive Era, and intensifying in the mid-1960s, Progressive elites inside and outside our government centralized governing authority in a "fourth branch," the executive branch's agencies and bureaucracies. These institutions and those who run and staff them are the heart of the administrative state.

Administrative state rule is fundamentally anti-democratic and anti-constitutional. Its animating "expert consensus" derives from and carries the authority of science. In practice, this amounts to elevating the research universities into the highest sources of political, moral, and spiritual authority (with a supporting role played by think tanks, NGOs, and small circulation intellectual journals, all of which take their cues from the universities). Their holy writ is the peer-reviewed journal article.

One must be careful, however, not to be too hard on the original Progressives. Their actual policy agenda was mostly sensible—and vastly preferable to what our contemporary progressives ram down our collective throat. Those original Progressives sharply curtailed immigration, spurring the most successful wave of assimilation in American history; built infrastructure throughout the country, prioritizing underserved rural communities; rooted out corruption in cities and towns; instituted competitive civil service examinations that greatly bolstered the honesty and competence of government; busted up oligarchic trusts to check runaway corporate power and enable fair competition; cleaned up the country's food and water supplies; enacted scores of policies supporting morality and the family; instituted sensible workplace safety and other pro-worker regulations; and built the National Park system—among many other great achievements.

Progressivism was also not without its notable failures and missteps. It suffices to mention Prohibition and America's unfortunate acquisition of an overseas empire, our questionable and costly intervention in World War I, and Woodrow Wilson's disastrous attempt to redraw the map of Europe in his image.

But Progressivism's most enduring legacy is the damage it wrought on the functioning of our political institutions and on elite understanding of politics. Casualties include federalism, the separation of powers,

limited government, and enumerated powers. The Progressive amendments to the Constitution have enabled the scope and size of the federal
government to grow exponentially—for instance, the Sixteenth by autho-
rizing the income tax and the Seventeenth by reducing the power and
influence of the states in national affairs.

Progressivism eroded popular control—democratic accountability—
almost to the point of obsolescence. The net effect is very similar to that
intended by "concurrent majoritarianism": whatever the majority does
or does not want, if its will contradicts the interest or preference of the
ruling minority—that is, progressives and their administrative state
apparatchiks—it is ipso facto illegitimate and not allowed.

Worst of all, at the theoretical level, Progressivism entirely upended
our elite's understanding of justice, of good and bad. The hidden cause
of that upending is the contradiction at the core of Progressivism, which
at once denies a fixed human nature and hence a standard of goodness
independent of human preference or will but also insists that progress is
good. "Historicism"—the belief that values change from era to era—is
Progressivism's indispensable foundation. By this, the Progressives did
not mean simply that people's preferences and habits change over time.
They intended something much more fundamental: the underlying structure of right and wrong, of morality itself, changes over time. But if
morality is always changing, then no one morality can be simply true—
much less good.

There is thus an implied relativism at the heart of Progressivism.
Leading Progressive intellectual John Dewey explicitly denied that morality has any fixed meaning. We must "advance to a belief in a plurality of
changing, moving, individualized goods and ends," and "growth itself
is the only moral 'end.'" Woodrow Wilson agreed: "The hope of society
lies in an infinite individual variety, in the freest possible play of individual forces." In other words, true morality is letting everyone choose
his own morality.

But in actual practice the Progressives were strong moralists who
pushed policies to strengthen the family, attack corruption, and uplift

workers and the poor. Dewey himself denounced "capricious or discontinuous action in the name of spontaneous self-expression." He and his fellow Progressives would very likely be shocked and revolted by Weimerica 2020. But why, and how, on the basis of their own stated principles? One may despise what the Progressives despised and admire what they admired—one may esteem Progressive policies as good—but one cannot consistently do so on the basis of Progressive ideology.

Progressivism never managed to square this circle. It instead was pulled in one direction by its moralistic, busybody practical streak, and in the opposite by its theological hostility to every religious, philosophic, or traditional conception of morality. It was left to Progressivism's heirs to combine these two contradictory impulses into a new morality, a new idea of the good.

"The Sixties"

"The Sixties" are here understood broadly to include all the lefty trends that originated as "counter-cultural" in that era but now *are* the culture.

The Sixties are such well-trod ground that anything one tries to say about them will seem old hat to someone. Perhaps no era in the history of the world has been more analyzed, debated, chewed over, lionized, and (occasionally) criticized than America in the 1960s.

But mostly lionized. The literature—histories, memoirs, biographies, cultural appraisals—on the period is vast but almost uniformly rapturous. The Sixties are nearly always portrayed as a time of necessary liberation and creative ferment, a new dawn, the moment when America finally began its long overdue march toward redemption for its ugly past. A whole prestige television series—*Mad Men*—had this as its explicit, unsubtle theme. As one critic put it, "*Mad Men* shows why the '60s *had* to happen"—by "had," meaning that the country faced a moral imperative to overcome and even sweep aside what had come before.

There's something to that interpretation, of course. In reality and in the mythology, the cornerstone of the Sixties is civil rights—the effort to end Southern segregation, outlaw discrimination, and fully integrate American blacks into every aspect of American life. A majority of people outside the South saw segregation as a stain on the country—unfair, morally wrong, contrary to American principles, and an international embarrassment at a time when we were waging a cold war against what was effectively a slave state. Most were happy to see it go.

To most Americans, the purpose of civil rights in 1964—and thereafter—was to redeem, finally, the unfulfilled promise of emancipation. Segregation once defeated—civil rights once secured—the letter and spirit of America's founding principles would at last be fulfilled. Henceforth the country would go forward guaranteeing basic rights, living up to "all men are created equal," and judging everyone according to the content of his character rather than the color of his skin.

Yet that's not exactly the way things worked out. Instead, the extension of civil and voting rights to blacks was treated not as a necessary corrective but as a down payment, a beginning. More—much more—would be demanded, and not just from genuinely aggrieved blacks but from groups few had hitherto believed had any cause to be aggrieved. A reviewer of Christopher Caldwell's *The Age of Entitlement: America Since the Sixties*, puts it this way: "[T]he broadly accepted direction of thought throughout the West has been consistent since the 1960s: to bring within the pale of the constitution and civil society those who had hitherto been marginalized or excluded."

That, indeed, has been elite interpretation of the 1960s for more than half a century: America was not merely unjust to blacks through segregation; America was exclusionary to virtually everyone other than heterosexual white Christian males. And "inclusion" in this understanding has turned out to mean not the removal of de jure or even de facto barriers but efforts to ensure equality of outcomes across groups.

That's not what the American people were sold in the 1960s, nor what they thought they were getting. Had they been told the real plan outright, they would surely have said, "No." It's hard to say whether the deception was intended from the beginning or opportunistically grafted on later. President Lyndon Johnson's famous 1965 Howard University commencement speech, delivered scarcely a year after the passage of the 1964 Civil Rights Act, suggests the former:

> But freedom is not enough. You do not wipe away the scars of centuries by saying: Now you are free to go where you want, and do as you desire, and choose the leaders you please.
>
> You do not take a person who, for years, has been hobbled by chains and liberate him, bring him up to the starting line of a race and then say, "you are free to compete with all the others," and still justly believe that you have been completely fair.
>
> Thus it is not enough just to open the gates of opportunity. All our citizens must have the ability to walk through those gates.
>
> This is the next and the more profound stage of the battle for civil rights. We seek not just freedom but opportunity. We seek not just legal equity but human ability, not just equality as a right and a theory but equality as a fact and equality as a result.

Six years after this announcement of a new core goal of American liberalism, Harvard professor John Rawls would provide an elaborate justification for redefining justice along these lines. Rawls helpfully sums up his 560-page tome *A Theory of Justice* in one sentence: "All social primary goods—liberty and opportunity, income and wealth, and the bases of self-respect—are to be distributed equally unless an unequal distribution of any or all of these goods is to the advantage of the least favored."

Throughout the book, Rawls refers to equality of result simply as "equality," as if to scrub from the memory banks any other definition or understanding. He dismisses equal treatment before the law as mere "formal" equality. Genuine equality requires equal outcomes.

But only to a point. The second half of Rawls's formulation—inequality is OK if helps the "least favored"—he calls "the difference principle." Of these two core tenets, he writes that

> the first requires equality in the assignment of basic rights and duties, while the second holds that social and economic inequalities, for example inequalities of wealth and authority, are just only if they result in compensating benefits for everyone, and in particular for the least advantaged.

Rawls variously calls his political philosophy "justice as fairness" and "social justice."

In this understanding, the purpose of public policy—of government itself—must be to achieve genuine equality through the redistribution of goods such as power, wealth, and honors from the "advantaged" to the "disadvantaged." Policies are deemed good only to the extent that they help the disadvantaged—especially the most disadvantaged.

This is obviously incompatible with civil rights understood as a once-and-for-all removal of formal barriers to access. "Justice as fairness" rather demands that civil rights transform from grants of nature to be guaranteed by an impartial government into entitlements to various goods and honors. There is, of course, a fundamental kinship here with the Progressive conception of negative versus positive rights or liberties.

Rawls himself identifies the least favored or "most disadvantaged" not by who they are but by what they lack: opportunity, wealth, and honors. In principle, then, a disadvantaged person could be from any racial or ethnic group—say, a lower-middle-class West Virginia kid whose parents never went to college and whose father has been unemployed for years.

But the modern left, which took over Rawls's theory and reformulated it in furtherance of their interests, heatedly denies this. In their view—which is authoritative in our time—a straight white male absolutely cannot be disadvantaged. To the contrary, all such men are inherently and permanently "advantaged." Everyone else, by contrast, may lay some claim to being disadvantaged, if not necessarily to being among the "most disadvantaged." There is a hierarchy of disadvantage, whose precise rankings the left keeps mysterious, both for purposes of coalition management (naturally every member thinks she occupies the top spot) and to keep the "privileged" guessing.

But this understanding is subject to immediate and obvious commonsense objections. How is our young West Virginian in any way more "advantaged" than (say) the black billionaire founder of a cable TV empire? Or a gay billionaire Silicon Valley CEO? Or the female heiress to a financial services behemoth? Still more intricate justifications had to be elaborated—sort of like the way medieval astronomers invented epicycles to explain why, despite what you see the planets do in the sky, the earth really is the center of the universe.

The heart of those justifications can be seen from the subtle shift in language: from "favored" and "advantaged" to "privileged." To be favored implies a person or institution doing the favoring. An advantage may well be a grant of nature: superior strength or a high IQ. Or it may be something earned: wealth accrued through a lifetime of hard work. Privilege, by contrast, is much easier to connote—and condemn—as inherent, undeserved, unearned, even somehow unnatural.

Aristotle distinguishes between two forms of justice: distributive and corrective. The former concerns who deserves, and therefore gets, what. That is to say, it addresses the distribution of fundamentally scarce goods. The latter redresses actual wrongs: a thief is caught and punished, his victim's property is restored.

One could easily justify Rawls's original project—or any program of generous liberalism—solely on distributive grounds: those who have long had less should now get more. But America's contemporary left is not content to leave things there. It insists that what the country most needs—good and hard—is a massive helping of corrective justice. America was founded in racism, sexism, greed, and bloodlust, a litany of original sins the expiation of which the country—or at least a big part of it—must dedicate itself to overcoming (assuming redemption is even possible).

This is a new layer to the theory. Rawls himself is most concerned to alleviate what he considers disadvantage that arises from arbitrary factors or circumstances. By contrast, to the modern left, disadvantage has only one cause, and it is definitely *not* arbitrary. The sole reason why some have more and others have less is oppression: both oppression in the past, which continues to do harm in the present, but also oppression in the present. To many—perhaps most—Americans, the claim of present oppression sounds dubious, given the systematic repeal and stigmatization of unfair laws and practices over the past fifty-six years. The left has an answer to that, too: oppression has gone not away but rather has gone underground. It is "structural"—in the very DNA of our country— and also "subconscious": embedded in the hearts of the "privileged" whether or not they admit or even realize it.

Here's where the concept of "group rights" reappears. Rawls's original theory is perfectly consistent with limiting redistribution to an individual basis. Wherever there is poverty, constrained opportunity, or low status, simply take from those who have and give to those who don't.

But once "advantage" is redefined as illicit "privilege," and "disadvantage" as resulting solely from oppression—and especially once past oppression is accepted as a cause of present disadvantage—then justice ceases to be a matter of fairness to individuals but instead becomes a matter of group redress. The "disadvantaged" as a group become in effect the plaintiffs in a societal class action lawsuit—except that as individuals they need show no specific harm to themselves. Simply by virtue of being in the class, they have been and are being harmed and therefore have a "right" to the goods of the "privileged" defendant.

If woke justice were simply distributive—an endless robbing of Peter to pay Paul—the resulting injustices, resentments, and inefficiencies would be bad enough. But making redistribution not just "corrective" but based on birth—insisting that robbing Peter to pay Paul is not merely justified but required because Peter was born to an advantaged group and Paul wasn't—essentially tells Peter that his government, his society, his country is a revenge plot with him cast as the villain; that no amount of apologizing, payment, or pleading will ever let him off the hook; that he will forever and fundamentally be judged not for what he *does* or *does not* do but for who he *is*. How is he likely to respond to *that*?

For now, suffice it to say that modern leftism does exactly what it accuses America and Americans of doing and having done from the moment the first slave set foot in Jamestown: it racializes everything it touches. While the formal theory is even more complex than the above account, its core can be summarized in six words: Whites bad, people of color good.

CHAPTER THREE

Our Present Regime

The ideology of "the Sixties" at its most distilled—liberation from all restraints, sneering disdain for tradition and Christianity, contempt and hatred for America and its history, recasting of whites as the archvillains of their country's story—would have been destructive enough on its own. But when combined with Calhounite "group rights" and Progressive rule-by-experts via leviathan fiat, it has proved deadly.

Let us, then, contrast how our government is *supposed* to operate—and used to operate, if not always perfectly or consistently—with how it actually *does* operate today. But first we must understand the principles, stated and otherwise, by which it rules.

MODERN AMERICA: "PRINCIPLES"

The foundational principle of the American regime—the heart of its claim to being based on true morality and the true standard of political legitimacy—is supposed to be human equality. Which means that the government is supposed to treat people equally before the law, not use the law to try to equalize everyone and everything. But the latter is what, in fact, it does, or tries to do—though not to the ruling class, who largely exempt themselves from the lefty social engineering they push on everyone else.

The Transformation of "Civil Rights"

The American government enshrined in the parchment is based on—and was established to protect—the natural rights of its citizens. A "natural" right is one that a person possesses simply by virtue of being a person. These rights are the grant of God and nature and are "unalienable." That is, they are not given by man or law, and cannot justly be taken away by either—except in cases of just punishment and insofar as men freely cede to a just government a portion of their rights to secure the remainder. That is, upon entering the social compact, men surrender the complete freedom they enjoy in the state of nature in exchange for government protection of most of their natural rights.

Civil rights in this understanding can be understood in two complementary ways. What makes a right "civil" as opposed to simply a right? The first distinction between civil and natural rights is that the former are legal rights, the codification of the latter. All men by nature enjoy the right to life. In practice, protection for their lives takes the form of laws against homicide, plus effective policing to prevent, and punishment to deter, that crime. In the state of nature, one has natural rights but not civil rights because there is no written law backed up by credible state enforcement.

Second, our founders distinguished between rights the government is obligated to protect for all—citizens and non-citizens alike—and those it is required to secure only for citizens. Since all human beings possess unalienable rights to life and property, the government may not justly decline to prosecute the murder of, or theft from, a foreign visitor on the grounds that he is a non-citizen. But non-citizens do not possess, for instance, the right enshrined in the First Amendment to "petition the Government for a redress of grievances." Non-citizens have no claim to any say in the functioning of a government not their own, beyond the expectation that it secure their basic rights while they are present on its soil. Social compact theory and practice exclude—indeed, are rendered meaningless by—the notion that foreigners can direct any government but their own.

A coherent concept of civil rights does not distinguish among classes of citizens. Between citizens and non-citizens, for certain rights, yes; among fellow citizens, no. As Justice John Marshall Harlan stated in his famous dissent in *Plessy v. Ferguson*:

> [I]n view of the Constitution, in the eye of the law, there is in this country no superior, dominant, ruling class of citizens. There is no caste here. Our Constitution is color-blind, and neither knows nor tolerates classes among citizens. In respect of civil rights, all citizens are equal before the law. The humblest is the peer of the most powerful. The law regards man as man, and takes no account of his surroundings or of his color when his civil rights as guaranteed by the supreme law of the land are involved.

The civil rights movement of the 1960s seemed at first to proceed according to this understanding. That is to say, it appeared to seek the removal of formal barriers to fellow citizens' enjoyment of equal natural rights, as codified by law into civil rights. Or, in language the movement's leaders used at the time, they sought to compel America to "live up to its promise," to honor the pledges enshrined in the parchment.

But the movement quickly transformed into one seeking special privileges and accommodations for some. Former chair of the United States Commission on Civil Rights, Mary Frances Berry, explains:

> Civil rights laws were not passed to give civil rights protection to all Americans. . . . Instead they were passed out of a recognition that some Americans already had protection because they belong to a favored group; and others, including blacks,

Hispanics, and women of all races, did not because they belonged to disfavored groups.

Note the almost word-for-word Rawlsian formulation.

It is beyond the scope of the present undertaking to determine whether Berry's assertion is correct as a historical matter; that is to say, to ascertain whether the civil rights movement was from the beginning an effort not to end dual-class citizenship but rather to remove its worst features and then reverse the classes, or whether it began to end dual-class citizenship but was later transformed. Whichever the case, that's what "civil rights" means today: formal inequality before the law for citizens, and erasure of the distinction between citizen and non-citizen.

Equality versus "Protected Classes"

As far as I have been able to discern, the phrase "protected class" was coined by conservatives as a derisive taunt against policies such as affirmative action that divide people into groups, offer benefits and privileges to some, and deny them to others. If so, the left has managed to "own the insult." "Protected class" is now not only said without irony; it is official government terminology.

According to the United States Equal Employment Opportunity Commission, "Every U.S. citizen is a member of some protected class"— but also "Equal Employment Opportunity laws were passed to correct a history of unfavorable treatment of women and minority group members." Well, which is it? Indeed, how can "every U.S. citizen" be a member of a "protected class"—unless American citizenship is coterminous and synonymous with "protected class"? How can we all be members of a "protected class" unless there is only one such class: American citizens?

Theoretically, it might be possible to have numerous distinct classes that, taken together, cover the entire population if their protections differed from class to class—say, members of one group were protected against job discrimination while those of another were shielded from housing discrimination. But the protections offered by civil rights law do not vary from class to class. The classes rather identify who receives the benefits and—by omission—who does not.

Most of our laws remain formally "blind" to categories such as race, sex, religion, and sexual orientation. But some specify which groups are to receive which benefits, such as set-asides in contracting. This self-contradictory jumble of color blindness and color specificity makes our laws, on paper, an incoherent mess. The way they are enforced, however, is entirely coherent: one group—and only one group—does not qualify as a "protected class": straight, white, Christian males under a certain age (old enough, they may qualify for protection against age discrimination). Christopher Caldwell puts it this way:

> Those who lost most from the new rights-based politics were white men. The laws of the 1960s may not have been designed explicitly to harm them, but they were gradually altered to help everyone but them, which is the same thing. Whites suffered because they occupied this uniquely disadvantaged status under the civil rights laws, because their strongest asset in the constitutional system—their overwhelming preponderance in the electorate—was slowly shrinking, because their electoral victories could be overruled in courtrooms and by regulatory boards where necessary, and because the moral narrative of civil rights required that they be cast as the villains of their country's history. They fell asleep thinking of themselves as the people who had built this country and woke up to find themselves occupying the bottom rung of an official hierarchy of races.

Since discrimination is unpopular with the majority of Americans, our rulers try to deny out of one side of their mouths that any discrimination is taking place. But that is difficult to maintain, since everyone knows that a great deal is taking place—all of which, out of the other side of their mouths, the rulers insist is a positive good.

The way they try to reconcile this obvious contradiction is to assert that no one is being harmed by unequal treatment; it's just that some people are being helped while others are not. That help is essential redress for past wrongdoing and is necessary to overcome present "structural racism" and unjustly accumulated "privilege," which act as a kind of omnipresent oppressor.

For every American who savors the castigatory nature of this new arrangement, there is at least one—perhaps two—who find it, at best, distasteful. To make it more palatable, a layer of sugar is added: while discrimination is, first and foremost, necessary redress for past and ongoing injustice, it also brings the benefits of "diversity," which is "our strength," into every corner of the country. That old America was bland, boring, stultified. "Diversity" livens it up and expands its horizons with "vibrancy," fresh perspectives, alternative ways of thinking and doing, and better restaurants.

But all that is just backfill public rationalization. Once the meaning of equality is transformed from equality before the law or equality of opportunity into equality of result—and specifically equality of result across groups—then achieving equality paradoxically *requires* unequal treatment before the law.

Hence the dizzying and byzantine ecosystem of quotas, preferences, and set-asides in hiring, promotions, contracting, and myriad other aspects of modern life, all of which violate the letter of civil rights law but have become its spirit. Inequality before the law—based on race, but also on sex and sexual orientation—is the true animating principle of the American regime as it exists and operates now.

This is true not merely at the governmental level but also in the private and nonprofit sectors. By means of court decisions, bureaucratic mandates, and threat of lawsuits—both from the government and from individuals whom the law and the bureaucracy encourage to sue—the government ensures that discrimination reigns in virtually all aspects of public, and even much of private, life.

Not that it necessarily needs to do so in every case. Nearly all of America's most powerful institutions—big corporations, finance firms, foundations, and above all the universities—don't need to be prodded to discriminate; they do it willingly, even eagerly.

Public and private bureaucratic fiat is only one way the present regime imposes discrimination. The legal system is also an engine of enforced inequality via the doctrine of "disparate impact." If, say, a certain job requires certain aptitudes, and the employer selects for those aptitudes through a test, that test can be invalidated if too few of this or that "protected class" pass it. The burden of proof is then on the employer to show (a) that the things being tested for are absolutely necessary to the job, and (b) there's no other way to screen for them but the test. If the employer cannot, then the disparity will be deemed ipso facto "racist" (or "sexist" or one of the other -ists) and the cudgel of civil rights law will be used to even it out. The same "logic" is applied across the board in modern America: to "positive" factors such as admissions, hiring, contracting, lending, board seats, and so on no less than "negative" ones such as incarceration, school discipline, and poor health.

"Color Blindness" as "Racism"

The logical outcome of the above understanding is that not taking race into account is now insisted to be "racist." To be sanctified as "not racist" in Bizarro America requires being "racist" in the dictionary sense. The key—and only—questions are: which races do you favor and which do you target?

The left could easily have stopped at the argument that, given past discrimination, not to take race into account going forward would inevitably fail to address racial inequities, and therefore as a prudential matter race should be considered. And for a while they did seem to stop there. But no more. Martin Luther King's "dream" is dead. Indeed, under the new understanding, King must himself have been a "racist."

If that sounds insane—and it should—consider a graph popular on the woke Web, endorsed by (among others) tenured academics at our leading universities. It shows a pyramid bisected near the top by a thick, dark line. Above the line, under the heading "Overt White Supremacy (Socially Unacceptable)," are ten practices arranged in five groupings. Below the line, the heading is "Covert White Supremacy (Socially Acceptable)," followed by fifty-seven practices in nineteen groupings. At the top of the pyramid is the most "socially unacceptable" practice of all, "lynching." In the top grouping just below the line, "colorblindness" is identified as the worst "socially acceptable" form of "white supremacy."

The spiritual, if not literal, author of our civil rights regime would thus seem to be Lewis Carroll's Humpty Dumpty, for whom words mean just what he chooses them to mean; the only question is who is to be the master—that's all.

Equality of Result: The Results

One purpose of all this discrimination is to ensure—or at least work toward—equality of result, less for individuals than for groups. Yet just as ending discrimination proved insufficient to achieve that goal, so did reversing the groups against whom it is practiced. Lyndon Johnson's "War on Poverty" and similar initiatives at the state and local levels were intended—by means of massive spending on health, education, job training, welfare, housing, transportation, urban development, community organizing, and much else—to complete the work that preferences could only advance so far.

Yet here we are, five and a half decades and trillions of dollars later, and inequality is still with us. In fact, it is in many ways worse. Though not every group is worse off, at least not in an absolute sense.

Partisans of the leftist approach insist that, without their reforms, social and economic life in America would be a catastrophe—Tsarist Russia but with serfdom based on race. And, indeed, it's not hard to identify great gains—in income, wealth, educational attainment, and social standing—across "protected classes." Much controversy continues to swirl as to the causes and their relative impact. Which did more good, the removal of formal barriers or preferences and redistribution?

The left insists it was the latter. In their telling, the persistence of systemic racism means that certain groups can never thrive unmolested because such groups are never unmolested. Which is why these policies must go on forever.

That wasn't always the claim. Our rulers used to reassure Americans that discriminatory and redistributive policies would be temporary. It would take a few years or decades, but sooner or later inequality would be vanquished and these extraordinary measures could be retired. The Supreme Court on more than one occasion has said exactly this about racial preferences, most recently in 2003, when Justice Sandra Day O'Connor, writing for the majority, declared that the "Court expects that 25 years from now, the use of racial preferences will no longer be necessary to further the interest approved today." Twenty-five years from 2003 is 2028. Does anyone expect our rulers to voluntarily end racial preferences by then?

In any event, few in power say anything like that anymore. To the contrary, they denounce as "racist" and retrograde anyone who does. This is a key difference between the emerging leftist overclass in the heady days of the 1960s and the left today, after a half-century in power: back then they were optimistic. "We Shall Overcome" was not just a song but a mindset, an anthem of hope for a better future that would surely arrive. But listening to the left today, all one hears is that America has never been worse, our race and inclusion problems never greater. Indeed, the left has radicalized considerably since the 1960s and no longer admits that America ever had any promise. Whether and to what extent they really believe that or merely calculate that it's useful rhetorical fire to keep the pressure on for more "reform" is an open question.

The problem is that while, in absolute terms, incomes and outcomes for "protected classes" have mostly improved, the "gap" between their outcomes and those of the "privileged" has remained stubbornly large. And in present-day America, there is only one allowable explanation for disparate outcomes: oppression. This notion was fringe in the 1960s but is now orthodoxy, which means that programs initially billed as temporary and ameliorative have subtly but unmistakably shifted to being permanent and punitive.

And not simply punitive, but punitive against America's one "unprotected class." Some members of that class try to argue that since they personally never owned a slave, never bolstered Jim Crow, and never discriminated against anyone, they are not guilty of anything and do not deserve to be punished. But the "logic" of "privilege" does not allow that avenue of escape. In the ruling understanding, the majority of Americans are akin to a nation guilty of war crimes. It doesn't matter if this or that German never came close to committing an atrocity or even didn't participate in any way in the war: his nation is at fault and therefore he is at fault. Nor does, in this understanding, the past ever really become the past. Privilege in our regime's definition is not merely unearned but stolen. Corrective justice, remember, requires that stolen goods be returned.

By the left's own logic, preferences and redistribution should continue until Bad America has nothing left. Of course, the left heatedly denies this. And it's fair to take their denials seriously, for they both do and do not wish to carry their policies to their logical conclusion. Doing so would satisfy justice and vengeance but would also be difficult to implement and make the future . . . uncertain.

Their largest reason for hesitation arises from the question: how does all this get paid for? The initial answer in the 1960s was: out of rising economic growth. When that gave way, the answer became: debt. But even before the coronavirus shutdown, the American economy wasn't growing nearly fast enough to finance all the commitments the country has taken on; our foreign creditors are not idiots and most can do math. It remains to be seen how bad the effects of the shutdown will be. One thing is certain, though: however much time we had to keep coasting on debt before, we now have less.

Which means that to keep the whole thing going, the regime will eventually have to come after accumulated domestic wealth.

"Neoliberalism"

But not everyone's. It is a curious fact that, after more than half a century of the most ambitious leveling and redistributive undertaking since the Russian Revolution, American society is more unequal today than when the project started.

The main reason is that the American economy over the same period was remade: deindustrialized and financialized, with massive privileges granted to capital at the expense of labor. Some will interject that this process was inevitable and even desirable: an obsolescing manufacturing economy gave way to a twenty-first-century information-service economy. Admittedly, in a free economy some of this transformation was indeed inevitable.

But hardly all. Everyone recalls the Reagan reforms that liberalized financial regulation and woke up a slumbering Wall Street. Few any more connect them to the Johnson administration's massive borrowing to fund the Vietnam War and the Great Society or to Nixon's scuttling the Bretton Woods agreement and unmooring the dollar from any fixed standard of value, which in hindsight looks like the opening gambit of a long-term play to elevate the financial sector from well-paid servant to plutocratic master. As much as the liberalization and lionization of Wall Street were reviled and excoriated by the left at the time, they were quickly ratified and amplified by Bill Clinton, just as Eisenhower ratified the New Deal.

Clinton also proved a more ardent free trader than any Chamber of Commerce Republican. He rammed through the North American Free Trade Agreement (NAFTA) when his predecessor couldn't—granted, with Republican votes—and went on to spearhead, at the behest of our business class, American economic collusion with China. There seemed to be no concession to China that Clinton was unwilling to make—from lifting restrictions on selling sensitive American military technology to giving Beijing its way on the precise seating arrangements at a White House state dinner. The granddaddy, though, was clearing obstacles to China's accession to the World Trade Organization—a policy that, like George H. W. Bush's beloved NAFTA, Clinton would need his successor to get through. Before George W. Bush's first term was half over, the old protectionist-labor wing of the Democratic Party was dead—as Dick Gephardt learned the hard way when he dropped out of the 2004 presidential race the day after the Iowa caucuses.

In hindsight, the fierce political battles of the 1990s, 2000s, and the first half of the 2010s recede into insignificance when one realizes the bipartisan near-unanimity across a range of the most important issues. Trade? Benefits everyone! Haven't you read Ricardo? Outsourcing? Good for business, and we'll retrain the "losers" for "today's economy"! Financialization? That's not even a thing. But a strong banking sector is crucial to maintaining American economic hegemony and the dollar's reserve status! The tech sector? America's crown jewel and the true engine of future growth!

Mass outsourcing of virtually every job beyond bond trader, app designer, busboy and hotel maid would have been bad enough. Combined with wide-open, low-wage, low-skill immigration, America's lower-middle and working classes faced catastrophe.

A catastrophe with disastrous effects on Americans of all races. There was, and remains, no way to exempt members of "protected classes" from the relentless downward pressure on wages exerted by mass immigration. This is especially true of illegal immigration, whose beneficiaries are almost always paid under the table and thus below minimum wage or union scale. But members of "protected classes" at least benefit from all the other ways government and the private sector favor them.

Members of the unprotected class do not. That's not the main reason why their fortunes have declined over the last generation—deindustrialization, outsourcing, and mass immigration are the primary causes—but it hasn't helped.

And yet some—those who benefit from deindustrialization, outsourcing, and mass immigration—have managed to do better than ever. More specifically, the closer one is to the real centers of power in New America—financial institutions, tech firms, multinational corporations, elite media, universities, and administrative state bureaucracies—the better things have gotten, and the better off one is.

A great irony of modern America is that more than a half century of warring against inequality has produced an America as unequal as it was in the so-called robber baron era—perhaps more so. The fabled Gini coefficient—a measure of wealth and income inequality—has been rising for at least a half century. It's not a coincidence that this rise began more or less precisely when old American social, political, and economic arrangements began to give way to what has come to be called "neoliberalism." A more precise name might be "managerial leftist-libertarianism," for this movement is top-down, bureaucratic, and anti-democratic, committed to social engineering and grievance politics, and undermines virtue while promoting vice. But that's something of a mouthful, and "neoliberal" has, for better or worse, gained widespread acceptance.

Neoliberalism elevates as a matter of "principle" the international over the national; it rejects the latter as narrow, particular, cramped, even bigoted, and celebrates the former as cosmopolitan and enlightened. Neoliberalism is (for now) forced to tolerate nations and borders as unfortunate and unhelpful obstacles, but it looks forward to a time when such nuisances are finally behind mankind forever.

Until that time, neoliberalism works to warp state power into instruments whose primary mission is not to secure the well-being or interests of individual peoples or nations but instead to enforce the international neoliberal order—in particular the movement of capital, goods, and labor across borders in ways that benefit the neoliberal ruling class. In practice, this amounts to widespread, close-knit cooperation between business and government—or what neoliberals euphemistically refer to as "public–private partnership." They leave out the little detail that big business is the senior partner. Conservatives, still fighting "government regulation" as if America were stuck in Groundhog Day 1981, have yet to grasp the reality that the majority of the country's domestic and foreign policy is oriented around securing trade, tax, and labor ("migration") policies that benefit finance and big business.

The real power in the neoliberal order resides not with elected (or appointed) officials and "world leaders"; they—or most of them—are a servant class. True power resides with their donors: the bankers, CEOs, financiers, and tech oligarchs—some of whom occasionally run for and win office, but most of whom, most of the time, are content to buy off those who do. The end result is the same either way: economic globalism and financial-ization, consolidation of power in an ostensibly "meritocratic" but actually semi-hereditary class, livened up by social libertinism.

This combination works well for the oligarchs, whom it both enriches and enables to indulge their appetites—sophisticated and tawdry alike. As for the latter kind, oligarchs and their progeny have both the wealth and position to buy themselves out of whatever stupid fix into which their degeneracy may (briefly) dump them. The poor, working, and middle classes . . . not so much. Which is one reason why 1960s liber-tinism has been a disaster for the latter while leaving hardly a dent on the ruling class, for whom adolescent and young adult hard-partying is seen as a harmless rite of passage.

This "neoliberalism"—more than formal inequality before the law, more even than attempts to achieve group equality of result—is the true "principle" of the American regime as it actually operates today. Aggres-sive social leftism, which has two primary parts, legitimizes neoliberal-ism as it conceals its true nature. Libertinism excuses and even encourages all kinds of self-indulgent hedonism, which anesthetizes people into not noticing that, in concrete terms, their lives and their country are getting worse. It also makes the oligarchs seem "hip" or "cool" or whatever kids today call toleration of licentiousness. And our overlords' aggressive promotion of "wokeness" makes them seem moral, and hence deserving of their wealth, power, and status.

MODERN AMERICA: PRACTICE

Modern America is thus no longer a "democracy" (if it ever was) or a republic (which it certainly once was) but an oligarchy whose real rulers project an illusion of "democracy" to mask the essentially undemocratic character of their rule. Their implicit claim to rule is based on supposed expertise and superior morality; their rule's true foundation is monopoly over the levers of governmental power, control of elite institutions, election manipulation (when necessary), and propaganda—all underwritten by superior wealth.

Now that we understand the nature of this regime and its principles, it's time to examine its practices—how we are actually ruled in America 2020.

The "Consent of the Governed"?

For a people fit for liberty, consent is a requirement of legitimacy. Consent is also fundamentally a means by which the governed control their government, which is a necessary but dangerous instrument. Without government, men live insecure in the harsh state of nature. But government—any government, indeed government qua government—is also prone to abusing its powers and easily coopted. Here is Madison in *Federalist* No. 51:

> In framing a government which is to be administered by men over men, the great difficulty lies in this: you must first enable the government to control the governed; and in the next place oblige it to control itself. A dependence on the people is, no doubt, the primary control on the government; but experience has taught mankind the necessity of auxiliary precautions.

"Dependence on the people" is not the only control—there are others, including the separation of powers, checks and balances, and the "extended sphere" described in *Federalist* No. 10. But it is the primary control—that is, popular consent is the chief means for keeping government in its proper sphere, exercising only its lawful powers.

Popular consent also produces an important practical benefit. As the founders were well aware, every decision the government makes will be opposed by someone. For that decision not to be seen by the losing side as illegitimate and tyrannical, the losers must feel that they had their say, that their objections were heard, that they lost fair and square, and that they will have other chances—that the system is not rigged against them.

Consent is granted initially by the social compact and then continually granted and regranted via elections. Do we still have government
by consent? I here submit that the answer to this question is, more or
less, no.

First, there are large parts of the country where voting simply doesn't
matter. Demographically, one side or the other is so numerous that its
opponents are effectively disenfranchised. While there are red and blue
examples of this phenomenon, as a practical matter in modern America,
blues dominate reds in far more instances than the reverse. The modern
left likes to complain about small red states exercising influence disproportionate to their small populations. This effect is, of course, exactly
what the founders intended to protect state, regional, and minority
interests—"minority" here meant not in the sense we use it today but
any constitutional and lawful interest unthreatening to the safety of the
republic but potentially unpopular with the majority.

The founders, however, did not intend massive concentrations of
lockstep voters to overwhelm the votes and preferences of everyone else
through sheer demographic might. When Jefferson and Hamilton skew-
ered one another over the pros and cons of big cities—home of dangerous
urban mobs to the former, engines of economic dynamism to the latter—they agreed on the potential danger from massive voting blocs easily
controlled by monied interests.

Needless to say, voters did not "consent" to the last fifty years of
mass immigration, which has entirely transformed the electorate of the
country. It was foisted on them by the ruling class in order to squash
consent by effectively voiding their votes. Indeed, in order to bypass
consent, the ruling class explicitly misled the American people about
what immigration "reform" would do. Here is Senator Edward Kennedy
on the Immigration Reform Act of 1965 (also know as Hart–Celler):

> What the bill will not do: First, our cities will not be flooded
> with a million immigrants annually. Under the proposed bill,
> the present level of immigration remains substantially the

same. . . . Secondly, the ethnic mix of our cities will not be upset. . . . Contrary to the charges in some quarters, [the bill] will not inundate America with immigrations from any one country or area, or the most populated and economically deprived nations of Africa and Asia.

Every word of the above is false; everything Kennedy assured Americans would not happen has in fact happened. One result is that, in today's America, for every Wyoming senator casting a vote on behalf of a mere 578,000 people, there are millions of red Americans living in blue states who may as well not even bother to vote, ever. Their voices are never heard.

States such as California, Colorado, Illinois, New York, and now Virginia are one-party owing almost entirely to mass immigration. A few big cities and counties are crammed with the recently arrived who—together with the oligarchs and valet-class liberals who beckoned them in—overwhelm the votes of everyone else. This is how a state like Virginia—cradle of the American Revolution and home to four of our first five presidents—suddenly, just like that, became implacably hostile to the first two amendments to the United States Constitution. Five cities and counties—three adjacent to Washington, D.C.—essentially dictate to the other 128. This is the sort of brute-force majoritarianism that our founders warned against and took pains to prevent.

Once the blues have power, they waste little time. Coastal Californians, for instance, impose their environmental enthusiasms—some of them eminently reasonable for addressing coastal issues—on interior red counties with entirely different problems and priorities. Farmers can't irrigate their crops because Sacramento dictates water policy as if the whole state were Marin County. Developers can't build in fast-growing Bakersfield because Malibu—also not unreasonably—insists on remaining exactly as it is. Newly minted Virginia state legislators who've never hunted or been to a shooting range in their lives suddenly strive to restrict gun rights statewide in a commonwealth whose rural precincts have lived peaceably and profitably with firearms since long before the American Revolution.

As Joel Kotkin has remarked, "The worst thing in the world to be is the red part of a blue state."

Virtue and Wisdom versus Consent

One supposes, though, that it's pointless to get too upset about this, because even when and where red America does have the numbers to outvote the other side, elections no longer change the direction or substance of the government.

A claim to rule is different than a principle of rule. The former legitimizes the rulers; the latter justifies the regime itself. For our founders, the principle of the American regime is equal natural rights; the rulers are the elected representatives of the sovereign people; their claim to rule is the consent of the governed.

By contrast, our current overlords rest their claim to rule on a twofold and mutually reinforcing assertion of superiority. The first is expertise: their purportedly superior understanding of the complexities of modern life, grounded in their purportedly superior intelligence and elite education. These claims dovetail neatly with their moral claim, because to twenty-first-century America's elite, virtue is less a matter of what one does or does not do than what one believes and does not believe. To be smart and educated is to hold the correct opinions; to hold the correct opinions is evidence of intelligence and education.

This is one reason why election results such as Brexit over Remain and Trump over Clinton so anger neoliberal oligarchs: these outcomes are not merely wrong "factually"—contradicting expertise—but "morally," offensive to what elites "know" is the "just" outcome. Hence the "backward" parts of Britain and America (everywhere, really) deserve to lose, while the "enlightened" parts deserve to rule. The rubes' racism, sexism, xenophobia, and much else obviate any claim they may assert to having a say over how they're governed.

Our rulers' claim to superior morality is just a foreshortened version of the classical notion that virtuous rulers are better than vicious ones. Similarly, modern expertise is really just an updated (and simplified) version of the ancient philosophic argument that ultimately wisdom is the only just title to rule. With one major difference: the ancient philosophers qualified and caveated their claim; our virtuous experts mean it in deadly earnest. They consider themselves wise and brook no challenges—indeed they regard any questioning as tantrums from petulant children. Important matters are hashed out in rarified settings—faculty lounges, international conferences, C-suites, government meeting rooms—and then "decided." Once decided, they are final; opposition and even questions are illegitimate. You don't question that 2+2=4—and you certainly don't make policy based on any other answer.

This is not to dismiss all claims to expertise as ipso facto illegitimate. Government in the complex modern world needs expertise—but confined to its proper sphere. Many problems cannot be solved without recourse to specialized information, which experts—and often only experts—possess. But in a system based on the consent of the governed, expertise may *inform* policy, but it can't justly *make* policy without first persuading democratic majorities. Our elites ignore or override the latter when they contradict elite consensus. This is an undemocratic and illegitimate use of expertise.

Separation of Powers?

The administrative state takes elite expertise and moral consensus and channels them into policy, which it then enforces. While nominally part of the executive branch, in reality administrative state bureaucracies operate on their own and without accountability—certainly without political oversight. The constitutional first branch—Congress—in practice defers to this unconstitutional fourth branch. The "laws" Congress passes are in fact just directives to the administrative state to write "rules," which are the real laws.

Having abdicated its fundamental legislative role, Congress is all too happy also to jettison its oversight powers over the executive branch. Part of the point of deferring to expertise is to shirk hard work, dodge tough decisions, and focus instead on fundraising and campaigning. Theoretically, the elected and politically appointed members of the executive branch also oversee—indeed run and implement—the "rule-making" process. In reality, they are too few, too weak, and serve too short a time in their jobs to do much. Plus, most of them either agree with administrative state diktats or else are, for one reason or another, not up to fighting them. And many are simply bought off by lobbyists fronting for corporate, financial interests.

We see here the first and fundamental breach of the separation of powers: Congress neither legislates nor oversees. The executive does both, although it's not supposed to legislate at all, and the way it oversees is anti-constitutional. The constitutional way would be for presidentially appointed—and Senate-confirmed—statutory officers to run executive branch agencies according to their constitutionally and statutorily enumerated powers. The real way these agencies are run is by unelected bureaucrats accountable not to elected or appointed officials but to "expertise," which is to say to elite opinion. It is these bureaucrats who are—through the "rule-making process"—the real legislators.

They are also in many respects the real executives, since they often get to decide when, how, and against whom their rules are enforced. And sometimes administrative state agencies act as all three branches at once: a "legislature" that drafts its own "administrative law," an executive that enforces that "law," and a judiciary that tries, convicts, and sentences offenders under the guise of "administrative hearings." This is, needless to say, the precise concentration of authority that the founders feared and implemented the separation of powers to prevent.

Kritarchy

"Kritarchy" is a Greek neologism that means "rule of judges." Strictly speaking, we don't live under a regime in which judges rule alone.

It's more precise to say that modern American judges are a vital node of the neoliberal oligarchy who exercise far more power than they ought to have, in ways the founders never intended.

According to the parchment, judges are supposed to rule on individual cases and—in extraordinary circumstances—may invalidate laws that clearly flout the plain text and meaning of the Constitution. This is not what our judges actually do. They profess themselves loyal to the Constitution, in part as a diversionary tactic but also in part out of genuine sincerity. The problem with their sincerity is that their loyalty is not to the actual Constitution but to a rival constitution of the left's own devising. That constitution is not written in the same manner as the formal Constitution, but neither is it completely unwritten. Its tenets are explained in various books and journal articles, in certain laws, and in administrative rules.

But mostly they are memorialized in judicial rulings that purport to interpret the de jure Constitution but which really outline the parameters of today's true, de facto constitution. I was unable to identify who coined the term "legislating from the bench," but it's an apt description of what modern judges do. In the guise of "interpreting" the law, judges very often make the law, inventing new "rights" as they go.

Alan Dershowitz—lately a hero of President Trump's impeachment show trial, but at heart a lifelong extra-constitutional judicial liberal— writes of his experience clerking for David Bazelon, long-serving chief judge of the U.S. Court of Appeals for the District of Columbia, which is widely regarded as the country's second most powerful tribunal:

> If a defendant deserved compassion but no writ of habeas corpus—or other formal legal remedy—was technically available to him, Bazelon would wink at me and order that I find some ground for issuing a "writ of rachmones." Rachmones is the Hebrew-Yiddish word for "compassion."

In other words, a judge who could find no support in law for the outcome he wanted resorted to his own personal sense of morality to achieve the desired result. That basically sums up the history of constitutional jurisprudence since the 1960s.

The beginning of this trend is most often identified as the Supreme Court's 1965 decision *Griswold v. Connecticut,* which invalidated a state anti-contraception law on the ground that it violated a non-enumerated yet somehow inherent constitutional "right to privacy." But the United States Constitution does not mention a right to the former, nor does it require invalidating a properly enacted law against the latter. Those who believe there ought to be a constitutionally enumerated right to privacy have a constitutional remedy: amend the Constitution. Similarly, those who oppose anti-contraception laws have a democratic remedy: elect legislators who will repeal them.

Judges don't like either of these remedies, partly because they can take a long time but mostly because they are, in many cases, not likely to occur at all. Kritarchy is a means to an end, the end being the enactment and defense of the progressive elements of neoliberal oligarchy. If those policies can't garner enough support to win popular or legislative majorities—or worse, are overturned by legislative majorities—the role of the judge is to impose them in the first case and reinstate them in the second.

So, for instance, when the people of California voted 60–40 to deny welfare benefits to illegal aliens, a federal judge blocked the measure on the ground that it violates the new, de facto constitution under which illegal aliens have not merely natural rights, but also American constitutional and civil rights. The people's new law never took effect; judges rule.

Sometimes judges overturn popular will and invent new rights in the same action. After the U.S. Congress, followed by several states, specified in law that marriage is between—and only between—one man and one woman, judges not only invalidated all those laws but declared a constitutional right to same-sex marriage.

At other times judges block the implementation of lawful and constitutional executive branch policy. Witness, for instance, the continuing kritarchic assault on President Trump's lawful order temporarily banning travel to the United States from countries with inadequate vetting procedures for their citizens. The rationale is, again, an alleged civil and constitutional right for foreigners to enter the United States.

Another important role for judges in a kritarchy is to use sophistry to justify policies that are obviously unconstitutional under the actual Constitution and/or that contradict statute law. Perhaps the most famous recent example is the Supreme Court's reimagining the ObamaCare individual mandate as a "tax" to declare that the law passed constitutional muster. But the supreme example is the forty-two-year (and counting) effort to affirm that racial preferences are somehow not barred by federal law, which explicitly prohibits discrimination by race. The only consistent thread here is the end: the progressive outcome must always prevail.

Finally, the kritarchs sometimes even assume executive powers. This is typically done via consent decrees and the like, through which judges issue orders that municipalities, states, and sometimes even federal agencies must follow. For instance, judges have mandated bussing; directed cities to build schools in certain areas, even mandating how much those cities must spend; forced towns to build "low income housing" and mandated where; and taken over prison systems and mental hospitals. To this day, judges dictate to the executive branch how it must deal with foreigners who enter (or try to enter) our country illegally. Again, whatever one thinks about any of these policies— though I need hardly add that kritarchy is never used for conservative ends—they are all properly enacted only through the elected branches of government. Kritarchy imposes them by fiat, without even the pretense of democratic accountability.

"Federalism"?

The Declaration of Independence declares the new country to be a union of "free and independent states." The question of how close that union should be has loomed throughout American history.

Our founders sought to establish the weakest possible federal government capable of performing its essential functions, for three fundamental and intertwined reasons. First, government is inherently dangerous, so the less power it has the better. Second, the states—being closer to the people and more responsive to regional differences and needs—are better equipped to handle most matters than a far-off centralized administration. Third, the states were prior to the federal government; the people, through their states, created the latter to serve them, not the other way around.

We owe the Constitution of 1787 to the failure of the Articles of Confederation, which formed too loose a union. In the do-over, the founders gave the federal government more power but strictly limited those powers and reserved everything else to the states as inherently local matters.

But today there is hardly anything—neither criminal nor civil justice, not welfare, not schooling, not transportation—that the feds consider "local" enough to leave to the states. The states still have governments, which spend a lot of money on these and other activities. But often they do so as federal satrapies, at federal direction—whether legislative, judicial, or administrative. Even much of the money the states spend comes from the feds: taxed out of their own citizens and economies, sent to Washington and skimmed, then sent back at pennies on the dollar.

For any matter the oligarchs deem important—and as America gets "woker," fewer and fewer matters are deemed too unimportant for federal notice—they make sure to use federal power to impose their will nationally. Sometimes the method is carrots—the promise of easy money—at other times sticks: threats of lawsuits, consent decrees, and outright takeover.

As a result, the states' role as so-called "laboratories of democracy" is increasingly illusory. Essentially, the state governments are allowed but one freedom: to be more progressive-left than the federal government and elite opinion. But never less.

In fact, things tend to go in the other direction. Whenever a progressive state enacts some fresh enthusiasm, the feds are almost certain to view such "progress" as "a model for the rest of the nation" and force the other states to go along. See, for instance, same-sex marriage, which began at the state level in Massachusetts before finally being imposed on the entire country by the Supreme Court. This process, however, does not work in the case of non-progressive outcomes—not even in defense of constitutionally enumerated rights. Hence the Court's finding in *District of Columbia v. Heller* that the Second Amendment forbids draconian gun restrictions was applied only to the District of Columbia and not to any other states or municipalities that limit citizens' gun rights. Advocates had to go back to court to force other states to honor the Constitution. They won again (*McDonald v. Chicago*), but anti-gun states pretend the ruling never happened and continue to restrict citizens' rights.

Then there's direct executive branch interference. Consider the case of "Affirmatively Furthering Fair Housing," an Obama-era HUD program that, in the words of commentator Stanley Kurtz,

> gives the federal government a lever to re-engineer nearly every American neighborhood—imposing a preferred racial and ethnic composition, densifying housing, transportation, and business development in suburb and city alike, and weakening or casting aside the authority of local governments over core responsibilities, from zoning to transportation to education. Another way of looking at Obama's AFFH is to see it as a way of allowing big cities to effectively annex their surrounding suburbs—siphoning off suburban tax revenue and controlling suburban planning as well.

You'd think, or hope, that the Trump administration would have shut this down, but you'd be wrong. I don't mean to single out the president for blame, only to make the point that the federal behemoth runs

on autopilot, according to a flight plan decidedly not of Trumpian origin
or direction. It exists to implement and nationalize the elite agenda, and
it does so no matter who is nominally in charge.

"Limited Government"?

According to the parchment, the federal government is supposed to
field and fund an army and navy, protect the borders, make treaties,
regulate foreign trade and interstate commerce, maintain a sound common currency . . . and that's about it.

But if you hadn't noticed, there is today almost nothing the federal
government doesn't do—or try to. The fact that it fails embarrassingly
at most of the tasks it sets itself never circumscribes its ambitions, which
seem to multiply by the year.

I won't belabor the topic because endless books and articles have
been written on this. Except to say: the United States government
spends nearly five trillion dollars per year, roughly a quarter of that—
twenty-three trillion and counting—financed through debt. The biggest
items in the budget are entitlement programs (Social Security, Medicare, and Medicaid), followed by defense, non-defense discretionary
spending, and debt service. That leaves about a trillion for means-tested
welfare—which, like Social Security, Medicare, and Medicaid, are not
constitutionally authorized; they are also of dubious and uneven effec-
tiveness at best.

If only waste were the worst accusation we could levy against our
federal overlords! No, the worst is that they spend so much of our hard-
earned money on intrusive, busybody social engineering—backed by the
fearsome powers of the administrative state, its "civil rights" enforcement
arm, and the criminal justice system. Once the feds get it into their heads
that some new crusade is the "civil rights struggle of our time," you had
best get with the program—or else.

Essentially, the average middle-class American pays about a third of
his income to a government which then spends a big chunk to discriminate against, hector, and harass him. Is there another example from

history of a state that so gleefully hounds the single largest demographic bloc of the population it nominally serves? And of those people not only not objecting, but paying for the privilege?

"Equal Justice under Law"?

Those noble words are carved in marble above the entrance to the gloriously neoclassical Supreme Court building. Do they still hold?

Inequality is the fundamental animating principle of New America—so long as one gets the hierarchy right. And on that score, only one ranking is certain because the left has a difficult time agreeing who is entitled to occupy the upper ranks. But everyone knows who comes last. That fact alone is incontrovertible proof that "equality before the law" in modern America is a fiction.

Those words are also a sham in a more prosaic way. Consider two events from a single week in February 2020. First, the Justice Department filed its sentencing recommendation for Trump associate Roger Stone, who had been convicted of lying to the FBI in the course of the Russia hoax probe. The department initially sought seven to nine years—a recommendation reduced to four when the attorney general, claiming to have been misled by his own subordinates, intervened. A week later, Stone was sentenced to forty months. Second, that same Department formally notified former FBI deputy director Andrew McCabe that it would not pursue criminal charges against him for . . . lying to the FBI.

Here we have the exact same offense but two vastly unequal outcomes. One man was investigated, charged, tried, convicted, and sentenced. Stone may be, as many allege, a shady character. But at age sixty-six, with no criminal record or history of violence—or even evidence of ever having owned a firearm—he was arrested at gunpoint in a predawn raid on his home by a heavily armed posse, some in helicopters, others in a boat covering his backyard dock just in case he tried to swim away. Does mere shadiness warrant all *that*? Stone was then maximally charged with seven counts of process crimes—all of which substantially overlapped—unrelated to any alleged Russia "collusion," which was itself a ruling-class fabrication. In other words, they threw the book at him.

The partisan leftist judge who presided over Stone's trial imposed a gag order preventing the defense, but not the prosecution, from saying anything publicly. The jury forewoman lied about being unbiased and ignorant of the Russia probe; her robust social media presence revealed not just anti-Trump vitriol but specific anti-Stone sentiment, plus proof that she had, contrary to her own statements during jury selection, followed the Russia probe closely. In other words, she lied specifically about facts material to the case in order to get on the jury so she could stick it to Roger Stone. When Stone's lawyers pointed all this out to the judge, the latter brushed it off.

After Stone's inevitable conviction—the feds almost never lose—prosecutors attempted to throw another book at him in sentencing. Nine years is more than twice the average time served by *rapists* and *armed robbers*. Even four years—the government's more reasonable climb-down—is longer than many drunk drivers guilty of vehicular manslaughter get.

Still and all, Attorney General Barr's reduction of the sentencing recommendation was treated in the press and elite opinion as an absolute outrage. Barr has no right! Roger Stone must be destroyed! Those same voices exulted that Andrew McCabe had been "cleared." Nothing to see here!

At least McCabe was investigated. Other proven liars and leakers such as James Comey, James Clapper, and John Brennan haven't been and almost certainly never will be. As Mark Steyn said of our feds' crusade against Canadian publisher Conrad Black, even if one is not convicted, "the process *is* the punishment." Just ask my former boss Michael Flynn, who lost his career, his house, and his money—and endured three years of "impartial" justice because of our supposedly sterling "process." All for, again, allegedly lying to the FBI. But the FBI agents who interviewed him—including the corrupt Peter Strzok—told their bosses they didn't think Flynn had lied.

That's before you even consider the fact that the interview was a trap, a setup, convened under a misleading pretense on the second business day of a brand-new administration, without telling Flynn he was under investigation or informing him of his right to have a lawyer present. We knew this before—it was obvious from the circumstances—but the FBI's own notes confirm it. Flynn's lawyer had to wrench those notes out of the government's clutches with a crowbar: the general's tormenters resisted unto the last handing over evidence that would exonerate an innocent man. Then, after the attorney general finally dismissed charges that never should have been brought, the judge presiding over the case asked private parties to file briefs against Flynn in order to justify punishing him anyway: kritarchy as individual vendetta. Does it get any more banana republic than that?

The man who set Flynn's perjury trap, James Comey, later laughed and boasted about it from a public stage on the Upper East Side. But for his own lying and leaking, Comey remains uncharged and uninvestigated. As do—so far as all public evidence shows—the person or persons in the Obama administration who leaked the highly classified details of General Flynn's conversation with the Russian ambassador to get the whole sordid farce going. That's a felony—one our feds are fundamentally uncurious about finding out whodunnit. Whoever did was on the right team, you see. Then there's the question of why the government was listening to Flynn's phone calls in the first place, since FBI agents lied about having evidence that Flynn was a Russian agent. No one's ever been held to account for that either.

The supreme example of contemporary unequal justice, however, remains Hillary Clinton and her server. A retired four-star admiral said to me of that case that "an E-5 under my command who did something even one-tenth as bad would have been dishonorably discharged and locked up for years." An E-5, for those not familiar with military terminology, is a mid-ranking enlisted man or "non-commissioned officer"— someone who does most of the work but has very little real power.

Let us quickly review all the ways in which the Clinton "investigation" was rigged. The secretary herself was never interviewed under oath but was rather allowed to submit a written statement. When she was finally interviewed in person, it wasn't under oath—and the inteview took place two months after Comey drafted his statement exonerating her. At least one accessory to the act under investigation was not only not interviewed at all but allowed to serve as Clinton's lawyer, thereby according attorney-client privilege to both the former secretary and her lawyer-collaborator. When a tech specialist who worked on the server told the FBI that he had illegally deleted tranches of emails, the FBI gave him immunity as an inducement to change his story. Some of the classified material illegally on Hillary's illegal server found its way (also illegally) onto the personal laptop of top aide Huma Abedin, and from there to the personal computer of her husband, convicted child sex predator—and former Democratic congress-man—Anthony Weiner. Neither of whom, needless to say, paid any price for those particular violations of the law.

Conservadorks homed in on Comey's substitution of the phrase "grossly negligent" with "extremely careless" because the former carries legal ramifications while the latter does not. The fix was in! True enough, as far as that goes. But both phrases are risible lies. There was nothing "careless" or "negligent" about what Hillary and her cronies did. They very deliberately, premeditatively, and methodically moved her emails to a private server so that—in clear violation of federal law—the government could neither see nor archive them. That's the precise opposite of "careless" and "negligent." The use of those words is so offensively contrary to the truth that one can't help but suspect that the contradiction is intentional, meant to rub in our faces that the government can do and say to us whatever it damn well pleases. "We rule; screw you and shut up; we know we're lying, you know we're lying, we know you know and vice versa; eat it and like it." That's the message.

One could explore this theme forever; as President Trump likes to tweet, "Many such examples!" But we have to move on at some point. However, not quite yet.

One does not need to be a ruling-class Washington insider to benefit from unequal justice. Having some of them in your iPhone contacts can be enough. When actor Jussie Smollett was caught red-handed faking a preposterous hate hoax—MAGA hat–wearing rednecks, devoted fans of the rap soap opera *Empire*, prowling the Chicago Loop at 2:00 a.m. during a polar vortex looking for black TV stars to beat up?—things initially looked bad for him. But then Michelle Obama's former chief of staff, who knows both Jussie and the state prosecutor handling the case, made a few calls. That prosecutor, incidentally, had been elected on the wings of George Soros's money, precisely because she is ideologically opposed to enforcing the law. Charges were promptly dropped.

As this chapter was being drafted, word came down that Smollett had been indicted by another prosecutor after all. Maybe something will come of that. I doubt it, but who knows.

The principal beneficiaries of unequal justice in the individual sense are the well-placed and well-connected. But they're not the only ones. Our old friend "group disadvantage" also plays a role. An unstated but not absent reason for the initial clearing of Jussie Smollett was that he is a member of a protected class. The left has been complaining for years that the justice system is too hard on protected classes. Their remedy is simple: go easier on them.

This is part of the reasoning behind all that Soros money electing soft-on-crime DAs throughout the country: "law enforcement is racist." This is meant in at least three senses: the laws themselves are racist, the people and institutions that enforce them are racist, and the act of enforcing the law is racist.

So, increasingly, we don't—at least not with any pretense of consistency. In 2019, illegal alien Christopher Puente—who had already been convicted of burglary, forgery, trespassing, and domestic violence, and been deported—managed to make his way back to Chicago, where he was arrested for theft. Authorities then released him in defiance of an ICE directive. In early 2020, he sexually assaulted a three-year-old girl in a McDonald's bathroom. Hard-left, anti-cop Chicago mayor Lori

Lightfoot didn't bother to apologize to the little girl or her family, or to explain to the people of Chicago how letting career criminals go helps their city. Instead, she attacked ICE: "If ICE is complaining, then they should do their job better."

Get that? In New America it's now legal to sexually abuse toddlers, so long as you're a member of a "protected class"—and it's racist to complain. As more leftist mayors and prosecutors get elected and implement more "innovative" criminal justice reforms, such as waiving bail for violent felons, things are going to get worse before they get better (assuming they do get better).

In the spring of 2020, as Minneapolis burned, its leftist boy-mayor sided with the rioters—as did, even more openly, the state attorney general. The governor appeared at least to want to enforce the law, but obviously had no idea how—or simply lacked the will. The police entirely pulled back and even sacrificed one of their precinct houses, which was burned to the ground.

That was just in Minneapolis—and barely scratches the surface of all that transpired there. The same script played out in dozens of cities throughout the country. Perhaps most notorious of all, in Seattle, the mayor, the city council, the police, the governor—everyone in any kind of position of authority—gave over several city blocks to a mob and refused to enforce any law at all. At least one person was shot to death and at least one more critically injured. One might also cite 2020's orgy of nihilistic vandalism and desecration, which has met almost no resistance and often takes place under the authorites' watchful eye.

All this was a replay—but worse—of the Baltimore riots of 2015, which were allowed to continue as a matter of official policy. "We also gave those who wished to destroy space to do that," explained Stephanie Rawlings-Blake, the mayor of that unfortunate city. I am, of course, well aware that these and other riots were precipitated by the deaths of young men at police hands. In nearly all such cases, once all the facts are fully known, the initial, official line—innocent young man intentionally killed by racist cops—turns out to have been false, or at the very least incomplete and misleading. But even if it ends up being entirely true this time, who or what is helped—how is anything made better—when law enforcement and state power hold back and let a lethal and destructive mob rule?

America, or large parts of it, appears to have lost the will to enforce the law. This trend—the reversal of one of the great public policy triumphs of the last generation; namely, beating back the massive crime wave that began in the mid-1960s—is not merely making our cities dirtier, more stressful, and more dangerous. It's literally getting people killed. Homicide rates, which had been declining across the land since the early 1990s, began to tick up after a safely reelected Barack Obama let loose his inner "community organizer" and sided with the hard left against cops and law-and-order DAs. The trickle becomes a surge and then a flood.

So far, the victims of this nascent new crime wave have been disproportionately "of color" and poor. The leaders who claim to speak for such people don't seem to care. Certainly, the victims and their families and friends must. Does anyone else? If so, their voices are barely heard above the din of elite chatter urging that the criminal justice system be made even more lenient.

Though not in every respect. A few examples neatly convey our ruling class's priorities. First, they say—loudly and often—that they are against guns. But the single most effective "gun control" measure of the last several decades was the combined effort of New York City mayors Giuliani and Bloomberg to get illegal guns off the street by stopping, questioning, and frisking those suspected of carrying firearms and/or guilty of other infractions. Opinion on "stop-and-frisk" was divided. Most New Yorkers appreciated that it made the city safer. Tourists and business travelers naturally were all for it. Civil libertarians just as naturally hated it, as did some—but by no means all—residents of the neighborhoods most affected.

Opinion is no longer divided: to be a moral American in good standing today, one is required to hate "stop-and-frisk." Its effects were felt

too heavily by disadvantaged groups. That the practice also saved the
lives of thousands of members of such groups is either denied or not
allowed to be stated. Hence when Mike Bloomberg ran for president, the
most anti-gun American politician ever had to denounce his own successful effort to confiscate illegal guns. Which he did—with the apparent
sincerity of a forced confession before a Soviet tribunal.

The logical position for someone who hates guns as much as Bloomberg does would be to focus one's attention and ire on illegal handguns—
as his administration had done—and not on legal rifles, as
Bloomberg-backed state and local politicians are now doing. The vast
majority of gun crimes in this country are committed with the former;
very few—according to the FBI, less than 3 percent of homicides—are
committed with the latter.

Yet in Virginia—a state with relatively low crime overall and virtually none in its rural counties—the newly elected Democratic majority
in the state legislature targets gun owners in exactly those counties.
Moreover, they go after rifles, which those citizens own in far greater
numbers than handguns. Essentially, the ruling class is trying to outlaw
devices that law-abiding Americans have lawfully owned for years, and
their ancestors for centuries—their right to do so specifically enumerated
in the Constitution. Such laws instantly transform upstanding citizens
into felons.

Why would our elites do that? More specifically, why would they
target these particular guns and owners while insisting that public policy
not touch others? They say it's to make us all "safer"—but that hardly
passes the smell test, since neither these particular guns nor their owners
have much, if any, connection to crime. One can be forgiven for speculat-
ing that the answer is persecution.

Consider also the differing fates of Antifa thugs and the people they
beat up. In New York City, Antifa goons got into a fight—it's hard to
say who started it—with a group of men calling themselves "the Proud
Boys." Although no one was seriously injured, the NYPD expended
significant time and resources tracking down the Proud Boys, but none

whatsoever looking for any Antifa figures involved. Two Proud Boys were sentenced to four years in prison. No Antifa members were ever identified, much less charged with any crime, still much less tried or convicted. At most, the incident was a mutually idiotic brawl for which only one side was punished. The real distinction here is that the Proud Boys are regime dissidents while Antifa members are ruling-class shock troops.

It could be worse. In places where Antifa is strongest—Portland and Seattle above all—they can more or less riot at will. The police will do nothing—either because they're scared, sympathetic, or have been instructed not to.

Antifa aside, the fundamental right of self-defense—the bedrock foundation of all our other rights—is increasingly not honored if you're a member of a disfavored group and your attacker is not. For example, two years ago in Florida, a middle-aged man—perhaps unwisely—rebuked a young lady for illegally parking in a handicapped spot. For his trouble, he was assaulted by her much larger male companion, who slammed the elder man into the pavement before going at him again. The victim drew out his—lawful—firearm and shot his assailant dead. For this he got twenty years in prison.

One used to hear pro-gun conservatives mouth the slogan "Rather be tried by twelve than carried by six." I don't think that holds quite the same salience it used to.

Consider also the double standard now applied to due process: in sexual assault allegations, women receive due process and more. Men—like Spaulding in *Caddyshack*—"get nothing and like it." In the wake of ruling-class icon Harvey Weinstein's sex scandal and downfall, we've been told incessantly that we must "believe women." Not "hear them out respectfully and investigate, taking care to protect the rights of the accused." That's the Old America way. In New America, "believe women" means that if a woman levels a charge, the man must be treated as guilty. In practice, though, this amounts to "believe *certain* women": Christine Blasey Ford, yes; Tara Reade, no. Brett Kavanaugh? Clearly guilty. Joe Biden? Eh, maybe—but that was a long time ago and we really need to beat Trump. . . .

All this came into spectacular display in the Kavanaugh show trial. Here we had a "victim" whose story was obviously made up. She in fact changed her tale several times and claimed not to remember important details, such as when the alleged incident happened—not even what year—where it took place, how she got there, or how she got home. Every single witness she cited disputed her account, and her own family didn't seem to believe her. She even lied to investigators about having a fear of flying (she in fact takes vacations all over the world).

But the left and the leftist media insisted that we "believe the woman"—because she's a woman. Period. It (just barely) didn't work that time, but the whole ordeal was a disturbing harbinger of where the left wants to take us.

Corruption

The word "corruption" brings to mind big city machines, ward heelers and payoffs, "free" turkeys on Thanksgiving, Boss Tweed and Richie Daley. That kind of corruption—"honest graft" in the immortal words of Plunkitt of Tammany Hall—is peanuts compared to the real stuff.

Three types of corruption are meant here. The first is similar to the old style, but less blatant—and much more lucrative. Let's call it "soft bribery." A businessman donates to a politician's campaigns over the years and makes clear to said pol that when his time in government is up, he will be taken care of—provided he works for the businessman's interests while on the inside.

This arrangement is so common that its terms never have to be hinted at, much less stated. It's just understood that this is how our system works. Monied interests know what they must do to "get things done" while aspiring pols know that "government service" is the surest path to wealth for those who can't hack it in tech or finance. Occasionally, very blatant examples come to light—the "Keating Five" for instance, or Bernard Schwartz, head of the defense contractor Loral, greasing Bill

Clinton to lift restrictions on the sale of sensitive military technology to China. When exposed there is momentary outrage, sometimes even investigations, very rarely punishment—and never real reform.

Mostly, though, the linkage between service and payment is left unclear. The reason the ruling class can insist that Hunter Biden "broke no laws" in his business dealings with various foreign governments is because he didn't. That he was paid millions to do nothing in a field in which he has zero experience admittedly smells to high heaven, but as long as pols and their families are willing to brazen out a little bad publicity—and they always are—nothing will come of it.

I don't mean to single out the Democrats either; everyone operates this way. The reason the Republicans didn't want to go into the whole Biden Inc. scam during President Trump's impeachment is because they all do the same thing—or hope to, once they leave office. It's not so much dread of being called hypocrites that held Republicans back as fear of stopping the gravy train.

Nor is it only politicians who benefit from these practices. Recent revelations would seem to indicate that no institution in American life is free of pay-to-play corruption—everyone in a position of power or influence is on the take in one form or another. The Sierra Club, for example, dropped its long-held stance that mass immigration is a threat to the environment in exchange for $200 million from a woke billionaire. Foreign governments spread wheelbarrows full of cash around Washington to lobbyists and "research organizations" in exchange for favors and influence. Elite parents pay sordid bribes to enroll their otherwise unqualified kids into prestigious colleges, which have no qualms about cashing the checks. Cheap-date "conservative" think tanks shill—for a lot less than two hundred mil—for the tech oligarchs that attack and undermine conservative principles. Even the churches have gotten in on the action, with some denominations taking Soros and Koch money to preach for open borders. Granted, many men of the cloth would advocate that out of conviction—but, like good businessmen, they figure if they're going to say it anyway, why not get paid?

The worst, though, are the universities. They collude with the feds to steer billions of dollars in grants their way, all while charging exorbitant tuition and fees, funded with federally backed student loans that the universities lobby Congress to make un-dischargeable in bankruptcy. Nor do our campuses limit their greed to ripping off Americans; they're also on the take from our foreign rivals and even enemies. More than 1.1 million foreign students are currently enrolled in American colleges, most of them taking a spot that might otherwise have gone to an actual American—most also paying full freight, which is one reason why our colleges are happy to shaft their fellow citizens in favor of aliens.

Three hundred seventy thousand of those students—nearly one-third—are from China, America's greatest national security threat. Nobody knows how many of them are spies, but it's not zero: many are caught every year. On at least ninety American campuses, the Chinese government funds so-called "Confucius Institutes" that, according to Senator Josh Hawley (relying on data from the FBI), "spread propaganda, suppress academic freedom, and threaten the national security of the United States" by supporting espionage. A few universities have gotten rid of such installations, but most prefer to keep the revenue.

Student spying would be bad enough, but when teachers do it the results can be devastating. In the first half of 2020 alone, six professors at American universities—including the chair of Harvard's chemistry department—were arrested either for passing American defense and technology secrets to China or illegally taking money from the Chinese government or both. University administrators make a show of being appalled—it would look bad if they didn't—but otherwise don't do anything to try to curtail Chinese influence over their institutions, or our country. They're too invested in the money, their xenophilia, and their anti-Americanism.

The second type of corruption is far graver. Even when corruption at the state and local levels was rampant in some parts of the country, the United States could pride itself on the notion that our feds were incorrupt—and incorruptible. Recent events have blown that conceit right out of the water.

Look at what we've learned just during Trump's presidency. Our intelligence agencies—forbidden by law to spy on Americans—not only did exactly that, but spied not just on ordinary citizens, which would have been bad enough, not even just on incoming officials in a new administration, which is even worse, but on a major party presidential candidate in the middle of a presidential race. And did so at the direction and with the full knowledge of the incumbent president and his most senior cabinet officials and aides. The FBI—supposedly the sterling example of American rectitude—contrived a phony criminal investigation to justify the spying, lied to judges in order to get warrants, then lied to Congress and, later, lied to the American people about their ginned-up handiwork. When the judges found out they had been lied to, they did, and said . . . nothing. Ditto Congress—with the honorable exception of Devin Nunes.

The exposure of the largest political scandal in American history— an inside job to frame a presidential candidate as a Russian spy and rig a presidential election—has thus far reaped almost no repercussions except for a few witnesses caught up in perjury traps and one campaign operative convicted for entirely unrelated tax and disclosure offenses. Oh, and also people like Carter Page and Michael Caputo, who were never charged with anything but still had their lives ruined. But the people who ran the hoax? Two mid-level players got fired, one on the day before he was set to retire. That's it. The big dogs? Scot-free.

I am sorry, and even a bit trepidatious, to have to say this, but the most storied and powerful agencies in our government—the Justice Department, the FBI, the CIA, the entire "intelligence community"—are, all of them, corrupt. Their leaders do not operate for the common good or in the public interest but in furtherance of their own, and of the ruling class's, which is the same thing. They need not—and often do not—obey the law. If they believe or even suspect you might be a threat or an obstacle to their rule, they will use their vast powers to crush you.

Remember how Senate Minority Leader Chuck Schumer taunted President Trump for challenging the spies who nominally work for him?

"Let me tell you, you take on the intelligence community, they have six ways from Sunday at getting back at you." Let that sink in for a moment. Here we have one of the most powerful men in the United States, a pillar of the ruling class, a titan within our government, openly bragging that our most powerful, secretive, and unaccountable agencies mete out private vengeance—including against elected presidents—to serve their institutional interests. It's hard to know which is more shocking: that statement's accuracy or the fact that a leading United States senator boasted about it publicly.

At any rate, Schumer is right. No one can or will stop them. You may seek recourse in the courts, but the courts are part of the system and behave as such. Judges defend the interests of their allies—the government and the rulers—not ordinary Joes who've gotten out of line and had the temerity for one reason or another to take on their overlords.

The most palpably obvious example of official corruption—the one that ripped off the mask—was the arrest, slap on the wrist, rearrest, and "suicide" of pedo-sex-criminal Jeffrey Epstein. First the government let him skate on very serious charges, either because of his extensive connections—which included Bill Clinton, who travelled twenty-six times on Epstein's aptly nicknamed private jet, the "Lolita Express"—or because the intelligence community ordered prosecutors to back off because Epstein was somehow useful to them. Then, more than a decade later, Epstein was rearrested out of the blue for the same crimes. No one quite knows why, or why then. Perhaps his usefulness had come to an end? Then he "killed himself" in what is allegedly among the most secure detention facilities in the country, while all the guards supposedly responsible for keeping him alive weren't paying attention, *after* he had already made one "suicide" attempt. Oh, and the security camera footage covering the period of his first attempt was "lost."

When an institution is this brazen in lying to the public—when it doesn't think it needs to bother to come up with a plausible alternative explanation for what everyone can plainly see—that is but another sign that the attitude of its leaders is: "Screw you; we rule."

No doubt all of these agencies employ many thousands of patriotic, conscientious, impartial people who strive every day to do the right thing for their country. But just as doubtless, none of them are in positions of real power or authority, and none ever seem to rise to one. Nor, I am also sorry to say, do any ever expose and condemn the pervasive corruption and blatantly illegitimate actions of their bosses. Nearly all remain silent. The few who speak up do so only to defend "the institution" which "may have made some mistakes" but which is also "on the front lines of protecting Americans every day" and whose patriotic employees' dedication to their mission should never be questioned.

The third type of corruption, the gravest of all, let's call "meta-corruption." In the founders' conception—indeed, in the view of virtually every political thinker and practicing statesman who ever lived—the core purpose of government is to promote the common good, traditionally understood as policies that benefit the whole citizenry. We now have almost the exact opposite: a government and elite institutions that either deny there is a common good or insist that it is identical with their own narrow sectarian interests. Few—if any—American institutions see their role as promoting the good of the American nation as a whole. Fewer still—if any—actually try to do it.

Electoral Manipulation

Elections are supposedly the "bedrock of our democracy." That bedrock is crumbling.

Outright voter fraud—ballot stuffing, ballot tossing, and the like—is not (yet) the norm. But it does happen. For instance, in the 2012 presidential election, in fifty-nine Philadelphia precincts literally zero votes were cast for Mitt Romney. Now, Philly is no one's idea of a Republican stronghold. But zero? Simple human error—especially given the rates at which the elderly vote—would produce at least a few Romney votes. That, indeed, may have been how Al Gore lost Florida in 2000: nice old ladies going to vote for that nice young man running for vice president but forgetting to bring their reading glasses and—oops!

More common are attempts to manipulate the rules so that Democrats always win. This includes "positive" efforts, such as mail-in voting, "motor voter" laws, and giving children, felons, and illegal aliens the vote, and "negative" ones such as challenging any and every measure intended to increase election security and integrity.

Given all the recent ostentatious bleating about the sanctity of our elections, you'd think our elites would support taking extra special care to ensure election integrity. You'd be wrong. Simple commonsense reforms such as requiring people to show ID to prove who they are before they vote are denounced as "racist" and rarely enacted. I voted for twelve years in New York by simply showing up and being given a ballot. I actually was registered and voted only once in every election, but there was nothing preventing me—or anyone else—from abusing the system. When measures are enacted to prevent such abuse, the left relentlessly attacks them by means of lawfare—the use of strategically placed and timed lawsuits to tie up enemy resources and force outcomes that can't be achieved at the ballot.

Or consider so-called "ballot harvesting"—the practice of canvassing nursing homes, housing projects, and poor and immigrant neighborhoods with absentee ballots. How those ballots get filled out and whether the candidate chosen is really the "voter's" choice is impossible to say. Also unknowable is how many such ballots filled out the "wrong" way get tossed before ever reaching the polling station. Harvested ballots—ones filled out with the "assistance" of people working for a specific campaign—are anything but secret. The harvester can throw out ones that don't further the cause.

The now infamous 2018 Republican wipeout in California's Orange County—long one of the nation's GOP strongholds—was driven in part by this practice, which the Democratic supermajority in the state legislature legalized in 2016. In that one county alone, a quarter million harvested ballots were dropped off on Election Day—and tipped several races that the GOP had been winning at the voting booth. How many of those harvested ballots were legit? There's no way to know, and that's the point. The ballots served their purpose—that's what matters.

When states try to pass laws to end or even limit this practice, here come the lefty "public interest" lawyers! Indeed, the left files lawsuits to challenge every measure that might make electoral fraud harder. Increasingly, they file Election Day challenges in every close contest in the country, always with one aim: to ensure a Democratic victory—whether through additions or subtractions or both. Every late-arriving box of Democratic ballots in the trunk of some activist's car must be counted or else our democracy is a fraud, just as every Republican absentee ballot must be scrutinized and discarded for the slightest irregularity. Whatever works.

Trust in our electoral process is also supposedly the bedrock of our democracy's legitimacy. Then why do Democrats attack that process relentlessly with omnipresent cries of "voter suppression" and claim that any election they lose was rigged? Stacey Abrams lost the 2018 governor's race in Georgia—one of the few states with fairly strict election security—by fifty thousand votes. Yet to this day she claims that she "won."

Why? Genuine conviction is one possibility, and she does seem sincere. But there are other motivations. One, constantly crying "suppression!" and "fraud!" gins up the base. Second, it salves losers' egos.

The Big Fish—as yet uncaught—is of course the Electoral College. If the Democrats can get that sucker on the deck and gut it, they know they'll never lose another presidential election.

Controlled Opposition

Lenin is supposed to have said that "the best way to control the opposition is to lead it ourselves." Chesterton really did say that the "whole modern world has divided itself into Conservatives and Progressives. The business of Progressives is to go on making mistakes. The business of Conservatives is to prevent mistakes from being corrected." These two quotes explain virtually all you need to know about the bulk of today's "conservative opposition."

Start with the GOP (about which we will have much more to say in the last chapter). It accomplished great things in the 1980s and arguably into the mid-1990s. But in the intervening two decades before Trump, it distinguished itself in only two ways: selling out its base in favor of its donors, and bending over backward to secure—nearly always unsuccessfully—good press. On the issues that mattered most to its voters' daily lives—especially trade and immigration—the Republicans consistently sided not just against their voters' desires but against their interests. Worse, Republicans cynically fundraised on moral and religious issues they knew to be dear to conservative hearts—and then folded like cheap tents whenever the left mounted a fresh offensive in the culture war.

Conservative media isn't much better. True, there are some good shows on Fox: above all Tucker Carlson, whose program is the focal point of opposition to New American woke tyranny. Rush Limbaugh remains the best at what he does—and, crucially, one of the few voices on the right capable of understanding, and evolving with, events. (As a friend of mine likes to put it, "He knows what time it is.")

So much of the rest of the right-wing airwaves, though, is dismal— either out of entropy or by design. Paeans to "freedom" and tributes to heroic veterans are all well and good—I occasionally enjoy both—but grave times require more serious and urgent messaging. "Socialism" is bad—yes!—but warmed-over 1980s rhetoric glosses over all the ways that working-class Americans are being shafted by Big Capital and need help.

The worst, though, are the institutionalized parts of the "conservative movement," above all the think tanks and magazines. I can't see much evidence that any thinking has gone on in any of them for some time. They mostly churn out erudite justifications for current arrangements and "explanations" for why things couldn't possibly be any different; that is, apart from lower taxes, less regulation and more trade deals.

None of this is "oppositional" in any coherent sense of that word. The record, if nothing else, demonstrates that. What has Conservatism Inc. successfully conserved, what leftist advance has it prevented, over the last thirty years? Its fortunes rather seem to have risen and fallen—but mostly risen—alongside those of the neoliberal oligarchy. That might be a coincidence, but it's much more likely to have been the whole point.

PROPAGANDA AND CENSORSHIP: NARRATIVE, MEGAPHONE, AND MUZZLE

Our rulers are not above using force to maintain power. But, like Bartleby the Scrivener, they prefer not to.

Their preferred instrument of rule is propaganda, through their deft use of which they have proved that one can, indeed, fool many of the people most of the time. Here is a potentially book-length topic which we have space to treat only briefly. But I shall do my best to explain how modern propaganda works.

There are three core elements: the "Narrative," the "Megaphone," and the "Muzzle." The first term has been in circulation for a while and, as far as I can tell, no one remembers who coined it. Steve Sailer definitely came up with the second. The last, and least clever, is mine. It'll have to do.

The "Narrative" is the meta-story—the message—that elites want every American to accept unquestioningly. There are also sub-narratives pushed to support the meta-Narrative, and/or to meet ruling-class exigencies in a given moment. The "Megaphone" is the collection of instruments through which the Narrative is broadcast: newspapers, cable channels, streaming services, social media, aggregators, late-night talk shows, TV series and movies, the education system—basically any institution whose primary purpose is the creation and/or dissemination of "content." The word "information" will not do as it implies underlying truth. "Content" by contrast can be, and very often is, entirely fake—especially when it purports to be the truth. The "Muzzle" is the censorship arm. This has many facets, some formal—social media sites and banks de-platforming dissenters—others informal: massive societal pressure to shun and even "cancel" wrong-thinkers. Online wokerati are one of the rulers' not-so-secret weapons: they sniff out and persecute dissent for free, out of zeal.

There is no "Ministry of Truth" (yet) that sets the Narrative, beams it out to the world, and punishes dissent. The propaganda system is rather a decentralized network—with greater and lesser centers of power, to be sure, but no single dominant node or executive or even committee in charge. A more accurate way to understand the Narrative is as the product of a hive mind. The people who set and sell it all essentially come from the same socioeconomic class, received the same education, grew up in or move to the same neighborhoods, work in the same industries, and share the same tastes.

A few of them make it into what might be termed the "Inner Party" of the ruling class: those who actually pull the levers of power and reap the greatest rewards. But seats in the Inner Party are relatively few. Therefore a great many from this class find themselves in universities, where first drafts of the Narrative are crafted while others end up in the media, holding and shouting through the Megaphone. To use a Hollywood analogy, the ruling class are the producers, the academics are the writers, senior politicians and deep-staters are the directors, media personalities and other celebrities are the actors, activists are the crew, and you and I are the (captive) audience.

The Narrative

The core message of the meta-Narrative is that America is fundamentally and inherently racist, sexist, homophobic, xenophobic, Islamophobic, transphobic, and so on. The flaws and sins of America derive directly from those of its founding stock, who are natural predators, inherently racist, and malevolent. They never decline a chance to harm "people of color" unless prevented by force. Moreover, everything they have is stolen— "plunder," in the word that Narrative super-spokesman Ta-Nehisi Coates repeats incessantly in his über-woke bestseller *Between the World and Me*.

The Narrative distinguishes between those who acknowledge and make some effort to atone for their "privilege" and those who do not:

"deplorables" in Hillary Clinton's clarifying terminology. The former don't endeavor to make amends by giving up their slots at the top of the pyramid; let's not go nuts. They do so rather by pushing leftist social policies that undermine deplorables and appeal to people of color, so long as those policies don't jeopardize the bottom line—at least not the ruling class's personal bottom line. But spending shareholder cash on wokeness is A-OK. As Xenophon explained more than two thousand years ago, the wise ruler is always liberal with other people's money but tightfisted with his own.

This explains the explosion in recent years of what has been termed "woke capital": ham-fisted propaganda pushed by corporations on topics that have nothing to do with their products. Woke propaganda is a way for the Inner Party to buy off those who might otherwise resent their student debt, dead-end job, or lack of any job at all. For instance, by relentlessly pushing "Pride Month" messaging throughout June, billionaires and CEOs signal to leftist mobs that they're really the good guys and shouldn't be resented in an age of rising wealth concentration and inequality. Amazingly, it works—on all but a few Bernie Bros.

In contrast to their betters, deplorables revel in their privilege—according to the Narrative, at any rate. In reality, this "reveling" can be as innocuous as not engaging in constant self-flagellation. No matter; deplorables are useful—necessary—foils. This is another way elites justify their position, wealth, and honors: it's not just their expertise that entitles them to rule; they also serve as the principal and indispensable bulwark against the deplorables, who would surely come after the oppressed if only the good guys weren't holding them back. It's a feudal claim: you peasants would be dead without us to protect you, hence we deserve our privilege.

Since the mostly-white elite sets and broadcasts the Narrative, naturally its members would prefer to target only deplorables. But as the Narrative becomes ever more explicitly anti-white, that becomes more and more difficult. Elites must therefore constantly affirm their deep belief in the Narrative in order not to be consumed by it.

But the Narrative also holds that society itself—and all its institutions—are irredeemably infused with racism, which it posits as a kind of inexpungible white original sin. Hence it's not exactly clear whether, and if so why, white elites are to be forever exempt from the Narrative's Last Judgment. This little problem is, for the moment, looked past, for the same reason that playground fights instantly divide the class: people instinctively know, from a very young age, who's on their side and who isn't. But the cognitive stress that the Narrative exerts on its own followers increases daily, and one wonders for how long the distinction between deserving elites and deplorables can be maintained.

The foundational purpose of the Narrative is to obscure who the ruling class really are and to misdirect potential resentment and class hatred in other directions. This points to another contradiction. At the same time that the Narrative holds America to be irredeemably racist, it also insists that the present ruling arrangement is a "meritocracy"; everyone in a position of power, prominence, or wealth got there on talent alone and thus deserves her status. There is no ruling class per se, just a collection of very smart, driven people who through sheer grit worked their way to the top. Envying or resenting them is therefore irrational. And self-defeating, because in a "meritocracy" anyone can make it. Including your kids! Don't rail against the system; join it and reap the rewards!

The crafters of the Narrative are not unaware, however, that to large portions of the American population, this part of the message rings hollow. Top slots in modern America may theoretically be open to all, but somehow most of them keep ending up in the hands of the same types of people—basically the sons and daughters of the current ruling class, plus a few well-chosen and obedient outsiders plucked from poverty and obscurity to demonstrate the rulers' "fairness," "openness," and "commitment to diversity." Year after year, decade after decade, millions and their progeny are consistently left behind. The Narrative therefore needs a villain to blame for this obvious injustice.

That villain is "white privilege." Maintaining a fine and mysterious distinction between "white privilege" and white *people* is necessary, given the fact that the ruling class remains overwhelmingly white. The unspoken formula is: all whites have privilege; those who, in 2020, have the most deserve it because they have the correct views. Those others? The truck drivers, plumbers, cops, nurses, and teachers? They're the real villains.

The Narrative seeks to unite at the same time that it seeks to divide. Uniting the entire nation would be dangerous; that much concentrated power, if enough people ever got wise, might upend ruling-class domination. Constant denunciation of the unearned, unrepented privilege of deplorables provides a fault line through the heart of American social and political life, ensuring that no 50+1 electoral coalition can ever threaten to dislodge the ruling class.

But the denunciations also unite all those who oppose the deplorables' alleged "privilege." No ruling class can long rule without foot soldiers. There are, broadly speaking, four ways to motivate soldiers: patriotism, fear, hatred, and spoils. The ruling class doesn't even try to use the first, for obvious reasons. It instead relies on the others, particularly the second and third, which go together: one tends to hate what one fears, and vice versa. As we shall examine in detail in the following chapter, the ruling class's army would seem to have a lot of its own fault lines. The glue that holds it together is animus generated and intensified by the Narrative.

A secondary focus of the Narrative is demonizing men and dividing men and women—especially young men from young women.

As Heather Mac Donald has observed, the Narrative insists that somewhere between 20 and 25 percent of girls who go off to college will be sexually assaulted during their time on campus. Barack Obama himself got into the act, repeating the lie—which he is plenty smart enough not to fall for—that "one in five" college women are raped or otherwise harmed. That's a rate many multiples worse than the most dangerous cities in America—places that no one who can avoid sets foot in, and which everyone who can afford to leave does. Yet every year, hundreds of thousands of girls, aided by their eager parents—Barack and Michelle

Obama included!—carefully prepare college applications into which they pour every detail of half a decade of earnest academic and extracurricular achievement in anxious anticipation that they might be admitted to an institution—with a rape rate hundreds of times that of Detroit.

If this calumny were even remotely true, it would be—by far—the largest public safety crisis in the history of the United States. All federal, state, and local power would be dedicated to crushing the scourge—and parents and their daughters would avoid campus in terror until the perpetrators were all caught, removed, and punished.

The lie is so huge, so preposterous, so insane, so monstrous, one wonders what the point is. But we know the point. The lie is repeated in order to increase the power of leftist commissars, to tighten the federal grip on our education system, and above all to demonize young men—especially young white men.

Perhaps the most ridiculous hate hoax thus far in our young century—one anyone not blinded by prejudice could instantly see was entirely phony—was the claim made by a young coed that a gang of fraternity brothers raped her for hours on a pile of broken glass. Local police and campus authorities could not substantiate the charge, and the coed herself, knowing full well her story was false, wasn't eager for them to try. But that didn't stop *Rolling Stone* magazine from treating her preposterous tale as gospel truth, nor the rest of the media from blaring it through the Megaphone. Even the Obama White House got in on the action.

When—inevitably—the whole thing unraveled, the media tried to wave the story aside as a dull lesson in journalistic process failures. An associate dean at the university implicated in the article eventually won a libel lawsuit. No matter. Never explain, never apologize. Then, when the need arises—for example, when it's time to derail a Supreme Court nominee—do it all over again.

Narrative ideas are initially crafted in the universities—to which, admittedly, most people pay no attention. But this lack of popular scrutiny is actually a great advantage: it allows academics to formulate malevolent doctrines in complete freedom, without fear of consequences such as falling donations, denial of funding, or declining enrollment. (While it's true that a few of the furthest-left liberal arts colleges are going out of business, the big public and private universities where the Narrative really gets written are doing just fine.)

Once drafted, these ideas are then refined at conferences, published in academic journals, and memorialized in academic-press books. In the next stage, elite intellectuals sanitize (slightly) and popularize emerging doctrines for elite consumption. This typically takes the form of prestige books from commercial publishers, essays in elite nonacademic magazines, and interviews on shows with elite audiences such as NPR and (before he got #MeTooed) Charlie Rose.

The most important example of this process at work is the transformation of the definition of "racism." The dictionary and commonsense understanding of that term was, not long ago, that "racism" is judging people by their race rather than by their moral qualities and talents, and/or harboring ill will toward an entire race, and/or believing that one race is somehow superior or inferior to another. In the mid-1980s, university sociology departments changed this definition. The core of the old understanding was retained, but "racism" was now said to be possible only from those "in a position of power." And for post-1960s leftism, deplorables are always and will forever be "in power" no matter how much their average incomes and lifespans may decline or how many billionaires or presidents of color there may be. Hence only white people can be "racist"; people of color, by definition, cannot. What seemed kooky in 1987 is now not merely mainstream but utterly dominant.

The Megaphone

From here, the Megaphone takes over. Its role is to disseminate doctrines that the elite has already adopted. The principal Megaphone is the mass media. It's hard to overstate the importance of the *New York Times* in pushing the Narrative, simply because of its reach, prestige, and influence. It goes without saying that the *Times* is utterly dominated by

Ivy Leaguers and other ruling-class apparatchiks. So its "coverage" would probably look the same regardless.

But surely it's not irrelevant that, in the depths of the 2008 financial crisis, Mexican rentier billionaire Carlos Slim—who would soon become, for a time, the richest man in the world and is still the richest man in Latin America—rescued the *Times* from bankruptcy. By 2016, he was, and remains, the paper's single-largest shareholder. If you were the single largest shareholder in the world's most influential media company, wouldn't you use it to promote your business and personal interests and those of your country and region? Especially if you knew the entire staff was already inclined to do so? A telecom monopolist who makes his money by overcharging Mexican nationals living in America when they phone relatives back home, Slim obviously profits from open borders and globalization. But then again, so does Mexico—and so does the *New York Times*. So it's all good.

The *Times* has outsize power, which it uses in two ways. The first and most obvious is choosing what to cover and how to cover it. Other media institutions seemingly also have this freedom, but in practice nearly all follow the *Times*, which—not for nothing—has been called the "assignment editor to the world." This power is ultimately the more important—and subtle—of the two.

The second is essentially blunt force propaganda: scream as loudly as possible through the Megaphone and hope—assume—that a non-trivial number of people will be brainwashed. What else explains the notorious "1619 Project"? It can't be "news": 1619 was four hundred years ago. The *Times* has always been liberal, but it's impossible to imagine even the crusading Howell Raines *Times* of 2003 giving over huge sections of the world's most valuable newsprint real estate to a cheap knockoff of an Oberlin College senior thesis. The whole purpose of "1619," errors and all—errors especially—is to push the Narrative: to attack the legitimacy of the nation, its history, its government, and especially its historic majority. It's a form of domestic intellectual terrorism—conceived and pushed by the nation's most prestigious and influential opinion-making organ. Has any society in the history of the world ever been subjected to such deliberate internal treachery from one of its own commanding-heights institutions? Though, of course, from the perspective of the *Times*, it is not "treachery" at all but fealty to the one true faith, for which it is not enough that New America succeed; Old America must be destroyed.

We may quickly also note that as scholars exposed one "error" (or lie) after another, the *Times* neither corrected nor retracted any of them. Instead, in a perfect illustration of elite back-scratching, it was awarded a Pulitzer Prize. A curriculum based on this morale-sucking, cohesion-destroying, incendiary calumny is now being adopted by school systems across the country. *That's* influence.

But back to "reporting." As noted, the *Times* leads, and others follow, each in a manner peculiar to its specific institutional strengths. For the *Times*, that means a drumbeat of gray-toned but ideologically slanted "reporting," plus front-page more-in-sorrow-than-in-anger "news analyses" that explain correct thinking on the topic at hand. Jeff Bezos's personal newsletter to the beltway elite, the *Washington Post*, is much less subtle—it pumps out the straight party line—perhaps because its readers are a bit more obtuse. Television's role is to shorten, simplify, and amplify the message. Cable and social media ensure saturation coverage.

Thus, in support of the Narrative that deplorables are both "in power" and predatorily racist, the media scours the nation in search of ordinary crime blotter stories that it can blow up into national panics. Hence the Trayvon Martin, Michael Brown, and Freddie Gray cases (and many others) were covered with the zeal the press used to reserve for events of the magnitude of Pearl Harbor. And, it must be noted, in every instance they got the story wrong. For the media's core role is not to report the news but to push the Narrative. Hence any story that can be spun as "innocent lamb killed by racist white cop" will be so spun, even if the victim was an adult with a criminal record, was in the process of committing a crime, and moved to assault said police officer, who in turn wasn't white.

Tom Wolfe's 1987 mega-bestseller *The Bonfire of the Vanities* demonstrates how it all works in vivid detail that manages to be hilarious, depressing, and prophetic all at the same time. It often feels as though America is stuck reliving that book's plot over and over, a harrowing, real-life illustration of Nietzsche's eternal return.

Thus far, in all such cases, prosecutors have failed to secure convictions of assailants. Exoneration, however, tends to take months or even years, by which time the public will remember only the initial story—which was blared through the Megaphone—and may not even learn of the eventual outcome, which the media will bury in a half-column story on page B18 if they cover it at all.

But the media won't back down even when it is immediately caught red-handed in a lie, as the Covington fiasco illustrates. To recap, a deplorable high school student attending the annual March for Life in Washington, D.C., was filmed standing still and smiling while a left-wing American Indian activist chanted and pounded a drum in his face. The media initially "reported" that the boy and his friends were somehow aggressors. The Indian activist was eagerly booked as a cable news guest and lied about what happened in order to implicate the students. About two days of nationwide angry vituperation against a group of fifteen-, sixteen-, and seventeen-year-old boys ensued, in which virtually every media outlet and figure, along with woke-left politicians, joined a Twitter mob in denouncing them as "racist" and "privileged." So-called "conservative media" wasted not a nanosecond in joining the mob. A writer for *National Review*, Conservatism Inc.'s flagship magazine, called the students "evil" and wrote that they "might as well have just spit on the cross." The boys and their families received so many threats that, for a short while at least, they didn't dare set foot in their own homes. Their school had to close, only to reopen under heavy police protection.

But soon a longer video surfaced which showed that the Megaphone-approved account of the incident was a lie from beginning to end. The boys had themselves been, and were still being, harassed—viciously and profanely jeered by a group called the Black Hebrew Israelites. Not only that, but they were hardly "privileged"—just ordinary middle-class kids from a part of Red America with (at the time) an unemployment rate about 25 percent above the national average. Nick Sandmann, the boy targeted with the most abuse, eventually settled a lawsuit with CNN—sum unknown—which at least amounts to a tacit admission of guilt from one media organ. But—with very few exceptions—neither anyone in the media nor the politicians nor the Twitter avengers who slandered and smeared those kids ever formally apologized or corrected the record. They never do.

So thirsty is the press—and our elites generally—for stories that further the Narrative, they constantly fall for obvious hoaxes. We mentioned above the absurdity of the Jussie Smollett hate hoax, which the press pushed relentlessly until so much counter-information came to light that continuing to do so became impossible. In fact, as hate hoaxes become more and more common, the press seems to fall for more and more of them—it *wants* to believe.

In June 2020, the Megaphone pushed yet another preposterous story, this one alleging that a racially mixed (his mother is black, his father white) NASCAR driver found a noose in his garage. The Megaphone naturally maxed out the volume. NASCAR vowed to fire everyone involved. The FBI sent fifteen agents to investigate and determined that the "noose" was in fact the loop to a garage door pull. No one—not the driver, not NASCAR, not the media—apologized or even admitted that they had gotten anything wrong. In fact, not only does the media never stop amplifying hate hoaxes and never apologize when the hoaxes are inevitably revealed to have been phony, they refuse even to admit hate hoaxes are a phenomenon worthy of coverage. "Not a thing!" is the Narrative-approved take.

The Megaphone mostly pushes the meta-Narrative but can be used to push any Narrative that serves ruling-class ends. Examples include "We must fight them there to avoid fighting them here" to justify the American military's unending conflicts and presence in some forty countries. Another perennial is "Trade barriers are immoral and will crash the economy, while free trade is indispensable and benefits all," even as free trade contributes to the decimation of manufacturing, destroys communities, hollows out the middle class, stomps down wages, fuels the opioid crisis, and causes mortality rates to spike.

But the ultimate recent example is, of course, the Russia hoax. This one was cooked up not on campus but in the "intelligence community" and our "law enforcement" agencies (see "Corruption" above). We all know this particular Narrative: as presidential candidate, Donald Trump "colluded" with Russia to steal the 2016 election. There was never any evidence for this; the whole story was a lie from the beginning. But that didn't stop the ruling class from using the Megaphone for three years to broadcast incessant propaganda to the contrary. When the investigation they cheered and enabled found nothing, they simply whipped up a new Narrative: Ukraine! Bribery! Or extortion . . . or abuse of power. Or something.

You might think so-called "news organizations" that chose the Russia hoax as the biggest story of the twenty-first century and then proceeded to get it entirely, demonstrably wrong—over and over and over—would lose their viewers, their credibility, their money, and eventually go out of business. You'd again be wrong. Because they're not "news organizations." First and fundamentally, they're the Megaphone—the essential transmission apparatus for ruling-class propaganda. You can't broadcast the Narrative without the Megaphone, and the point isn't to get the story right, it's to broadcast the Narrative. Seen in this light, the media not only did their jobs those three years; they excelled. They hammered away at President Trump's legitimacy and greatly impeded his ability to govern. Sure, they would have been happier had they been able to remove him from office. But from their perspective the effort was win-win—or, heads, big win, tails a smaller win. But either way, a win.

One may say the same thing about all ruling-class propaganda and "political correctness" generally. There's a serious upside to never retracting a refuted lie. In the widely quoted words of English physician and author Anthony Daniels:

Political correctness is communist propaganda writ small. In my study of communist societies, I came to the conclusion that the purpose of communist propaganda was not to persuade or convince, nor to inform, but to humiliate; and therefore, the less it corresponded to reality the better. When people are forced to remain silent when they are being told the most obvious lies, or even worse when they are forced to repeat the lies themselves, they lose once and for all their sense of probity. To assent to obvious lies is to co-operate with evil, and in some small way to become evil oneself. One's standing to resist anything is thus eroded, and even destroyed. A society of emasculated liars is easy to control. I think if you examine political correctness, it has the same effect and is intended to.

"Fact-Checking"

The Megaphone is also a tool for setting the parameters of truth itself. There's no end to the way the media does this, not least through the modes just discussed. But the most overt are so-called "fact-check" articles and "explainer" sites. Through these immensely hubristic tactics, the press assumes for itself the mantle of sole arbiter of fact.

Just about every media outlet now has a "fact-checking" arm whose ostensible mission is to subject politicians' words to rigorous, dispassionate analysis. There are even entire—officially "nonpartisan"—organizations that do nothing but this. They all strike the same pose: "We're just umpires, calling balls and strikes." In reality, they're all systemically biased by design; their real purpose is to push the Narrative and undermine, distort, or attack any corrections, refutations, or counterclaims.

They do this in at least three ways. First, Republicans and conservatives get "fact-checked" exponentially more often than their opponents. For those on the other side, it takes a real whopper to rouse the fact-checkers to weigh in, and even then they mostly don't. A quick glance at the front page of "factcheck.org"—"a nonpartisan, nonprofit 'consumer advocate' for voters that aims to reduce the level of deception and confusion in U.S. politics"—on May 26, 2020, found seven anti-Trump items, one anti-Republican item, one item critical of both candidates' ads for a Senate race, and one Biden "exaggeration." Or 8.5 anti-Republican entries out of 10.

Second, the fact-checkers' definition of "fact" is elastic. When a Democrat speaks, he almost has to dispute the laws of physics to draw the attention of a fact-checker. A conservative's every utterance, by contrast, will be scrutinized under an electron microscope. Third, for Republicans—but only for them—arguments are critiqued as if they were offered as facts. Statements such as "Cutting taxes will lead to economic growth" are thus given "four Pinocchios" based on the expert testimony of tenured economists while "Raising the minimum wage will ease poverty" gets a pass.

Similarly, "explainer" articles purport to take complex subjects and boil them down to tell you what's really going on; in reality, they just encapsulate the Narrative. Everything is "explained" through that lens—especially conservative ideas. Conservatives never get to explain themselves, or if they do, their explanations are "fact-checked" into pulp. Then the "explainers" rewrite the conservative script and certify their version—and only their version—as the officially acceptable account.

Fact-checkers and explainers are now working in open collusion with social media to censor speech. Their role is to give a veneer of legitimacy—of "nonpartisan expertise"—to all the bannings and deletions that the social media companies want to do, would do, and are already doing anyway. This ties back to the Progressive imperative of redefining all political questions as ones with correct and incorrect answers. Those "answers" may be "based" on "data" or "science" or "expertise" or "consensus"; the main point is that each question has only one, the one the oligarch-left wants.

Conservatives complain endlessly about all this but get nowhere. They stack examples of media bias like cordwood—indeed, whole think tanks have for decades been doing exactly this—and the left never gives a millimeter. Why would they? They've made themselves the sole arbiter of truth. If they say bias doesn't exist, then it doesn't. Who's going to challenge them? One or two right-wing outfits where interns watch TV all day and compile lists? Just write another "explainer" article explaining that those organizations' money comes from deep-pocketed conservative donors and therefore all their conclusions are illegitimate, whereas the foundation and oligarch money behind the fact-checking sites is purely disinterested and nonpartisan. Or trot out that tired bit of sophistry that says the media cannot be biased to the left because it's owned by corporations, and corporations are inherently conservative. Whatever works in the moment.

Nor do the conservatives who spend countless hours—years, really—compiling examples of media bias realize that they are playing the left's game. Part of the strategy is to provide so many examples of bias that tallying them up is like counting grains of sand on a beach. The left challenges conservatives to "prove" media bias exists, and the conservatives run off like dogs fetching tennis balls, eager to bring back examples for a pat on the head—and start the game all over again. The differences are that dogs know fetch is a game, and in their case the game is actually played for their benefit.

As a friend of mine likes to say, "The left is expert at using its pawns to tie up our bishops, knights, and rooks." The more of our resources and man-hours the left can trick us into squandering on Sisyphean tasks like "proving" media bias, the better for them and the worse for us. The "debate" will always take place on leftist ground, under leftist rules, with leftist umpires. And no matter how many balls are fetched, the charge will never be admitted. The point is to keep you fetching—forever. In well over fifty years, the right still hasn't figured this out.

The Muzzle

Which brings us, finally, to the Muzzle. There are several ways it operates. The most common is the way it chooses what "news" is "fit to print." The Russia hoax? Definitely fit! In fact, go wall-to-wall for three years with it. Local crime blotter stories that fit the Narrative? Yep. Interracial crime that does not? Definitely not! In fact, it's become a cliché that any time you read a crime story in the prestige press and the races of the people are not mentioned, the victim is white and the assailant is not.

Or consider the fact that the so-called "White Death"—a decline in white life expectancy for the first time in decades, mostly owing to opioids and alcoholism—was ignored for two decades. White mortality began to climb for the first time ever in the late 1990s. When two married Princeton economists noticed and wrote about it, they described being "told, in no uncertain terms: *How dare you work on whites*," and getting "really beaten up." Their research doesn't fit the Narrative.

Tech companies—which increasingly control news dissemination—are doing the same thing with their algorithms: suppressing stories that contradict or undermine the Narrative and promoting those that support it.

Another form of Muzzling is "de-platforming." Say the wrong thing on social media, have your account locked. The informers—who are nearly all volunteers—aren't content to silence people on Facebook or Twitter. Increasingly, they want to "cancel" heretics: get them fired, cut off from the financial system, even denied medical care. A new regulation in the United Kingdom—which we must assume will be proposed here sooner or later—would allow Britain's National Health Service to deny non-emergency care to those deemed "racist, sexist, or homophobic." Government bureaucrats, naturally, will be the ones doing the deeming. The word "National" in the NHS's name means that it's supposed to serve the entire country. Everyone pays taxes to support it. Will those denied care for their alleged "racism" get a refund?

The major employers in this country—public and private—are all too happy to play along. A big part of the reason why cancel culture is so effective is that corporations voluntarily enforce its diktats with ruthless efficiency. At the front end, they indoctrinate workers on what can and can't be said (and thought) and make clear the price of noncompliance. On the back end, they fire—without references, and often with a public shaming—anyone who steps out of line.

Look what happened to Amy Cooper, the now infamous Central Park dog walker. Perhaps she overreacted by calling the police on Christian Cooper, though his own recording of the incident shows him using vaguely threatening language. Amy Cooper became the instant target of a social media mob, was denounced as a racist by the mayor, fired from her job, and had her dog taken from her. At the time of this writing, authorities are mulling over whether to charge her with a crime; civic leaders have proposed that she be banned for life from Central Park. She will almost certainly have to move out of the city and is probably unemployable for life, all over a trivial dispute about a leash. This is America 2020.

Private companies join these orgies of personal destruction—immolating their own employees—in part out of fear of social media mobs and Megaphone bad publicity, in part to avoid government lawsuits, but also out of conviction: the commissars in HR who enforce the norms are true believers.

One wonders, logically, where this ends. If heretics are to be denied not just the right to speak but the ability to make a living and see doctors, how are they supposed to stay alive? Or is that the point? To create a sort of virtual gulag that allows zeks to roam free, but starves them and refuses to treat their illnesses or injuries? What's next? Should we brand such people on the forehead so that strangers not in the know don't unwittingly commit some act of kindness toward them?

The Celebration Parallax

The most difficult aspect of the Muzzle to explain is the way it imposes a laughably unfair and contradictory double standard on certain kinds of speech. A close cousin to what I am about to describe is Rod Dreher's "Law of Merited Impossibility," which he coined to describe the left's tactic of at once dismissing and confirming any Christian's concerns about the effects of extending legal protections to homosexuality:

It's a complete absurdity to believe that Christians will suffer
a single thing from the expansion of gay rights, and boy, do
they deserve what they're going to get.

The Law may be usefully applied to any number of issues on which
conservatives were instructed to take leftists at their word and ask no
questions about where leftist enthusiasm is headed.

Not to take anything away from Dreher, who was right about what
the left was doing at that time, but his law has become a bit passé. It
assumes that leftists still go to the trouble of reassuring their targets with
platitudes they don't really mean. They don't do that anymore. Today
their preferred tactic is to say what they really mean—and then persecute
anyone not on their side who dares quote their own words back to them.

On no subject is this tactic more prevalent than immigration. The
left insists that concerns from certain quarters that immigration policy
in America (and Europe) amounts to a "great replacement" is a "dangerous," "evil,' "racist," "false" "conspiracy theory." But a leftist *New
York Times* columnist can write an article entitled "We Can Replace
Them" and . . . nothing. Same fundamental point, except she's all for
it and her targets aren't. Depending on who's doing the talking, the
demographic transformation of the United States is either a glorious
trend that portends a permanent Democratic majority and a more
"vibrant" future . . . or else a "conspiracy theory" that is not happening
in any way at all, no-how.

Similar two-track rhetoric has long defined the affirmative action
"discussion." People of color must be granted explicit preferences to
overcome America's "legacy of racism," so that we may "diversify"
America's power centers and end white male dominance, a move that—in
addition to being necessary to address the country's inherent racism—
improves those institutions by infusing them with different and hitherto
neglected points of view. Also, kids of color need "role models" who
"look like themselves." But there is no such thing as "reverse discrimination," which is itself a racist term.

Call it the Celebration Parallax. A parallax is the apparent difference in position of the same object seen from different vantage points. For instance, an analogue speedometer that reads sixty miles per hour to the driver, but fifty to the passenger—even though the needle itself is only in one place.

In the case of contemporary speech, the decisive factor is the intent of the speaker. If she can be presumed to be celebrating the phenomenon under discussion, she may shout her approval from the rooftops. If not, she should shut up before someone comes along to shut her up. Note also that the key distinction here is celebration versus non-celebration, not support versus opposition. One need not actually, clearly oppose the subject under discussion in order to be blameworthy; declining or neglecting to celebrate it forcefully enough will do. As in Stalin's Russia, lack of enthusiastic clapping is regarded as opposition. In other words, the legitimacy of one's right to state the same identical fact, in the same identical language, depends on who one is and what one thinks of it.

Since the left presumes that all persons of color approve of the phenomena covered by the Celebration Parallax, the parallax is really a test to distinguish allies from deplorables. That, and a way for the ruling class to rally their troops and tamp down intra-coalition discontent, while at the same time discouraging and demoralizing the opposition. Crowing about leftist intentions and the inevitable leftist triumph helps keep the foot soldiers happy and united. But that same crowing also tends to rouse the other side, who might finally organize in their own defense. Since the crowing can't be dispensed with, the possibility of opposition must be suppressed. The left's strategy is: any time anyone who is not "one of us" and doesn't love our plan for them repeats what we say, destroy them. The rest can't be allowed to get wise.

Dissidence = Terrorism

The most potentially sinister manifestation of the Muzzle is the way our corrupt intelligence and law enforcement agencies increasingly allege that "white nationalists" pose a threat to the nation as great or greater than deadly foreign enemies or domestic terror cells. The Megaphone does its part to magnify the alleged "threat." As of June 2020, googling "white supremacy" yields 42.4 million hits, "white nationalism" 35 million, and "white terrorism" an astounding 135 million.

The formal effort began with the Obama administration's so-called "Countering Violent Extremism" (CVE) program, an effort to fuzz up the definitions of "terrorist" and "terrorism" by equating the severity of threats from well-organized—and often foreign-supported and directed—enemies of America with homegrown or domestic extremists. But not just any domestic extremists—many of those are after all motivated by Islamism, leftism, or some other anti-American ideology. No, the only domestic extremists meant were right-wingers. Who undoubtedly exist, but are just as undoubtedly less numerous, less well-organized, less well-funded, and much, much less deadly.

Nonetheless, out went the cry: Threat level the same! Same response and resources required! But all that was a lie. The true purpose of CVE's equivalence rhetoric was to dial down the pressure on suspected Islamist terrorists—the Narrative is exquisitely sensitive to charges of "Islamophobia"—and dial up the pressure on alleged "white supremacists," even those with no history of violence or even of advocating violence.

Recently, this trend was taken up a notch. In February 2020, the director of the FBI testified that his agency has placed "racially motivated violent extremism . . . on the same footing in terms of our national threat banding as ISIS." ISIS—a fanatically violent Islamist sect that until recently controlled vast swaths of the Middle East, including oil fields—has killed tens of thousands in its own region and at least 2,000 in overseas terror attacks; wounded tens of thousands; enslaved 3,500 women and children from the Yazidi community; beheaded dozens of people at a time; trapped 30,000 families on the Sinjar Mountains, causing at least 70 children to die of thirst, killed 500 of the men and sold the remaining women into slavery; filmed the beheading of American journalist Steven Sotloff; and displaced millions. Are there any Americans—however misguided or evil—who even remotely compare to *this*?

How many "neo-Nazis"—real ones—are there in this country? Enough to fill a single high school gymnasium?

Counting terror deaths is hard, but terrorism expert Timothy Furnish ran the numbers, choosing as his start date the 1993 attack on the World Trade Center. Furnish found that, since then, Islamic terrorism has murdered just under 28,000 people worldwide. The global death toll over the same period from all white violence even plausibly—that is, not necessarily definitively—connected to "white supremacy" is 346. Or 1.5 percent of the Islamist butcher's bill. This is the "grave, urgent threat" that the Megaphone insists our government should immediately pivot toward crushing.

It should go without saying that of course cops should, if they can, stop any form of extremist violence before it happens, and—if they can't—crack down hard on the perpetrators. But why, then, does the FBI—along with most local law enforcement—consistently allow Antifa, America's most violent domestic terror group, to run amok? Because it knows that the ruling class doesn't want Antifa shut down, because Antifa's violence serves the Narrative.

In June 2020, as first Minneapolis and then dozens of other cities burned partly at the hands of Antifa shock troops—many of whom flew in for the fun—the Megaphone not only went out of its way to avoid any use of the word "riot," it also laughably flogged the Narrative that the arsonists, looters, and shooters destroying the city were "white supremacists" and "Trump supporters." Ample evidence to the contrary—above all live video—got scrubbed off social media almost instantaneously. Thus are Narrative, Megaphone, and Muzzle utilized and advanced all at once.

The risk here is obvious. So long as law enforcement believes one of its roles is to enforce the Narrative, feds and cops will be tempted to target nonviolent dissenters—people who consider themselves in every respect patriots and loyal Americans—under the guise of stopping "violent extremism." The hard left already considers displaying the American flag to be a sign of hatred and violence. How long before the FBI agrees?

Perhaps the greatest irony of modern American politics is that those most attached to America—the physical country, its history, and its symbols—are those its government least serves, while those most vocally dissatisfied or even angry with America are precisely those whom the government has been transformed to favor. The former can't stop cheering for a country whose institutions and elites, as every day passes, more openly despise and work against them. The latter can't stop complaining about a country that they've successfully remade in their own image to serve their own interests. At least the latter know that their complaints have a strategic purpose: to continue to punish the former and further transform America to their liking. The former are, emotionally, living in the past.

CHAPTER FOUR

The Ruling Class and Its Armies

It will perhaps appear to some that I have too often used the phrase "ruling class" without defining it. It's time, then, to explain who they are and what they want.

But here the road divides. First, we must distinguish the ruling class from its foot soldiers. Second, we must differentiate what the former want from what the latter want. Third, we must discern the ruling class's three categories of foot soldiers and what each of *them* want. For, like the explorers who set out for unknown waters and lands seeking, variously, gold, God, and glory, the ruling class's crew is comprised of people with different, and sometimes competing, motivations. Some just want money. Others, true-believing utopians, strive for the perfection of man on earth. And others (here the analogy breaks down a bit) seek revenge.

Nor are all their desires always compatible with ruling-class interests. In some cases, even the wishes of those within a given foot soldier faction are internally contradictory: some want, or believe they want, X and not-X at the same time. For instance, many want to punish America for its alleged sins but also continue to reap benefits from America's historic productivity—as if a prostrate, anguished America can keep producing at anywhere near its accustomed clip. All this makes the future uncertain, and likely tumultuous.

WHO—REALLY—RULES US?

In classical political philosophy, the fundamental political question—the answer to which defines the regime or political structure—is: Who rules? Secondary, and related, is: To what end? Generally speaking, the ruler(s) may be one, few, or many; and they may rule for the common good or for their own private good.

According to the parchment, in America the people are sovereign, and they are to exercise their sovereignty in furtherance of the common good, to "promote the general welfare." The government is their servant, which they direct and control through elections that choose the officers of their representative institutions, who then steer the state in the direction indicated by the people. There is no "ruling class" per se, though the founders did hope that the cream would rise to the top; that is, that the people would select as their representatives and officials the best from every region and background. As Jefferson put it in a letter to Adams:

> There is a natural aristocracy among men. The grounds of this are virtue and talents. Formerly bodily powers gave place among the aristoi. But since the invention of gunpowder has armed the weak as well as the strong with missile death, bodily strength, like beauty, good humor, politeness and other accomplishments, has become but an auxiliary ground of distinction. There is also an artificial aristocracy founded on wealth and birth, without either virtue or talents; for with these it would belong to the first class. The natural aristocracy I consider as the most precious gift of nature for the instruction, the trusts, and government of society. And indeed it would have been inconsistent in

creation to have formed man for the social state, and not to have provided virtue and wisdom enough to manage the concerns of the society. May we not even say that that form of government is the best which provides the most effectually for a pure selection of these natural aristoi into the offices of government?

This noble vision is not what America has now. We have, instead, an artificial aristocracy, founded partly on wealth and birth—but informally, and thus disguised. Our ruling class flatters itself into thinking it is not a caste but a cadre of deserving "meritocrats": "natural aristoi" whose "virtue and talents" entitle them to rule. What they are in reality is a smallish minority who rule in furtherance of their own private interests.

Angelo Codevilla's analysis in *The Ruling Class* (first an essay, then a book) distinguishes the ruling from the "country" class, though not all of the latter are specifically rural (but it's safe to say that just about every rural American is part of that class). The country class lives in many places, professes many faiths, and hews to many different habits and traditions, yet its members are alike in two fundamental ways. First, while some of them are rich and/or prominent in their own fields and communities, none has any influence on national politics, elite discourse, or the culture. They are acted upon, not actors. The apparent exceptions—red-state congressmen—on examination nearly all turn out to be defanged kittens doing the bidding of their ruling-class masters. The rare genuine country-class congressman like Matt Gaetz is marginalized by the Republican leadership. Second, people in the country class don't like being bossed around. Codevilla explains that:

[T]he country class' . . . different sectors draw their notions of human equality from different sources: Christians and Jews believe it is God's law. Libertarians assert it from

Hobbesian and Darwinist bases. Many consider equality the foundation of Americanism. Others just hate snobs.

Which makes their dislike of the ruling class especially understandable. Contempt for the country class is a bedrock criterion—almost the distinguishing characteristic—of our overlords.

At first glance, it may seem that "wealth and birth"—traits inherent to a landed aristocracy—do not define America's present elites. But that would be wrong; one simply has to understand wealth and birth in a new way to see how they determine who rules in modern America. Birth matters in two fundamental ways: *to whom* one is born, and *where*.

Our elites are increasingly hereditary. Not formally: there are, obviously, no inherited titles. But as America's economy increasingly shifts to reward intelligence above all else and Americans increasingly practice "assortative mating" (smart people marrying smart people), since intelligence is partly heritable, economic and social success is increasingly confined to a narrow caste.

The ruling class's opinion on intelligence is, however, complex. Outwardly, they seem to believe that smarts are not merely a virtue but the preeminent virtue. Their own fancy degrees are proof of their superior intelligence and knowledge, which in turn are the foundations of their title to rule. For the ruling class, intelligence is not simply a matter of ability but also of opinions and tastes: smart people all think the same way about the most important things because to be smart is to understand, and to understand is to agree. Therefore those who disagree are either dumb or—if obviously intelligent in a raw-horsepower way—crazy. As for processing power itself, too much tends to make one a dork, hence intelligence turns out not to be the supreme virtue after all. Intelligence marshaled in the service of, say, solving some century-old higher math problem is unobjectionable but frivolous. Applied to something like sequencing the genome—a task far beyond the intelligence of anyone in the ruling class—it is dangerous and even evil, since the discoveries might contradict ruling-class dogma.

One may therefore amend the above formulation to increase its accuracy without changing the point:

> As America's economy increasingly shifts to reward ~~intelligence~~ **performance on standardized tests and success navigating elite "education"** above all else, and Americans increasingly practice "assortative mating" (~~smart~~ **highly credentialed** people marrying ~~smart~~ **highly credentialed** people), since ~~intelligence~~ **the ability to do well on standardized tests and successfully navigate elite "education"** is partly heritable, economic and social success is increasingly confined to a narrow caste.

Hence up-and-coming members of the ruling class are almost exclusively the children of established members.

As to where one is born, America's new elite is overwhelmingly concentrated in blue enclaves: the expensive parts of coastal cities, "super zip" suburbs, and college and resort towns. It's not essential to be born or raised in one of these places; the ruling class keeps an eye out for a limited number of talented outsiders—especially from "protected classes"—to welcome into the ranks. That way they can deny the otherwise obvious, and grave, charge that they are a closed, self-perpetuating caste and, with the same gesture, pay some danegeld to "diversity." But mostly the ruling class replenishes itself from within. This is partly a matter of affinity—most everyone prefers the familiar to the alien—partly a matter of snobbery (flyover rubes are uncouth and uncultured), and partly a matter of safety: giving power to outsiders is not the way to maintain your own.

As for wealth, as a prescient man said within my hearing nearly thirty years ago, in the New America, "If you can choose whether to be born rich or smart, choose smart." But increasingly, to be born smart is to be born rich, and vice versa. Not necessarily oligarch-rich, but comfortably upper-middle class at least—rich enough to be able to afford the sine qua non amenity of the ruling class: elite schools for your children.

In practice that means either expensive private academies or an elite public school district with stratospheric home prices and property taxes, followed by an elite private college or, failing that, one of the "good" (defined as "one elites don't find embarrassing") public universities if you're lucky enough to live in a state that has one (California and Virginia, yes; New York and Massachusetts, no). Best of all is the Ivy League or Stanford, which to attend as an undergraduate is equivalent in New America to a title of nobility in Old England. Not all such titles are equal, of course. We may say that a Harvard (and perhaps Stanford) degree is a dukedom while one from Dartmouth is maybe an earldom and Brown a baronetcy. But compared to the Great Unwashed, a peer's still a peer.

The Ruling Class's Citadel: The Universities

It's worth considering the nature of these schools, which even more so than home-and-hearth are the true incubators of the ruling class. As everyone knows, they are hard to get into, and most who make it have something on the ball. Yet there is a curious hypocrisy to these universities' admissions policies. Leaving aside Harvard's and Yale's origins as seminaries to train clergy—in important ways, they still are!—all of these colleges used to serve, more or less explicitly, the old WASP upper class. Hence legacy admissions—generations from a single family all attending the same school—were not only common but unabashedly part of the institutional mission.

Then, in the mid-1950s, Ivy League administrators and trustees had a change of heart and changed the mission: instead of serving a quasi-hereditary upper crust, they would scour the nation for talent. They quietly condemned their institutions' old policies as unfair, unworthy of elite institutions purporting to lead a great nation locked in a titanic struggle for liberty, and also shortsighted. To win the Cold War, America would need its best, wherever they happened to come from. As a result, greater reliance was placed on standardized test scores. Ivies' share of legacy admits declined, and the ethnic composition and geographic base of the student bodies broadened significantly.

Listening to these schools' deans, you'd think their policy is still to scour the nation, looking for the best and brightest wherever they may be. But the reality is closer to the older practice, except instead of favoring WASPs they favor the children of the current ruling class. For instance, nearly 30 percent of legacy applicants to Harvard get in; the overall rate is only 6 percent, and thus even lower for non-legacies. At Stanford, legacies are three times more likely to be accepted than unconnected nobodies.

Beyond the literal legacies are those whom we may call the meta-legacies. Say dad went to Harvard but you don't quite have the chops; or mom went to Brown but you aced the SAT, took only AP classes your senior year, and can document a hundred more hours of community service than she could. In the former case, you might have to settle for a lesser title; in the latter, you might be able to trade up. In both cases, though, you're still in the club. For all its paeans to "diversity," the ruling class takes care of its own. As the dean of Harvard College helpfully explained when challenged on why upper-income students outnumber poorer kids six-to-one, "We're not trying to mirror the socioeconomic or income distribution of the United States." Diversity has its limits.

Once the ruling class's own are taken care of, next in line are promising members of certain demographic groups, followed by athletes. Dead last are deplorables from the country part—they're "privileged," and these preeminently privileged institutions see their mission as "dismantling privilege." Hence by far the most underserved demographic on elite campuses are rural and red-state whites—a fact confirmed by simply comparing National Merit Scholarship data (a record of the highest-achieving high school seniors every year) with elite college admission rates by race and region.

The case of Asians is both complicated and illustrative. On one hand, they are obviously not white and therefore under the current understanding not "privileged." Asians tend to do extremely—frustratingly—well on standardized tests. "Frustratingly" because if admission to elite schools were granted purely by "merit" (grades and test scores), their student bodies would be substantially more—perhaps even plurality or majority—Asian. That's exactly what happened at California's public universities after a referendum banned race-based admissions in 1996: Asian enrollment zoomed up across the system, especially on the most elite campuses. (That's one reason why the University of California Regents voted in 2020 to drop standardized testing altogether.)

The ruling class can't allow the same thing to happen to its private citadels: where would their own kids go? More to the point: what would happen to their iron grip on those economic, political, and cultural institutions to which the Ivy League is the pipeline and which are the ultimate sources of ruling-class power and prestige? Today's elites have absolutely no interest in repeating the generosity of the WASPs who gave away the Ivy League in the 1950s. That means keeping competitors—and potential usurpers—out.

Which is the reason elite universities discriminate heavily against Asian applicants. When challenged—Harvard was recently sued for exactly this practice—their defense is that they know best the type of students they're looking for and endeavor to evaluate each "holistically," on the basis not just of grades, test scores, and extracurriculars, but also "personality" and other "leadership traits." The implication—to be clear, *their* implication, not mine—being that Asians somehow have deficient personalities or lack leadership traits.

Elite universities' defense that they should be allowed to choose those whom they can best serve, and who can best serve them, sounds reasonable and was employed by any number of American institutions—colleges, companies, clubs—before the 1964 Civil Rights Act effectively stripped freedom of association out of the First Amendment. A stripping which, needless to say, Harvard and all the other Ivies entirely supported and still do. It's OK for *them* to discriminate however they like; but if you so much as attempt to evaluate applicants or candidates without regard to race and end up with too little "diversity," bureaucrats and/or the legal system will crush you. Like nearly all elite institutions, the universities' formal—if implicit—policy is: freedom of association for me but not for thee.

The other core purpose of admissions policy is to screen for wokeness. As one admissions bigwig at Yale put it, "For those students who come to Yale, we expect them to be versed in issues of social justice. We encourage them to be vocal when they see an opportunity for change in our institution and in the world." The preeminent consideration for admission, then, is whether an applicant is a good bet to become—in terms of opinions, voting patterns, priorities, donations, and activism—a reliable member of the ruling class. Is she already, or can we make her, "one of us"? Few for whom this answer is not a clear "yes" get in.

And once you're in, you're in. As Codevilla explains, "Since the 1970s, it has been virtually impossible to flunk out of American colleges. And it is an open secret that 'the best' colleges require the least work and give out the highest grade point averages." That certainly jibes with my personal and anecdotal experience. I'm looking at you, Stanford, where an A- is considered an intolerable affront and a B+ may as well be an F.

The true purpose of this "education" (one must put the word in quotes because few these days learn anything substantive from it) is twofold. First is the continuance of ruling-class habits and tastes, the basics of which the students get from their parents but which calcify when drilled home by their surroundings and peer networks. Second is certification: to have been initiated and schooled in the mysteries means you really belong, are in the club.

The ruling class, then, are not so much exceptional as above-average and conformist. The former quality is what gets them into college; the latter is what college exists to make them. Yet however banal and unimpressive, members of this class run everything important in modern America. Some of them—the tech oligarchs, hedge fundies, private equity barons, and CEOs—are spectacularly rich, with net worths exceeding the GDP of whole countries. Others—banksters, Big Law partners, C-suite also-rans—are ordinarily rich, able to live as well or better than

the dukes and earls of old. Still others—salaried Davoisie coat-holders—
are "affluent."

And a few are akin to that staple of English literature, the "impoverished
aristocrat," someone whose income—sadly—doesn't quite measure up to
her social status or self-conception. "Impoverished" in this context therefore
does not mean "unemployed and broke" or even "living paycheck to paycheck without health insurance in a double-wide outside Omaha" but rather
"doesn't have enough to enjoy all the trappings of upper-middle-class ease."
Just as Trollope's "impoverished" gentry never had to live in tenant farm-
houses or industrial slums, our ruling class's lowest rung still somehow
manages to bed down in blue coastal metros—and wouldn't be caught dead
anywhere else. Mostly their "poverty" arises from their choice of a career—
for example, journalism, government, academia, or activism—that doesn't
pay all that well.

But don't kid yourself: they're still ruling-class. First, because they
came from that milieu and got the education. Second, and fundamentally,
because—while their betters may be more likely to move the levers of
power—these are the people who set the cultural norms and tastes, and
increasingly the agenda, for everyone else.

WHAT THE RULING CLASS WANTS

This one's easy: the ruling class wants to stay in power, maintain its
status, preserve its wealth, and increase its share of all three.

That doesn't mean, however, that its members favor the status quo—
not entirely. They favor it insofar as it favors *them*. Now, it might seem
laughably obvious that the status quo favors them; didn't they build it
specifically to favor themselves? Yes, they did—but they don't yet feel
certain that their project is complete.

Machiavelli explained this seemingly paradoxical fear this way:

> It [is] much disputed who is the more ambitious, he who
> wishes to maintain or he who wishes to acquire; for either one

appetite or the other can easily be the cause of very great tumults. Yet nonetheless they are most often caused by those who possess, because the fear of losing generates in them the same wishes that are in those who desire to acquire; for it does not appear to men that they possess securely that which man has unless he acquires something else new.

This insecurity drives the ruling class to keep the pedal to the floor with globalization, mass immigration, propaganda, political correctness, censorship, de-platforming, and all the other forms of personal enrichment, corruption, harassment, persecution, and unfairness endemic to their rule. They proceed hell-bent with the project because, as Corporal Hicks said seconding Ripley, it's the only way to be sure.

You and I might think that the ruling class are plenty rich and powerful enough, but that's not how *they* feel. Again, Machiavelli:

[A]mbition . . . is so powerful in human breasts that it never abandons them at whatever rank they rise to. The cause is that nature has created men so that they are able to desire everything and are unable to attain everything. So, since the desire is always greater than the power of acquiring, the result is discontent with what one possesses and a lack of satisfaction with it.

Montesquieu makes much the same point when he describes man as "a being whose greed for power keeps increasing the more he has of it, and who desires all only because he already possesses much."

The issue for the ruling class, then, is not merely how to *secure* their power and wealth but how to *increase* it—because, in their minds, the latter is necessary for the former. Their solution is, first and fundamentally, to transform the United States into a deracinated economic-administrative zone with one-size-fits-all "rules," whose surface impartiality masks an unbending bias toward capital over wages, management over labor, words over actions, ideas over things, the new over the old, cosmopolitanism over the familiar, foreigners over the native-born. Second, it is to persuade or bully as much of the developed world as possible into going along; and third, over time to amalgamate all such economic-administrative zones into one big zone, so that the lines on the map hitherto known as "borders" recede into historical curiosity, like the county boundaries of Olde England which—after progressive "reform"—no longer carry any political significance. The twentieth-century Russo-French philosopher and bureaucrat Alexandre Kojève, borrowing from Marx and especially Hegel, articulated this vision and named it the "universal and homogenous state." This is the end state the ruling class seeks.

The ruling class knows that while their desired transformation has come a long way, it still has a ways to go. Shocks such as Brexit, Trump, and the Yellow Vests reveal dangerous pockets of resistance that threaten the whole project. In particular, lots of Americans still regard their country as a country, not an economic-administrative zone.

Homogenization

To our elites, all this variation and specificity are at best nuisances and at worst obstacles. Steeped in economic theory, they see the world as a set of abstractions. Differences and distinctions among peoples and countries are thorns to be sliced away, lumps to be milled, knots to be sanded down. The ruling-class "celebration" of "diversity" masks, and even leads to, their underlying and fundamental push for homogenization.

Efficient markets require—or at least run best with—interchangeable consumers and workers. The expense of differentiating products to satisfy differing cultures, tastes, and needs undercuts economies of scale and drives down profits. The ability to hire and fire at will—which requires fungible workers who never stand up for themselves—drives down wages (that is, costs). One class of consumer buying one product, made by machines that never take breaks or demand raises, is the profit-maximizing neoliberal Platonic ideal.

Except, that is, for the ruling class themselves. This is the first of many contradictions—or, let us say, tensions—that bedevil ruling-class ideology and preferences. Our elites like variety, especially gradations of luxury—the higher up the scale the better. These two qualities obviously do not easily coexist with mass homogenization. So far, however, the ruling class has managed to have its cake and eat it. Retail and restaurant chains, food purveyors and supermarkets, real estate developers and home builders, box stores and the consumer brands that fill them—really, any business that sells to the middle class and below—become more alike by the year, as do their products. The ruling class owns and runs most of these businesses and so reaps the rewards.

It then lavishly spends the rewards on luxury goods and services—including necessities such as food, but at a rarified level—from a much smaller network of high-end suppliers. The purveyors to the rich constitute a kind of parallel economy, made up of small and medium-sized enterprises ("SMEs" in banking terminology) that exist to serve only the ruling class and, to a lesser extent, its well-salaried valets: lawyers, lower–upper management, mid-level bankers, and the like. Fifty years ago, firms at this scale served and employed millions of ordinary people in every region of the country while making their owners comfortably, but not spectacularly, rich. Today nearly all such companies are gone—either run out of business or absorbed into corporate behemoths whose workers are paid much less, and top management much more, than they were in the firms subsumed or replaced. C-suite denizens, needless to say, don't buy their own companies' products, much less set foot in the stores.

Indeed, one metric of whether you've "made it" in New America is whether you're ever under compulsion to shop at Walmart, Target, CVS, or Kroger. Despite being much closer income-wise to the down-market middle than to the Davoisie whose coats they hold, the clerical upper-middle class, if it can, avoids those places as if everyone in them had COVID-19, preferring to flirt with personal bankruptcy shopping alongside their betters.

Similarly, the ruling class spends lavishly on homes and on "communities" that are compact, safe, clean, orderly, and chocked with independent businesses and excellent public schools. Their houses, too, tend to have been built before World War II and hence don't all look and feel identical. Most of these abodes are quite attractive and many downright gracious. This is another—and much harder to surmount—cutoff line between the upper-middle class and their socioeconomic inferiors, who live at best in cookie-cutter exurbs but, the further one looks down the ladder, in drab apartment buildings that look like Motel 6s without the towering signs.

In other words, in where and how it lives, in what it consumes and where it shops, the ruling class pays through the nose to experience America as if the calendar still read 1955—and a particularly upscale 1955 at that. In its professional life, it works hard to make sure that you can't afford to live the same way. What Americans of all classes—admittedly, at varying degrees of elegance—could enjoy throughout most of the twentieth century is now available only to the rich, whose ethos is: identical pods, box stores, processed junk, and drive-thrus for you but not for us.

Pacification

Homogenization, though, isn't simply a matter of money. It's also a very effective way to make the population pliant and controllable. For rulers in a nominal democracy who still rely on elections to gain, keep, and legitimize power—who don't (yet) dare dispense with the spectacle of voting—inuring voters to misrule is essential. The tried-and-true method for doing so is to anaesthetize them: "bread and circuses," in the Roman formulation. In our case, the "bread"—far from nutritious Roman pane—is junk and fast food: heavy on sugar and processed starch, low on protein, healthy fats, and vitamins. The "circuses" are video games, ever-more-vapid action movies and streaming TV, "sportsball," and—above all—porn.

"Entertainment" is at least as old as rhapsodes reciting Homer. And complaining about innovation is as old as philosophy. In Plato's (written) dialogue *Phaedrus*, Socrates—sounding a bit like Abe Simpson— denounces writing on the grounds that books relieve men of the necessity of memorization and thus undermine knowledge retention.

Yet it's fair to say that the sensory overload endemic to our times— "devices" and "screens" everywhere, almost never out of view—is unique in the annals of man. Cinema may be a great art form—I'm a fan myself—but the big blockbusters of today are virtually content-free exercises in sex, gore, gross-out humor, and/or retina-searing "action." Popular music hasn't evolved or produced anything new (much less good) in what feels like thirty years. Rooting for one's favorite team devolved from a pastime into an obsession and now is the center of many people's lives—even as the athletes on those teams live at a further and further remove from anything like ordinary American experience. Willie Mays— one of the two or three greatest baseball stars of the twentieth century— used to live blocks from his home field and play stickball with kids on his street. Can one imagine any of our pampered faux-gladiators leaving their gated compounds to do anything remotely similar? Once a year, maybe, in a well-choreographed stunt carefully staged by the player's agent and "covered" by a compliant press.

But the worst is porn. Here I have no choice but to sound (even more) like a fuddy-duddy. So be it. The statistics are all over the map. Is porn responsible for 5 percent of global Web traffic? 30 percent? 80 percent? You can find studies alleging all three—and every number in between. Is it a $10 billion industry? $100 billion? More? Less? Again, you can find support for virtually any number. According to one ranking, porn sites occupy the seventh, ninth, and tenth most-visited destinations on the internet.

Whatever the actual stats, here's what we know. Porn is ubiquitous, easily accessible to anyone—including children. Its purveyors and those in positions of public responsibility do nothing to restrict access. We're not talking about lewd watercolors, bodice-ripping novels, "naughty French postcards," or even a *Playboy* stash in the attic. Today's porn is a fire hose of billons of terabytes of graphic sex acts—any you can imagine, and many you mercifully have not—instantly available on any desktop, laptop, tablet, or phone.

The human urge for sex is the strongest inborn natural passion, and, while by no means absent in women, it tends to be stronger in men, especially young men. The keenest observers of humanity—including the decidedly non-fuddy-duddy Jean-Jacques Rousseau—have long agreed on that. Properly channeled, this passion is the foundation of families, communities, and whole societies and spurs great individual and collective happiness. Unchanneled, it can be a source of loneliness, misery, violence, and despair. At best, a man gluttonously indulging in porn is reduced to a slave of his basest appetite.

I know some will condemn me for dismissing the plight of young men today. Porn is more effect than cause, they will say, and charge that it's heartless to blame men with no jobs, no prospects, and no chance at a real family life for whiling away the years however they can to get by. But my purpose here is less to blame young men than the ruling class.

Porn is a moral and spiritual disaster for society, and everyone knows it. Pornographers themselves know it, which is why they obscure and even deny how they make their money or else concoct elaborate rationalizations such as "It reduces rape!" They know they're destroying performers'—mostly young women's—lives just as surely as they know their product drains the substance and charm out of young men's.

Rivaled only by drugs, porn is moreover the ultimate standing refutation of the libertarian idiocy that everyone is best-off maximally free from any authoritative guidance to wallow in whatever body- and soul-destroying solvent he likes so long as it "doesn't harm anyone else." Of course, *every* vice harms someone else—from the loved ones who suffer in sadness watching addicts waste away to the communities rent by dysfunction, from the societies that must make do with fewer productive citizens to the taxpayers who subsidize pathology and then fork over more to clean up the wreckage. Libertarians, acutely attuned to the value of a dollar, are moved by that last consideration, but can only snark at the others.

The ruling class doesn't merely allow all this: they've actively loosened every legal, regulatory, societal, cultural, and moral restraint that used to stand in the way of nonstop indulgence of basic appetites. With few exceptions—notably, the Meese prosecutions in the Reagan era—the state and the elites have been bulldozing a path for porn for the last fifty years. Now they're doing the same for drugs, starting with marijuana. Will they stop there?

What kind of leaders harm their own citizenry by design? The answer is: ones with reason to fear them, who wish to strip them of any restiveness that might coalesce into threats to elite rule. The current porn-drug tsunami is an evil much too great and deliberate to be called a failure. Its purpose is to deaden you—to drain you of any sense of dignity, self-worth, fighting spirit, or inner belief that you are worthy of respect. Above all, it's to render you unwilling to stand up and demand—to fight for—what you're owed as a human being and citizen.

This is not to absolve the users. Porn—no less than legal pot—is a drug, and its purveyors are pushers. Just because the ruling class enables the pushers doesn't mean you have to indulge. Just because our ruling oligarchs have made your lives terrible doesn't mean their porn and drugs will make you feel better—much less be better. They make you worse. Which is what the ruling class wants: you, on a couch, fat, ill-nourished, out of shape, stoned, playing games, watching porn, and consuming their cheap garbage—on credit. And hence no threat. Don't give them the satisfaction.

The ultimate aim of pacification, though, is to prod you into crying out for big government and high finance to take care of things and carry you through the tough times. They both want you dependent; the latter salivates at the prospect of lucrative late fees and interest payments, the former at more clients. Neither want you to grow up. They're like those horror story parents who deliberately stunt their children's growth to keep them dependent—forever.

Demoralization

Third in the Great Triumvirate of ruling-class devices for protecting their power by making you inert is demoralization. The word is
meant in two senses. The first denotes the literal decline of moral
behavior from one generation to the next. Not to sound once again
like an old man ranting "Get off my lawn," but George Washington
was right:

> There is no truth more thoroughly established, than that there
> exists in the economy and course of nature, an indissoluble
> union between virtue and happiness, between duty and
> advantage, between the genuine maxims of an honest and
> magnanimous policy, and the solid rewards of public prosper-
> ity and felicity. . . . [T]he propitious smiles of Heaven, can
> never be expected on a nation that disregards the eternal rules
> of order and right, which Heaven itself has ordained.

Want to feel better? *Be* better. Act better. Live better.

Our ruling class doesn't want that for you. They prefer you doped-
up, drunk, obsessed with consumerism, spectacle, sex (if you can get any;
porn if you can't), and other forms of private indulgence. Their approach
to the people they ostensibly lead is 180 degrees opposite from that of
our founders. The epic debate between Hamilton and Jefferson over the
relative merits and drawbacks of industrialization versus agrarianism
mask their underlying agreement. Their paramount concern was how
best to inculcate lasting moral and republican virtue in the citizenry. Our
ruling class, by contrast, seeks to make us incapable of self-government.
They're more interested in docility than morality—except for their own
valet class, whom they understand must behave themselves to a degree,
so as to maintain their utility.

No doubt, to some, this all sounds crazy. The ruling class couldn't
possibly want that! You're making them out to be some kind of supervil-
lains! And, to be fair, I think few see themselves this way. They're Jedi

masters at talking themselves into believing that every move they make in their own self-interest serves some higher good.

Just not the common good of fellow citizens. "Citizen" is an alien—almost hostile—concept to our ruling class. Except when they cite that dubious quote attributed to Socrates in which he claims to be "neither Athenian nor Greek but a citizen of the world." They like that one because it relieves them of any obligation to their actual fellow citizens—Americans—in favor of airy assurances to people on the other side of the world whom they'll never see.

Not to imply that they have no ties to such people whatsoever; just no personal contact. Institutionally, the ruling class is all in for the Third World. They consider outsourcing jobs and underpaying foreign workers acts of virtue for which they deserve pats on the back—which they are happy to provide themselves. A stunning *Atlantic* article from 2011 gave some ruling-class apparatchiks rein to say what's really on their minds, unfiltered and—apparently—uncoached by their high-priced PR teams. Here's one revealing passage:

> The U.S.-based CEO of one of the world's largest hedge funds told me that his firm's investment committee often discusses the question of who wins and who loses in today's economy. In a recent internal debate, he said, one of his senior colleagues had argued that the hollowing-out of the American middle class didn't really matter. "His point was that if the transformation of the world economy lifts four people in China and India out of poverty and into the middle class, and meanwhile means one American drops out of the middle class, that's not such a bad trade," the CEO recalled.

And another:

> I heard a similar sentiment from the Taiwanese-born, 30-something CFO of a U.S. Internet company. A gentle, unpretentious

man who went from public school to Harvard, he's nonetheless not terribly sympathetic to the complaints of the American middle class. "We demand a higher paycheck than the rest of the world," he told me. "So if you're going to demand 10 times the paycheck, you need to deliver 10 times the value. It sounds harsh, but maybe people in the middle class need to decide to take a pay cut."

This mercenary ingrate—whoever he is—is right about one thing: it does sound harsh! But it is also revealing. It gives the lie to the notion that the ruling class "couldn't possibly" intend the destruction of the middle class, the historic core of the American nation. They're on record saying they do.

And has any other country in the history of the world so deliberately played the sap for overclass foreigners? "American exceptionalism" has come to mean welcoming arrogant oligarchs who come to cut our wages while sanctimoniously lecturing us that our meagre salaries—mere fractions of one of their car payments—are still too high. As comedian Yakov Smirnoff used to say, in that far-off time when immigrants were still grateful, "What a country!"

Even if we could ignore the ruling class's plain statements of intent, we'd still have to look at the effects of their policies, chief among them being precisely "the hollowing out of the American middle class." One is free to insist that this is not the plan and the point. But what difference would that make? The result would be the same. And results are the strongest possible evidence for intent. If it were all a big unintended consequence, a tragic mistake, wouldn't the ruling class have wised up and corrected course by now? Would they have fought—and continue to fight—Trump so bitterly, lashing out at any small measure that might curtail their further accumulation of wealth and power?

The second, and related, meaning of "demoralization" is the deliberate lowering of morale, enthusiasm, belief in the future, confidence that whatever difficulties lay ahead, the outcome will be worth it. A demoralized population feels the opposite: that its best days are behind it, that the future holds only further decline.

The ruling class demoralizes the citizenry first and most obviously by impoverishing them. Not literally starving them, but cutting wages, outsourcing jobs, importing foreign competition, driving up the cost of housing and other essentials—in short, eroding their standard of living. The unmistakable trend—felt, over the last half century, everywhere but the big blue metros—is that things are a little worse this year than they were last year, and next year will be a little worse than this one. The old belief taken for granted by every generation of Americans until yesterday, that one's children will have it better than oneself, has been shattered.

Reagan seemingly managed to turn things around, but his boom was chimerical, fueled by debt and financialization. All the big trends that define American society and the American economy today— outsourcing, mass immigration, de jure and de facto amnesty, Wall Street and tech dominance—either got their start or intensified in conservatives' hallowed 1980s. The subsequent Clinton and Bush booms made no pretense of serving ordinary, heartland Americans; they were winner-take-all affairs that consolidated the gains of the New Economy into its strongholds.

The Trump administration—which, at least until the COVID recession hit, was actually driving up wages from the bottom and incentivizing insourcing, onshoring, and renewed manufacturing—provided the first respite from the broad trend in a generation. For it to have lasting impact, it will have to outlast Trump and extend into a new and long-lasting nationalist-populist consensus. But that's a topic for the final chapter.

The hurdles are high. For the principal way the ruling class demoralizes America is by our education system, which they've taken over and transformed into a transmitter of anti-male, anti-Western anti-Americanism. This is an adjunct of propaganda—the Narrative—but is distinct and thus requires separate treatment.

By now you know the basic contours: Christopher Columbus was a genocidal maniac. Jamestown was a slave colony (at least this one they have partly right). The superstitious and misogynistic Pilgrims, for all their blathering about "religious freedom," burned "witches"— all of them women—at the stake. The first "Thanksgiving" was actually an anti–Native American massacre. The American Revolution was fought to defend slavery, or to ensconce a squirearchy, or a rapacious merchant class, or some combination of the above, but in any case to protect monied interests and exploit everyone else. Slaves and immigrants "built" the country; everyone else just lived off their toil. The Civil War was about . . . well, anything but slavery. All the great achievements of the Industrial Age were stolen from inventors of color and/or built with exploited immigrant labor. The real story of World War II is first and fundamentally America's indifference to and inaction over the Holocaust, and also Japanese internment; of the Cold War, cynical capitalists bullying a nobly intentioned regime trying out a new way to uplift the poorest; of the moon landing, the "hidden figures" who did all the math. That, and it was a jingoistic waste of resources which a just country would spend on its poorest. And so on and so forth.

The point is twofold, and contradictory: to drill into young, potentially patriotic Americans that they must never, ever, feel proud of their country's achievements, but also that they damned well better feel guilty about its sins—real, imagined, and exaggerated. To the question "Why can't we feel proud of our past accomplishments?" the Demoralization Narrative gives a threefold responses. First, because it's not your past; none of you personally accomplished any of that and it's unreasonable to be proud of something you didn't do. Second, it's not even your ancestors' past; they—and you, through falsifying history—stole that past from its real heroes. Third, because your past is shameful and evil. To the inevitable follow-up—"If it's irrational to be proud of past actions we personally didn't do, why should we feel guilty about things we didn't personally do?"—the response is: shut up and feel as you're told.

A big reason why so many Americans buy this propaganda is that they've been trained to in school.

This toxin was brewed in the universities, then took over the education schools where teachers are trained and curricula developed, moved down to the high schools, and finally captured the elementary schools.

The latter present the material a bit more gently, befitting their captive audience's tender age, but nonetheless manage to get the main point across. Forget the Pilgrims, Washington, Lincoln, and all the rest of those phony "heroes"; everything good about America (if indeed there is anything) arose from groups your parents' teachers marginalized or ignored. Now let's look at this picture book about Harriet Tubman, Martin Luther King, and Cesar Chavez. (We won't mention the part about the latter being fiercely anti–illegal immigration to protect the wages of the farm workers whose union he led.)

Private education, by and large, offers no respite. Indeed, the opposite is mostly true. Being more elite on average, these schools tend to follow the lead of prestigious universities with more zeal than their public counterparts—and voluntarily, without having to wait for bureaucratic edicts to tell them what to teach. As a result, there is now hardly any school in the nation, public or private, that does not indoctrinate students to hate their country: some because they're the villains of its gruesome story of rapacity and oppression, others because they're told they're the former's victims. Thus are the latter encouraged to hate not only the land in which they live but well over half its population, and in some cases even many of their own classmates.

It must be asked again: has this ever happened before? Has any other nation in history dedicated its entire education system to teaching its own children to hate their country, its history, at least half of their fellow citizens, and even—a portion of them—to hate themselves? More to the point: has there ever been a racially, ethnically, and religiously diverse society whose ruling class, as a matter of policy, used the schools to attack and demonize any semblance of a common national identity? Nor is this a purely American phenomenon—Western societies around the world are afflicted—though I think it's safe to say we got the ball rolling. Even the communists—no slouches in the propaganda department—sought to "unify" the USSR in part by asserting the idea of "Soviet Man," a figure who could (at least in theory) encompass not just Russians but all the various ethnicities and captive peoples ruled from Moscow. (They also, not incidentally, never touched the Russian literary canon.) We do precisely the opposite. Are we the first? If not, no record of any other example appears to have been preserved, which should tell us something about the long-term viability of present arrangements.

So why do they do it? To demoralize. In any society not actually based on slavery, being taught that your country is a slave plantation and you the overseer is profoundly demoralizing. Healthy societies preach the precise opposite: they aim to engender pride among the citizenry.

Yet the old, prideful account, scholars will rush to tell you, often elided or left out a great deal. Indeed, this is the door through which our demoralizing treatment of past and present snuck through. "We're just filling in the gaps!" the reformers insisted. American history must be "inclusive" and tell the whole story. Of course, in this, they were right. Students *should* know about Crispus Attucks, the Trail of Tears and Wounded Knee, Frederick Douglass and Harriet Tubman, Booker T. Washington and W. E. B. DuBois, Seneca Falls and Selma—and many, many other persons, places, events, and trends. To quote Faber College's motto, "Knowledge is good."

But filling in gaps—telling the whole story—was never really the point. The next stage was to insist that the old account of American history is filled with myths and falsehoods that must be exploded. Some of those making this claim do so from a sincere love of truth. Like Plato's Socrates, they hate above all the "lie in the soul"—the lies we tell ourselves, those deeply held beliefs that we never question but that turn out to be wrong. False history must be "demystified" in the name of "truth." I confess to a certain sympathy for this view. While I appreciate the pedagogical and moral intent behind, for instance, Parson Weems's story of George Washington and the cherry tree, if it isn't actually true, I personally would rather know than not know.

But today the official account of American history goes well beyond "demystification" and myth-busting and instead charges headlong into distortion, omission, exaggeration, puffery, unjust denigration, and straight-up demonization. Even liberal historians have started to gripe. Several with impeccable liberal credentials—including James McPherson, Sean Wilentz, and Gordon Wood—have pointed out the many factual errors of the "1619 Project." Of course, to no avail. Their objections will have exactly the same effect as five decades of conservatives' pleading with the left to slow down, take stock, and be more "balanced."

The "inclusion" and "demystification" arguments were almost always made in bad faith. For most proponents, the end state—the goal—was always demoralization. A demoralized population is unlikely to rise in its own defense, to assert its rights, to insist on a say in how it is governed, or to demand a share of the future. From the ruling-class perspective, if you're not already one of them or capable of becoming one—preferably to serve them in ways that make them money and/or solidify their rule—they have no use for you. They certainly don't need or want you as workers. You cost and demand too much; immigrants are cheaper and more pliant. Besides, machines will eventually be able to replace people altogether. You're useful, for now, as consumers—at least until such time as globalization has made the domestic and international markets large enough that your meager purchasing power can be safely dispensed with. Look at the way, for instance, that Hollywood and our entire "entertainment" complex—including big-league sports—aggressively kowtow to the Chinese government while force-feeding woke propaganda to the domestic market. They either don't care about or are actively hostile to your needs, wants, and tastes. Most of all, they want you to sit still and shut up. And then die, preferably without reproducing.

Centralization

The overarching goal, recall, is the transformation of the United States, the West, and as much of the rest of the word as possible into an interconnected economic-administrative zone. That in turn requires centralization—as much as possible. You can't have people willy-nilly making their own decisions, either individually or collectively. That ruins the whole project.

Just look at what some of those people tend to choose—or would, if they were allowed to: carrying guns, praying in schools, preventing the public library from hosting "Drag Queen Story Hour." Some are so obdurate as to prioritize their own religious superstitions over others' fundamental right to a wedding cake.

While stopping such troglodytism is, of course, a moral imperative, those issues are really sideshows. The core goal is to ensure the smooth operation of markets and prevent revolt, rebellion, or revolution—except when such can be marshaled in support of the current regime. For keeping down the other kinds, though, centralization is not merely nice to have; it's an imperative. Competing power centers cause confusion and can delay or even weaken the project. A society or zone or empire—whatever you want to call it, so long as you don't say "country"—works best when power is concentrated, decisions are swift and irrevocable, and dictates uniform and universal. In the event that people, or some of them, decline to be docile, it's much easier to remind them of their place when a centralized power holds the whip hand—as the Yellow Vests in France have learned to their dismay. The purpose of homogenization, pacification, and demoralization is to make us less fit for and capable of liberty and increasingly indifferent to, even unaware of, lost freedom.

HIGH + LOW v. MIDDLE

That's what the ruling class wants—the "vision"—and how they're working to get it: the means. The end state is both already present and still looms in the future. It's here in the sense that our society looks and operates now in many ways according to ruling-class wishes. But things could also get much worse along the same lines—and the ruling class's foot is on the pedal, hard, to ensure they get that way.

To maintain, strengthen, and perpetuate its grip on power, the ruling class maintains an army of rank-and-file soldiers. Not to denigrate overmuch the "life of the mind," but a relative handful of scrawny (or, as often as not, pudgy) Ivy Leaguers can't by themselves rule a population of 330 million. They need muscle.

In a nominal democracy, that means voters. In a quasi-open society, it also means people to generate and disseminate the propaganda, maintain the Narrative, and punish dissidence.

This is the real nature of the modern American regime: a high-low coalition against the middle. The high—the oligarchs and their (relatively) impecunious but "educated" culturati—team up with the so-called "disfavored" or "disadvantaged" or "marginalized": the fringe, the poor (but not the taxpaying working class!), single women, the unemployed and unemployable, welfare recipients, immigrants, and anyone unhappy with or angry at America.

Of course, none of these groups really are officially or legally disfavored, disadvantaged, or marginalized anymore; our entire system has been upended, successfully, to do the opposite. Their claim to "disfavor" rests on, first, the (real or alleged) unfair treatment of their ancestors and, second, the "gaps" that remain between the outcomes—above all, earnings and wealth—for some groups versus others. The only acceptable explanation for those gaps is "privilege," and the only acceptable solution is more redistribution and social engineering.

On this basis do high and low team up to squeeze the middle. Their tacit understanding is that, in exchange for votes, the oligarchs share (a little bit of) the wealth. Not their own, of course—or at least as little of their own as possible. But the goods have to come from somewhere, and this is how the middle gets it from both ends. The regime taxes the daylights out of the middle class and then, what it can't extract from taxation it transfers in other ways, such as outsourcing and more immigration. The daily delights that can't be covered by direct and indirect wealth transfers are backfilled with low interest rates and loose credit, which, not coincidentally, fuel an oligarch-friendly asset bubble: security and real estate prices rise or stay high, while the lower orders think they're richer than they are thanks to easy money.

WHAT THE RULING CLASS'S MINIONS WANT

Broadly speaking, the ruling class leads, employs, and utilizes three categories of minions or foot soldiers. There is much overlap. Many—in some cases all—of the opinions to be sketched below are held simultaneously by the same person(s). To repeat a point made above, since many of those opinions are in tension with, and even flatly contradict, one another, this presents problems for the ruling class—and for the future stability of America. All of that will be explored in due course. For now, it's paramount to understand the three different schools of thought in their respective essences.

The Freeloaders

These people are the simplest to understand: they just want free stuff. Some of them can't work, many don't want to work, others don't mind working a bit but prefer not to work too much, still others can't find work (or enough work, or the kind of work they want), and yet others work plenty but just want more than the returns from their work can provide.

This is not necessarily to restate the old conservative critique of "welfare queens" and the like. It is rather to acknowledge two trends that have been running in parallel for the past several decades.

The first actually began nearly a century ago with the advent of the New Deal. Say what you will about that project—and it's not our purpose here to pass any sort of definitive judgement for or against—there can be no question that it fundamentally set the politics of the nation on a more redistributive course. Indeed, that was the whole point. One can hear some leftist invoking the Celebration Parallax to condemn this banal observation—"redistribute" is a conservative bogey-word, hence he's not in favor, so deny, deny, deny and denounce, denounce, denounce! But it remains a fact that the New Deal was sold as necessary redress against "economic royalists" who hoarded wealth unto themselves and cheated the middle and especially working classes. In this understanding, the solution to wealth concentration is—or was, in that particular circumstance—active government interference.

Perhaps that argument was correct. I confess that in my earlier days, I would have greeted any such assertion with a typically conservative backhanded dismissal. But after watching, for thirty years, a new class of "economic royalists" enrich themselves at the expense of their—and my—fellow citizens, all the while praising the glories of the "free market," I am no longer quite so confident that the conservatives have this one right.

Be this as it may, the net effect of the New Deal and its successor programs has been to accustom people to rely on outside forces for their "needs." Now—again—say what you will about this fact, but it can't be denied without also contradicting the rationale for redistribution. One cannot in the same breath insist that the unadjusted economic system inadequately provides for most people's needs, advocate for government redistribution, and then, when that's achieved, deny that anything has changed and maintain that people are just as self-reliant as they always were.

The question is not whether the increased dependency took place, but whether or not it was necessary and what its effects have been. As is well-known to anyone who follows politics, conservatives have long argued that those effects have been bad: increased dependency goes hand in hand with decreased self-reliance. Something-for-nothing, even when necessary, saps the spirit over the long term.

The results of the country's vast experiment (launched in the 1960s) with widespread, generous, no-strings welfare suggests that this is true, at least in part. As do the results of the marginal reversal of that experiment in the mid-1990s: welfare rolls down, employment up. The question would then be whether there is a "sweet spot": an amount of generosity, or dependency, that is "enough" to cover "needs" the market cannot (or will not), but not so much as to weaken initiative.

That is, assuming you think such enervation is a problem. Many of those most passionately committed to the dole as a matter of policy manifestly do not. To these people, welfare recipients are clients—in effect, a market—and so the more the better.

The aforementioned welfare reforms partially rolled back this situation, but not entirely. The Obama administration did all it could to return the country to the status quo ante but didn't quite make it. The true believers await with anticipation the next Democratic administration to take the country all the way back—and then much further in the direction of mass distribution and dependency.

The other major factor in increasing dependency has been the toxic—and intentional—bundling together of outsourcing, mass immigration, financialization, and decimation of manufacturing. People who would prefer not to receive assistance—and who in former times never would have thought of it—now consider that they have no choice. There's no other way to make ends meet—at least not at anything remotely comparable to their accustomed standard of living.

Attentive readers will note that, throughout this discussion, I have placed the word "needs" in quotes because "needs" are elastic. Not, again, to sound too much like a let-them-eat-cake conservative, but it's true that things today considered "needs"—cars, air-conditioning, high-speed internet, flat screens, smartphones—didn't exist in prior generations, some not even within the living memory of this generation. Yet all these, and much else, are considered indispensable to modern life.

Perhaps they are. But they cost money. And much of the remunerative work available in the twenty-first-century American economy does not return quite enough in the form of wages to pay for all these "needs." The reasons for this are complex, but at least two warrant attention.

First, once you start filling the marketplace with free or cheap money, prices inevitably rise. The economists have a saying: "Too much money chasing too few goods." Lots of money in the system means more is required to buy just about anything.

The second reason is the restructuring of the U.S. economy to reward labor less and less (and less), and capital—emphatically including cash from overseas—more and more. So domestic wages drop and jobs disappear while ever-compounding capital floods into every asset class, further hiking prices across the board, especially for housing and education.

The result is that for those aspiring to a "middle-class" standard of living—a modest home in a decent school district, one or two cars, a rustic vacation in the woods or by a lake once a year—redistribution or debt or both are necessary, not to live but to enjoy what prior generations could easily afford on one income.

Without "blaming" anyone, or even taking a position on the relative costs and benefits of wealth transfer as a social and political principle, it should at least be clear that our current economic and governing arrangements have created a massive constituency for such transfers. We're giving away "free" money, and we've made it extremely difficult to maintain a modest, and formerly within-reach, standard of living without free money.

All this is just the baseline, before one even considers the more specific focus of this section, which is the core Democratic-left constituency for more—of your—stuff. This is exemplified above all by the Bernie Bros, but also the devoted followers of Elizabeth Warren, AOC, and the rest of "the Squad." A short time ago, it might have been tempting to hope or wish that the more "moderate" wing of the Democratic Party— exemplified by, say, Joe Biden—could reel the party back from this rapacious impulse. But you wouldn't know that from listening to Biden, who throughout the 2020 primary season busily jettisoned his former "moderation" in favor of rhetoric every bit as socialistic—minus that one word—as Sanders's. One wonders what the real difference is. The Democrats have moved so far to the left that any candidate would be under the same pressure from the core Democratic base to "deliver" more or less the same outcome: masssively increased government largesse.

The free-stuff constituency is large and growing. The more unfair, unbalanced, unequal, and winner-take-all our economy becomes, the larger this constituency will become and the more it will transcend traditional Democratic voting blocs and make inroads among Republicans.

There are only two ways to satisfy the desire for free stuff: borrow or take from someone else. The current governing arrangement relies on both—for now, more on the former than the latter. But nations can borrow only so long as lenders—above all other nations—believe they have a reasonable prospect of being paid back. After that, to continue the gravy train, "taking" in some form or another—taxation, inflation, expropriation—must take over.

The potential damage from such a trend—to individual bank accounts and to the economy generally—should be obvious enough. The ruling class knows this, which is one reason they went all out to stop or co-opt Bernie and the core reason why they prefer to borrow rather than tax, and to target labor over capital when taxing. Hence the obscene preference given to finance tycoons paid in equity and interest, which is then taxed at the far lower capital gain rate rather than as ordinary income. All you salarymen paying a third or more of your six-figure incomes to the feds are suckers; the top oligarchs pay half that rate on their annual nine figures.

To keep that going in an age of socialism, the ruling class will have to dramatically increase taxation on the middle and salaried classes. Those people don't earn enough to finance socialism long-term, but sqeezing 'em till the pips squeak might buy some time while the oligarchs attempt to think through what to do next. But, as should by now be clear, there's an inherent tension in the votes-for-stuff corrupt bargain that they've not even begun to figure out how to resolve.

The Wokerati

The Wokerati are true believers. They want stuff, to be sure; and they want revenge, to a degree, but less for themselves than for others—more for the expiation of American sins broadly than for anything done to themselves personally.

What they most want is perfect justice. They don't have a coherent, non-contradictory definition of justice but feel that they know it when they see it. The contradiction at the heart of their vision is that any claim that something—whether an action, institution, individual, or circumstance—is unjust presupposes a standard of justice. X is wrong, but the absence of X would be right. Lack of Y is wrong because Y is right.

But such claims are meaningless absent a fixed standard of justice. If discrimination is wrong, then non-discrimination must be right—and so on, across a range of issues; the logic is the same. All of which presupposes and/or indicates an end point. Indeed, the popular left-wing slogan "Justice delayed is justice denied" implies exactly that: justice exists, can be known, and can be achieved.

All of this the Wokerati do, yet also do not, believe. An interesting thought experiment: If you could strap one of them into a chair and shoot her up with an infallible truth serum, what answer do you think you'd get to the following question? "Is there such a thing as perfect justice—an end state which, if it could be achieved, would redress all wrongs and treat everyone fairly?" My hunch is that she—or any of them—would reveal themselves as believing two things at once: (1) there is perfect justice, because there must be—or else what are we all working toward?—but also (2) there isn't, because if there were, then the project would eventually have to end, and what fun would that be? Hence what they want to believe is that "justice" may be achieved over this or that injustice—to the barricades, comrades!—but never in toto. At least not as a practical matter. This is also why they never quite have an answer to the question, "What do you want?" They can tell you what they want right now, but not overall.

To the Wokerati, rectifying "injustice" is a vocation. Vocations don't just end; they are lifelong. We may here pass over as a side issue the fact that much of the "injustice" the Wokerati rail against, none have ever suffered personally. Depending on your point of view, this makes them either selfless altruists or officious busybodies. Either way, this phenom-enon has been going strong at least as long as affluent white kids began trekking down South in the early 1960s to protest segregation. I would hardly be the first to point out that a nontrivial portion of those who never face serious problems of their own glom on to the very real prob-lems of others in order to give their lives moral purpose. For some, build-ing families, strengthening communities, worshiping God, enjoying friends, and tending to their own are simply too pedestrian to provide real meaning.

Nor would I be the first to observe that it's probably not a coinci-dence that the phenomenon really started to gain steam as traditional religious faith and observance fell off a cliff among the credentialed classes. It's not so much that this newfound enthusiasm for justice *replaced* faith as it supplanted the old type of faith—for the new version is no less a faith, however secular and "rationalistic" its adherents believe themselves and their beliefs to be.

The new faith transforms justice into "social justice" to distin-guish it from the traditional kind: fulfilling one's duties, obeying the law, being a good citizen, paying one's debts, helping one's friends, preventing harm where possible, inflicting it when necessary to the defense of the good—that is, doing right by everyone. But that's hard, and kind of dull to the woke mind, which judges moral worth not by how one treats those around oneself but by how loudly one agitates on behalf of those furthest away. Or to be more precise, there is a moral hierarchy on which agitation occupies a high rung, but merely holding the right opinions is enough to secure a spot on the ladder. Whereas to hold the "wrong" opinions—say, to believe the biblical teaching on marriage—even if one behaves irreproachably in every other respect, is to be a Bad Person.

There is another element, too, exemplified by the intoxication enjoyed by those who triumphed in the civil rights movement. To win a real victory over real injustice is a heady experience. Those who lived it once want to relive it. Those who only observed it, or read about it, or watched it in a documentary, want to live it for themselves. In the same way that certain men too young to fight in World War II were actually glad when the Korean War broke out—now I get my chance!—young(ish) Wokerati today look forward with hunger to the next "defining civil rights struggle of our time." They want to participate, to be able to boast, perhaps to their grandchildren, in the unlikely event they ever have any (Wokerati are not known for their fecundity) . . . but at any rate to someone, that they were there . . . at the ramparts!

Only, you know, within reason. "Ramparts" today has a different meaning than it did in, say, 1963, when marching for civil rights actually meant risking beatings, imprisonment, and much else. Today, no one goes to jail for supporting the latest "civil rights" craze. You're much more likely to be punished—fired, shamed, silenced, ostracized—for questioning it. Those daring or foolish enough to express outright opposition up their risk exponentially. The (scant) good news on this score is that America is not (yet) England, Canada, or parts of Europe, where dissent has been outright criminalized and people go to jail for blasphemy against the reigning orthodoxy. But if the Wokerati have their way, we'll get there.

This cost-free "fun" in being "on the right side of history" is a big part of the reason why every achieved triumph leads inexorably to the next struggle, why every fresh enthusiasm immediately becomes the next "defining civil rights issue of our time." The process is familiar. Begin with the demand for the removal of formal barriers; implement a system of nondiscrimination; follow that up with formal recognition and, finally, elevation to "protected class" with all the privileges pertaining thereto. Sometimes different struggles happen in parallel: "our time" is apparently capacious enough to accommodate several defining civil rights struggles at once.

Like the votes-for-stuff corrupt bargain, these enthusiasms have the potential to put the ruling class in another bind. So far, they've managed to channel all this leftist energy into causes that satisfy the Wokerati's passion for "justice" without endangering the bottom line.

In some cases, the opposite even holds: wokeness can expand markets and even create new ones—exemplified above all by what in the 1970s was called "women's liberation" (from what?) but has since been rebranded as "women's empowerment." Of course, in a free society all persons should be free to choose their own life paths; I merely point out the non-coincidental facts that, as the ruling class has encouraged, even browbeaten women into staying in school longer, prioritizing their careers, and delaying or avoiding marriage and children, women's disposable income has risen while their obligations to spend those earnings on people other than themselves have declined. This has proved a boon to consumer products brands, pharmaceutical companies, fashion houses, handbag makers, department stores, bars and restaurants, real estate developers (more singles mean more demand for separate housing units), plus airlines, cruise lines, hotels, and resorts. A lot of folks are making a lot of money off all this "empowerment," the root meaning of which turns out to be "indulge oneself." Nothing against profits, but when one factors in the concomitant rise of women's unhappiness and antidepressant use (by some accounts, a quarter of American females take some form of these drugs), one is entitled to wonder whether the net effect has been altogether positive.

At any rate, this is one of the games "woke capital" plays: identify a previously undifferentiated and untapped "market segment," peel it off from the rest of society—including those to whom it would otherwise be closest to—flatter it, and then sell to it. Women being slightly more than half the population, that market is the biggest prize. But the possibilities are endless and include demographic categories that actually exist in nature—Modelo selling beer to immigrants by flattering them that they're more American than the Americans—and ones that do not. Five years ago, transsexuals seemed at best tangentially relevant to the concerns of most Americans. Today they're on the cover of glossy, ad-driven magazines, and a whole burgeoning industry has appeared seemingly out of nowhere, selling new wardrobes, puberty blockers, hormone "therapy," and "gender-reassignment surgery"—in ascending order of cost. Somebody's making a lot of money off all that, too, and it's not you or I.

Three birds are killed with this stone, and others like it. First, ideally—though not in every case—new markets are created, or existing ones expanded. Second, the Wokerati's passion for identifying—and charging after—fresh monsters to destroy is channeled away from potential resentment over the rise of neo-feudalism and instead into outlets that don't threaten ruling-class power or profits. Third, letting the Wokerati have their way over non-threatening enthusiasms provides them with the illusion of new, and hard-won, "rights" or "benefits," which satisfies the human passion for "recognition" and substitutes for actual, material success in the new order.

This perhaps requires a bit of explanation. I'm not much of a Hegelian, but I do think Hegel was onto something with his concept of "recognition." The basic idea is a variation on the biblical truth that man doth not live by bread alone. Man's essential humanity is a mixture of appetites and passions—here Hegel's thought is little different from that of the Bible or the Greeks—and one of those passions is an insistence that other men acknowledge or "recognize" his individual humanity, his distinctness, his freedom. In case the following helps to clarify, in street gang or prison yard terms, "recognition" is the same thing as "respect."

The Wokerati are, in a way, more Hegelian than Hegel. The master posited, somewhat implausibly, an absolute moment in which all men mutually recognize the essential humanity of all others, with existential conflict forever confined to the past. The Wokerati's utopia, by contrast, far more resembles Hegel's primordial state in which would-be "masters" seek to be "recognized" themselves without having to recognize others in turn. "Recognition for me but not for thee," decrees he with the whip hand.

"Recognition," though, is cheap—especially compared with 1789-like upheaval and redistribution, a fact the ruling class understands in their bones. So far, their bait and switch has worked spectacularly well. How long can it go on? How many "injustices" that pose no threat whatsoever to the ruling class still lurk in the woods, waiting to be slain, to die unmourned and unmissed, with no adverse or unintended consequences? How long before the Wokerati take up an enthusiasm that the oligarchy considers a dagger pointed at its very heart?

So long as all the destructive energy is aimed at tradition, religion, and culture, the ruling class aren't worried: half of them despise that stuff as much as the Wokerati do, and the other half figure they can wall themselves off from whatever downsides may arise from acid-washing away all historic supports for productivity, morality, and order. Some of the ruling class even revere tradition, savor culture, and practice their religion behind their walls.

But can those walls keep out the forces of chaos forever? A—perhaps *the*—distinguishing characteristic of the Wokerati is the firm belief that their utopian vision carries no disadvantages. There are no trade-offs. Every (American) tradition upended, every (Western) culture destroyed, every (biblical, especially Christian) religious tenet discarded leads only to broad, sunlit uplands.

To what extent does the ruling class really agree with all that? They pretend to, partly to appease the woke rank and file, and partly out of fashion. As Tom Wolfe once remarked, betraying a conservative opinion at a Manhattan dinner party provokes a stunned, appalled silence, "as if [you] had just said, 'Oh, I forgot to tell you, I'm a child-molester.'" But on some level, mustn't our elites wonder what effects a complete moral collapse will have on their own quality of life? To a nontrivial degree, the ability to spend and enjoy massed wealth depends on the character of the surrounding society—and that of the worker-serfs who smooth passage from the Upper East Side to the Hamptons, Palm Beach, Mayfair, Gstaad, and beyond. Tall gates and armed guards can protect one to an extent, but if there's no one left capable of producing the goodies, what will be left to spend all that money on? Who will pilot that G650—and to where?

I believe that, on some level, the ruling class is aware of the problem. More than once I've heard some tycoon complain that he'd love to employ native-born Americans of any race but can't because whenever he's sentimental enough to hire some, they either don't show up or do a lousy job before quitting without notice. The American working class is hopeless, they say; we have no choice but to hire immigrants!

Such plutocrats may be venal, but few are so dumb that they can't see a connection between lack of individual and collective fortitude—virtuous people, strong families, tight-knit communities—and a dysfunctional workforce. On some level they know, or fear, that the universal solvent of wokeism—especially when piled on top of declining wages, lost jobs, and crushed industries—shreds the social fabric.

But for now, woke witch hunts seem to be "working," so the ruling class gives them a pass and even eggs them on. At some point our overlords may wish to change course, but when and if they reach that fateful conclusion, it might be too late. There may, indeed, be a great deal of ruin in a nation—but a great deal is still finite.

The Avengers

At first glance, there would appear to be so much in common between the Avengers and the other two groups that one might wonder whether a separate category is warranted. Like the Freeloaders, the Avengers want free stuff. Like the Wokerati, they condemn America as fundamentally evil. We might even say that social justice requires both positive policies—the Wokerati agenda—but also punitive ones: the Avengers' wish list. Aren't they then just two sides of the same coin?

Perhaps—but the present discussion is more about motivations; therefore, stipulating again the considerable overlap among groups, let's examine those that are specifically vengeful.

The Avengers look more backward than forward. Their hope for a glorious future is secondary to their lust for redressing the past. The free stuff is necessary recompense for past and present wrongs.

To the Avengers, everything good in America—and I do mean everything; they seem to admit no exceptions—is either the result of oppression, corruption, and theft, or else the product of hard, honest work by "disfavored groups" who deserve all the credit but never get any. The real story of America is, first and foremost, slavery, but also genocide against Native Americans, religious bigotry against all non-WASPs, anti-Asian racism, Jim Crow, sexism, anti-Mexican racism, anti-Hispanic racism, homophobia, Islamophobia, transphobia—you get the picture.

In the revenge-oriented mind, these sins *are* America. They outweigh, by far, all the accomplishments and glories—or are even the true cause of them. There is nothing good in or about America, the Avengers insist—and at the same time allege that every American good was created by someone else and stolen. Those wars you think you won? They were all in the service of imperialism—and all those victories were achieved by mistreated groups and on the backs of the oppressed back home. Inventions? Stolen, or the result of exploitation, and then hoarded by the privileged and denied or rationed to the disfavored. Prosperity? Sure—for the 1 percent. All that blather about America being "a middle-class country" is just cover for wealth concentration. "Freedom?" Don't make us laugh. Maybe for you—at our expense—but can you seriously and with a straight face call Jim Crow, back of the bus, literacy tests and poll taxes, omnipresent racism, hiring discrimination, on-the-job harassment, unequal pay, glass ceilings, redlining, and microaggressions "freedom"?

Pick virtually any claim to American greatness (or goodness), the script is always the same. First, denial: it wasn't great, it was bad; it wasn't a victory, it was a loss; it wasn't an achievement, it was sordid or trivial. Second, grudging concession coupled with denigration: OK, the "victory" may have been real, but it furthered an evil end; the "achievement" empowered and enriched a few at the expense of the many; the few then used this new wealth and power to further oppress the rest. Third, claim credit: actually, the victory was won, the achievement accomplished, by our people; you guys just stole it and covered up our central role.

Obvious and blatant contradictions pile up from one postulate to the next. We could chase our tails debating whether the Avengers see those contradictions or not, but the answer doesn't matter. The contradictions

serve their interests. To the Avengers, consistency is not merely the hob-
goblin of little minds but an obstacle to be bulldozed.

The Avengers are not racially monolithic—plenty of whites self-
identify in this category and are among its most passionate adherents—
but they are primarily motivated by racial concerns. The core of their
worldview is that everything whites have is stolen, the result of oppression, depredation, slavery, colonialism, and expropriation. Anything
people of color lack—every manifestation of inequality or differing group
outcomes—is also the result of these crimes. The entire country—its
Constitution, its laws, its traditions, its culture, its institutions, and above
all its (white) people—are all geared toward one thing, and one thing
only: oppression and rapine of people of color.

Non-Avengers tend to deny that this sentiment and the resulting
rhetoric exists—a not-atypical human response to any phenomena too
horrible to confront squarely. In this, the deniers are assisted by the
Celebration Parallax, which punishes those who notice and especially
those who discuss what they notice. "No one says or believes that!" goes
the cry, "and only a racist would suggest that anyone does!"

Oh, but many *do* believe that—and they say so. Examples are too
numerous to catalogue—start looking and what you find will shock
you—but here's a little taste just to give you an idea. On Christmas Eve
2016, a (white) American professor tweeted, "All I want for Christmas
is white genocide." Then, on Christmas Day, to ensure no one misunder-
stood, he reportedly followed up with, "To clarify: when the whites were
massacred during the Haitian Revolution, that was a good thing indeed."
After complaints, he received a mild rebuke from his university's administration but nothing more. (He eventually resigned but not, apparently,
under pressure from his employer.)

The typical response is to blame the complainers: if you're worried
about this fine person venting some righteous steam, you must be crazy
and/or race-obsessed yourself. Yes! Those who object to loose talk about
genocide? They're the real racists! In this way is the climate encouraged
to become ever more vitriolic and extreme.

Conservatives are all too happy to play along; indeed, to an embarrassing degree, they do the Avengers' work for them by issuing preemptive denials on their ostensible opponents' behalf. Nothing makes a "conservative" squirm more than being confronted with explicitly anti-white rhetoric. They try to pretend they didn't hear and, if that fails, forbid any mention of what they heard. It's a kind of intellectual-rhetorical Stockholm syndrome.

However, the credibility of these denials is undermined by the Avengers' liberal usage of the Law of Merited Impossibility: "None of this is happening" is followed up with "But given whites' inherent racism and centuries of depredation, resentment and anger from people of color are completely understandable." When that fails, gaslighting denial is the order of the day. On the rare occasions when someone is brave (or foolish) enough to throw an Avenger's own quotes back at him, the latter's whole team leaps into overdrive with hairsplitting parsings of every phrase—insisting, like unfunny Inigo Montoyas, that plain words do not mean what we think they mean.

Denial, though, is increasingly untenable as the Avenger-left has become more unguarded about what it really believes and wants. Whether because they tired of the effort, got sick of insincerely appeasing their enemies, or concluded they were finally powerful enough not to have to bother, they've stopped sugarcoating the hate.

In 2018, Sarah Jeong, hired as a *New York Times* editorial writer, gained instant fame when her litany of anti-white tweets—for example, "Are white people genetically predisposed to burn faster in the sun, thus logically only being fit to live underground like groveling bilious goblins?"—was thrust under the eyelids of normie-America. Elite intellectuals rallied to her defense, not to deny what she said—her bluntness made that impossible—but to excuse it and "put it into context." A few elites did express concerns—that conservatives' unfair scapegoating of a righteous, oppressed sister might retard progress.

Jeong was only expressing—in a puerile, Very Online way—sentiments that have been mainstream on the left since the 1960s. One may say that she was returning her side to its roots. When anti-American revenge-hate first came out into the open in the 1960s, it was expressed clearly, without euphemism or misdirection. Susan Sontag's most famous paragraph, published in 1967, may not have been its first expression but remains the gold standard for clarity and comprehensiveness:

> If America is the culmination of Western white civilization, as everyone from the Left to the Right declares, then there must be something terribly wrong with Western white civilization. This is a painful truth; few of us want to go that far. It's easier, much easier, to accuse the kids, to reproach them for being "non-participants in the past" and "drop-outs from history.". . . But from a world-historical perspective, that local history which some young people are repudiating (with their fondness for dirty words, their peyote, their macrobiotic rice, their Dadaist art, etc.) looks a good deal less pleasing and less self-evidently worthy of perpetuation. The truth is that Mozart, Pascal, Boolean algebra, Shakespeare, parliamentary government, baroque churches, Newton, the emancipation of women, Kant, Marx, Balanchine ballets, et al, don't redeem what this particular civilization has wrought upon the world. The white race is the cancer of human history; it is the white race and it alone—its ideologies and inventions—which eradicates autonomous civilizations wherever it spreads, which has upset the ecological balance of the planet, which now threatens the very existence of life itself.

At that time, the ruling class didn't bother to deny either the words or the underlying sentiment. And Sontag was hardly a lone voice in the wilderness. Similar fusillades were penned, published, or shouted by Stokely Carmichael and Huey Newton, Fay Stender and Angela Davis, Bill Ayers and Bernardine Dohrn, *Ramparts* and the *Berkeley Barb*; even the elbow-patched *New York Review of Books* got into the act, with its infamous how-to-make-a-Molotov-cocktail cover. The rhetoric was so raw and voluminous that any hint of denial would have been met by its targets with angry incredulity, like a man standing in a monsoon being told he's not wet. Instead, intellectuals insisted that the hate was justified—and also nothing to worry about. Justified because of centuries of oppression; nothing to worry about because mainstream Americans still had all the power. All they needed to do was acquiesce to the liberal project and the nation would be healed.

Americans did acquiesce, but the nation didn't heal—and still hasn't. Much progress has been made in terms of removing formal barriers, raising incomes and education levels, and so on. But gaps remain, resentments over which only intensify when the sole permissible explanation is deliberate injustice.

Jeong's hostility was notable only insofar as she's not a complete nobody: Berkeley, Harvard Law, *New York Times*, #bluecheckmark on Twitter. Spend half an hour on that or virtually any social media platform and you can easily find tens, perhaps hundreds, of thousands spewing the exact same stuff, and worse. Which points to the second (after denial) typical non-Avenger response: dismissal. These are just anonymous cranks blowing off steam!

The left is happy to agree—and bait you into playing the same game of "prove it!" so that you'll waste hours compiling tweets that they can wave away as inapt or "out of context," all the while compiling their own lists to show that "your side does it too." Which they do, to a degree. But the differences are nontrivial.

For one thing, the right is much better self-policed. Indeed, over-policed. As the Jeong incident illustrates, the left never jettisons one of their own over mere words, no matter how inflammatory or evil. But the right betrays its own all the time, over trivialities. All the left has to do is raise a stink and demand a scalp, and here come the "conservatives," knives out, sharp and eager. Trent Lott buttering up a senator of five decades' standing on his hundredth (!) birthday? Git 'im! Jason Richwine empirically demonstrating that Mexico is not sending their best? Off with his head! And so on, and on. It's the new blacklist—with "conservative" activists and intellectuals as the snitches. Every writer and editor at *National Review*—and throughout much of the rest of the "conservative movement"—seems to consider Buckley purging the Birchers to be the single most heroic act of the twentieth century—more important than Lindbergh crossing the Atlantic or D-Day. In seeking endless purges of their own ranks, the "conservatives" not only think they are imitating the Great Man; deep in their hearts they hope that today's left will praise them just like they praise Buckley (but only for purging). It's incredible that anyone with even an indirect, passing familiarity with the left could possibly believe that, but all you have to do is read one G-File to see that some do.

Second, Twitter and all the social media companies ruthlessly censor any account even vaguely associated with the right for infractions that pale next to offenses with which #bluecheckmarks get away with impunity. For example, (black) conservative activist Candace Owens retweeted some of Sarah Jeong's rants nearly verbatim, replacing "white" with "black" for rhetorical effect. Owens's account was suspended; no such action was ever taken against Jeong. Most of the time, the platforms don't even give a reason; they just cite unspecified "violations of our terms of service."

Most important, left-wing revenge-hate gets a pass because it's not merely part of modern America's cultural-intellectual paradigm; to a large degree, it *is* that paradigm. Sarah Jeong's and her cohorts' tweets are downstream not just from Sontag and the Sixties, but from the dominant discourse of our time. The intellectual history of the idea is complex and stretches back not just to 1960s radicalism but also to the founding of "critical race theory" in the academy.

We may say that its rise to mainstream dominance began in 1995, when Noel Ignatiev, a Communist-turned-anti-white-intellectual, published his Harvard dissertation as "How the Irish Became White." Weren't they always? No, said Ignatiev; they "became" white when they learned—in and from America—how to oppress blacks. Ignatiev went on to found the journal *Race Traitor*, whose motto was "Treason to whiteness is loyalty to humanity." In a *Harvard Magazine* article entitled—with admirable clarity—"Abolish the White Race," he wrote that "[t]he goal of abolishing the white race is on its face so desirable that some may find it hard to believe that it could incur any opposition other than from committed white supremacists."

The temptation, again, for normie-America is to wave this all away as fringe stuff, not worth worrying about. Except it isn't fringe anymore, as the careers not just of Ignatiev and Jeong but also Michelle Alexander, Richard Delgado, Robin DiAngelo, Roxane Gay, Michelle Goldberg, Amy Harmon, Nikole Hannah Jones, Mari Matsuda, Suketu Mehta, Angela Saini, and Tim Wise (among many, many others) testify. In politics, there is of course "the Squad," who are bleeding-edge radical to be sure, but the supposed "mainstream" of the Democratic Party genuflects in their direction, not the reverse.

The supreme example among "thought leaders" is, of course, Ta-Nehisi Coates. Since the publication of *Between the World and Me* in 2015, Coates has been showered with honors like few figures in American life since Neil Armstrong, and in letters since Steinbeck or Hemingway—perhaps even Twain. He has been called "America's foremost public intellectual" by both the *New York Times* and the *Washington Post*, named a MacArthur Fellow and given a "Genius Grant," and awarded the National Book Award and a Kirkus Prize, to name only the most prestigious. This partial list understates the esteem in which Coates is held by our elites, who not only can't bring themselves to criticize even his most risibly impenetrable utterances—"whereas his forebears carried whiteness like an ancestral talisman, Trump cracked the glowing amulet open, releasing its eldritch energies"—but trip over themselves in a mad race to see who can trowel on the most praise.

What is the program of "America's foremost public intellectual"? Coates never states it all that clearly, either because he's deliberately obscuring his radicalism or else just isn't a very good writer. Thankfully, we have Christopher Caldwell to interpret:

[Coates's] key concept is "plunder." White Americans did not, as the heroic narrative of civil rights would have it, move from enslaving blacks to excluding them, and then, starting in the 1950s, steadily break down the exclusion until we reached the more equal world of today. No—Coates's argument is one of "structural racism." To this day, society is structured so that whites can continue to rip off blacks. Indeed, they cannot do without blacks, whose exploitation is their main source of prosperity. America's entire democratic Constitution was built on goods robbed under color of law and still rests on that robbery. "By erecting a slave society," Coates writes, "America created the economic foundation for its great experiment in democracy." Reparations are owed because today's system is the same system in essence, and all whites participate in it. "White supremacy," he writes, "is not merely the work of hotheaded demagogues, or a matter of false consciousness, but a force so fundamental to America that it is difficult to imagine the country without it."

And, crucially:

The reparations under discussion will not discharge the debt whites owe to blacks. "We may find," Coates writes, "that the country can never fully repay African Americans." What he is proposing is ultimately less a regime of reparations for blacks (since nothing can be fully "repaired") than a program of infinite penance for whites. To judge from the reaction to Coates's book, white intellectuals are ready to endorse this idea almost unanimously.

This might sound alarming enough, but it's also *so five years ago.* The substance of the Avenger mindset—it's perhaps not coincidental that Coates moonlights as a comic book writer—has not changed. Permanent reparations to redress "plunder" is still the order of the day—though Coates's circumspection ("we may find") has been discarded and replaced with certainty. Post-Coates, a (white) commentator in the *New York Times* informed readers, "White debt . . . can never be repaid."

A rational person might conclude that there's no point in trying to repay a debt that can never be repaid—isn't discharging unpayable debts what bankruptcy law is for? But, no—just as bankruptcy courts work to recover and distribute whatever assets they can scrounge even if creditors recoup only pennies on the dollar, "woke justice" intends the same. Debtors may not be able to pay in full, but justice reqires that they hand over what they have.

Coates may, in hindsight, turn out to have been less the apotheosis of the American intellectual than a historical figure, a waypoint on the ongoing journey to Wokevana. Already his wordiness and obscurantism have come to seem embarrassingly timid to the bomb-throwers who've followed in his wake. When *Politico* asked Ibram X. Kendi—2020's It-Radical, who is to Coates what Stokely Carmichael was to James Baldwin—to contribute, in 100 words or less, a single idea to "fix" one of the foremost problems facing America, he sent back 154, which are worth quoting in full:

> To fix the original sin of racism, Americans should pass an anti-racist amendment to the U.S. Constitution that enshrines two guiding anti-racist principals [sic]: Racial inequity is evidence of racist policy and the different racial groups are equals. The amendment would make unconstitutional racial inequity over a certain threshold, as well as racist ideas by public officials (with "racist ideas" and "public official" clearly defined). It would establish and permanently fund the Department of Anti-racism (DOA) comprised of formally trained experts on racism and no political appointees. The DOA would be responsible for preclearing all local, state and federal public policies to ensure they won't yield racial

inequity, monitor those policies, investigate private racist policies when racial inequity surfaces, and monitor public officials for expressions of racist ideas. The DOA would be empowered with disciplinary tools to wield over and against policymakers and public officials who do not voluntarily change their racist policy and ideas.

If that sounds more than vaguely Soviet to you—with admixtures of Orwell, Koestler, Mao, and the Black Panthers—you're not alone. Each new entrant into the blame-then-fleece-America sweepstakes is more frighteningly aggressive than the last. At this rate, we're not far from the day when elite, Overton Window–setting intellectuals descend all the way back down into the muck of uncut Sontagism.

You might be wondering: What happens if the Avengers get what they want? Strictly speaking, that's a topic for a later chapter. For now, it's necessary to consider how the Avengers' desires undermine elite interests and goals and stress the ruling-class coalition.

The fundamental paradox or tension is little different than the one that strains the ruling-class alliance with the Freeloaders: How do the former find the sweet spot between "enough" redistribution to satisfy the latter but not "too much" that eats away at their own wealth and power? Ruling-class rapacity is actually tempered by a measure of prudence—or, we might say with more precision, what modern political philosophy calls "enlightened self-interest." The ruling class know that they have to give up some to keep most, or at least refrain from taking all, and thus are willing to compromise—so long as the settlement greatly favors themselves.

The problem is that the Avengers aren't very amenable to compromise. In disposition, they have more in common with Veruca Salt than Henry Clay: they want it all, and they want it now.

The ruling class benefits, for now, from the fact that the Avengers' top priority is not—for now—material well-being. Sure, they want stuff—the more the better. They also want honors: awards, accolades, tributes. Most of all, though, they prioritize punitive action against their putative enemies; this is the core way they differ from the Freeloaders. An old saying variously attributed to La Rochefoucauld, Somerset Maugham, and others holds that it's not enough for oneself to succeed; others must also fail. The Avengers are easier to please. If reaping benefits turns out to be too difficult, they'll happily settle for seeing their enemies suffer. They're all for making everything worse so long as doing so punishes the objects of their hate.

Avengers also seek maximum leniency for themselves. One conclusion they draw from the "centuries of oppression" and "America-Is-Racism" narratives is that they have a right to be given a pass for most, if not all, transgressions of the law. What is law, anyway, but the illegitimately imposed will of the oppressor?

This sentiment drives the "criminal justice reform" craze: the dialing back of criminal sanctions on acts that used to be felonies carrying significant penalties; the nationwide, Soros-funded election of soft-on-crime prosecutors; the increased use of "prosecutorial discretion" to let bad guys off easy, or even scot-free, so long as they're members of a "protected class"; and—on vivid display in 2020—the sight of American cities being repeatedly, night after night, sacked and looted by mobs while authorities either do nothing (perhaps because they were ordered not to by city hall) or else try to restore order only to see everyone they arrest let go without charges. All of this the Avengers would very much like to see intensified. The logical conclusion of such "criminal justice reform" is that members of "protected classes" become exempt from the law.

The ruling class prefers this focus to material redistribution; it's confident it can much more easily shield itself from the consequences of lawless dysfunction than protect its assets from a real socialist revolution.

But over time that may prove a miscalculation. The last major capitulation to Avenger impulses—in the 1960s and 1970s—unleashed a crime wave that lasted nearly thirty years, reduced certain major cities to the modern equivalent of ancient ruins, and took hundreds of thousands of lives. Because the underlying society was so much more stable then, and our economy's fruits so much more evenly distributed, most of the country was spared the consequences. Yet today, owing to ruling-class rapacity, the traditional working and middle classes—who got us through our last experiment with anarchy—are much smaller, poorer, and weaker than they used to be, while those motivated primarily by anti-American revenge are much more numerous and powerful.

DON'T WORRY; SHE'LL HOLD TOGETHER

Even if the ruling class can, Brazil-like, retreat behind walls, gates, helicopter pads, and armed guards to spare themselves actual violence, what happens to the surrounding economy on which their wealth and status depend? What happens when and if the Freeloaders are fully fed? Wokerati enthusiasm fully indulged? Avenger animosities taken to their logical extremes?

You may think things will never come to that—how preposterously alarmist! And perhaps they won't. But if not, the reason is unlikely to be because any of the ruling class's foot soldiers realize the immoderate unreason of their desires and back off. It will rather be owing to one of three other possibilities.

First, the ruling class might turn out to be right after all. Perhaps the globalized nodes of the finance-tech economy—the islands of the Davos Archipelago—are so rich, talent-saturated, and hyper-competent that elites can afford to be infinitely generous and indulgent. And perhaps their generosity and indulgence will produce the regime of universal peace, justice, and happiness that some on the left predict.

Alternatively, perhaps the ruling class has made a bet that however antisocial the behavior of their surrounding serfs and barbarians may get, their own lives will never suffer. The Great March of Progress, led from the top, will go on. The implicit wager here is that states don't matter, that the Davos Archipelago is a kind of quasi-independent and self-sufficient Hanseatic League. The countryside is nothing but a syphon or leech; the things it once produced can be made better and purchased more cheaply elsewhere. If one producer stops delivering value for price, then it is easy to move on to another "supplier." Strip-mining social capital out of one's own nation-state carries no downsides; there's always another source somewhere else.

But then *some* states must matter, because after society—and then, inevitably, production—is destroyed in one, for production to be relocated elsewhere, that new location must have a functioning society. Bankers, traders, venture capitalists, and coders aren't going to manufacture RAM chips and circuit boards—much less harvest "green energy" or weld together electric cars—with their own soft hands. But somebody has to do all the grunt work, which means there must be at least a few countries left whose people are capable of it.

If it turns out that the ruling class's wager is wrong—that the Davos Archipelago can't survive indefinitely surrounded by dysfunction, chaos, and violence—then only one option remains: shut down the foot soldiers, and their works, by force. Does the ruling class have the will or the power to accomplish that? The riots of May and June 2020, still ongoing at the time of this writing, provide reason for doubt.

What's clear so far is that the ruling class hasn't even tried to tap the brakes. Disinclination, inability, or approval of present trends are equally plausible explanations for why not.

CHAPTER FIVE

Immigration

*"The ambitious brought entire cities and nations to Rome
to disturb the voting or get themselves elected. The assemblies were veritable conspiracies; a band of seditious men
was called a comitia. The people's authority, their laws
and even the people themselves became chimerical things,
and the anarchy was such that it was no longer possible
to know whether the people had or had not adopted an
ordinance."*

—*Montesquieu*, Considerations on the Causes of the Grandeur of the
Romans and Their Decadence, *IX*

We could easily have counted immigrants as the fourth category of
ruling-class foot soldier—they certainly fill that role in the workplace and in the voting booth!—but the consequences of mass immigration are so enormous and important that the topic deserves its own
chapter.

UNPRECEDENTED IN HUMAN HISTORY

Since the United States "reformed" its immigration laws in 1965, at
least fifty-nine million newcomers—legal and illegal—have moved to
our country.

I say "at least" because we can only count those whom we keep track
of; we really have no idea how many have come illegally. The number
incessantly cited for most of the last decade—"eleven million"—does
not, of course, include those previously amnestied or who managed to

legalize their status in some other way; they get counted in official figures, such as the census.

And, curiously, that eleven million figure never seemed to rise even as the years ticked by and the border remained, for all intents and purposes, open. Finally, in 2018, researchers from Yale University published a new study claiming that the real number of people currently living in the country illegally was closer to twenty-two million, double the long-accepted official figure. So we don't know how many newcomers—legal and illegal—have resettled here. It might be sixty million. It might be seventy-five million. It might be higher than that.

In any case, it's not lower than fifty-nine million; that's the Pew Research Center's most recent (2015) estimate, which all our wise and good accept as gospel. And that figure does not count the children of immigrants; newcomers tend to have higher fertility rates than the native-born. According to the Migration Policy Institute, factor in the kids, and the number rises to ninety million. That's larger than the population of all but fifteen of the world's 197 countries and territories. And that figure itself may still be an underestimation.

Ninety million is in any case a lot—especially considering that when this latest wave began, the U.S. population was only 193 million. Today it's around 330 million. That, at any rate, is the current estimate. When the 2020 census is made public, the real number will likely turn out to be higher, which means that at least two-thirds of all population growth in America over the last two generations has come from immigration. And probably more than two-thirds, considering how our system deliberately undercounts illegal immigrants and that native-born birthrates have been at or below the replacement level—which demographers define as an average of 2.1 children over each woman's lifetime—since the end of the baby boom.

A mass migration of this scale and speed has never happened before in human history. Don't believe me? Will you accept Bill Clinton as a fact witness? Here, the then-sitting president, in 1998:

But now we are being tested again—by a new wave of immigration larger than any in a century, far more diverse than any in our history. Each year, nearly a million people come legally to America. Today, nearly one in ten people in America was born in another country; one in five schoolchildren are from immigrant families. Today, largely because of immigration, there is no majority race in Hawaii or Houston or New York City. Within five years there will be no majority race in our largest state, California. In a little more than fifty years, there will be no majority race in the United States. [Applause.] No other nation in history has gone through demographic change of this magnitude in so short a time.

He's right. The closest equivalent would be the fourth-century invasions of the Western Roman Empire. But this is at best an imperfect parallel, first, because those invasions took centuries, and second, because those newcomers were for the most part arriving from the same region, directly adjacent to Roman territory. Our mass immigration, by contrast, is happening in the blink of an eye, and our immigrants—legal and illegal—come from every corner of the globe, profess every faith, and speak every language.

An event unprecedented in scale, scope, and nature is bound to have unprecedented consequences. Have all—any—of those effects been thought through? The reasons stated by proponents of the current wave of immigration for why continued mass immigration is necessary and good don't stand up to close scrutiny. That doesn't mean that our elites don't have a plan, only that their real plan isn't what they say. Make no mistake, there *is* a policy—deliberate neglect and lack of enforcement are as much policies as any duly enacted law.

WHY OPEN THE DOORS?

Immigration, whenever and wherever it occurs, takes two to tango: people who want to leave where they are and live somewhere else, and the people already living there who want to welcome them, whether openly and formally or by passive acquiescence. Immigration, then, is always deliberate—on both sides. And on the receiving side, there's always a reason why immigration is welcomed or allowed. Let's examine the historical reasons in the American case.

The Founders

There were, arguably, two periods in American history when the country needed to increase its population at a rate faster than natural growth could have produced. The first was in the founding era. The American population at independence was less than three million citizens. Those three million owned and nominally controlled eight hundred thousand square miles of territory, for a population density of under four persons per square mile. To put that into perspective, Great Britain has an area of about ninety thousand square miles; its population in 1783 was about seven million, for a population density of nearly eighty per square mile. France, with an area of a quarter million square miles, in 1783 had about twenty-five million people, for a population density of one hundred per square mile.

It was clear to our founders that if their fledgling nation were going to hold on to all its land—some of the most fertile, navigable, and resource-rich in the world—it was going to need more people. Four per square mile was laughably inadequate to settle and utilize the inherent productivity of the United States' western territories— much less to prevent their seizure by far richer, more populous, and militarily stronger imperial powers. That prospect risked the reversal of what the founders had just fought the Revolutionary War to achieve: independence from far-off colonial domination. They were also keen to protect their lands from invasion, seizure, raids, and other forms of insecurity that ultimately only a settled population can prevent. Early immigration mitigated this potentially grave problem.

The Ellis Island Wave *

The second period of "need"—the post–Civil War industrialization and economic boom—is more arguable. It's plausible to assert that the country's economy would not have developed and grown as fast as it did without this influx. The question is whether that level of growth was necessary.

Certainly, it made a lot of people very rich—above all the so-called "robber barons"—but ordinary Americans and millions of immigrants also prospered. In all likelihood the country could have industrialized without immigrants, though perhaps more slowly. Western expansion might also have been slowed without immigrants to backfill—at lower wages—industries and jobs left behind by those departing the East. But it's also plausible that the United States would not have achieved great-power status in the twentieth century absent the demographic might that the Ellis Island wave provided to both our labor and military manpower pools. Though acting in the world as a great power incurs high costs, which may or may not always outweigh the benefits.

In any case, all this is before we even consider the effects of the Ellis Island wave in changing the cultural and political character of the nation. When that wave really began to surge, around 1880, the U.S. population was just over fifty million. Over the next three decades, the country added about forty-two million immigrants. It simply beggars belief to suppose that a near doubling of the population in so short a time would not change the country—*any* country—fundamentally.

---

* I realize that the use of "Ellis Island" in this context is slightly anachronistic, since the first federal immigration station at Ellis Island didn't open until 1892. But—especially since that facility's renovation and reopening as a museum in 1990—"Ellis Island" has been synonymous in the American mind with "immigration," especially the post–Civil War wave dominated by Southern and Eastern Europeans. Before Ellis Island opened, millions of immigrants had already passed through nearby Castle Clinton, to say nothing of other entry points into the United States beyond New York. For the purposes of the present discussion, "Ellis Island wave" refers to all of these immigrants plus their descendants—including my ancestors and me.

Here we bump against yet another instance of the Celebration Parallax. In elite discourse and popular culture—in intellectual journals, in literature and movies and television—the Ellis Island wave has become one of the most romanticized events in American history. Browse Amazon for ten minutes and you can find book after book, film after film—*A Nation of Immigrants*, *Shaping our Nation*, *Faces of America*, *A Nation of Nations*, *The Huddled Masses*, *The Great American Melting Pot*, *Ellis Island: A History of the American Dream*, I could go on for pages—lauding all the ways in which nineteenth- and early-twentieth-century immigration "transformed," "enriched," "enlivened"—the list of verbs is potentially endless, so long as they're positive—a drab, bland, benighted America. If that's not a frank assertion that mass immigration "changed America," what is—or would be?

We may say that America's mythology of itself has passed through four phases. The first celebrated the initial settlement of North America and the founding of the country. The second focused on the Civil War and westward expansion. The third lionized the industrial-economic boom and our two world-bestriding military victories in the first half of the twentieth century. In each instance, people living through a given phase tended to derive inspiration from the one just prior. Hence during the sectional crises of the early republic, and during the Civil War, Americans looked back with pride and awe on the Revolution. The heroic sacrifices of the Civil War fueled Americans' self-conception as a continent-settling people. In the twentieth century, veterans of the World Wars couldn't get enough Westerns—in the pages of pulp novels and on the big and little screens.

The descendants of the Ellis Island wave were the first major generational cohort in the country who could not plausibly trace their ancestry to those who fought the Revolutionary or Civil Wars, settled the West, or spearheaded America's emergence as a world power. The first—and second, and in many cases even third—generations of this wave were intensely grateful to America for delivering, and then some, on its "promise of a better life." As a result, they almost universally assimilated and became intensely patriotic. But at a certain point—around a quarter century after America's victory in the Second World War—some of the descendants of this wave began to feel . . . let us say, left out . . . of an American mythology that did not, because it could not, literally reflect the contributions of their ancestors.

Let a grandchild of Ellis Islanders describe these sentiments in his own words. Here is Allan Bloom—product of, and professor at, some of America's most elite universities, millionaire bestselling author and superstar public intellectual—recounting to a Harvard audience how much he and his family and friends enjoyed Franklin Roosevelt's taunting the Daughters of the American Revolution:

> Roosevelt was gently ridiculing those ladies for believing that in America old stock constitutes any title whatsoever to privilege. That notion is a relic of the aristocratic past which this democracy supplanted in favor of equality or of privilege based on merit. Roosevelt was urbane and witty, this century's greatest virtuoso of democratic leadership. We, the immigrants or the children of immigrants, loved his act; he was on our side. Our enjoyment of his joke was enhanced by the *acid of vengeance* against those who thought they were better than us. [Emphasis added]

The FDR speech Bloom so appreciates was delivered in 1938, Bloom's own exactly fifty years later, by which time Ellis Island idolatry in literature, the arts, and popular culture had achieved total dominance. Two decades prior, the Western had died as an American genre—or else had been transformed from heroic accounts of a founder-pioneer past in which hard-yet-principled men established law and justice on the frontier, into the brutal, exploitive origin story of a fundamentally prejudiced and unjust country. In this telling, America did not begin its path to redemption until the first Ellis Islanders glimpsed the Statue of Liberty—which at the same time was "retconned" from a commemoration of the centennial of American Independence into a "Statue of Immigra-tion" celebrating the transformation of America into, finally, some-thing less rotten to the core.

Descendants of pre–Ellis Island America have almost no influence over the broader culture anymore—they began to surrender that when they gave away control of the elite universities. Those who do have influence wield their power to rewrite American history, glorify immigration, and demonize anyone who dares question it.

Hence to suggest that the Ellis Islanders might have carried some drawbacks with them across the Atlantic, stashed in their steamer trunks, is . . . well, it can't be "racist" because they were all white, but it's definitely "hateful" and not true! Those heroes didn't change America at all, you bigot! Except to make it better!

But consider: there was no Mafia in the United States before the Ellis Island wave. There were ethnic gangs and ethnic conflict, to be sure—but importing more ethnic groups caused both to increase. When you pack different tribes cheek by jowl that aren't used to one another and find on contact that they don't much like each other (at least at first), friction is one, inevitable, result. That's before we even consider the ethno-specific gangs imported by mass immigration. The rejoinder that "America had that already" is hardly compelling: if one such manifestation is a problem—and it's hard to see how gangs and street crime can be good—then more make the problem worse.

Second, just as George Washington warned in his Farewell Address, when portions of the people take sides over foreign con-flicts, domestic factions form. He gave that warning way back in 1796, when the country was much more homogenous than it would become. Each new ethnic group transplanted to America brought with it, to varying degrees, the grudges, animosities, and quarrels of the Old World. Many grew to insist that their personal beefs inform American policy, even in far-off controversies in which America has scant, if any, interests. Several of America's foolish and wasteful foreign entanglements can be attributed to this impetus. It is, for instance, hardly obvious at first or second glance exactly what interest the United States has in sticking its neck into the near millennium-long quarrel between England and Ireland. And yet we have, repeatedly, driven by domestic rather than international considerations.

Finally, and most consequential, the Ellis Island wave shoved the American political center well to the left—permanently. There would, and could, have been no New Deal without the votes of millions of immigrants and their descendants who transformed the American electorate.

Here the Parallax rears up again. Historians, political scientists, intellectuals, artists, and the culturati will beam with pride as they credit the Ellis Island wave and its votes for making possible the first political realignment since the Civil War, which produced five consecutive Democratic presidential terms and a new liberal consensus for America. But question that influence—or the effects of the New Deal—from the perspective of the founders' regime of constitutional limited government? Don't you dare!

I may as well note here that all of the above constitutes what the lawyers call an "admission against interest." Not one strand of my DNA was present on American soil before 1890. In making these arguments, I am speaking of my own ancestors. Yet my first—and only—national loyalty is to the United States and its people; and my intellectual loyalty is to the truth. Whether or not one favors the leftward cultural, political, and economic shift caused, in part, by the Ellis Island wave, it's either ignorant or (far more likely) intentionally intellectually dishonest to deny that it happened.

The relevant point for our purposes, though, is less about the past than the future. The consequences—*all* the consequences—of immigration must be thought through and weighed as we shape immigration policy going forward.

1965 AND COUNTING: THE "RATIONALES"

Whatever one's final judgment of the Ellis Island wave—all upside, the good outweighed the bad, vice versa, a wash—it's much more difficult to discern the benefits to the existing American citizenry, much less the necessity to our well-being, of the current ongoing influx of new immigrants. Far more evident are the effects they're having on our cultural, economic, and political life—but since those effects are often negative, the ruling class and its propaganda-enforcement arm do not allow them to be discussed.

But *somebody* must be benefiting, or else this wave wouldn't be happening—wouldn't be allowed to continue, and those who raise questions wouldn't be consistently demonized and de-platformed.

In contemporary America, the only acceptable answer to the question "Who benefits from mass immigration?" is "We all do!"—sung out with a Stepford-wife, hostage-video-style grin. Liberals and "conservatives," leftists and rightists (with a few exceptions among the latter) all agree: immigration "enriches" America. They mean this in the tangible and prosaic sense—immigration helps our economy—and also spiritually: immigration makes us better people, collectively and individually.

The economic arguments are put forth—of course—by the ruling class and all who benefit from neoliberalism, but also by certain "conservatives" for whom the object of conservation par excellence is free market ideology. To this cast of mind, "the economy"—especially the statistics that measure its alleged health—is infinitely more important than the people, communities, industries, or country that the rest of us are foolish for thinking it exists to serve. As one exceptionally blinkered libertarian ideologue memorably put it, "We're an economy with a country, not a country with an economy." But that is merely an extreme way of stating a position which—at root—every "economic conservative" at least implicitly believes.

The economic case for mass immigration ultimately rests on the assertion that, since America's fertility is declining, we need more people. The reasons we are said to need more people in turn boil down to two:

to "do the jobs Americans just won't do" and to shore up our entitlement and retirement systems, especially Social Security and Medicare. Let's turn first to the foundational assertion.

Declining Fertility

Having insufficient babies to replace, and even exceed, a nation's current population is often said to be the ultimate societal catastrophe. I suppose that could be true if said society simply ceased to exist owing to a lack of children. Has that ever happened? Civilizations do die, of course, but in all cases I can think of, conquest, famine, natural disaster, or some other external impetus is always involved. Even civilizations that lose the will to live as such—that is, to carry on their customs and traditions—don't simply die out for lack of fecundity. People still have babies; those children just grow up as part of a different or new or emerging civilization.

Yet to listen to immigration boosters, you'd think a birth dearth coupled with mass die-off is the number-one threat facing America. I very much doubt that, but suppose for a moment that it's true. Is there a flip side: a danger from overpopulation? Famous population doomsayer Thomas Malthus may have been wrong in a lot of particulars, but he was surely right that no land—no finite territory with finite resources—can sustain unending population growth in perpetuity. One reason why foreigners want to come to America is because in many cases their homelands are overcrowded, with resources so stressed by population growth that living standards remain very low and in some cases have even declined over decades. Countries as dissimilar as the Philippines, Bangladesh, Egypt, and Haiti are examples. The population of sub-Saharan Africa is exploding—at the same time Africans are attempting to flee en masse. Population growth to infinity and beyond would appear not to be a thing to seek for its own sake.

It would seem, then, that too much growth can be at least as bad as not enough. But immigration boosters focus only on the latter and ignore or dismiss the former. They point to sub-replacement fertility rates in the United States as proof that we "need more people." Do we?

Let's first understand that low birthrates are hardly unique to America. Without exception throughout the developed world—across races, cultures, religions, regions, and just about any other demographic trait you can think of—the richer and more technologically advanced a population becomes, the fewer babies it has. Even theocratic but relatively sophisticated Iran has a low—and falling—birthrate.

I don't mean to wave aside the concerns raised variously by Pat Buchanan, Mark Steyn, David Goldman, and other careful analysts of this potentially dismaying phenomenon. If, as some fear, birthrates in the West have entered a death spiral from which they cannot recover, that would indeed be decisive—and is a possibility we can't dismiss.

But is recovery from such a spiral impossible? To answer that, we must first understand its causes.

The cause most commonly asserted is that wealth breeds self-indulgence. There is some truth to this. But past aristocracies—hardly poor even by modern standards—used to produce lots of children, and not simply for lack of contraception. Birth control in one form or another has been around since the ancient world, if not always in pill form, and the upper classes have always had more access to such things than the lower. Another data point that undermines the wealth hypothesis is that, in the so-called "advanced" countries, as children have become (as one wag put it) "luxury consumption items," the affluent are the only demographic besides the devoutly religious having three or more kids. Indeed, surveys asking men and women alike how many children they'd like to have yield a mean closer to three than to two, even as total fertility remains under two. This more than suggests that depressed birthrates are not solely, or even primarily, driven by a society-wide loss of interest in reproduction.

So if money is driving down birthrates in high-income societies, it's not wealth per se that's the cause. It is rather that a skewed wealth distribution bids up the costs of parenthood's prerequisites—sufficient income for a comfortable but hardly luxurious home in a safe neighborhood with good schools, with the option available for one parent to be primary caregiver—until they are unaffordable for all but the solidly upper-middle class and above.

That primary caregiver used to be known as "mom." The furies will object, but what economists call "revealed preference" tells us something different from the harangues of the womyn's studies departments. Women who can afford to stay home with their children by and large do—at least when their kids are young. Surveys also bear this out: when asked whether they'd rather work or stay home with their little kids, a majority of women say they'd rather stay home, at least until the tots go off to school. But in modern America's winner-take-all economy, most mommies can't. Speaking anecdotally as someone who lived for many years among the Davos-valet upper-middle class, nearly every mother of young children I knew who could afford to stay home did.

Even more causal than money would seem to be feminism and the sexual revolution, which together decoupled procreation from sex, continue to push up the age of first marriage for both sexes, and emphasize career over family. The little-noticed irony here is that it's the upper caste whom these trends have affected least. Elites prioritize their careers and get married later, but also manage to stay married and typically squeeze out two or more babies in the process. By contrast, their all-but-forgotten high school buddies—who either didn't go to college or else had to settle for a state school—are far more likely to have kids out of wedlock or, if they manage to get married at all, to end up divorced.

At any rate, the question is begged: exactly *how* does immigration solve the fertility problem? Yes, it stocks the country with more people— as if human beings were interchangeable items to be moved around in inventory as necessary. Which, as we saw above, is exactly the way the ruling class sees things. But such a view runs against normal, human, familial feelings.

Think of it this way. You likely have a family. Perhaps you also get together with them on holidays. One year there are twelve of you, the next eleven, and a few years later, nine. Elders passing is a sad but inevitable part of life. Typically, they are "replaced" by marriages and children. Another way to replace them, though, would be to invite more people to holiday gatherings. Suddenly, you are twelve again! If dinner goes well, you could even formalize things by adopting your guests into your family.

In a certain sense—legally, and perhaps even emotionally—they would indeed then be part of your family. But how far can that principle be stretched? Could you replace all twelve and still be the same family? Six? The surname, the house, the dinner table, even the holiday menu might all be the same. But would it really be the same family?

This is not—of course—to run down adoption, which has been honorably practiced since Roman times. It is rather to point out that there are limits. It's one thing for the hypothetical Smiths of Plymouth, Massachusetts, to adopt a child—even more than one over the course of generations. But would the Smiths still be the Smiths if they entirely replaced procreation with adoption?

That's what the argument that "we need immigrants" boils down to: the assumption that native birthrates will never reach or exceed replacement levels again, hence the population of the country will crash—and eventually die out—and can be kept going only by continuing immigration flows. In this understanding, a "nation" is nothing more than whichever people happen to live on some particular stretch of dirt at any given time. Hence France is just a plot of land in Western Europe bordering Spain, Germany, Italy, and a few others. France would still be "France" no matter who lived there.

But does that make sense to anyone who is a not a rank open borders ideologue? France, fundamentally, *is* the French—who, indeed, are shaped by French soil, but who also decisively shape it. There are historical examples of nations being separated from—even driven off—their land and surviving as a nation. But a land without a people is not a nation; it's just a country, an area, a region, a place. Some in Quebec call this notion "mapism," as if there can be a Quebec without Quebecois. The Smith House without any Smiths might still be called the "Smith House," but if so, only for antiquarian reasons.

The rejoinder will surely be: No one is talking about France without any French or America without Americans. There's that racist "Great Replacement" conspiracy theory again!

But let's fully think through the argument that low fertility means we "need" immigrants. This assumes that low native fertility never again rises above replacement. If that's true, then without immigrants, the land will eventually go empty. Not only does the argument demand this conclusion, immigration boosters sometimes state it openly. And not just about the United States but about Japan, Spain, Italy, Singapore—any nation with low fertility. They're going extinct!

Maybe. But the conclusion assumes that present trends continue forever. It's at least possible that after a generation or two of low birthrates—and concomitant reduction in overcrowding and resource competition—family formation will once again become a more attractive and affordable option for young people.

But stipulate the immigration-booster case: native-born fertility never recovers and the only way to keep people living and working on the land is immigration. Then—by the logic of their own argument—"the Great Replacement" is true. If a people dies out while another occupies the space where they used to dwell, the former—by definition—have been "replaced."

Is America without any Americans in any appreciable sense still America? Or American? The sound you hear is conservadorks howling. How dare he! Immigrants *are* American! They're more American than Americans!

There is a kernel of truth in this. I personally know—as I'm sure many others do—people who have fled foreign tyranny, found refuge in America, and come to love this country, its people, its history, its institutions, and its symbols as much or more than some of the native-born. Indeed, fostering such patriotic assimilation used to be one of our country's greatest strengths and often produced citizens with amazing zeal for the health, strength, and welfare of their adopted home. We need to get that back.

But it must also be admitted that human nature in general resists casting off long-held allegiances, political beliefs, and cultural mores in favor of new ones. Not everyone is capable of that; it's safe to say that a majority are not. Much more important: so what if this or that immigrant can name all forty-five presidents in order, recite the Gettysburg Address, or give a precise explanation of the Ninth Amendment? Good for him—and for us, I suppose, if we've already taken him in. Better he has an intimate knowledge of America in all its facets than not.

But that in itself does not make him "more American" than someone born here—any more than my profound (and sincere) love of French food and wine makes me more French than de Gaulle. As much as it pains neoliberals and neoconservatives alike even to contemplate this fact, America—no less than France or India or Israel or Japan or Mexico—*is* a nation. Our Constitution—so beloved of propositionists—begins with the phrase "We the People of the United States," not "of the entire world," and states that its purpose is to serve "ourselves and our Posterity."

American xenophiles often snark that many a native-born citizen could not pass the citizenship test required for naturalizing immigrants. While admittedly a terrible indictment of the country's civic education, this in no way obviates the fact that the native-born—many with generations behind them on this soil and no other allegiance to speak of—still fundamentally belong here in this country, and it to them. To suggest otherwise is simply offensive—and, I note, never said of the peoples of any other nations. When was the last time you heard someone even imply that, say, a Guatemalan doesn't really deserve his citizenship because he can't regurgitate on the spot factoids about Guatemala's history or government?

But stripping Americans of their citizenship is something our ruling class daydreams about out loud. Court sophist and *New York Times* house-trained "conservative" Bret Stephens called for expelling native-born American citizens to make room for more immigrants: "So-called real Americans are screwing up America," he wrote. "Maybe they should leave, so that we can replace them with new and better ones." He went on to say that was just a joke, but even his walk-back reveals his contempt: "Who would take them?" If you didn't already know what your betters think of you, now you do. Unbridled class and ethnic animus is A-OK when the overlords express it against red-state hicks, but it's an urgent cause for cancellation if some trucker "punches down" by deadnaming a Soho fashion designer.

In sum, America is for the Americans—just as France is for the French, India for the Indians, Israel for the Israelis, Japan for the Japanese, Mexico for the Mexicans, and each of the world's countries for its particular people. That's not to say, necessarily, that America should never take in immigrants—though I personally think that, after fifty-five years and at least ninety million newcomers and their descendants, a moratorium is warranted, not least in order to assimilate this latest wave. It *is* to say that America is not the common property of all mankind, that every one of the world's nearly eight billion people is *not* "more American than the Americans." If everyone in the world is American—actually or potentially—then no one is. The logic of immigration absolutism leads to its own unraveling: in insisting on the universality of Americanness, it strips Americanism of all distinction or meaning. The ruling class welcomes that outcome. Have any of the "conservatives" thought it through?

But what if the fundamental premise of the xenophiles—shared by those who reject open-borders absolutism but also fear the "death of the West"—is wrong? Why is a continued American birth dearth necessarily inevitable?

Economic and social factors drive, or at least contribute, to low fertility. Those factors might be reversed or mitigated. We could at least try; we're not trying now. It is surely odd, and notable, that neoliberals and their allies on the hard left have trouble identifying a single social problem that government can't solve. Yet when confronted with low fertility, they throw up their hands. There's nothing to be done except import the world! But other countries—such as Hungary and hated, sinister

Russia—have demonstrated that policies which encourage family formation can help raise birthrates. The problem (for us) is that such policies
don't favor oligarchic interests and so are never discussed, much less
adopted, here.

In fact, the opposite is true. At the same time the neoliberal-far-left
alliance insists that the only way to ensure continued occupancy of
American soil is to bring in more and more immigrants, they do everything they can to discourage native births: from promoting endless
"education," careerism, consumerism, and late marriage to restructuring
society and the economy to make families less affordable. Another
important way they discourage fertility is with never-ending propaganda
that "overpopulation" is killing the planet. Needless to say, this message
is only broadcast (and heeded) in the developed world, which has already
long had the planet's lowest birthrates and cleanest environmental record.
But scolding the rest of the world over baby booms or pollution? Unthinkable! The much-discussed and revolting "Great Pacific Garbage Patch"—
an estimated 1.6-million-square-kilometer expanse of ocean containing
some 87,000 metric tons of cast-off plastic—overwhelmingly originates
from just five countries, 30 percent from China alone. But our overlords
insist that the "real threat" to Mother Earth is Americans having babies.

Nor do the xenophiles ever acknowledge immigration's effects in
driving native birthrates down. Immigration depresses wages by increasing the supply of labor. Poorer people, to the extent that they're responsible, have fewer children. Immigration also increases demand for
housing, pushing up prices and rents. Americans, at least since Williams-
burg and the Lower East Side went hipster, prefer not to cram large
families into two-room railroad flats. They want space. When they can't
afford it, they have fewer kids. Immigration stresses public schools by
filling them with non-English speakers who consume a disproportionate
share of educators' time and resources. When the native middle classes
find urban schools unusable, they respond one of three ways. First, enroll
their kids in expensive private schools—assuming any exist, their kids
can get in, and mom and dad can afford the tuition. Second, move to a

suburban district with "good" (read: English-speaking and crime-free) schools—assuming they can afford the hefty home prices and property taxes, constantly driven up by those fleeing urban cores; don't forget to factor in the extra costs in time and money from commuting. Third, have fewer kids, or none at all.

Across the board, whichever path is chosen, "more expensive" translates to "fewer children." Simply reducing—or better yet, halting—immigration would remove a major upward driver of costs and might raise native birthrates all on its own.

Never ones to give up easily, immigration boosters point to America's sheer physical size. Sometimes this is meant as a brush-off, as if concerns about immigration were simply and solely a matter of where to put everyone. Don't worry; we've got room! Well, OK, so we do. Does that mean we're obligated to fill every square inch? Would it be wise to try? America may have a lot of space, but even our land is not infinite. More to the point, not all of it is ideal for human habitation. Is it reasonable to expect the Dakota Badlands or the Sonoran Desert—virtually empty for centuries—suddenly to support huge populations? Where will the water come from? How will those people earn livings? Will their local economies still be in the black after factoring in the cost of trucking in food and other essentials?

Often, though, empty or sparsely populated space is asserted to be a problem in and of itself, one that only immigration can "solve." Bret Stephens argues that America needs immigrants to repopulate dying small towns in the heartland. But surely even he knows that immigrants mostly crowd into parts of America that are already crowded—and then crowd out the Americans already there.

Much of rural America has been depopulating for decades—a trend partially reversed by the recent fracking boom, which (naturally) most of those who favor mass immigration want to strangle with regulation. (At least most conservative immigration boosters, dumb as they otherwise are, don't want to kill America's one booming blue-collar industry.) The same economic forces prompting Americans to flee the interior apply as much to immigrants as to the native-born. The American government, unlike China's, doesn't (yet) have the power to force people to live where it wants them to. Perhaps better policy could revitalize the American heartland and make its towns more attractive; I'm actually optimistic on that score. But if that's possible, isn't it worth doing to help the native-born people still there—and to entice back their family and friends who left? Rather than once again give away huge sections of the country to foreigners?

When all else fails, the last refuge of the immigration-fertility Eeyore is the shopworn example of Japan's "decline," allegedly caused by its shrinking population. Which, it is said, can be turned around only, or at least most easily, by opening the borders—a step the Japanese have always been loath to take.

But before we accept that claim of Japan's "decline" at face value, let's ask: compared to what? The peak of the Tokyo property bubble in 1989? Certainly, Japan's economic growth rate over the subsequent three decades has been lower than America's. But—leaving aside the question of whether a country's GDP growth is the true measure of its health (it's not)—Japan's economy over that period has *not* declined. Its per capita GDP remains behind America's, but when measured not against the whole population but per working-age adult—a key measure of productivity—Japan's is actually on par with ours. Perhaps that has something to do with Japan's relative lack of hedge-fund and high-tech oligarchs whose titanic fortunes inflate economic statistics while doing nothing for workers or communities. Consider also that CEOs' pay in Japan averages one-tenth that of their American counterparts—who often lead weaker companies turning out inferior products.

Anecdotally, let me add that I've been to Japan a number of times as a tourist and on business. The country looks remarkably "first world," with a very advanced economy, well-developed goods and services, superb infrastructure (much better than ours), and technology that makes parts of their landscape look like the Jetsons compared to our Flintstones. Standards of living are very high, with one major exception: living space.

There ain't a lot of it, but what do you expect in a rocky archipelago? Japan's birthrate is indeed low. But wouldn't raising it exacerbate that particular problem? Perhaps—in addition to the downward fertility experienced in all advanced nations—Japan's birthrate has dropped owing to the Japanese people's sentiment that their country got a mite too crowded and they'd prefer a little more personal space.

In any case, Japan is very far from the dystopia that the open-borders crowd so often portrays it as being.

"Shoring Up Entitlements"?

OK, maybe the case for "more people" falls short in a few places. But the one respect in which it's absolutely sound is the need for more taxpayers to pay for America's expensive entitlement systems, which are already functionally bankrupt and can't possibly meet the obligations that, on paper, they owe to the American population. Right?

Not so fast. First, those who most closely study entitlements insist that our system is unsustainable even with a vastly larger U.S. population. Promised benefits are too generous, kick in too early, the boomers too numerous, and modern life spans too long. By some estimates, we could cram six hundred million people into the United States and still not solve the problem. But we would create a lot of other problems!

This points to the second reason this argument fails: it implicitly accepts (some actually make this explicit) that, unreformed, Social Security and other entitlements are Ponzi schemes. Economist Paul Samuelson confirmed this openly—and approvingly—in 1967:

> Social Security is squarely based on what has been called the eighth wonder of the world—compound interest. A growing nation is the greatest Ponzi game ever contrived.

What that quote implies but doesn't quite make explicit is that such schemes only work so long as workers (the young) always outnumber retirees (the old)—in other words, only so long as the population never stops growing. *Never.* Does a future America in which the population is counted in the *billions* sound good to you? Is the carrying capacity of the fifty states infinite? One needn't be a Malthusian to see that the answer is an emphatic "No!"

Even if we're willing to accept dramatic declines in living standards—which overpopulation would certainly cause—America would still eventually run out of sufficient space, water, clean air, and food and the land on which to grow it to support a population without limits.

Endless population growth, then, cannot be the solution to the entitlement problem. At some point sanity, necessity, and self-interest all require that the American population stabilize. Somehow or other, we'll have to come up with a way to solve our fiscal problems without bringing in immigrants ad infinitum.

Third, the argument that endless immigration will "fix entitlements" assumes that all or most immigrants are young or at least of working age and over their lifetimes will pay sufficient taxes into the system to bolster its balance sheet. But, while many are relatively young, most don't earn nearly enough to contribute the level of taxation the system needs to keep going. We're importing a lot more gardeners and nannies than bankers and coders; the former don't make nearly enough money to "save Social Security." Also, thanks to our idiotic "family reunification" policy, immigrants are not limited to the young. Younger newcomers sponsor their parents, grandparents, aunts, and uncles, many of whom are past working age—and end up collecting the very entitlement benefits that their tax dollars are supposed to pay for.

Finally, even if we could make the math work, taxing working immigrants to finance the retirements of the native-born is to invite social strife. In an increasingly balkanized country—toward which the USA took several giant leaps in 2020—ethnic and other demographic and interest groups increasingly see themselves as loyal only or above all to their own and are indifferent to, and often suspicious of, other groups. Intergenerational wealth transfers only work if the whole citizenry conceives of itself as one body, one population, one citizenry. Otherwise, such transfers breed resentment. The more the U.S. population embraces identity politics, the more that younger generations will ask of American retirees, "Why am I paying for your condo in Boca?" If we keep the borders open to finance entitlements, that sentiment will not only increase but is likely to take on a racialist tone. Indeed, the question is already beginning to be asked: How is it fair that young, poor people of color just starting out in life should subsidize old, (relatively) rich whites? There aren't any terrifically convincing answers that will satisfy those asking.

"Jobs Americans Just Won't Do"

We come finally to the hoariest pro-immigration cliché of all. Crops rotting in the fields! Assembly lines grinding to a halt! Construction sites abandoned like ancient ruins! If business can't get enough workers, our economy will screech to a halt!

This is of course nonsense, on several levels. First, as anyone who's taken high school economics knows, the availably of any good or service is a function of price. Can't find what you want at the price you're offering? Offer more. That emphatically includes labor. Hence to be accurate and not (deliberately) misleading, our hoary cliché must be amended to: "jobs Americans just won't do—at the low wages corporations and other businesses want to pay, which poor immigrants will accept eagerly."

Labor is the largest cost for most businesses. It's no wonder, then, that management is always looking for ways to minimize that cost— and/or to shift it onto the shoulders of others. Mass immigration does both. "Sophisticated" neoliberal economists would have us believe that the law of supply and demand applies to everything but labor. That's hogwash—illogical, contrary to common sense and observation, contradicted by the very theory they cite in support. And also contradicted by the revealed preference of employers, who always prefer the broadest possible labor market, in part because a large pool of workers maximizes their choices but mostly because it depresses wages. Employers may be liars, but they're not idiots; they know that they have to pay workers more in tight labor markets, hence they know that mass immigration serves their interests. The idiots are those who sincerely believe the neoliberal lies that the price of labor neither rises with scarcity nor declines with abundance.

The other reason employers love mass immigration can be summed up by another economic slogan: privatize profits, socialize costs. It goes without saying that the money employers save by hiring immigrants—especially illegals—they keep. The costs—in healthcare, schooling, policing, and other government services—are borne by taxpayers. Other costs include laid-off native-born workers and the resulting social pathologies, hopelessness and despair, all of which can be mitigated somewhat by public assistance (also shouldered by taxpayers) but over time builds up throughout society and can't be effectively offset by anything.

The bottom line is that there are few—if any—"jobs Americans just won't do." Americans do, however, understandably resent having their wages relentlessly undercut by foreign labor in their own country.

"They Enrich Us"

Demographic and economic arguments exhausted, all that's left is culture. Mostly the left—but to a nontrivial extent also the right—falls back on some version of "Immigration enriches us."

The implicit—and sometimes explicit—presupposition here is that America as-is, and as it has been, is boring, benighted, drab, dull, colorless (in every sense of that word), lifeless, and unworthy. But an immigration-enriched America is "vibrant." This has become a buzzword whose meaning in this context is never made clear beyond "nonwhite and not dull." All you need to know is that immigrants are vibrant, vibrancy is good, and America without vibrancy is bad.

Mostly, though, the left—unlike the right—doesn't feel it has to make a case for mass immigration. Its own adherents are so all-in that they don't require any convincing. Their position is simple: mass immigration is good, full stop. Here is Bill Clinton again, summing up elite conventional wisdom:

I believe new immigrants are good for America. They are revitalizing our cities. They are building our new economy. They are strengthening our ties to the global economy, just as earlier waves of immigrants settled the new frontier and powered the Industrial Revolution. They are energizing our culture and broadening our vision of the world. They are renewing our most basic values and reminding us all of what it truly means to be an American.

Leaving aside the dubious assertion that it was immigrants who "settled . . . the frontier" or "powered the Industrial Revolution," confronting a litany like this, one must wonder if there's anything immigrants *can't* do.

Though, to be fair to the former president, to read the entire speech (Portland State commencement, June 13, 1998) is to grasp immediately that portions of it could not be spoken aloud by any Democrat, nor 99 percent of Republicans, today. He condemns illegal immigration and calls on newcomers to assimilate and learn English, among other heresies—all of them apparently sincere, at least insofar as that word can be applied with a straight face to Bill Clinton.

But overall, the tone of that speech is rhapsodic—as is every elite utterance on the subject. Yet it's reasonable to ask why, if immigrants possess such superhuman powers, they don't use them to make their own countries into places that no one would ever want to leave. You know: rich, clean, safe, advanced, innovative, and attractive. Not to suggest that all contemporary sources of immigration are, er, sinkholes. But there must be something deficient, or at least not great, about them or else people wouldn't leave. No doubt there are lots of talented individuals in these countries whose potential is unrealized, held back by the underdevelopment of the surrounding society, school system, infrastructure, and so on. But for the immigration-booster fairy tale to be true, *all* immigrants, or at least the majority, must be potential superstars whose full capabilities can, and will, be realized only upon arrival in the United States. To our great benefit!

But you're not supposed to think about any of this. The point to take to heart—as a theological matter—is that immigrants are coming here *for us*, to enrich us, spiritually no less than materially. In the immortal words of Jeb Bush, immigration—especially the illegal kind—is "an act of love." Immigrants selflessly come here to make our country better, something we cannot do for ourselves. What of those who don't think America is bad, who don't think it needs to be fundamentally transformed? Well, too bad. Those people are wrong. And racist. They deserve what they get.

"You Deserve This"

But wait—what can that possibly mean? Immigration is supposed to be good for us. So how can those who oppose it "deserve what they get"? And here we run into yet another lefty paradox—the central paradox of modern leftist immigration enthusiasm.

If there's one thing all contemporary American leftists—native-born and recent immigrant alike—agree on, it's that America is racist and oppressive to the core: in its origin, in the design of its government and institutions, in its actual practice throughout history, and in its present operations and practices. Indeed, there is a thriving literature in which recent arrivals to the United States complain about their horribly benighted new home.

Yet it is precisely to this horribly racist country that more than a million immigrants of color flock every year, and to which leftists insist they *should* flock year after year.

The implied presupposition would seem to be that America is not bad but good—or at least better, on some level, by some metrics, than the countries immigrants are leaving. Who leaves a better place for a worse one? Especially when the place being left is one's lifetime and ancestral home, in many cases all that one has never known?

We are told constantly that immigrants "come here for a better life." I for one do not doubt that for a second. But how can the average Wokerati or Avenger possibly believe it? How is that "better life" achieved by moving to a country that's the functional equivalent of a concentration camp? If Mordor—a land "ruinous and dead, a desert burned and choked," populated by cannibalistic orcs—is the source of all evil in Middle Earth, which must repay hobbits, elves, dwarves, and men for the destruction it has wrought, then how can it be right or good to pack hobbits, dwarves, elves, and men off to Mordor?

Fictional hypotheticals aside, something does not add up here. If leftist anti-Americans are sincere, shouldn't they be shouting from the rooftops to would-be immigrants to stay away from this racist hellhole? Which is not, to say the least, the message that the Megaphone actually broadcasts.

The circle is squared by the following "logic": immigration makes America less racist by making it more diverse. To the extent that immigrants change the culture and help force changes in the law, that's all to the good. Immigrant griping—which on the surface seems so ungrateful and offensive—actually serves a noble purpose. Left to their own devices, Americans will not change America in the ways it needs to be changed. But prodded by immigrant complaints—which needless to say are always reinforced by the Narrative—Americans can be guilted into going along with the necessary reforms. When the country changes to accommodate the demands and preferences of immigrants, it gets better. Hence immigration is in a sense good for us, or for some of us—even beyond all the other ways described above in which it's said to be good for us. But in this respect, it's good for us in the way that deserved punishment is good. Immigration is the indispensable way that America can make partial amends for its past and present racism and oppression.

One may reasonably ask: even if one were to accept the charge that America is fundamentally racist and agree that American racism must be expiated, why must that expiation take the form of mass immigration? Especially by people, many of whom don't seem much to like America, its people, or its culture? Why is demographic transformation the only way for the United States to redeem itself? Why couldn't we instead make amends via—just to spitball a few ideas—affirmative action, the Great

Society, the War on Poverty, Head Start, and massive welfare spending? Not enough? OK, let's throw in a few decades of mass self-flagellation.

But, no, neither these nor any other remedies short of keeping the borders open will do. The real reason is still kept somewhat hidden but is beginning to be made more explicit. Suketu Mehta, author of *This Land Is Our Land: An Immigrant's Manifesto*, explains the thrust of his book: "I claim the right to the United States, for myself and my children and my uncles and cousins, by manifest destiny. . . . It's our country now."

Got that? Forget "We the People" and "ourselves and our Posterity." America is not ours. It's *theirs*. Who are "they"? Mehta clarifies with the following anecdote:

> So my grandfather, who was born in India—he was sitting in a park one day in North London minding his own business. And this elderly British gent comes up to him and wags a finger at my grandfather and says, why are you here? Why don't you go back to your country? And my grandfather, who came from a business family, said, because we are the creditors, because you came to my country. You took all my gold and my diamonds. You prevented our industry from growing, so we have come here to collect. We are here because you were there.

We have come here to collect. "We" and "they" have switched places. "They"—foreigners—are the new "we." They define themselves as anyone wronged—actually or in their own accounting—by the American past. And not only by the American past, as the anecdote illustrates. You might ask: how is it that the United States (Mehta himself lives in New York and teaches at NYU) is in any way to blame for British colonialism in India? *We* didn't colonize that country. If anything, American pressure following World War II accelerated the end not just of the British but of all the European colonial empires.

The answer is that Mehta—who I here single out simply as a clear advocate for what has become the dominant pro-immigration, anti-American position—aggregates the entire West and declares it (us) guilty. It doesn't matter who, specifically, did what to whom. A kind of collective bloodguilt attaches to us all. Nor does it matter that the alleged sins for which we must atone were committed, in the vast majority of cases, by people no longer alive. The bloodguilt is hereditary.

"To collect" *what*, exactly? That's never spelled out, but Mehta does helpfully raise the good old "plenty of room" argument, noting at one point that "[t]here is enough space in the United States alone to hold all 7 billion of our species." That's preposterous, of course—before one even makes the necessary correction that the population of the world is today closer to eight than to seven billion. But one wonders: are those words intended as an observation? A threat? Or is that the *plan*?

The logic of all this would suggest the latter, or something like it. If guilt is so pervasive that atonement requires that working-class people who never colonized anyone, and whose ancestors never did either, must turn over portions of their country to anyone and everyone *in the entire world*—if people in Peoria owe the people of Pakistan because some Prussians once colonized a part of Puerto Rico—then it's hard to see what any limit might be. And I think that's the point. There is no limit. Immigrants must be allowed to keep coming, with no regulations or restrictions, indefinitely.

Here we must recall the meaning of the transformation of "civil rights." When applied to immigration, the new understanding turned out to mean the inherent "right" of foreigners to emigrate to America regardless of American law or the democratically expressed will of the American people. Elite framing of America's (and the West's) immigration "debate" presupposes the illegitimacy of any objection to, or wish to limit, further immigration. It's not simply that the burden of proof is placed on the American people to justify limiting the supposed "rights" of foreigners; that would be bad enough (but better than what we have now). The deeper presupposition is that any such burden of proof cannot be met. Limits on immigration violate the civil rights of foreigners and are therefore illegitimate. Over time, the courts have fully endorsed this view—though the Supreme Court has yet to rule decisively either way.

But this new understanding's origin was political. It's not a coincidence that America's most sweeping and transformational immigration law ever was passed barely a year after the 1964 Civil Rights Act. Here is Robert F. Kennedy interpreting the former in the light of his (arguably mistaken) interpretation of the latter:

> [T]he central problem of immigration today [is] that the law
> . . . has not recognized that individuals have rights irrespective
> of their citizenship. It has not recognized that the relevant com-
> munity is not merely the nation but all men of goodwill.

Actually, the former senator was wrong: as we saw in chapter 3, American law from the beginning has always recognized that "individuals have rights irrespective of their citizenship." But, as we also saw, our law distinguishes between basic rights properly guaranteed to all men by virtue of their being human beings and civic rights properly exercised only by citizens. Senator Kennedy's statement erases this distinction and begins the adoption of *aller menschen verden brüder* as American public policy.

Which is where we remain today. Once you assert, as everyone on the left does, that everyone in the world has a "right" to move to America, then immigration becomes a kind of perpetual motion machine. Curtail it ever, for any reason, and you have sinned and must atone— through more immigration.

Thus the 1924 immigration law, which sharply limited new entrants, is consistently cited as a core reason why we're morally obligated today to keep the "golden door" wide-open.

But even supposing one accepts the unpersuasive argument that it was somehow wrong to exclude immigrants at that time, then the sup- posed wrong would have been committed against those actually excluded: the specific people who wanted to come here but were denied. Why and how would redressing that wrong require letting in later generations—the majority of whom have no connection to any specifically excluded person? It would be one thing if, say, Francoise Sakho of Senegal and Francisco Lopez of San Salvador were denied their dream of moving to the United States in 1935, but we did our best to make it up to them by admitting their great-grandchildren. The logic of that also makes no sense—but it makes more sense than the left's insistence that because we once excluded some people, we must now admit all people.

In the leftist mind, sentiment in favor of immigration restriction arises from only one motive: racism. You or I might think ourselves within our rights to say to a would-be immigrant, "No offense, you seem like a fine person, but right now our country has pressing problems that require all of our attention and resources, and we need to focus our efforts on helping our own citizens." To the left, if said would-be immigrant is a person of color, to deny her entry not only violates her fundamental right to immigrate to the United States but is also ipso facto "racist."

Which brings us back to the as-yet unanswered question: if one truly believes in permanent, hereditary Western bloodguilt stemming from omnipresent racism and oppression, how is anything made better by urging people of color to move to a racist country that allegedly hates and mistreats them? If America is as bad as the left says it is, wouldn't moving here be a punishment?

No explicit answer is ever given, in part because the question itself is never allowed to be explicitly asked. But the implied answer is clear enough: there is money in America, money "plundered" not just from native-born blacks but from all people of color, foreign and domestic. Immigration redresses, in part, that plunder. How? First, by simply allowing immigrants to partake in the American economy and enjoy an American standard of living; second, by redistribution from Americans to immigrants and their descendants. This latter effort has yet to begin in earnest, but it's what the leftist vanguard wants—and intends.

We begin to understand—finally—what "we are here to collect" really means. What's to be collected is *your stuff*, which—despite what you might think—you didn't really earn and isn't really yours. Mehta writes approvingly of what "Ta-Nehisi Coates [says] America owes its black citizens" and then adds, "Globally, too, a giant bill is due." The bloodguilt for colonialism is racial and extends even to the descendants of the first European colony to throw off its colonial master!

The central paradox of course remains. If immigrating to America raises an immigrant's standard of living, that would seem to tell against the repeated assertion that America is racist to the core. Why would a racist country let in millions of people of color and reward them with incomes many multiples of what they could earn at home? "America is racist," it seems, is only meant half seriously. *Part* of America—let's call it the red part—is racist, but there's also an enlightened, non-racist blue part. It's owing to the good graces of the latter that immigrants are welcomed into America to help the former atone, to the extent it can, for its historic sins..

To restate the essence of the argument: America is and has been for its entire existence the most racist and predatory nation in the history of the world; its guilt is inherent in its being and its sins can never be expiated; nonetheless, morality requires that the attempt must be made, and one essential way is for America to welcome endless immigrants from the very populations Americans allegedly hate.

Don't look to resolve the contradiction; that isn't the point. The first half of that formulation is there to cow you into accepting the consequences of the second. In the words of British immigration skeptic Douglas Murray, "[A]ll major demographic change in the West starts with denying the facts, moves to admitting the facts (with the assertion that it's good for us), and only at the last stage claims that even if it's not good for us we deserve it." We are well into that last stage. My only revision to Murray's otherwise axiomatic truth is that, on our side of the pond, the left manages to assert at the same time that mass immigration is good for us *and* that those who suffer its bad effects deserve it.

Former vice president Dan Quayle, of all people, coined the Orwellian slogan used as a cudgel to enforce this orthodoxy and suppress dissent. "Diversity is our strength," he intoned after, of all things, the 1992 Los Angeles riots. We can thank Suketu Mehta for updating and clarifying Quayle's nonsensical pronouncement: diversity is your punishment.

Immigration versus Capitalism, and Vice Versa

One might detect a tension between the two ways—getting to live and work here, and redistribution—that immigration is supposed to remediate American plunder. The indispensable presupposition of the first is that every immigrant's standard of living goes up upon arrival in America. After all, for immigration to function as reparations, immigrants have to do better in America than they did in the place they left.

But for immigrants to get what America allegedly owes them, the American economy must remain, if not the strongest in the world, then at least very, very productive. Yet unless all the known laws of economics—above all those concerning incentives—are false, then the goal of redistribution conflicts with the imperative to maintain high productivity. Conventional conservatives may be unequal to the present moment, but they're not wrong about everything. Confiscatory taxation does tend to suppress economic activity, stifle growth and innovation, and make countries poorer. The woke left hasn't yet figured out a way around this problem.

It's possible, I suppose, that some of them simply don't care and view America as a plump, dead fowl to be stripped to the bone and consumed, its carcass discarded. But one does in that case wonder: what countries would the left go on to fleece next? Europe and the Anglosphere are the obvious targets—and are already being targeted. After that? Most of the world's remaining wealth would at that point be in East Asia, whose nations—whatever their individual culpability for colonialism—are not nearly as susceptible as the West to guilt trips and so likely can't be hectored into giving away their countries as atonement.

So if the plan is simply to seize and spend, what happens after that? The question once again comes to mind: if would-be privateers like Mehta were any good at creating and sustaining productive economies, why don't they do so at home? The question may sound impolitic, but it naturally follows from the immigration-as-reparations premise: if you're going abroad to take from others—if that's your explicit program—then you've tacitly admitted that you can't create wealth, or at least not as much as you'd like, yourself. Which would also seem to be borne out by the fact that America's per capita GDP is exceeded only by petro-states and tax havens. The countries sending most of today's immigrants don't even come close.

Once the reparations checks have been spent, and if the borders remain open, what follows must be a broad equalization of global standards of living—which is to say, the American, European, and Anglosphere medians and means must decline toward those of the "Global South."

If in fact that *is* the plan, it's perfectly consistent with revenge as a motivator. But it doesn't square up nearly as well with reparations as "debt that can never be repaid." For those kinds of debts, you want the checks to keep coming—and clearing—forever. Which means the Western economies need to keep chugging along.

But how to ensure *that* when the incentives to work, produce, and innovate take a whole magazine of bullets to the kneecaps? Why is it reasonable to assume that the American economy will produce at or anywhere near historic levels as it becomes more explicit that everything certain people earn is going to be taken by others? Are Americans so altruistic they'll keep working—just as hard, indefinitely—to support an endless stream of foreigners whose leaders explicitly say that the product of Americans' labor must be handed over as reparations?

Another consideration, all but unmentionable in elite-controlled discourse, is: to what extent is American economic success the product of American (and Western) cultural habits and mores? You'd think that the people who reap most of this economy's fruits would be the most concerned about jeopardizing it, but apparently not. Or if they are, they don't talk about it—or allow anyone else to. For, I think, two reasons: first, they really do believe that human beings are interchangeable—the "supply chain" of labor—hence it can't possibly be true that this or that cultural practice has actual relevance in the real world and might affect productivity or wealth. The important thing is to pay the lowest wage—period. Second, they've internalized the Narrative's insistence that to make distinctions based on culture is to "discriminate," and discrimination is not merely bad but the worst thing in the world. So the ruling class simply does not allow any such thoughts to be thunk.

But what if they're wrong? What if American habits and norms—emphasis on nuclear over extended families, high trust, dedication to the rule of law, and abhorrence of petty corruption—are central to American economic productivity and hence to America's high standard of living and aggregate wealth? Not to say that these traits are absent from other societies, or even from all or most immigrants. But we're not allowed to screen for them, are we? That would be discrimination!

If it's true that American success depends on these and other habits, and we're not allowed to choose immigrants with them in mind, then the only way to ensure America's continued prosperity—even if only as a means for delivering reparations—would be to Americanize all immigrants. But today, not only do we not even even try. What the left used to call the "dominant paradigm"—as in the old bumper sticker "Subvert the Dominant Paradigm"—insists on the opposite. Immigrants are implored to retain their entire cultural inheritance—in part to "enrich us" but mostly because even suggesting that they assimilate is "racist."

Many implausible things have to be true for current levels of immigration, along with the American economy and the society that underwrites it, to remain sustainable. If only one of them turns out not to be, Houston will have a problem.

WHO *REALLY* BENEFITS?

Post-1965 mass immigration has primarily benefited and continues to benefit four groups: 1) immigrants themselves, 2) the bureaucrats who serve them, 3) financial, big tech, and agricultural oligarchs, and 4) Democratic politicians and their leftist allies.

How bureaucrats benefit from immigration is obvious. Immigrants and their children—even the children of illegal entrants, who under a mistaken interpretation of the Fourteenth Amendment are automatically granted American citizenship—are about 50 percent more likely than the native-born to live below the poverty line, making them ideal clients for government welfare providers. According to the U.S. Census Bureau, 63 percent of immigrants utilize means-tested welfare, compared to 35 percent for the native-born. Government agencies more than businesses—much more so, since they can't judge success by profits, productivity, or innovation—measure their importance and worth by the size of their clientele: more clients mean bigger budgets and more bureaucrats. Poor immigrants are to welfare bureaucrats what unhappy couples are to divorce lawyers.

How immigrants themselves benefit has mostly been explained. As a general—and logical—matter, a person does not uproot himself or his family from a country where his ancestors have lived since time immemorial unless he perceives that he, and they, can do better elsewhere. As I reply when asked about the background (and, implicitly, social class) of my own Italian, Greek, and Lebanese ancestors, "They must have been peasants or they wouldn't have left. You don't leave if you own the joint."

In a chapter of Machiavelli's *Discourses* entitled "The cause why people leave their ancestral places and inundate the country of others," he cites three: famine, war, and oppression. Many of today's immigration boosters try to force upon us the impression that most, if not all, immigrants to America are fleeing precisely these plagues—the better to inculcate sympathy and a guilty conscience, to make us feel that any misgivings are evidence of heartlessness, cruelty, stinginess, and are otherwise just plain un-American. "That's not who we are."

Machiavelli's account leaves out the most common motivator for nearly all contemporary immigration and most historical immigration to America as well: economics. Sure, some people flee war, oppression, or natural disaster. But most—the vast majority—simply want to live better. Not that there's anything wrong with that desire, but let's not kid ourselves into romanticizing a fundamentally material considerations into something inherently selfless, noble, or moral. Our culture's mawkish glorification of crossing an undefended border or overstaying a visa as the ultimate acts of selflessness obscures this otherwise obvious fact.

Yes, there are other reasons to flee certain countries—in particular high crime, poor infrastructure, and bad governance. But all of those still fall under the broad rubric of "quality of life." As in, "If I can move to your country, my quality of life will improve." What happens to the existing citizenry's quality of life is not a consideration.

Yet to acknowledge this obvious truth is, once again, to run straight into the buzz saw of the Celebration Parallax. Immigrants, we are incessantly told, "come here for a better life." Well, what does that "better life" entail? Conservadorks of course insist: Freedom! Inside every day laborer the spirit of George Washington is struggling to break out! That may be true of a few, but overall—come on. Also, if "freedom" is so paramount to America's post-1965 immigrants, why do they consistently vote for the anti-freedom, nanny-state party?

In truth, few immigrants come here—or go anywhere—for "freedom." Some flee oppression, but that oppression so often so neatly correlates with grinding poverty that disaggregating the two motives can be impossible. In the relatively rare cases for which it's not, the immigrant typically flees less to seek freedom than to avoid persecution. And most immigration attributable to bad governance consists of flight not from persecution but from the depredations of incompetence or anarchy. Both of these motives are perfectly understandable and blameless, but—again—let's not lionize or romanticize what are, at root, acts of self-interest. "They come here for freedom" is nothing but propaganda intended to bamboozle the gullible professional right—which desperately wants to be bamboozled. Mass immigration's true beneficiaries know they must tailor their message for different audiences; they further know that what roadkill is to flies, appeals to "freedom" are to conservatives.

In any event, there is a great deal of bad governance in the world, along with a not-inconsiderable amount of persecution. There always has been and always will be. Depending on how you define either, at least half the world's eight billion people must suffer one or the other or both. Why must it be the special mission of the United States of America to offer refuge to them all? According to that vision, we are not a country but a "haven," a kind of international charity—like one of those preserves for endangered animals, but for people, lots of them, and on a national scale. It's just another version of immigration-as-punishment but, instead of being stated punitively, given a high-minded gloss. Aren't I wonderful for being so "welcoming!" The measure of one's goodness as a person, and ours as a society, becomes our degree of willingness to hand over our country to foreigners. To the extent that we're not, we're scolded for being selfish and bad.

OK, the conservative-economist axis will respond: Sure, immigration helps immigrants. When did we ever deny that? But it helps *everyone*—all of us—and not just in the "enrichment" sense pushed by the left. It also specifically helps our economy.

Of course, there is an extent to which this is true. Immigration lowers wages, which are a cost, thus booting corporate profits. This is especially true in the service industries—especially hotels and restaurants. It's all but universally true in agriculture. And it's increasingly true in many of the upper (or upper-middle) reaches of the white-collar economy, especially tech, whose oligarchic leaders exploit various visa programs to import virtual indentured servants to do jobs that Americans most emphatically *would* do if they could get them—but they can't because immigrants hold them all and perform them for much lower wages. One 2018 study, looking at census data, found that 71 percent of workers in Silicon Valley are foreign-born. Is it really so difficult to find, in a country of 330 million that invented the modern computing industry (and much else), no one born here who wants to and is capable of working in tech? Oligarchs will, of course, say yes and cite a paucity of (for instance) native-born CompSci grads. And then turn away when it's pointed out that when the wage they're offering is insufficient to meet a coder's rent or student loan payments, many rational people will choose another career. Native-born Americans who do manage to get a job in the tech sector are often replaced with foreigners—and then stuck with the final indignity of being ordered to train their replacements or else forgo their meager severance pay.

Another way that immigration helps that abstract data set known as "the economy" is by increasing the size of the population—which neoliberal oligarchs refer to as the "domestic consumer market." More consumers mean more spending, which boosts corporate earnings.

Thus the "benefits" from immigration to "the economy" accrue mostly to businesses—especially to the five hundred largest corporations that control two-thirds of the American economy—plus smaller banks and other financial institutions such as private equity firms and hedge funds that either own, lend to, or invest in the companies whose bottom lines improve by crushing wages and selling more stuff. More to the point, the benefits accrue to the people who run those firms.

Immigration admittedly does tick up the numbers—the statistics that run across the bottom of the screen on CNBC and appear in every morning's *Wall Street Journal*, allowing business reporters, economists, and politicians to crow about "the economy." But these statistics are either abstractions that mean nothing to average citizens or else are goodies that float to the top like golden balloons.

The closest one can come to a class of "ordinary citizen" who benefits from mass immigration are metro-affluents who want to pay the lowest possible price for their organic produce, who rely on immigrants for their housekeeping, lawn care, childcare (and, increasingly, elder care), and whose lives of abundance and ease depend decisively on the value of their assets. More immigration means more people, which means higher housing prices; it's not a coincidence that the most expensive real estate markets in the country are in the areas with the largest concentrations of immigrants. Higher housing prices are tough on those seeking to buy, but great for those who already own. Similarly, when "the economy" improves, stock and other asset prices rise, which is catnip to 401(k)-rich boomers. But these people are, at best, a narrow slice of the citizenry—as are the other direct beneficiaries of mass immigration.

But—"Studies Show!"

The above is all just common sense, confirmed by observation. Yet the data your lying eyes transmit to your brain is daily contradicted by endless "studies." As in "studies show that immigration does not lower wages" and "studies show that immigration does not contribute to high home prices" and "studies show that immigration boosts the economy" and "studies shows that immigration benefits everyone." Amazingly, "studies show" that immigration is 100 percent positive for everyone and never imposes any costs or negative effects on anyone.

It's important to see this for what it is: weaponized social "science," bought and paid for by the ruling class—often literally, in the form of generous grants to "think tanks" and other research institutions that dutifully produce "studies" that conclude precisely what their patrons want you to hear. Other such "studies" are pumped out of the universities, which don't have to be told what to say because they haven't, in the last fifty years, hired anyone who harbors the slightest doubt about immigration's benefits.

The major exception is Harvard's George Borjas, an immigrant himself, whose research finds that immigration shifts about $50 billion annually from "losers" (native-born workers) to "winners" (techies, banksters, upper management, and the rich). He also shows that the $50 billion immigration adds annually to "the economy" is easily offset by the more than $50 billion immigrants consume in public services, above what they pay in taxes.

Another frequent assertion is that immigrants are particularly entre-preneurial—especially compared to the sluggish native-born. Former Minnesota governor Mark Dayton—who married into the Rockefeller family and is also an heir to the Target discount store fortune—once told the citizens under his charge, "Our economy cannot expand based on white, B+, Minnesota-born citizens." There's that prioritization again of "the economy" over pesky people, with a good helping of condescension thrown in. One must wonder: what does Governor Dayton think of C+ Minnesota-born citizens? D+? Should they be expelled along with all the other Americans Bret Stephens wants to kick out?

"The economy" needs better people. Don't you know that Google, the greatest start-up (so far) of the twenty-first century, was "founded by immigrants"? This one example seems to serve as all the proof for immigrants' alleged superior entrepeneurialism that's ever needed.

Leaving aside the questions of whether and to what extent Americans really owe Google any gratitude or whether Google should be on its knees thanking America, the "studies" that "show" all this immigrant entrepreneurial energy are based on sleight of hand. Jason Richwine—a public policy expert who focuses on immigration—explains that one way to up the immigrant-entrepreneur count is to call a company "immi-grant-founded" so long as one founder happens to be from abroad. Hence Uber—founded by one Canadian and one American—is an "immigrant-launched" firm, as is Palantir, founded by German-born Peter Thiel and four native-born Americans. Nor should it be necessary to point out that a genius of Thiel's caliber is hardly representative of the typical immi-grant. Immigration boosters like to insinuate that because Thiel was an immigrant, all immigrants are (at least potential) Thiels. But in the real world, there aren't that many Thiels to go around.

A better measure of entrepreneurship might be self-employment. But here we find that immigrants slightly trail the native-born. At best, their share of business ownership tracks their participation in the labor force.

I don't, however, want to imply that skepticism of immigration's economic benefits would be illegitimate absent studies confirming the premise. That kind of thinking plays directly into ruling-class hands: no opinion can possibly be valid unless "studies show." The people and institutions behind the studies all share the same interests—including an interest in ensuring that you believe what they want you to believe. A quick Google search of words such as "immigration," "jobs," "economy," "benefits," "drawbacks," and "downsides" illustrates the point nicely. The results? One "study" after another, either conducted or reported by a prestige institution—the U.S. Chamber of Commerce, the Anti-Defamation League, the National Urban League, *Forbes* magazine, the *New York Times*—"showing" that immigration "benefits everyone." I got to page ten, a hundred hits in, without finding a single example of immigration skepticism. Deliberately seeking such skepticism—for example, a search of words and phrases such as "debunk," "myth," and "immigrant entrepreneur"—turns up the precise opposite of what is being sought. Apparently, the only myths about immigration are those which question whether mass migration is really the solution to every social and economic problem.

All of this is just another example of the way that rule of experts is used to promote elite interests and squash yours. But—leaving aside the facts that "studies" which "show" are more often than not compromised and false and that "social science" is basically a fraud that doesn't come close to equaling the precision or reliability of the natural sciences—some issues are inherently political and not properly resolvable by any kind of science at all. They should rather be deliberated politically, in their totality. Empirical or "scientific" criteria of course have their place but must be evaluated alongside—and in some cases balanced against—other criteria, emphatically including what a sovereign people does and does not want.

Suppose it could be "proved" that immigration does indeed "benefit the economy"—and yet a majority of citizens still wanted immigration reduced or stopped. Which, indeed, the majority does today. In a country in which "expert" consensus is the highest authority, the citizens' desire is illegitimate and not to be heeded if it contradicts the experts. We see this insistence most glaringly on display with respect to "climate change." Global warming is "settled science," our betters shout, and your desires to keep your lousy coal-mining job or drive gas-guzzling muscle trucks are therefore immoral.

The same line of argument is also used to stifle and distort the immigration debate. "Studies" have "shown"—end of discussion! But it's not merely that bought-and-paid-for "science" has "empirically validated" exactly what the ruling class wants. It's also that the ruling class gets to choose the ground on which the constrained, truncated "debate" takes place. Economics? Yes! That's a numbers game, and we can "prove" our case empirically. Culture? Hell no! There's nothing empirical here at all, no numbers to massage until we get the "right" answer. Therefore—illegitimate! Racist! Nativist! Bigoted!

The intended result, as we have seen, is to disguise fundamentally political issues as merely empirical questions. Whether to take in immigrants is, of course, a fundamentally political issue, which is properly debated by considering a whole host of issues—economics emphatically included. But culture, language, religion, tradition, habits, talents, skills, and propensity for republicanism, as well as desired population size and density, effects on local schools and other services, even traffic congestion, are all no less legitimate. The "experts" rule them out of bounds because they know that if such considerations are allowed to be part of the conversation, their position weakens to the point of collapse.

But it's OK—perfectly legitimate—not to wish to see your country "fundamentally transformed," by immigration or anything else, into something it has never been and that you don't want it to be. The whole purpose—the definition—of politics is collective action to secure a common good.

This—of course—does not mean that a people can do whatever it wants, that a state is just a street gang writ large. The people's will is rightly constrained by natural moral limits—above all by the obligation to respect the natural rights of others. But simply disallowing some people from taking up residence in your country in no way violates anyone's rights. There is a natural right to *emigrate* but not to *immigrate*. A government based on the social compact must allow the unhappy to leave; it can't guarantee that they'll be able to settle in the country of their choice. That's a decision for the sovereign people of that other country to make for themselves—a decision they may make on whatever basis they choose, no matter what the "experts" say.

Neither "science" nor "studies" carry the authority to choose and direct our lives for us—including our political lives. A few elites—mostly the scientists themselves—believe that they do, but most press the claim merely as cover for getting what they want. Either way, the end result—and purpose—is to deprive you of what *you* want.

Electoral Lock

We come, finally, to immigration's most important beneficiaries: Democratic politicians and their various constituencies. The overlap among the four categories of beneficiary should by now be clear, as should the synergistic relationship between them all. The Democrats are now the party, if not of big business simply, then certainly of the top echelons of the private sector: tech companies, finance firms, and Fortune 500 C-suites, whose leaders all donate generously to the Democratic Party and serve in Democratic administrations—whose elected and appointed officials take care to ensure that public policy furthers elite interests. Bureaucrats are, of course, nearly all Democrats, working as cogs in the machinery of a government that increasingly serves only the very top—through favorable tax treatment, open trade and open borders, "research" grants, and other means—and the bottom, through public assistance and social engineering. Business-friendly policy creates more clients for welfare bureaucrats on both sides of the ledger: poor immigrants who use the system at disproportionate rates and native workers pushed out of their jobs and suddenly finding themselves with nowhere else to turn.

But above all, immigrants provide votes. The single greatest correlative factor of an electoral district's propensity to vote Democrat is its percentage of foreign-born: the higher the latter, the higher the former. This is the main reason why California turned, politically, from pale red—which it was for most of the twentieth century—to deep blue, which it will be for as long as the current two-party system lasts. It's also the reason why formerly reliably red, or at least purple, states such as Connecticut in the North, Virginia in the South, and Colorado in the West are now solidly blue. And it's why, sooner or later, longtime Republican stalwarts Arizona, Georgia, North Carolina, and even Texas will soon be blue too. Once Texas is gone, barring a history-making realignment, Republicans will have no hope whatsoever of ever winning the presidency again.

"Fantastical" is the only word to describe the Republican response, which ranges from ignoring the trend to hoping for the best and talking themselves into believing that if only they find exactly the right words, blocs who've never voted for them before will suddenly break their way en masse.

And who knows? Every event is unprecedented until it happens the first time. But "who knows?" is rarely the way to bet. Nor is it a reliable foundation on which to place one's hopes for the future.

Yet that, in effect, is what Republicans have been doing since at least the 1986 Reagan amnesty, over which time the connection between immigration and Democratic dominance became absolutely undeniable.

Since mass immigration into the West really got going in the decades following the Second World War, newcomers in all such countries—not just in the United States, but also in Britain, throughout the Anglosphere, and in Europe—have voted and continue to vote overwhelmingly for left-of-center and/or outright leftist parties.

This should not be surprising. The very word "conservative" points to the reason. Right-of-center parties attract those who are happy, or at least happier, with the status quo. To the extent that such people are dissatisfied, they tend to want to go back to older ways, not forward to something new. They're far more likely than those in leftist parties to love their country as it is, and has been, and much less likely to seek "fundamental transformation." They tend to come from "old stock," tracing their ancestry back generations in the same nation, with the same neighbors, on the same soil—often literally on the same spot, or very close by. They enthusiastically and emphatically self-identify with their country and assume that its government's interests are the same as their own.

Left-of-center parties, by contrast—and by definition—attract those less satisfied, even dissatisfied, who feel peripheral or marginalized, who want change. These can include both old-timers and long-termers; indeed, in the American case, the core of what would become the Progressive-Democratic-left coalition was formed by Yankee reformers, many of whom traced their ancestry to the Puritans. But while old-stock populations are sometimes divided between left and right, they never, en masse, side with the left.

Newcomers, by contrast, always do. The sole exception tends to be first-generation refugees with direct experience of Communism, such as, in America, Cubans and Vietnamese. But over time even those communities—the refugees' children and grandchildren—drift leftward, and their voting patterns come to resemble those of other immigrant blocs.

Beyond these relatively fleeting examples, in no parts of the developed, democratic world do immigrants now give, nor have they ever given, their votes to conservative parties consistently over time. Even one-off electoral successes are rare. The Spanglish-mangling Hispanderer-in-chief ("family values don't stop at the Rio Grande") George W. Bush barely got 40 percent** of the Hispanic vote in his reelection campaign—even after successfully hectoring lenders into loosening credit standards for minority borrowers, an act which helped fuel the financial crisis that closed out his second term.

** Exit polls at the time reported that Bush received 44 percent of the Hispanic vote; most websites still cite this figure as settled fact. Which, it's hardly irrelevant to note, is still a loss, and a big one. But post-election analysis revealed that 44 percent figure to have been at least four percentage points too high.

And Bush Jr.'s 2004 performance with Hispanics remains the Republican high-water mark, the best any GOP candidate has ever done with that demographic. Even his father, who won forty states, got only 30 percent.

Forty percent is, of course, a crushing loss that would guarantee any candidate's defeat—if that voting bloc were a large enough slice of the electorate. Which, for a long time, the Hispanic vote was not. But increasingly it is, in a growing number of states. And compared to other demographics, 40 percent for the Republican (not that it's ever been repeated) is very good! Asians, for instance, voted for Trump in 2016 at only 27 percent—slightly behind the president's share of the Hispanic vote that year.

THE STUPID PARTY

The Republican response to this is basically twofold. First, shrug and take for granted that mass immigration is a trend over which no political control can or should be exerted, like the change of seasons. Nothing can be done, therefore trying to do anything is a pointless waste of resources. But more than that, any thought of taking steps to stop or slow immigrant inflow—legal or illegal—is illegitimate, racist, and evil. One wonders: why is the demonization necessary if the assertion of futility is true? Why not just leave it at "Can't win, don't try"? Perhaps addressing immigration inflow would not be *entirely* futile; some measures might work—therefore best to forbid their public airing and unperson anyone who talks about them.

Why are Republicans so passive when their own electoral prospects depend on them doing *something*, when their own voters tell them over and over that they want immigration into the United States to be vastly lessened—and, lately, in the wake of the COVID unemployment spike, stopped altogether? It's tempting to conclude that they acquiesce because they're paid to. And there's something to that. Most Republican donors are still ideologically, or self-interestedly, committed to "free market," "pro-business" policies—emphatically including open immigration. The politicians they give to know that and aim to deliver what they're paid for—most of them in hopes of landing a cushy lobbying gig when their period of "public service" winds down.

Yet at least half the GOP's traditional donor base has gone over to the other side—and most Republicans still haven't noticed. Republicans are, in a sense, the last true Marxists. They still believe that the "base" of any economy and society is the "means of production." The only difference between a contemporary Republican and a 1950s Red is that the former openly sides with the owners of said means. We're the "business" party! Hence all businesses must, out of self-interest if not always from conviction, support us. We're trying to get the government off your backs and let you keep what you earn!

Except that, in Marxian terms, the "superstructure"—the cultural and zeitgeist-forming organs that in the old understanding feed off the "base"—has *become* the base. Or at least has become dominant, taking the place of factory owners in orthodox Marxist theory. Cartoon capitalists such as Monopoly mascot Rich Uncle Pennybags, Scrooge McDuck, and C. Montgomery Burns are laughably out-of-date as caricatures of our true overlords. The economy fundamentally changed right under Republicans' noses—and they still haven't caught on.

First of all, government at all levels consumes nearly two-fifths of U.S. GDP. That means that almost 40 percent of "the economy" is institutionally indisposed to the stock Republican message. Second, the private sector itself is starkly bifurcated in two fundamental ways: first, between industries that depend decisively on, and benefit from, government largesse versus those that do not; and second, between those that mostly move paper or process "information" or create "intellectual property" versus those that produce real stuff or deliver tangible services. As a general matter, the more concrete your business, the less dependent it is on government. The interests of the "information economy," on the other hand, almost entirely overlap with those of government, and vice versa.

This new reality—and the Republicans' inability to grasp it—is most clearly exemplified by the financial sector. Republicans desperately want to believe that since banking is the ultimate business—it's all about money!—and bankers the ultimate fat cats—you know you want that tax cut!—Wall Street must be on their side. But since the Medicis at least, finance has been the ultimate paper-pushing, non-producing industry. The only difference today is that bits and bytes have replaced paper. Even more decisive, though, in turning finance to the left has been the adoption of government-backed central banking and fiat currency, which make private banks effectively appendages of the state. If anyone had any doubt about the truth of that observation before 2008, the TARP bailouts should have put the matter to rest for all time.

Finance is only one pillar of the paper economy; most of the rest of blue-metro industry also qualifies, as does virtually the entire nonprofit sector and—above all—the cultural-university-intellectual complex.

Contrasted with all that, the Republicans have ... let's see ... energy, pharma, defense, agriculture, what's left of manufacturing, and perhaps a few others. These sectors are a much smaller share of the economy today than they were when the GOP "pro-business" message actually resonated. Once upon a time, Republicans could plausibly argue they were paladins standing up for productivity itself. It's not so easy to make that claim today on behalf of hedge funds, derivatives, diversity consultants, outsourcing, hookup apps, and global supply chains. Yet the GOP reflexively serves Chamber of Commerce and C-suite types whether the favor is returned or not. The one thing Republicans are good at is extracting federal concessions—tax breaks, pork projects, defense appropriations—for their donors, and often even for those who never have and never will give to them. One thing they aren't good at, because they have no muscle memory from even making the attempt, is governing in the interests of their actual voters, who overwhelmingly favor—and benefit from—immigration restriction. Republicans aren't called "the stupid party" for nothing.

Still, the main reason Republicans are so daft on immigration is that a majority of them have completely internalized the rewritten Narrative of America as a "proposition nation": an idea, not a country, with a racist past that must be atoned for. In other words, they accept in almost every particular the leftist/ruling-class Narrative designed to "fundamentally transform" the county in leftist/ruling-class interests and against the interests of Republican voters, constituencies, and communities. In this, Republican politicians' minds are formed and then continually reinforced by the "conservative intellectual" establishment—above all the D.C. think tanks and magazines—whose primary role is to spoon-feed the Narrative to newcomers to Washington, especially congressmen and senators, and punish instances of apostasy *pour encourager les autres*. Conservatism Inc. is especially effective at the latter, if not at much else.

This points to the second Republican response to demographic change. Since they have convinced themselves (however dubiously) that immigration can neither be stopped nor slowed and that it would be illegitimate to try, they conclude from this that the primary purpose of the Republican Party should be to win over immigrant voters. There is, of course, nothing wrong with this impulse per se; breaking the Democrats' iron grip on minority voting blocs would be a boon to the Republican Party, to the country, and—in my opinion—to those members of those voting blocs themselves. We'll explore that possibility in the final chapter. For now, I note only that the way to do it is not to keep allowing in a million-plus per year while attacking as racist the very idea of assimilation and rigging the economy to favor capital and screw labor.

Meanwhile, Republicans have decided to bet their entire future on doing something they've never come to close to achieving before—and that has never been accomplished in any country whatsoever. The old saw "If you're in a hole, the first thing to do is stop digging" appears never to have occurred to any of them.

The usual (or anticipated) response to this line of argument is to protest that, no, Republicans haven't seriously courted such voters. If only they were to do so, Hispanics (for instance) would reveal their

"natural conservatism." One wonders what form of "natural conservatism" fueled the Hispanic voting surge for socialist Bernie Sanders or the
General Social Survey result showing that 39 percent of Hispanics sympathize with socialism. In that same survey, 60.3 percent of the foreign-
born in America said they support socialism. "Natural conservatism"!

At any rate, "It hasn't been tried" is mostly trotted out as a form of
concern trolling. We're truly worried that you Republicans don't get
enough of the minority vote. We know just the way to fix that: adopt all
of our positions so that you'll be more appealing to those constituencies!
Left unsaid: that way, even if you win, we win, and your constituents
lose. But we both know that you won't win. You'll just demoralize your
own side, and then we'll outbid whatever you propose to court our voters
and call you heartless and racist for not offering enough.

Republicans fall for this every single time. Barry Goldwater's 1964
slogan was "In your heart, you know he's right." The unspoken Republican slogan ever since has been "In our hearts, we know we're wrong.
And racist. And so is America."

Some Republicans talk a good game—especially in the age of Trump.
They've learned from experience the importance of lying to their constituents, and some have gotten pretty good at it. The apotheosis of Republican
insincerity must be John McCain's reelection ad in which he visits the
southern border with federal enforcement officers, squints toward the
camera, and says—in an accent cribbed from a John Ford movie—
"Complete the danged fence." Yes! Amnesty John, who never met a
"comprehensive immigration reform" he didn't cosponsor, a Republican
whose commitment to open borders lagged behind only that of George W.
Bush, looked right into the camera—and lied just as brazenly as Bill Clinton. That's par for the Republican course. But when it comes to action,
Republicans emulate not McCain-at-the-fence but McCain-on-the-Senate-
floor. Judging their legislative record, one can't discern that Republicans
support any limits to mass immigration at all. Anything big business
wants, they line up eagerly to provide. They're often stopped in their tracks
by populist revolts, but they always rally and try again.

The Republicans' true position on immigration—their "revealed preference"—is that inflows of a million or more per year should continue . . . well, forever. The real purpose of the Republican Party is, then, not to represent the interests of those who actually vote for it, much less to deliver for those suckers. It is rather to import millions from poor countries with little or no tradition of liberty and then judge its own worthiness by whether or not it can convince the newcomers to vote for the (ostensibly) bourgeois-patriotic center-right party over the redistributionist-resentment far-left party. If Republicans can't manage to do that, they've apparently concluded that, Well, then, we deserve to go extinct.

If history is any guide, and/or present trends hold, they will.

The Democrats, their ruling-class masters, and their foot soldier constituencies are laughing all the way to the bank. "To win without fighting is best," said Sun Tzu. Essentially, the Dem-left coalition dictates terms to its ostensible opponents—"keep the borders wide open, don't restrict any existing immigration or visa program; in fact, expand them"—and the Republicans salute and do what they're told.

Is there another historical example of a political party, or any political entity, not defeated on the battlefield, still (on paper) numerically, monetarily, and politically strong, taking all of its opponents' "advice" at face value as if it were well-intentioned and for its own good? Doing exactly what its adversaries say to do, voluntarily? If so, I can't think of it.

But that's what the Republicans are doing and have been doing at least since the 1986 amnesty. Sooner or later—sooner more likely than later—this shortsightedness will destroy them as a national party, the same way that unchecked mass immigration has made Republicans irrelevant, if not quite yet extinct, in California, New York, and many other solid-blue states.

DEMOCRACY, THEN AND NOW

All of this will be—and already is being—defended, vehemently, as "democracy" and therefore good. Those who question it are attacked, even more vehemently, as "anti-democratic" and therefore bad. It's worth, then, taking a brief look at what this word "democracy" used to mean versus what it has come to mean today.

The word is, of course, Greek and literally means "rule" (*arche*) by the "common people" (*demos*). That is to say, democracy is rule of the whole political community (*polis*) by a part of that community. For there are other parts: principally the few—whether understood as the rich, the powerful, the moral, the wise, the brave, the strong, or some combination thereof. There also may be a "one," in the de jure sense of a monarch or the de facto sense of someone so preeminent in virtue that all, or nearly all, recognize his innate superiority—for example, Pericles in nominally democratic Athens.

Classical philosophers and historians alike condemn democracy as a bad form of government, in part because of its partiality but mostly because of the specific nature of the *demos*, which they contend is the *polis*'s least wise and least moderate part.

The classics instead recommend what Aristotle calls a "mixed" regime, in which no one part of the political community has the upper hand but all share power, each contributing its particular strength(s) and checking the others' particular weaknesses.

An updated version of this "mixed regime" is more or less what the modern political philosophers who inspired the American founders recommended and what our founders themselves worked to create. Sovereignty would rest with the people as a whole, but "the common people"—yeoman farmers, hired field hands, artisans, apprentices, factory workers, shopkeepers, domestic servants—as a class would not predominate. Power would be shared across regional, factional, social, and economic lines, with no one constituency ever gaining total control.

Our founders avoided the word "democracy," in part because of its bad reputation but also because they didn't believe the government they built was—strictly speaking—democratic. Yet over time, "democracy" came to mean something like their solution to the political problem: popular sovereignty, a government whose fundamental course is set by voting yet whose powers are limited by natural rights, enumerated powers, checks and balances, the separation of powers, federal versus state and local spheres of authority, and so on.

More recently, "democracy" has come to mean one thing and one thing only: majority rule. Of course, the core purpose of democratic—and republican—rule is to ensure a voice for the collectivity, to prevent the state from becoming an instrument that purely serves the few, or the one.

But pure majority rule takes us back to square one—to the original meaning of "democracy": the rule of a part over the whole. Which is essentially what "democracy" means in blue cities and states now. Sure, all the red folk get to vote. As far as the ruling oligarch-plus-foot-soldier alliance is concerned, that alone satisfies the requirements of justice, of "democracy." That the reds are outvoted every time, their preferences never considered, their interests never respected is irrelevant. There was a vote, you lost, and that's that.

This is why fundamentally republican but not purely democratic institutions and norms such as the Electoral College are so viciously attacked and despised. They hinder the operation of "democracy" thus understood. In this understanding, the 2016 election was illegitimate simply because Hillary won the popular vote. But consider: she won California alone by 4.3 million votes—and lost the other forty-nine states by 1.4 million. Of course, the founders created the Electoral College specifically to prevent brute-force voting from crushing underfoot all regional, sectional, cultural, religious, economic, and other differences. But that matters not a whit to our overlords—except as proof that the Electoral College is "anti-democratic" and so must go!

Similarly, the uncomprehending angst of people who've lived the same way, in the same places, for generations and who suddenly find themselves harassed by a hostile government—ostensibly "theirs"—that curtails their natural and historic rights? Their concerns are attacked as laments over "lost privilege." Virginia flipped from purple to blue in one election in 2019, entirely owing to mass immigration and the growth of the administrative state, which together have packed hundreds of thousands of loyal

Democrats into three D.C.-adjacent cities and counties. Immediately the state enacted, in the cradle of the American Revolution, draconian gun restrictions that flew in the face of centuries of tradition and peaceful practice. Too bad! You lost! That's "democracy"!

We should not, however, give the powers that be too much credit for principled consistency. If and when popular majorities produce outcomes they don't like, their devotion to "democracy" instantly evaporates. When, on the other hand, voters can be counted on to vote the right way, then voting becomes the necessary and sufficient action for sanctifying any political outcome. It doesn't even matter where the votes—or the voters—come from, so long as they vote the right way. Indeed, the fact that they vote the right way is sufficient to justify and even ennoble their participation in "our democracy." Immigrants and their children vote the right way, hence immigration is "democratic" and good. It's really just that simple.

Blues perpetually outvoting reds and ruling unopposed: this, and only this, is what "democracy" means today.

CALIFORNIA, HERE WE COME?

The Democrats' main goal all along for mass immigration has been precisely this: to eliminate the Republican Party—or any potential successor party—as anything but token opposition, allowed to hang on by a thread to give the illusion of two-party competition but incapable of winning elections or of governing if they do. To be sure, on this latter score, the Republicans didn't need much help, so inept and devoted to their real constituents—their donors—are they. But they still like winning, and extracting rent for their paymasters requires victories. Soon— very soon—they won't be able to win anymore, not in numbers that provide any share of real power. Then what?

Those expecting the answer "California on a national scale" might be too optimistic. The doyens of modern California—and New York, and all the blue states and metros—are not satisfied with those places as they are. America's elites believe their home turfs aren't progressive enough—are being held back by Republicans, rubes, and red states. Only once those forces are fully and finally defeated can the real transformation begin and the first steps toward utopia finally be taken.

But that's a topic for the next chapter.

CHAPTER SIX

If Present Trends Continue . . .

All of the above naturally inspires the question: what happens next? Like Yogi Berra, I find it tough to make predictions, especially about the future. I therefore generally try to avoid being pinned down. But I'm not above a little probabilistic speculation.

The first part of the answer, though, requires no speculation at all: either the ruling class can hold on to their power and keep their current arrangements going, or they can't. This chapter explores the possibility that they can.

NEOLIBERALISM FOREVER?

The most plausible—which is not necessarily the same as "likely"—outcome is the continuance of what we have now. "Assuming present trends continue" is supposedly a logical fallacy called "recency bias." So all the usual disclaimers apply: conventional wisdom is often wrong, correlation is not causation, past performance is no guarantee of future results, etc.

Yet present trends—whatever they are—typically become trends for powerful underlying reasons. Our particular present trends are, in addition, backed by powerful and wealthy interests. It's at least possible that our ruling class are not all total fools. To an appreciable extent, they might know what they're doing and know how to keep things going, if not forever, for a very long time.

Certainly, "history" is punctuated by major, memorable events. But only three truly big things have happened in my lifetime: the fall of the Berlin Wall and dissolution of the USSR, 9/11, and the one-two punch of the coronavirus shutdown and the woke-riots. Underneath those seemingly momentous events, it's clear now that the same trends have been intensifying inexorably since the end of the Cold War. If one charts the progress of neoliberalism like a stock price, there are some dips and even valleys along the way, but mostly it's been up, up, up. So it's not unreasonable to extrapolate forward and ask: what happens if present trends do, in fact, continue?

Only time will tell if 2020 proves a turning point that drives lasting change or ends up being just another spectacle that changes little—like when a big snake eats a whole pig and looks strikingly different for a short time, but all in the service of furthering its nature as a snake, to which familiar shape it soon returns.

No less than the shutdown and riots, Trump, Brexit, the Yellow Vests, and similar populist-nationalist movements may turn out to be major turning points. But it's too soon to tell and, for now, the oligarchs still hold all the commanding heights—except one. They want that one back. Their top priority for 2020 is to defeat Trump; for 2021 and beyond, to erase all traces of his influence on policy and politics.

Return to Normalcy

What would happen then? On one level, things would go back to "normal"—that is, to something like the post–Cold War neoliberal consensus. The sanctification of immigration, the glorification of "open" trade, jingoistic celebration of constabulary use of force in parts of the world tangential—at best—to the national interest: expect lots more of all that.

The basic contours of the back-to-normal regime will look much as they did at the height of the Obama administration—or, in hindsight, the Bush-Clinton-Bush-Obama imperium: a high-low coalition against the middle in service of big tech, high finance, and woke capital.

"Getting back to normal" will also require the Narrative to amp into overdrive on all the alleged "failures" of the Trump Interregnum. Getting out of the Trans-Pacific Partnership (which even Hillary Clinton had disavowed by 2016)? Disaster! Played right into the hands of China and alienated our allies! Blaming China for the coronavirus? Another disaster! Racist and xenophobic and alienated a key trading partner!

As we have seen ad nauseum, surface consistency is not a strong suit of the Narrative. There is, however, an underlying consistency: anything that serves the interests of the ruling class and hurts Trump is good. Period.

Hence you will hear endless denunciations of Trump's renegotiated trade deals as catastrophic—and inconsequential. Similarly, on immigration, the Narrative will be: Trump's racist xenophobia was a racist overreaction to a non-problem—that crippled our economy by depriving it of desperately needed workers . . . when the unemployment rate was nearly 15 percent. On foreign policy, the line will be (already is): Trump's recklessness risked calamitous war—while he recklessly pulled American troops out of combat zones in Syria and Afghanistan and tried to negotiate a peace deal with North Korea.

Only More So

All of the trends that defined the "post–Cold War era" and that Trump ran against and has opposed or sought to moderate will be intensified. The ruling class will get right back to elevating the international over the national while tolerating the national only insofar as state power is used to bolster the international neoliberal order and enforce its edicts to facilitate the movement of capital, goods, and labor across borders in ways that benefit themselves.

The economy will become even more artificial and jury-rigged. We shall test supposed iron laws of economic gravity—for instance, whether it's possible to maintain a fiat currency indefinitely with endless money printing and whether said currency can long maintain its global reserve status. The longer the rigging goes on, the more rigging will be required.

Overall, the economy will become more techified, more financialized, more concentrated at the coasts and in the cities, and more unequal. Expect the rich to get a lot richer and the middle class to disappear. Wages will fall. In the "gig economy," employer-provided healthcare will disappear for all but the senior-most executives, a trend that will in turn make some form of socialized medicine inevitable. Quality of care will fall for all but the people at the very top who can buy out of the government system. But eventually even their care will decline too, since there will no longer be enough money in the system to keep medical innovation going.

On Trump's big three—immigration, trade, and war—it will be back to the status quo ante, and then well beyond. At least at first, immigration levels will go dramatically up and there will no pretense of enforcement. We've already seen entire communities become demographically overwhelmed in the space of a decade or two. That will keep happening, but on a much vaster scale.

It will become much harder and more expensive to wall oneself off from the consequences, which means that the number, or at least the share, of "regime winners" who can afford the "good" suburbs or the private schools will shrink while the share of "losers" increases. As a result, native birthrates are likely to drop further, while pathologies such as addiction will increase and life expectancy will fall.

On trade, the government will revert to its accustomed practice of enacting policy to further enrich the rich, no matter the consequences for the middle and working classes. On war, the particulars are harder to foresee since it's never been clear what the ruling class gets out of endless, pointless, winless conflict. But they certainly have an affinity for it, which means we should expect more, with all the attendant negative consequences: more death, more of the nation's wealth sunk in wasteful adventures, the continued erosion of the military and further squandering of our national pride, international prestige, and many of our best young men.

So-called "public–private cooperation" will increase. This benign-sounding phrase—who could object to "cooperation," to government and business "solving problems" together?—masks a darker reality. What it really describes is the use of state power to serve private ends, at private direction. Hence foreign policy—that quintessentially public function, to "provide for the common defense"—will be further reoriented around securing trade, tax, and labor ("migration") patterns and paradigms that benefit finance and big business.

Government collusion with big business, especially tech and finance, and the ceding to corporations vast swaths of territory that the state used to occupy exclusively will intensify and expand. The "unpersoning" of dissenters will become ever more similar to what the government of China does through its "social credit system": ranking people based on their opinions—and Wokerati opinion *of them*—and then granting or limiting access to basic freedoms and services. This will be, and already is being, justified because it is done primarily by the private sector, whether by for-profit businesses that lock people out of entire sectors or "nonprofits" such as the odious Southern Poverty Law Center that identify targets.

If you think we have mass surveillance already, just wait. The government and the tech companies already work hand-in-glove, the latter helping the former in exchange for favorable tax, regulatory, and immigration treatment. When the last checks on such collusion from the Trump administration are gone, expect this joint censorship and oppression of dissent to increase by orders of magnitude. The left has finally found a way around the First Amendment: consolidate all "speech" and public expression onto a handful of private-sector platforms run by oligarchs and staffed by Wokerati; let them do whatever they want and when anyone complains, reply that "these are private companies that can

run their business however they want; you don't have to use their platforms and if you don't like it, start your own." The left knows it can
count on the moronic, friendly-fire-spraying libertarians to sing that tune
the loudest. Free speech as we have known it—as our founders insisted
was the natural bedrock of political rights, without which self-government is impossible—will not survive coming leftist rule.

The playbook is already being expanded to banking and credit. Getting on the wrong side of elite-woke opinion is increasingly to find yourself locked out of the financial system: no bank account, no credit card,
no ability to get a loan or pay a mortgage. Pay cash? The move to a
"cashless society"—purely to prevent drug lords and Russian spies from
laundering money, you understand—will obviate that option right quick.

There's no reason to assume the overlords will limit these types of
actions to speech and money. Why would they? Especially when the woke
vanguard will consistently clamor for more action and insist that any
company that does business with "racists" is complicit with evil—
"racist" being defined as anyone who hasn't bent the knee. China already
restricts travel for the disfavored. Why wouldn't U.S. airlines? Car rental
companies? Dealerships are independent, but they also depend on the
big automakers for their stock. And, anyway, who can possibly buy a car
if he can't get a job or a bank account?

As we saw, Britain's nationalized healthcare service is already moving to deny medical care to those deemed "racist, sexist, or homophobic."
What's to stop the Wokerati from pressuring America's patchwork of
public and private healthcare providers to do the same? And why stop
there? Why should "racists" even be allowed to buy food? That is, assuming they can even earn the money to pay for it. But that problem can
probably be taken care of by denying the bad guys credit or debit cards
and phasing out cash.

Not long ago, I thought the point of all this—aside from being punitive to enemies for the sheer pleasure of it—was to find the sweet spot
between too much overt oppression, which might provoke backlash, and
too little, which might allow opposition to gather strength. To expand

firings, un-personings, bank lockouts, and the like too rapidly might raise alarms; kept at the creeping level, they serve to keep most of red America locked into the blue system and thus dependent. A bit of caution would thus seem to serve ruling-class interests.

But signs of moderation, of magnanimity, of a recognition that "we won" and so can ease off are, to say the least, not common among the woke left. And the extent to which the ruling class can control its foot soldiers was very much called into question by the events of May and June 2020. Consider that New York City—the global neoliberal oligarchy's unquestioned capital and home to by far the largest share of America's elites—was sacked by mobs several times in the same week. Whether the ruling class allowed that, couldn't stop it, or lacked the nerve to try hardly matters.

Even if things keep going at present rates and don't accelerate, isolation, loneliness, desperation, addiction, and suicide will all increase as ostracization condemns heretic after heretic to a sort of internal exile. The most vocally strident among the left will call the resulting deaths just deserts; the rest will brush them off as perhaps sad, but the direct consequence of bad choices or bad natures. "That racist had it coming."

And every step of the way, the Narrative's reply to those who raise the alarm will be: That's *not* happening, and it's *good* that it is. You're a paranoid lunatic for even suggesting that censorship, de-platforming, or un-personing are problems, and also a racist who deserves it.

A Dark Age of White Noise

The ruling class has built a well-honed apparatus to inculcate docility in the people. Components include cheap, puerile mass entertainment, ubiquitous smartphones and social media, video games, porn, drugs, and so on across the whole dreary panoply of lowest-common-denominator "culture" in the current year.

We should expect all this to increase. Indeed, the ruling class's recent and ongoing enthusiasm for marijuana legalization and its total indifference to the opioid epidemic suggest that they're seeking to drug as many non-elites as they can out of any potential resistance.

Combine these factors with leftism's top-down, total control of thought, and the picture becomes bleak indeed. The times are already quite vapid; very little (if anything) of lasting merit has been produced in literature, philosophy, film, or the other arts in several decades. The trend seems to be getting worse.

But at least we still have that older stuff to fall back on, right? Not necessarily. The cherished and iconic works of our past are also threatened, in two ways. First, the movement that originated on campus more than a generation ago to get rid of core curricula and reinterpret those bits allowed to remain in light of leftist orthodoxy has borne fruit. We've now "educated" generations of students—even (especially) elite students—either (1) to have no familiarity with the Western canon; and/or (2) to despise it as inherently evil; or (3) to see it only through leftist lenses that make it seem as if it merely confirms current orthodoxy; or (4) to believe it was all "stolen" from other cultures. That last one is, of course, a lie, but one that at least implicitly concedes there's something valuable in the tradition. But the point is never made to spur anyone to actually read the books, rather only to validate in-group confidence. *My* people, and not *yours*, did that, hence *we* are great and *you* are not. The result is that the whole Western tradition is at risk of atrophy, and even death, simply from ignorance and neglect.

As if that were not enough, the left is starting to get even more actively hostile to the tradition. Certain elite intellectuals, led by Mark Zuckerberg's sister, have noticed that some young autodidacts have taken to reading the Great Books and listening to classical music. The elites see this as a threat. There are serious calls not merely to police how the canon is taught but to attack and even censor its "misuse" by "bad actors" who use it to challenge the Narrative.

It may not be long before Amazon, which virtually controls the entire book market, stops selling the classics altogether. Or perhaps a new industry will arise to bowdlerize them of all non-woke teachings. The worst-case scenario, which doesn't yet feel imminent but which cannot be ruled out, is that eventually such books get banned. Far more likely—and quite imminent in a world where Elizabeth Warren's nine-year-old trans friend gets to pick the Secretary of Education—is a time in which all the institutions that teach the canon, and the scholars who write about it seriously, will be attacked over petty and invented infractions. The real purpose of those attacks will be to silence those scholars and eventually shutter those institutions.

The climate of acceptable opinion in this country—already very narrow—will constrict further still. The necessity for self-censorship will dramatically increase. The core function of the Narrative will remain telling you what to think—and more important what *not* to think—but its message will get even more tendentious, hateful, omnipresent, and so, so much louder. Imagine a TV screen playing CNN, volume cranked to eleven, not just in airport waiting areas, but everywhere—forever.

Anarcho-Tyranny, Intensified

Those deemed "dangerous" by woke thought police will be dogged by authorities. Any suspected dissident not as scrupulous as Caesar's wife in his every interaction with the state will get the book thrown at him for minor, technical infractions of some law, executive order, or administrative rule. As the poor sucker is hauled away in cuffs by a heavily armed team of feds in windbreakers, CNNMSNBC reporters—tipped off in advance to get it all on camera—will intone that this "dangerous white supremacist" with "ties to neo-Nazi groups" was "planning attacks." Months or years later, after being held without bail, he'll be convicted of mail fraud and given the maximum sentence.

The left will seek to use this same combination of maximum Megaphone volume and maximum federal zeal to target lawful gun owners using the alleged threat of "domestic terrorism" as a pretext. "Red flag" programs operated by public–private cooperation will identify "potential terrorists" and the like who, to the extent that they don't suffer the fate described above, will at the very least have their guns seized. The future of the Second Amendment in the coming leftist regime is hardly any brighter than that of the First.

Meanwhile, other, much larger violations of the law will go unpunished, so long as the perpetrators are from "protected classes." This is another of those assertions that many will wish to dismiss as paranoid. Yet even before the 2020 riots, we had already seen tremendous pressure from the left for "criminal justice reform"—meaning leniency for the favored—and Soros-backed leftist "law enforcement officials" being elected all over the country.

Need evidence that going soft on crime is high on the agenda? Consider how, early in the COVID panic, leftist pols prioritized letting criminals out of jail, ostensibly because they were at risk of infection. The real reason, though, is explained by Rahm Emanuel's famous exhortation to his comrades to "never let a serious crisis go to waste." Governors, mayors, district attorneys, police chiefs, and sheriffs in blue zones across the country simply followed hizzoner's advice and did what they always wanted to do anyway but hiterto could, or dared, not. Emboldened by the crisis, drunk with power, and half-convinced that a scared population wasn't paying attention, they let the bad guys go. They got away with it, and they'll make the policy permanent once they have lasting power.

All that turned out to be mere prolegomena for what came next: the mass sacking and looting of major American cities from coast to coast, with little or no attempt by law enforcement to stop the violence. Nor was even that the end. Most of those who managed to get themselves arrested for rioting, looting, destroying of property, arson, or assault saw, to their great joy and Middle America's amazement, all charges against them dropped by leftist prosecutors. In the wake of mass violence at least as bad as the mayhem of the 1960s, cities from Los Angeles to Minneapolis to New York are seriously contemplating—with some elected officials outright demanding—the defunding or even complete abolition of their police departments. It would appear that in the very near future, basic criminal law will no longer be enforced in large parts of the United States of America.

Except against those who try to defend themselves. It's tempting to call this emerging America a "failed state," but it isn't really. The state is more than capable of acting on its own priorities, which emphatically include crushing known or suspected regime enemies. Far from being incapable of enforcing the law, the state rather chooses which laws to enforce, and which not to enforce, in accordance with the interests of the ruling class. That trend, too, will intensify.

Wish List

All of this is easy enough to predict because it is either what the left is already doing where it has the power, or what it says it wants to do. The lessons of California and New York show that when leftists no longer face opposition, they do whatever they want—or try to. The problem (for them, for now) is that they still face opposition from the red elements still extant in the federal government, from red states, and from red communities in their own states. Once the whole country has gone blue, though, things will be . . . different.

With opposition eliminated or neutralized, the left will gin up new enthusiasms with unprecedented zeal, which they will then impose nationwide and enforce approval of, even requiring feigned enthusiasm. Gay marriage and transgenderism were just the beginnings. We may speculate as to what exactly they will choose next, but they'll certainly pick something and force the wider society to accept it. Here's one guess: forcible removal of children from parents who resist their kid's demand to get on puberty blockers. At first silence will be acceptable—barely—but over time the left will insist on affirmative shows of approval for whatever it is they dreamed up yesterday and now insist is an eternal, inviolable principle. Everyone will have to wear the ribbon.

Humiliation is part of the appeal. While most lefties tend to believe in the urgency of whatever cause they happen to be worked up over at the moment, their deepest satisfaction arises less from seeing justice done than watching the retrograde submit. It lets the bad guys know who's boss. "How many fingers am I holding up, Winston?" Forcing you to call a woman a man, or vice versa, is all the more satisfying when those holding the gun to your head know you don't really believe it. That, and the constant ginning up of new hysterias keeps deplorables off-balance and on the defensive.

Religious persecution will necessarily have to increase because much of what the left is doing and wants to do directly contradicts the tenets of faith. We've already seen this with state orders forcing people to bake cakes for ceremonies that the bakers believe contradict their religion; we shall certainly see more of it, perhaps to the point where traditional Christianity will have to return to the catacombs.

However, there will be one major exception: a double standard will be ruthlessly enforced to allow Muslims (at least those who are regime allies) to do whatever they want in violation of leftist tenets. Leftism is incoherent in many ways, but it's clear on its priorities, and on the inter-sectionality pillar, Muslims rank very high—perhaps not at the tippy-top, but high enough to be exempt from leftist religious persecution, which will be directed only at Christians and Orthodox Jews. This is a reason to suspect polygamy might be the next leftist enthusiasm.

Other items on the wish list include abolishing ICE, not just halting the construction of Trump's border wall but tearing down sections already built before Trump's inauguration, and extending Medicare to the entire population—including all current and prospective illegal immigrants. Then there's the "Green New Deal," which would ban air travel by 2030 and eliminate America's entire energy sector, or at least the part that actually generates power.

And finally, the granddaddy of them all, "reparations"—long a fringe idea, revived by Ta-Nehisi Coates and recently endorsed by the venerable Brookings Institution, the premier "establishment," "respect-able," "moderate" center-left think tank in the country. Brookings scholars tend to be overrepresented in Democratic administrations, and the ideas they get behind tend to become policy. So when Brookings backs reparations, you can be pretty sure that once the Democrats are back in power, reparations will happen.

Goodbye, Constitution

Nothing gets a conservative's patriotic blood up more than effusive praise of the United States Constitution. God knows, I love it too—at least as much as any of them do.

Which is why it pains me to write that its future is bleak. To do what the left wants to do will require riding roughshod over our sacred parchment—even more so than we've already been doing.

The Constitution has been under explicit attack since the beginning of the Progressive Era, nearly 125 years ago. Those attacks exponentially intensified with the advent of 1960s leftism. They retreated a bit in the face of the Reagan–Gingrich counterattacks but are now back with a vengeance. If conservatives were to tally the score, we might take some consolation from the fact that from time to time we've been able to put points on the board. But we would also be forced to concede that we've been massively outscored, and that our losses are mounting and accelerating.

I take the liberty of quoting myself, from the "Restatement on Flight 93" (originally published on September 13, 2016), because the words remain apt and I can't think of a better way to make the point:

> For now, let's just ask ourselves two questions. First, how do the mechanics of government, as written in the Constitution, differ from current practice? Second, how well is the Bill of Rights observed? As to the first, we do still have those three branches of government mentioned. But we also have a fourth, hidden in plain sight within the executive, namely the bureaucracy or administrative state. It both usurps legislative power and uses executive power in an unaccountable way. Congress does not use its own powers but meekly defers to the executive and to the bureaucracy. The executive [at least when Democrats are in power] does whatever it wants. The judiciary also usurps legislative and, when it's really feeling its oats, executive power through the use of consent decrees

and the like. And that's just the feds—before we even get to
the relationship between the feds and the states. As to the
second, can you think of a single amendment among the Bill
of Rights that is not routinely violated—with the acquiescence
and approval of the Left? I can't.

This situation has gotten considerably worse since I wrote that. To
cite only two examples: free speech is under attack as it never has been
before. Right now, the battlefield is mostly social media sites, hence the
attacks are publicly justified as legitimate acts by private businesses. "The
First Amendment doesn't cover the private sector; property rights mean
they can do what they want!" Leave aside the extent to which the ruling
class cares about property rights for property not their own (answer: not
much); how meaningful is the distinction between public and private
speech when the modes of public discourse are increasingly concentrated
in the private hands of the ruling class? Answer: also not much. When it
comes to freedom of association, the government arm of the ruling class
is absolutely ruthless in declaring everything a "public accommodation"
so that said freedom becomes effectively nonexistent. But when half a
dozen (or fewer) big tech companies take over the means of disseminating
speech and ideas—oh, no! That's not a public accommodation! Those
are private firms and the rights of private firms are sacrosanct! As if this
were not enough, take a look at how free speech polls these days: the
younger the demographic, the less support one sees.

Consider also the incredible abuses of power from the Justice Department, the FBI, the intelligence community, and other agencies. Even with
Trump in the White House, the administrative state still does whatever it
wants while hampering the lawful directives of the elected chief executive.
So long as their targets are in the disfavored party, they can spy on American
citizens—up to and including presidential candidates—lie to and entrap
public officials, extort plea deals from the innocent, and leak highly classified
information for political purposes. (This is, needless to say, a very partial
list.) They get away with all this scot-free: no punishment, no correction, no

rebuke. They not only pay no price for shredding the Constitution and violating myriad statutes, they are lionized: the entire media and commentariat cheer them on. The fix is in, and has been for some time, but we still pretend we live in the age of Eliot Ness, the incorruptible G-man.

The fate of the Constitution is also inseparable from demographic change. Just as the least conservative and Republican areas of the country are the most foreign-born, so are such areas the places where the Constitution is least honored and operative. Lest someone object, "It's not about race!" I agree: whites themselves are sharply divided about the merits of the Constitution. A plurality at least, and all of the elite, despise constitutional limits. The only people in America who en masse still care about the Constitution and how it's supposed to work are conservatives, whose numbers—in absolute terms and as a share of the population—are dwindling. The bluer an area is, the less purchase constitutional principle holds.

If present trends continue, the Constitution has no future. Not only will neither its letter nor spirit be honored—either in ordinary circumstances or in the breach—not only will none of its guarantees be upheld nor any of its limits respected, but the document itself will be increasingly denounced as a hateful tool of racist oppression, a relic of a benighted, evil past best left on the ash heap of history. Indeed, that judgment is already the norm in academia and elite intellectual circles. And the history of the past fifty years shows that the left is extremely effective at ensuring that every fringe-radical idea to emerge from academia becomes mainstream. How many times have we scoffed at some academic insanity only, ten or twenty years later, to see it become federal law? Ivy League law professors explicitly argue in the pages of the *New York Times* that the Constitution is evil and has to go. We already don't govern ourselves according to its letter as a matter of practice. How long before what is today de facto becomes de jure? And even if it doesn't, what difference would that make?

Elective Monarchy

To give new practices a veneer of continuity, in the manner of Augustus Caesar insisting he was just another senator, the more the ruling class departs from the letter and spirit of the Constitution, the more they will (at least for a while) pledge ever greater fealty to the Constitution. Which in practice will mean only one thing: they will still hold elections every two, four, and six years, and the terms of office will remain the same length. These are, for the average American, still uncrossable lines and also impossible to fudge.

But politics—in the sense of reasoned deliberation about common ends—will cease. Instead, "politics" will be reduced to jockeying among Democratic officeholders and seekers for who gets what job when. There likely will still be general as well as primary elections, but only the latter will matter. The former will be mere formalities, as are gubernatorial contests in California and New York. It will probably take the Republican donor class a while to realize that their party is no longer viable at the national level, but they will eventually figure it out. After that, the party will become, for a few election cycles at least, what it is in New York and California: the plaything of billionaires who want to run for chief executive without the bother of a primary. All of them will lose. Then the party will die altogether.

The Democratic primaries will be the election. That is, to the extent that such contests actually *are* elections. It's safer and more reasonable to assume they'll be increasingly rigged, similar to the way the Democrats—twice—prevented Bernie Sanders from getting their party's nomination. Insurgency, outsider candidacies may still be attempted for a few cycles, but they'll get nowhere and pretty soon outsiders with anything on the ball will stop trying. We are, in a sense, headed back to the era of "smoke-filled rooms"—though naturally there will be no smoke, unless it's from pot.

To help us understand what's coming, a more precise regime category exists: the elective monarchy, in which the true electors are not "the people" but a handful of horse-trading elites. Historical examples include the Western Roman Empire (where hereditary succession was the exception to the rule), the Mamluk Sultanate, the papacy, and the Communist regimes of the USSR and the People's Republic of China. The grandees of the Democratic Party will get together every eight years (needless to say, no president will ever be denied reelection again) and decide who gets to "run." That person, facing no or token opposition, gets the big chair.

The fundamental question of every Democratic presidential primary season will simply be: Whose turn is it? That question will be asked in two senses: (1) which particular party luminary gets to run the show for the next eight years? and (2) which group gets to be in charge for a while?

The ideal—the plan—will be to keep the globalization gravy train rolling by sharing the spoils "more equitably," "spoils" in this case being both offices and remuneration (and, given the way our system now works, the former is the surest path to the latter). The economy's actual masters will naturally prefer to be more generous with offices than with money.

As for those quadrennial November contests, we'll still go through the formality of elections, but for show, like senate votes in imperial Rome. The less consequential elections become, the more our elites will insist on their sacrosanct significance. The mere fact of holding elections will become ipso facto proof that the regime is "democratic" and therefore legitimate.

This is another thing New America's rulers will share in common with their Communist forebears: the yearning for a veneer of democratic legitimacy. Near the end of the Cold War, columnist Charles Krauthammer coined the term "Tirana Index"—after Tirana, Albania, where tyrant Enver Hoxha once "won" an "election" 1,627,959 to 1—which holds that "the higher the score rolled up by the ruling party in elections, the more tyrannous the regime." The wonder is not that Hoxha won, nor even his margin of victory, but that he felt obligated to stage the sham in the first place.

I don't expect our coming overlords to rig our elections that badly; they won't need to.

REASONS TO DOUBT

Let me again caution the reader against placing unreflective bets against our ruling class. Machiavelli observed that "it is not reasonable that whoever is armed obey willingly whoever is unarmed," but our masters have managed to occupy, conquer, and co-opt every commanding height in our society, from which they rule us at will, all not merely without firing a shot but also in spite of their evident weakness according to almost every traditional or conventional measure of political strength. That achievement alone should inspire at least a grudging respect and serve as a warning against overconfidence or dismissive contempt.

So should the facts that the ruling class have managed to take things this far and keep them going this long. A thing achieved and operating is, ipso facto, more concrete than some speculative future. Some of the above might not even sound so bad. As long as "prosperity" can be maintained—bread and circuses consistently delivered—many will be content. A life of relative ease carries distinct advantages over one of backbreaking virtue.

Yet there are reasons to doubt that our overlords can remain in the saddle forever, or that the old nag underneath will never give out.

Downsides of One-Party Rule

Throughout history and around the world, the track record of one-party rule is, to say the least, not great. Most states that have either achieved or succumbed to it have failed sooner or later—mostly sooner.

A party in power that has every expectation of staying in power, that feels no threat—electoral or otherwise—tends to become arrogant, overweening, overconfident, greedy, hubristic, intolerant and dismissive of criticism, unable to correct course or even to see when it's gone wrong. Part of the benefit of real political competition is that facing opposition makes it harder to ignore one's own flaws and errors. One can, of course, always try to ignore criticism and dismiss bad news, but doing so is much easier when you're never forced to hear any.

This dynamic already prevails in America today. Complete domination of all public discourse and information is a massive benefit to the ruling class. But there's a downside. The rulers have almost no insight into the thinking, the beliefs, or the true sentiments of a large portion of the ruled. We cannot but know what our rulers think—we're bombarded with their propaganda 24/7. They have no idea what we think. This is why the 2016 election came as a complete surprise. They only ever hear what they want to hear, and what they tell themselves: that they're the greatest while anyone who doubts is some combination of evil and irrelevant. Even with all the commanding heights in safe hands, to be this out of touch is an inherently unstable situation.

Opposition also incentivizes competing parties to moderate their programs and scale back their wish lists; lack of opposition by contrast encourages maximalist thinking. No matter how just or equitable a given party endeavors to be toward the other side, the inherent tendency of politics is for parties to take care of their own. Unless it faces, and sees, a real prospect of losing power and knows that one day it will have to live under the rule of its opponents, a ruling party will never do full justice to the claims of its rivals. Only by ruling and being ruled in turn do the just claims of all have any chance of being honored.

By continually locking the other side out of all power and honors, one-party rule guarantees that half (or some significant portion) of the population will feel ignored and aggrieved, sentiments which then build like steam in a capped pipe. At a minimum, the legitimacy of the state erodes. At worst, the pipe eventually bursts.

Above all, in the absence of criticism, errors compound. Stupidity and incompetence are excused and even celebrated so long as their authors are people on the correct side. Things get worse. Discontent rises and must be squashed by more propaganda and oppressive action against dissidents.

History is, of course, depressingly replete with rickety regimes that nonetheless lasted a very long time. But every ruling class makes, and must make, a claim that justifies its rule. Ours alleges its superior hyper-competent technocratic expertise. How long can it last when the very machinery that it purports to operate with the precision of a race car engine creaks, leaks, sputters, and backfires in plain sight?

America the Incompetent

Americans—especially our politicians—love to pat themselves on the back over genuine accomplishments such as building the "arsenal of democracy," winning World War II, and putting a man on the moon. Hilariously, the same Green New Deal document that promises an end to air travel by 2030 also cites American aircraft production during World War II—from three thousand to three hundred thousand planes in four years!—as evidence of America's can-do spirit.

Which it was. Is that spirit still alive? An unsettling sign that maybe it's not is that Americans on the left and right alike always have to reach back a half century or more to find examples. More recent sources of inspiration are dismayingly thin on the ground.

Since the moon landing, America—and the West generally—appears to have made three fundamental "advancements": (1) low-cost, worldwide, ubiquitous mobile telephony; (2) exponentially cheaper, smaller, and more powerful computers; and (3) the internet. Some will dispute whether any of these have really constituted "progress." Without getting into that debate, there's at least no question that these things are all fundamentally new. In 1980, PCs were expensive, terrible, and could barely print your grocery list. In 1990, "cell phones" were as big as bricks, cost three grand, and worked in a tiny fraction of the county. "The internet" was mostly dorks on Usenet arguing over whether Picard was better than Kirk or vice versa.

Today all three of these technologies, and their intersections with one another, really have changed the world and make 1990 feel as distant from us as it was from 1960. But those are about it. Can you think of any others? I can't. Certainly nothing like the rapid advances that characterized America through the second third of the twentieth century. 1990 may feel a world away from 2020, but does 2000? Or 2010? Interestingly, all the telltale fashion, hairstyle, musical, and other cues that used to make one decade instantly distinguishable from others seem to have melted away. Ten seconds of any movie or TV show made before 1990 is enough to place instantly the decade of production, in some cases even the precise year. But from that point on, everything blends together. There's almost no point in making a "period piece" about (say) 2002; in what ways would the world depicted look any different? I believe these phenomena are related.

It would be one thing if we simply stopped "progressing" for a while but held our own at those things we had already accomplished. But that's not what's happened. In so many ways, America is worse today than it was a mere few decades ago.

Did you know, for instance, that most commercial flights take longer now than they did in the 1970s? That's both because the planes are slower and because of an outdated air traffic and airport system that can't handle congestion and incentivizes padding schedules. This is, of course, to say nothing of the horrible ordeal of getting through airport security or the purgatory-like environment and experience on board.

Apart from automobile quality—which admittedly has risen—there's hardly a single way in which our transportation sector is better today than it was a few decades ago. Distant exurbs with their ubiquitous six-lane surface streets aside, there seems to be no part of the country where the roads are anything above barely passable. In the big urban cores, streets resemble the lunar surface. Public transportation is hardly better. The New York City subway partially recovered from its 1970s nadir; city officials at least got the graffiti off the trains and chased out enough of the criminals that going underground to catch a ride was, for a time, no longer (in Tom Wolfe's mordant phrase) to "shoot dice with Fate."

But the subway is still dirty, smelly, overcrowded, slow, and always late. The MTA blames this on an "outdated signal system" that dates from when the network was originally built in the early twentieth century. And no doubt, technology from the ragtime era is probably no longer cutting-edge. But what does it say about New York—about America—that we've not managed to find a way to update it in *120* years?

Things are no better—and are in some respects worse—in other cities. No transportation system in the world beats Northern California's BART for per capita vomit, urine, and open drug use. BART and the Washington, D.C., Metro compete with one another for highest incidents of breakdowns and delays—derailed trains, electrical fires, oil spills, smoke inundations—mostly owing to crumbling infrastructure caused by deferred maintenance and worker incompetence.

For twelve years, I was a daily commuter on America's busiest rail line, Metro-North, which ferries office drones in and out of Manhattan. When I started riding, every train, every day, in both directions, was on time to the minute per the printed schedule. At some point in the early 2010s, I started to notice increasing lateness. Trains would either arrive late or else park mid-route on the tracks for extended periods. Curious, at one point I kept a log of every ride I took for a month. Not a single one either departed or arrived on time.

What's a few lost minutes? Perhaps not much, though they do accumulate. But soon it became apparent that those minutes were symptomatic of something greater. In one short stretch in the early 2010s, a series of derailments in and around New York—not just Metro-North, but also Amtrak and freight lines—killed five people and injured dozens more. Mussolini supposedly made the trains run on time; we can't even keep ours on the tracks.

The coronavirus that swept the world in early 2020 similarly exposed a combination of rot and negligence that should shock America out of its complacency. How is it that an alleged great power, the richest nation in history, inventor of the A-bomb and the Saturn V, with eleven aircraft carrier battle groups and the world's most sophisticated industries, could find itself unable even to manufacture something as basic as medical masks? Eight weeks into the crisis there was still a mask shortage. Our sophisticated supply chains struggled to find a way to meet demand. How hard can it be? Apparently, too hard for modern America. As President Trump used to say, "We don't win anymore."

Speaking of the Navy, in 2017 our fleet crashed or ran aground five of its ships, with fatal results in two cases—both of which the Navy later determined to be "avoidable." This is to say nothing of the aircraft crashes which also bedeviled the service that year.

A report on one of the ship crashes found that "[t]he crew was unprepared for the situation in which they found themselves through a lack of preparation, ineffective command and control, and deficiencies in training and preparations for navigation." The chief of naval operations further explained that "rising pressure to meet operational demands led those in command to rationalize declining standards . . . in fundamental seamanship" and that the crew responsible did not know "the basics of understanding the ship control console."

Did not know the basics of understanding the ship control console. I have no wish to cast aspersions against our brave sailors, the majority of whom no doubt (one hopes?) know what they're doing. But something is wrong here.

For decades, American society at all levels, across virtually all endeavors, has prioritized criteria other than know-how, skill, suitability, and even basic competence for placing persons into coveted, competitive positions—save, perhaps, for the choicest seats in ruling-class boardrooms.

For instance, when President Obama appointed Elena Kagan and then Sonia Sotomayor to the Supreme Court, the focus was all about what demographic boxes they checked. Justice Sotomayor herself described her approach to jurisprudence, and thereby justified her position on the bench, by declaring herself a "wise Latina"—that is, in terms of who she is demographically. By contrast, when Obama later nominated the white male Merrick Garland, he had to apologize to his base: "Yeah, he's a white guy, but he's a really outstanding jurist. Sorry." It's hard to say which conveys more about our ruling class and elite opinion: the "but" or the "sorry."

One could cite endless examples along the same lines. I shall leave it at just one more because it's so perfectly illustrative. In early 2020,

Washington governor Jay Inslee appointed Grace Helen Whitener to the state supreme court. News coverage was ecstatic:

> Whitener is a disabled black lesbian who immigrated from Trinidad. She joins Inslee's two other appointees: Raquel Montoya-Lewis, a Jewish Native American who previously served on tribal courts, and Mary Yu, an Asian-American Latina lesbian who officiated the first same-sex marriages in the state.

Are they "outstanding jurists"? Who cares! Though, to be fair, as the left defines "outstanding jurist," they surely are: they can be counted on always to rule the correct way.

The left's response has always been to assert that when the privileged are left to their own devices, they hire and promote only their own, deliberately excluding the deserving from other demographics. No doubt there is something to that; one doesn't even need to believe in omnipresent racism to accept that a part of human nature prefers the familiar and that this preference can override considerations of merit.

But for the left, strict scrutiny to ensure that individual bias not be allowed to act unfairly is not enough. They go much further and insist that know-how, skill, suitability, competence, and the like are just smoke screens to perpetuate privilege and exclude the disfavored. "Affirmative action" must be taken to ensure that the formerly disfavored become favored. And let no one think, or even suggest, that this entails hiring or promoting the un- or underqualified. No, there are scads of perfectly qualified—better qualified!—people out there who will excel in these roles if only given the chance, and the only way to give them a chance is to force the power structure to hire them because otherwise it wouldn't. (Suspend disbelief for the present and ignore the fact that the most prestigious institutions in America—from Harvard to Google to Goldman Sachs to the *New York Times*—not only don't need to be forced to emphasize demography in hiring and promoting; they require no encouragement whatsoever.)

In other words, it's win-win. We can admit, select, hire, promote, and honor people based on group membership, the focus on which over and above know-how, skill, suitability, and competence carries no costs or trade-offs whatsoever. We can have it all.

Can we? Consider the case of the Fire Department of the City of New York (which incidentally lost 343 of its members in one day on 9/11). As in California, in New York a job as a firefighter is one of the most coveted—especially by working-class men—in all the civil service. It's also especially demanding, both physically and mentally. To assess potential candidates' fitness according to the latter metric, the FDNY administers a test every few years. In prior years, the exam focused on extremely complex and arcane questions about firefighting knowledge, both to encourage applicants to study hard and to identify the strongest candidates.

The problem, according to the left, was that too many from the wrong demographic category and too few from the correct ones were passing. Those who did pass might have made "outstanding firefighters," but that wasn't the point. The (Republican!) Bush administration—which was defined by its response to 9/11—therefore sued the FDNY for "disparate impact discrimination" and found a simpatico federal judge to throw out those old tests and order up a new one, which was made so easy that 97 percent of all who took it passed.

Maybe the test was biased, as the Bush Justice Department, Judge Nicholas Garaufis, the "Vulcan Society" (of black firefighters) and their lawyers at the Center for Constitutional Rights, and the New York City Law Department all alleged. Maybe there's something inherently discriminatory about asking potential firefighters questions about firefighting and hiring them in part based on whether or not they know the answers. Maybe rewriting the test so that it instead asks them how to lay tile and measures their reading comprehension by having them summarize the contents of an aspirin label will have no adverse impact whatsoever on the quality of firefighting.

Or maybe there's a more direct connection between firefighting knowledge and success as a firefighter, and over time—as firefighters who took the old tests retire while those who took the new tests rise through the ranks—the FDNY will become less effective. Either way, New Yorkers are going to find out.

Every single one of us knows someone smarter and simply better at certain things than we are. Common sense suggests that allowing such people to rise as high as their talents will take them will benefit us all, and society itself.

Increasingly, however, American institutions prioritize factors other than qualifications. The ruling class have (while in part exempting themselves) placed a giant bet that this focus will not erode the overall competence and functioning of institutions that hire on such bases, or, eventually, of society itself. Either that or the bosses know otherwise but believe the inevitable costs are bearable and worth paying.

One wonders, though. Minneapolis has a large Somali population but, according to the city's powers that be, too few Somali police officers. So it set out to hire some. One of the new hires was a man named Mohamed Noor, who, according to the Minneapolis *Star Tribune*:

> was flagged by two psychiatrists during the pre-hiring evaluation in early 2015 after he exhibited an inability to handle the stress of regular police work and unwillingness to deal with people. . . . Noor was more likely than other police candidates to become impatient with others over minor infractions, have trouble getting along with others, to be more demanding and have a limited social support network.

He was hired anyway, and in 2017 shot dead Justine Diamond, an unarmed, barefoot, pajama-clad forty-year-old Australian lady who had called 911 to report hearing a woman's screams. It's hard to dismiss that particularly unfortunate bit of hiring as exactly "cost-free," much less as evidence that there are no inherent drawbacks to focusing on criteria other than suitability and competence.

Minneapolis looks to be on the verge of solving this particular problem by abolishing its police force. To say the least, that solution doesn't "scale up."

For the foreseeable future, America will still have institutions. But if the elite bet is wrong, then what we are likely to get, society-wide—starting in government but slowly spreading through the private sector, with the last holdouts being the tech companies and investment banks—is a sort of civilizational mega-DMV. Slow. Rude. Incompetent. Immense. Expensive. Arbitrary. Not merely unproductive but anti-productive. And, all too often, armed.

The Superpower Conundrum

When we consider America's "place in the world" and that place's relationship to ruling-class power, prestige, and position, two very large questions arise. First, to what extent does the stability of the regime—and the ruling class's position in the catbird seat—depend on the United States' status as a superpower? Second, to what extent does that status depend on a competent and coherent society with a united and patriotic population? To put the second question another way: is the ruling class vision of a deracinated economic-administrative zone conducive to or even consistent with America remaining a superpower over the long term?

Regarding the first question, we know from history that it's possible for a ruling class to exercise power and maintain their own predominance for a long time without their country itself enjoying anything like great-power status. But this typically occurs only in small(ish), isolated, and strategically marginal countries that geopolitical predators don't much care about. Any nation with something going for it typically has adversaries, actual or potential. Keeping them at bay and securing one's own interests requires some measure of military power and active engagement in international affairs.

But in the case of the contemporary United States, the calculus is complicated by the fact that this country is not merely a great power, nor even just a superpower, but the head and heart of an entire international system: the "liberal" or "rules-based" "international order." The wealth, power, and prestige of our ruling class derive in very large measure from their being the leaders of the world's leading country.

We have no precise, time-tested name for what, exactly, America is today vis à vis the rest of the world because no previous great power has ever operated as we do today. The word "empire," which many prefer, doesn't quite fit. Empire and imperialism are very specific things: rule over subject peoples by force or threat of force. If force were the decisive instrument of the "American empire," then Iraq and Afghanistan would be by far the most secure American imperial possessions today. It's also curious that our overseas allies no less than our domestic elites react with horror whenever Trump hints that he might reduce U.S. military commitments. This is hardly the response of cowering subjects straining under the yoke.

What the so-called "American empire" really is, then, is a voluntary alliance of neoliberal elites across nations to work together in their own interests, underwritten by American technological and financial might, backed up by the implied threat of American military force, and "legitimized" by an omnipresent propaganda barrage which insists that their cooperation benefits everyone. Note that the only truly "voluntary" parties to the alliance are the elites themselves; their peoples are rarely consulted and any objections they may raise are curtly overruled.

Members of this transnational ruling class all benefit from the current arrangement—and why wouldn't they, since they designed it in their interests?—which they all seem to understand cannot be maintained without a linchpin of sufficient size and power. The United States is, at present and for the foreseeable future, the only country other than China capable of fulfilling this role. Even before the coronavirus outbreak, the elites of no nation ostensibly within the "American empire" wanted to exchange American hegemony for Chinese. They want to even less now.

All this is to say: it's at least questionable whether our own ruling class (to say nothing of those of our "allies") could survive in power following the loss of America's preeminent (however precarious) global position.

Which leads to the second question: how long can a country that can't run a train or make surgical masks, that despises its past and antagonizes half its citizenry, sustain its position as global hegemon? How long can we maintain the technological and operational wherewithal and generate the necessary wealth?

Indeed, to what extent is the wealth necessary to maintaining our hegemony derived from that hegemony? Only a wealthy country can be the world hegemon, and being the world hegemon generates wealth. Which is more the cause of the other? Classical political theory holds that necessity gives rise to virtue, which enables societies to rise above poverty and use their strength to acquire empire, which makes them richer. If that's true, it would suggest that strength begets wealth more than the reverse, in which case American hegemony would seem precarious.

In the same vein, successful "empires" (at least so far) tend to depend on patriotic sentiment among their core citizens, especially those who form the backbone of the military. Hiring mercenaries can be a stop-gap for a while but is, over the long term, no substitute for a patriotic citizenry that directly benefits from their country's imperialism. It's not easy to see how a country that lacks this can long maintain its leadership position in the "world community."

Few elites in history (if any) have thought more highly of themselves and of their right to rule than ours. But in the same breath that they insist on their own personal superiority, they condemn the country they lead. To the ancient Romans or the Victorian Britons, the superiority of the ruling class and the superiority of their society were inseparable. Rome and Britain were great because Romans and Britons were great, and vice versa. Our elites, by contrast, love themselves but hate their country. Is that a recipe for long-term world domination?

If America is an "empire," then the foundations of our imperial rule can be traced to our victory in World War II, subsequent construction of the so-called "liberal international order," and leadership position—and apparent victory—in the Cold War. To say the least, all of these things (and many more) were accomplished by unabashedly proud, patriotic, unhyphenated Americans who were backed up by a fundamentally patriotic, confident, and united citizenry: ordinary people who did the work, produced the wealth, and supplied the soldiers. To what extent are the present American hegemons—who not only have no such support but openly despise ordinary Americans and their unsophisticated flag-waving—living off that prior success, spending down accumulated capital?

Roughly speaking, one joins the military as a job, or out of a sense of patriotic zeal—motivations not, of course, mutually exclusive. Patriotic zeal is far more likely to spur one to volunteer for a combat unit. The fact that thousands still do volunteer for such service every year, despite no evident threats of invasion or the like, is a testament to the enduring strength of American patriotism, but also a reason to wonder how long before this inherent patriotism begins to crack under constant reminders of elite disdain. How long before potential soldiers ask themselves whether fighting endless, constabulary wars in the Third World is "patriotic" or even "in the national interest," much less in their own or their families' personal interest and then decline to sign up?

"Becoming Brazil"

The argument that America is becoming a northern Brazil has been batted around for at least a decade.

The particular features of Brazil meant are: large; relatively rich but no longer the world's economic center; no longer the world's top technological innovator either, but also not a backwater (Brazil has Embraer!); very high wealth inequality; a tiny and shrinking middle class; pockets of extreme poverty far larger and more numerous than the historic American norm; ethnically diverse with no clear demographic majority but, roughly speaking, a European-descended upper class ruling over masses of poor people of other races; lower-trust with less social capital than America today, and certainly less than pre-1960s America; more crime, poverty, and general dysfunction; yet still, on the whole, in the top quintile or maybe even decile of countries, but no longer a great power, much less a superpower or hegemon.

Some make this argument as a warning. Others offer it as reassurance: see, Brazil is not that bad, hence our future won't be so bad!

While perhaps compelling as a prediction of America's future domestic, social, and economic structures, one must wonder if this analysis doesn't nonetheless fall short. For it seems at least plausible that Brazil's success, and that of many other countries, depends in decisive respects on the presence and backing of a friendly hegemon with a high-functioning society, economy, and military. Right now, that's us, and has been for a long time.

If the real Brazil is only able to be "Brazil" under the umbrella of American power, what country will play the "American" role after America "becomes Brazil"? The answer would seem to be: China or no one. Either possibility could prove dangerous for the United States.

Call it what you will—"rules-based international order," "American empire," or "neoliberal hegemony"—American preeminence is far from wholly disadvantageous to ordinary Americans. The way it's been implemented and furthered lately certainly has been, but it doesn't necessarily follow that the voluntary or forced surrender of the country's leadership role, much less its power, would redound to the American peoples' benefit. A power vacuum in the wider world is likely either to result in chaos or be exploited by a hostile state—for the simple reason that there are at present no non-hostile states with sufficient strength to fill the void.

Think about the chief ways today's American foreign policy negatively affects ordinary Americans: their sons get killed in pointless wars, their government spends vast amounts of money which the people either pay for in taxes or see saddled onto their children and grandchildren as debt, and America makes foolish trade deals that impoverish their communities.

All of that could be stopped, even reversed, without the country weakening its military or surrendering its robust presence in the world. Indeed, if, through sound economic and trade policy, we are to redomicile key industries and supply chains and revive our manufacturing sector, we'll need a robust military (especially a navy) and a confident foreign policy for all the reasons Alexander Hamilton diagnosed more than two hundred years ago: to protect our economic interests, maintain our prosperity, and prevent the world's trade routes, sea lanes, and conduits of commerce from becoming prey to pirates (literal or national). Worse fates such as territorial loss are more distant threats, but in the rare instances when they do arise, they tend to follow lesser disorders. Preventing them does not require being "the world's policeman" but merely strength and vigilance.

Even today, when America makes too little and imports too much, our underemployed and underpaid populace is better off with their own military underwriting the economic regime that supplies and to some extent even feeds them. As bad, unequally beneficial, and narrowly focused as today's American hegemony is, it's more beneficent than either Chinese rule or global anarchy would be. That's not an argument for continuing current arrangements, merely against blithely throwing away power scrupulously built up over centuries.

But isn't that exactly what "becoming Brazil" entails? And isn't America becoming Brazil an oxymoron if being Brazil presupposes American hegemony?

Still, our elites seem to want an America that, domestically, looks more and more like Brazil but that, internationally, operates like America circa 1950 or 1990. It's at least an open question whether that's possible. They seem hell-bent on conducting the experiment.

Potential Consequences of the Ruling Class's Unstable Coalition

The most important reasons to doubt whether our rulers can keep what is now "America" going indefinitely are the fractured nature and competing interests of the leftist-ruling-class coalition.

Leftist politics are fundamentally about dividing up spoils. Leftists see this as zero-sum: whatever you're getting, I'm not getting. This is one reason why infrastructure is the very worst in the bluest, richest states. The left no longer holds to any conception of a common good. Hence in the areas they control, politics is all about who gets what, and public projects either don't happen, take forever, and/or are ruthlessly exploited by rent-seekers.

It's reasonable to expect similar trends across the board, that the country will get dirtier, crumblier, uglier, and less functional. Private accommodations (some of them anyway) will remain splendid, and in some ways may even improve as money pours in to further insulate the rich from the surrounding dysfunction. But it will cost a great deal to buy one's way out, and there will be no way to do so fully. Though I half expect, as the roads continue to get worse and traffic continues to intensify (in part because of continued mass immigration), that the rich will increasingly turn to helicopters.

Leftism not being able to understand or accept any limits, it attempts to satisfy all its constituencies with unrealizable and even contradictory promises. To paraphrase Nathan Glazer's description of New York City in the middle of the last century, our government will increasingly stop trying to do things that government can do well in favor of trying to do more and more things that government can't do at all. Services will be plentiful and ambitious but poorly executed, often incompetent. The evident disconnect between what people are promised—and what they're taxed to pay for—versus what's delivered will cause public discontent and cynicism to rise.

This points to another potential fissure in the leftist coalition. Tech and financial oligarchs have thus far found clever ways to massively reduce taxation on themselves. This forces their political allies to increase taxes dramatically on the middle class wherever they can. But sooner or later—especially if financialization, outsourcing, and immigration continue apace—the middle class will be bled out. There's already a lot less there to tax than there used to be. Sooner or later, the poorer elements of the leftist coalition will notice that the middle class is broke and no longer really exists, hence the only way to keep the party going is to massively tax the rich, or even expropriate wealth. Indeed, we can already see the beginnings of this in, for example, proposals from Bernie Sanders, Elizabeth Warren, and Alexandria Ocasio-Cortez. Prior to the 2020 regime crisis, financial and tech elites seemed firmly in control and able to prevent this fissure from opening up wide. Their control is clearly more tenuous now. At any rate, those with the most at stake are the well-salaried professional classes, whom the poor-left will insist are "rich" and whom the left-oligarchs would prefer to stick with the entire bill by jacking up income taxes or raiding 401(k)s, 529s, and the like. But at least half that class is blue and might not want to go broke in the name of "justice."

If, on the other hand, blues can agree on—and stick to—an informal power-sharing arrangement, things might go more smoothly, and the regime could last longer. Under such a system it will be understood that every group gets a turn and that whoever is in power is obligated to work for the concerns of other groups. One interesting question is: under the rules of "intersectionality," will a president who checks more than one box count as a "turn" for all the groups "xe" represents? It seems doubtful that intragroup competition will be that easily resolvable.

In any event, such an arrangement can work only if and as long as the left-coalition's constituent members resist turning on one another. Some groups will undoubtedly feel more deserving—because more presently and historically victimized—than others. They may not rest content with the number or duration of the "turns" that the power-sharing arrangement allots them.

Multiple incidents in June 2020, when black activists demanded random whites to bow down to them, and were obeyed—when masses literally prayed to fellow citizens for the forgiveness of sins they hadn't committed but which they believe are inherent in their biology—suggest who will insist on being on top in the new hierarchy.

Such a diverse coalition, placed under the permanent charge of only one of its constituencies, which by itself cannot command even close to a majority, might be inherently unstable. But in an intellectual climate that elevates victim status to the highest moral good, it's hard to see how and on what grounds the other elements of the coalition could justify, even to themselves, retaking power from those above them on the intersectionality totem pole.

CIRCUMSPECTION AND RESTRAINT?

We must now consider two related questions—the first general, the second specific—whose answers could have decisive effects on the stability of the regime and therefore its longevity.

First, do any of our elites understand or agree with any of these reasons for doubt and, if so—whether out of prudence, self-interest, altruism, or some combination—might they tap the brakes?

Ultimately, there are only two ways to hold the current ruling coalition together: generate and distribute enough spoils to keep everyone happy, and stoke the constituent parts' common resentments.

The more that the former can be accomplished, the less necessary is the latter. The more the latter is allowed free reign, the more difficult it is to do the former. Since the left as yet lacks sufficient power to enact redistribution on the scale it says it wants, it has of late focused on stoking hatred, which we saw massively intensify since the beginning of Obama's second term, then intensify again at the beginning of Trump's first, and take a quantum leap forward in the spring of 2020 that shows no signs of slowing down.

It's a chicken-or-egg question whether the left elaborated the Narrative in order to unite its coalition, or if its coalition is united by a joint belief in the Narrative. Ultimately, it doesn't matter because the dynamic is likely to play out the same either way.

The priority for whoever truly believes the Narrative must be to take back what she's certain is rightfully hers. Thus we should not be surprised to see redistribution soon attempted at a scale never experienced in any modern Western country. That, at any rate, is where the logic of leftism leads. Only time will tell if the left has the wherewithal and the stomach—the courage of their convictions—to follow through. But it's not unreasonable to fear that the combination of seething resentment and the fiscal pressures of their utopian dreams will get them there sooner or later.

Should that happen, and if any of the laws of economics are actually true, then certain consequences must follow. With incentive structures overturned, GDP and standards of living must fall—and not just for those paying the bills but also for those collecting the checks. Innovation may perhaps not screech to a halt, but it will decline. What one wag called "the great stagnation" that we are currently undergoing may, in hindsight, seem like a golden age.

If, and as, society shifts from healthy competition into a group-versus-group spoils system, our level of civilization—measured by education, culture, technological progress, and basic competence at ordinary tasks—is likely to regress, not merely stagnate. Trust will plummet. No longer a nation in any sense but a conglomeration of disparate peoples out to get one another, we will become poorer, less accomplished, less cooperative, and more backward.

That doesn't necessarily imply or demand a collapse. History is replete with examples of nations and empires that endured a slow burn of accumulated social, cultural, political, civilizational, and economic capital and nonetheless lasted for centuries. The ne plus ultra example must be the Eastern Roman Empire, which stretched on for a millennium despite its inherent weakness. Indeed, the Byzantines also provide the supreme example of an elite content to watch their empire decline all around them so long as they remained top dog during the ride down. Whether that's possible in the American case is an open question, and in any event we all know how that other empire ended.

Yet some in our ruling class might foresee this outcome and seek to forestall it. What if, rather than trying to socially and culturally Manhattanize the entire country, they instead eased back and allowed red states, counties, towns, and people to remain red? You know, to pray openly, own guns, and segregate public bathrooms by sex. Refrain from unleashing torrents of national media hatred on innocent high school boys. Cease resettling foreign refugees far from the homes of those whose consciences demand they be admitted to the country. And, while they're at it, end the practice of relocating into red communities the urban underclass who happen to live on real estate that big-city builders are salivating to redevelop.

The Ottoman Empire practiced something like this: the "millet system," under which many of its very different ethnic and religious groups were permitted to govern themselves semi-autonomously. Obviously, such subjects had no control over foreign or military affairs, nor most aspects of internal security, and they had to pay taxes and obey all the major state laws. But in much of their everyday lives, they were free to organize their communities, practice their faiths, and resolve disputes as they chose. And many of those people, despite not professing the faith of their rulers, were nonetheless eligible for prestige positions in the central government.

Could our ruling class find it within themselves to tolerate something like this for the despised peoples of the hinterlands? They already allow kids from the sticks to flee their dreary homes for the brighter vistas of the blue coasts—provided they prove their worth by getting into an elite school. But can our elites stomach letting those who want to be left alone in the hinterlands govern themselves?

The answer to that depends in part on whether they can control their shock troops, who, inquisitor-like, will insist on meting out just punishment to heretics. For their own good, of course. Can they? All I'm willing to say confidently is that the ruling class hasn't yet tried. That could be from indifference, neglect, disinclination, fear, or underlying agreement with the leftist program. Probably all of these play a role—though we must amend that last one to *partial* agreement. The ruling class likes the aggressive social engineering but, as Bernie Sanders's fate illustrates, they don't like topsy-turvy redistribution. They seem also to love the propaganda—they certainly push it enough—but it's possible that eventually some of them will look in the mirror and realize that they, too, might be targeted by those it riles up.

How Long Will They Keep the Borders Open?

The acid test of whether the ruling class has a moderate bone in its collective body, and whether it has the will or the wherewithal to rein in its wokest vanguard, is whether it will ever take steps to curtail mass immigration.

The core purpose of mass immigration for the left specifically (as opposed to the ruling-class passion for cheap labor) is demographically to overwhelm red America so that, first and foremost, no Republican can ever win the presidency again and, second, the Republican Party becomes irrelevant in as many states, counties, and cities as possible.

The left is very close to accomplishing task number one. Indeed, their 2016 tantrum arose in part because more than a decade of talk of the "Emerging Democratic Majority" had convinced most of them that they already had achieved it. To learn otherwise, at the hands of Donald Trump of all people, was the shock of their lives.

One could argue that, once the left's lock on national power is assured, continuing to mop up resistance in every little red hamlet would be a waste of resources. One might also ask of our oligarchs: at what point would wages be low enough? Greed is powerful to be sure, but once the American population hits, say, four hundred million, might the bosses and the banks concede that yet another fifty basis point cut in their payroll outlays is no longer worth the diminishing marginal returns?

One could also argue that, past a certain point, not only would further immigration be unnecessary *for* the left, it would also be harmful *to* the left. It would make their own coalition more unstable; it would dramatically raise the cost, already quite expensive, elite blues incur to insulate themselves from disorders and inconveniences; it would further overwhelm America's already massively overstressed infrastructure and social services; and it would make the country, the economy, and society overall poorer, more atomized and balkanized, less united, less innovative, less productive, less law-abiding—and hence less able to deliver the goods domestically or maintain leadership internationally.

On the other hand, should an immigration moratorium be enacted, incomes and quality of life would likely stabilize—granted, at a far lower level than the middle class enjoyed a generation ago, but mere stabilization would help steady and extend the life of the regime itself. Such metrics might even improve slightly as one of the key downward pressures is removed.

Is there anyone in the ruling class who understands this and might be ready to declare "Mission Accomplished"? Certainly, there doesn't appear to be anyone who fits that description now. But this lack might be attributable to uncertainty that total victory has yet been achieved, and thus an unwillingness to take any chances. A few years down the road, might an awareness emerge that enough, finally, is enough?

Yet there will be powerful countervailing forces. The leftist desire for mass immigration, while at root cynical and self-interested, is couched in highly moralistic terms in which the left's shock troops devoutly believe. Therefore, should the ruling class ever conclude that it's time to cut off the flow, they're going to face massive resistance from their own base.

Which path is chosen will carry grave consequences. Keeping the border open will further erode quality of life for all but the immigrants themselves and the very richest, who will continue to have to buy their way out of the consequences with gated communities, private travel, private security, and the like. They already do that, of course, but the practice will have to intensify. Expect the super-elites' private security to act as a law unto themselves and not to be punished for whatever extra-legal violence they commit to protect their clients. Meanwhile, in a more anarchic and violent future, those reds who remain in blue areas with "defunded" or even abolished police departments will more and more find themselves in situations in which self-defense is necessary—but the regime will punish self-defense by reds against blues even as it refuses to enforce the law in other respects.

Keeping the borders open long-term will also, sooner or later, harm the left's clerical class, its low-six-figure urban wordsmiths and paper-pushers who already can barely afford a two-room condo in a blue metro. Without that class, the rulers' grip on power becomes precarious.

Even more important: that clerical-propaganda caste is mostly made up of the ruling class's own children—you know, the ones who didn't get in to Harvard or Stanford, or if they did, didn't make it to Goldman or found a Silicon Valley unicorn. The elite pyramid only has so many spots at the top; yet, like the second sons of dukes, also-rans have to be found places that befit their birth. Plus it helps bolster class solidarity to keep all these regime-maintenance positions—even the lower-status, lower-paid ones—entre nous.

Up to now, neither mass immigration nor any of the other policies that have gutted Middle America have much affected the ruling class's own children. White boys looking for their first job out of Bowdoin aren't applying at Iowa hog farms. Central American immigrants haven't thus far much competed against Wellesley coeds for internships at Vox.

But their children are starting to. More to the point, they and their children transform urban—and increasingly suburban—neighborhoods and school districts in ways that the ruling class, their praise of "diversity" notwithstanding, find hard to look past when it comes to their own kids. It's not hard to imagine an America sufficiently transformed that maintaining caste from one generation to the next becomes extremely difficult, and eventually a matter in which chance plays the decisive role. The ruling class has absolutely no problem screwing over their fellow citizens; to the contrary, they seem to relish it. Will they be as willing to limit the future prospects of their own children and grandchildren simply to maximize their own material comfort well into their declining years? Will keeping three homes plus a pied-à-terre, each with its own staff, be more important than seeing thriving grandchildren embark on fruitful, productive lives? Will ours become the first upper class in the history of the world to be not merely uninterested in the caste-status of its own offspring but instrumental in lowering it?

One wonders how many of them quite realize what they're doing. Given that ours is supposed to be a "cognitive elite," you'd think at least some of them would have an inkling. Do any?

Whether the ruling class eases off the accelerator could be the single most determinative factor of our coming fate. The following chapter explores what may happen if they don't.

CHAPTER SEVEN

. . . And If They Don't

A widely repeated aphorism holds that anything that can't go on forever won't. Often this is said in a tone of hopeful fatalism, as an excuse for inaction: why exert oneself when inevitability will do all the hard work?

Here, though, I mean it merely analytically. And—to repeat—we don't know that the current regime is a thing that can't go on forever. Maybe it can.

But if it can't, then broadly speaking its end may have five causes. First, the unrealistic nature of the neoliberal project might bump up against natural limits while the ruling class refuses, or finds itself unable, to correct course. Second, the unstable nature of the oligarch-left high-low coalition could spark regime-ending infighting. Third, Republicans, red-staters, rubes, and other dissidents and regime targets might revolt. Fourth, some unforeseen catastrophe, natural or man-made, could topple the whole house of cards. Finally, it may be true that there is a tide in the affairs of men, and perhaps ours is ebbing out.

Since I expect to be accused of wishing for one or another of the possibilities sketched below, I may as well answer that charge now. My fondest political dream is for a restoration of the American constitutional order—an order under relentless attack by the left for decades and defended fecklessly (if at all) by the right. My purpose in this chapter (for the whole book, really) is to deliver a warning to anyone who will listen, in hopes of advancing such a restoration. But, specifically, to the ruling class: your selfish, immoderate, pedal-to-the-floor insistence on more, more, more of every aspect of your agenda, coupled with your obvious inability or unwillingness, on vivid display in May and June 2020, to control your most radical foot soldiers may soon crash the very regime over which you rule and from which you derive by far the most benefit. And to the "conservatives": your constant surrenders, retreats, sellouts, and backstabbings—your refusal to stand up for your voters, your country, or the Constitution that you claim to love—amount to material support for those you claim to oppose. If America's constitutional order is overthrown through your cowardice and incompetence, you will have earned and will deserve a lion's share of the blame.

CONSERVATIVE HEGELIANISM

One can hear the "conservatives" snicker incredulously. What is this madman talking about? Collapse? Civil war? Secession? Revolution? Foreign conquest? Those things don't happen anymore!

It's amusing to recall how conservative intellectuals scoffed when Francis Fukuyama published his immensely famous essay "The End of History?" back in 1989. Fukuyama, they assured us, offered nothing but warmed-over Hegelianism, the silly old discredited theory of an absolute moment when all of man's, and society's, fundamental contradictions are synthesized and resolved, when the triumph of liberal democracy becomes permanent, first in the West, then around the globe. The author and his essay became—and remain—punch lines of an endlessly repeated joke. Whenever anything of note happened in the world, conservatives could be counted on to cackle "Oh ho! But I thought it was the 'End of History'!"

They all owe Fukuyama an apology, for today the conservatives themselves peddle the very same argument. Every time they dismiss the mere possibility of fundamental change, of some history- or regime-altering event, they implicitly accept Fukuyama's thesis: that history has ended and American democracy is its culmination.

That conviction arises from a variety of sentiments, not all of them bad, including patriotism; belief in "American exceptionalism"; identification of America with the best regime; confidence in the superiority of democracy to all modern alternatives, especially fascism and Communism; America's military victory over the former and apparent political-economic defeat of the latter; Reaganesque "optimism"; and the spectacle, especially since the Second World War, of so many countries turning to democracy while so few turned away.

Love of one's own is natural and mostly admirable. Yet there is a kind of blinkered hubris—especially for intellectuals—in being so confident that human possibilities which have bedeviled mankind throughout history can never happen again. Not here, anyway. We're too good for that; beyond it!

How else to describe such "thinking" except as conservative Hegelianism? Perhaps this unconscious yet fundamental acceptance of the left's core presuppositions over the last three centuries—the equation of goodness with "progress," the belief that the future is always better than the past, and that the mortal enemy of salutary liberation is bigoted and injurious constraint—explains why "conservatives" have been so ineffective at fighting or even checking, much less defeating, their ostensible opponents.

Conservative Hegelians simply cannot imagine any future other than what we have now, except maybe a little better—you know, with lower marginal and capital gains tax rates. Sure, they admit that America has some problems, but none that another symposium, half-day conference, white paper, or at most a book can't solve. Some even take consolation from the left's insane zeal: they've surely gone too far now! If a thing that can't go on forever won't, then sooner or later leftism will end and life can revert to "normal." Which to the conservatives means 1985: a popular Republican president, low taxes, 4.2 percent GDP growth, a strong military, a less vulgar pop culture, religion seemingly honored—and every facet of the 1960s revolutions in place, unquestioned, inviolable. But the kind of epochal change recounted in the histories and biographies lining conservatives' bookshelves is, to them, unthinkable.

For those who insist on the fundamental importance of virtue, morality, piety, liberty, industry, enterprise, thrift, decency, modesty, courage, and so on to any functioning and long-lasting polity, this is an odd stance to take. We know that "conservatives" are not unaware that the left is now at least fifty years into a scorched-earth campaign against virtue, morality, piety, liberty, industry, enterprise, thrift, decency, modesty, and courage; they complain about it all the time! "Stand[ing] athwart history, yelling Stop!" etc. But they still seem to think all it will take is a tweak here or a tuck there for a time-machine DeLorean straight out of 1985's most popular film to charge forth from a cloud of vapor and return them to the golden age.

Yet if conservatism's professed account of human nature, of the nature of politics and society, is true, then our current ruling arrangement must eventually break against the rocks of natural limits. Even force couldn't maintain it forever. More to the point, if conservatism's account of human *virtue* is correct, then it's hardly reasonable to assume that those fifty-plus years of forced and voluntary degradation have taken no toll but have instead primed society for a swift restoration of Reaganism.

If, on the other hand, Wokemerica can go on for decades or centuries, then honest conservatives must contemplate the possibility that their professed philosophy has been wrong all along.

Yet it's worth thinking about what might happen if the conservatives' own initial criticism of Fukuyama was right. For if "History" has not ended, then it must be true that certain neglected possibilities remain . . . possible.

However improbable the possibilities discussed below may be, they are all nonetheless classic "black swan" events: low probability but high impact. Were any of them to occur, we'd suddenly be forced to think about their effects and implications. There's no harm, and potentially much benefit, in getting a jump on things by starting to think about them now.

The potential outcomes here sketched are not necessary mutually exclusive, though some plainly are. For instance, there cannot simultaneously be a blue and a red Caesar, and the country cannot both break up and stay together. But other possibilities may indeed overlap. One might, for instance, envision a regime with both a blue Caesar and red banlieues.

Finally, I do not claim these are the only possibilities. They're just the only ones I've thought of (so far).

THE BIG SORT, ACCELERATED

Around the turn of the millennium, journalist Bill Bishop coined the term "Big Sort" to describe how Americans were self-segregating—by city, community, neighborhood, religion, and even media consumption, especially news.

In Bishop's original analysis, the "sort" was mostly intraregional and granular—more a matter of where you lived within a given metro area or state than in which metro or state. But in more recent years, as America has become even more polarized, the sort has become more regional, more state-to-state. As blue states, counties, cities, and suburbs get bluer, people not fully down with the program increasingly decamp to red areas. Yes, a few red states are getting bluer, but that's mostly owing to immigration or to blues fleeing (say) California only to bring their voting patterns with them.

If the ruling-class-plus-Dem-left coalition is able to hold itself together and achieve national supremacy, it's likely to press its agenda, hard. In which case the "sort" would accelerate: blue zones would get bluer, and reds redder.

Should this more deliberate, more explicitly politically motivated "sort" really pick up speed, it's not unreasonable to expect the big blue cities to become more sharply class-divided as wealth gaps widen—the highest Gini coefficients in America are all in deep-blue metros—housing costs rise, and living standards decline. Anyone not a big winner in New America with the means and spirit to leave will be tempted do so. The blue middle class—which has, for half a century, been shrinking like cotton in boiling water—could soon be all but gone, barely remembered by the remaining oligarchs and their serfs.

Furthermore, should blue-city pols follow through on their threat to "defund" and even abolish their police departments, it's hard to see how that won't lead to rising crime and further middle-class flight. America already tried this experiment once before, only less radically, and it didn't go well. What reason is there to believe that pressing it further this time will have a happier ending?

What happens to blue America then? The left has long enjoyed imagining—and sometimes even attempts to stage—little morality plays along the lines of "A day without immigrants" and "What would America be like without [insert demographic category]?" The purpose, of course, is to highlight all the things we wouldn't have, all the work that would not get done.

Taking a page from their own book, it's also fair to ask: what would America, or parts of it, be like with no middle or working class? Judging from the left's rhetoric, their utopia will be stocked with app designers, webzine editors, diversity consultants, foundation grant-makers, ethnic studies professors, artists, writers, and activists. The wiser understand that allowances must also be made for bankers, executives, mergers and acquisitions lawyers, and venture capital partners to pay the taxes and donate to woke causes. Then there's the urban poor, whom metropolitan lefties consider necessary for delivering takeout and likes to virtue-signal over but otherwise doesn't much think about.

They don't think about the middle and working classes at all. But we can. Imagine vacuuming everyone from those classes completely out of, say, New York and San Francisco. Granted, that's largely already been accomplished, but next let's also sweep them out of Yonkers,

Massapequa, Hackensack, Richmond, Vallejo, Fremont, and so forth. Who's going to drive the trucks, stock the stores, fix the power and sewer lines, lay the internet cables, wire the server farms, raise the cell phone towers, pave the streets, and do all the other things necessary to keep metro areas running? Will bluetopias establish super-commuter rail lines to ferry the proletariat back and forth from red redoubts? How long will the high-low coalition be viable when there's no longer any middle to define, and unite, itself against and despoil?

It's reasonable to wonder if a city so constituted is sustainable, even if it's backstopped by surrounding suburbs. But what happens if and when it no longer is? The woke left could easily use its electoral lock to put the screws to the purple 'burbs, with taxation of course, but also with woke edicts to enforce compliance with the Narrative. Let's see your entire employee roster—and board composition, while we're at it—so we can reward or punish you based on how well you've measured up to our ideal of "diversity." How much did you and/or your business give to charity last year, and to which causes? If the answers are: not enough, and the wrong ones—time to pay.

BANLIEUES ROUGES?

The Big Sort will likely improve life in red America—at least for those who don't care about ocean views, pride parades, or modern art exhibitions.

For a while, at least. But once the left has total, permanent control of the federal government, two things will undermine that advantage over time. First, the Democrats will enact most of the policies long on their wish list. And many of those have, to say the least, not been designed with economic growth or quality of life in mind, except for those who get richer by making everyone else poorer and for those fleeing countries where poverty is endemic and intractable. If your frame of reference is two bucks a day, then even a declining America feels bountiful. For everyone else, living standards will go down, as higher taxes, "green mandates," diversity requirements, payoffs, and other pointless government diktats squeeze efficiency and innovation out of the economy and basic competence out of everything else.

Second, leftists are likely to see outlier practices in red states and counties as intolerable challenges to their authority. If you think federalism in bad shape now, just wait. Once the government is safely back in blue hands, the left will try to federalize everything and reduce state and local governments to mere shells, or federal satrapies. And given the left's overwhelming power, and the gargantuan power of the federal government itself, they're likely to succeed, at least in the short term.

This assumes, of course, that the country has not cracked up already (more on that below). One way it might stay formally and nominally together, but informally more separated, is by an intensified Big Sort combined with what I shall call "red-state banlieues." *Banlieue* is a French word that means, more or less, "inner ring suburb." However, the phrase has taken on a second, now dominant meaning: the suburban cinder-block districts ringing French cities where many ethnically non-French immigrants and their children live. Those *banlieues* tend to be very poor, lawless, and dangerous. Another phrase for *banlieue* in French is *zone sensibles*, or "sensitive zone." Which is to say, what we call in America a "no-go zone," as in, no-go for the police or other authorities. Something like that might emerge in red America.

Appalachia, the plains and prairies, the upper Midwest, the Mountain West, parts of the South, and the eastern parts of the Pacific Northwest tend to be more Christian, more observant, more conservative, and more rural than America as a whole—populated with people who, in Barack Obama's immortal words, "cling to guns or religion or antipathy to people who aren't like them or anti-immigrant sentiment or anti-trade sentiment as a way to explain their frustrations." For ease of reference, let's call such people "clingers."

Most of them already live in red states. Should the left achieve permanent dominance, more are likely to move to one. And many—I would bet a clear majority—are not merely politically conservative gun owners serious about their faith but are also wary of federal overreach.

Clingers have been told for decades that "immigration enriches America," not that "immigration ensures a permanent blue electoral majority." Indeed, they've been hectored that the latter is a "racist conspiracy theory" which, to mention, proves you're a racist conspiracy theorist. But once that permanent majority is in place—as it already is in several states—the left crows about it. "California's changing demographics will further doom Republicans," exulted one *Los Angeles Times* headline.

If and when national politics finally and irrevocably turns against the clingers, and the left inevitably rubs their noses in it, some red-staters may conclude that they've been cheated, lied to, and had their country stolen from under their feet. Their respect for blue authority—already not exactly fulsome—might collapse. Outside the blue strongholds, the legitimacy of the state could erode.

Some clingers might then be tempted to try secession. But what if their resistance began as something smaller, unplanned, almost a stimulus response?

Suppose a rancher in the Rockies grazed his cattle in defiance of a federal edict, or a fisherman inadvertently destroyed the hive of some "endangered" insect, or a pastor on an alkali flat broke quarantine with a Christmas service, or an anti-vaxxer mom refused to stop tucking her flyers under windshield wipers in the shooting range parking lot. Then postulate the bluest, wokest, angriest president you can, say, Kamala Warren Ocasio-Cortez. She—or her attorney general, EPA administrator, or HHS secretary—might regard one of these acts not merely as criminal rebellion against the United States government but as a personal affront.

It's not hard to imagine such an administration blundering into a Ruby Ridge or Waco-like fiasco. The first federal hammer blows would very likely fall swiftly, decisively, and without opposition. But after that? After some obviously unjustified and disproportionate use of force against civilians, would the clingers necessarily sit back and suck up whatever followed?

Maybe. But maybe not. It's at least possible that red America might quietly—at first spontaneously, but later perhaps through more explicit cooperation—start to make federal operations on their turf more difficult. It might (say) become inconvenient for an FBI or ATF or BLM agent to buy gas, or get table service in truck stops, or friendly smiles from motel clerks in the hinterlands.

Over time, unfriendliness might give way to passive and even (mildly) active obstruction. What if red America started implementing its own version of woke lockouts and de-platforming? Sorry, sir, our credit card machine is down, and we don't take cash! The feds might appeal for help to the local police and sheriffs, but whose side would they take?

One obstacle to any such coordinated action would be that the government and its social media allies—or the social media companies and their government lackeys; it's hard to say who's really in charge—would crack down hard on attempts to organize or share information. In an era in which Big Tech all but monopolizes communication, this factor might seem decisive. And yet cooperation and coordination existed before Facebook and Twitter . . . before Usenet, even! The ruling class perhaps should not count on its control of social media to prevent covert organizing, at least not while speaking and writing are still practiced and permitted.

In any case, suppose further that the clingers were to turn up the heat a little. Not wishing to resort to violence against persons, they might instead decide to increase the feds' feelings of unwelcomeness by taking full advantage of their states' and counties' open carry laws. No one breaks any laws or makes any threats, but the message is conveyed: go too far and anything might happen. That alone might prompt a federal pullback, the same way that, in the wake of the various Black Lives Matter triumphs across America since the early 2010s, police officers have all but abandoned certain neighborhoods—even whole cities—because the residents have made clear that cops are not wanted.

Or the clingers could decide to remind blue America just how dependent it is on the heartland. What if necessary products stopped being shipped, routine deliveries stopped being made? Some truckers have already vowed not to deliver to any city that kneecaps its police force. There's no reason why that kind of deliberate inaction couldn't be used for political purposes.

But enough of this. Potential examples are endless. The question is whether the clingers would do something—short of violence but beyond meek acquiescence.

The core reason a *banlieue* is a no-go zone is not because the police feel unwelcome but because they feel unsafe; and they feel unsafe not because they *can't* use force to defend themselves but because they're unwilling to. They're unwilling because those against whom they'd be defending themselves are members of what in our country are called "protected classes," that is, people whom the entire ambient culture— national and international—would rally to defend no matter what they might have done to make defensive force necessary.

To say the least, that dynamic would not prevail in the United States. Were federal officials to use force against clingers, the immediate response from the media, intelligentsia, and ruling class would be loud, exuberant cheering. One might assume that fact alone determines the outcome.

Yet there are reasons to doubt. Federal agents did, after all, voluntarily de-escalate the infamous "Bundy standoff" of 2014—a Nevada dispute between ranchers and the Bureau of Land Management. True, in a similar incident in 2016, federal officers shot and killed one protester, but that man was definitely armed and apparently reaching for his gun. Otherwise, for five weeks agents waited out the protesters, who eventually voluntarily surrendered.

Looking toward America's hypothetical future, it's at least possible that (1) an insufficient number of federal agents would feel comfortable using force to crush disobedience, especially if no one in their own ranks had been physically harmed; (2) depending on the scale and scope of the resistance, the task might become too large for law enforcement alone and require the use of the military, whose soldiers might be even less inclined to follow such an order; (3) even under sustained propaganda onslaught, the broader American population might not support using violence to enforce what they judge to be trivial infractions of unimportant laws; and (4) the powers-that-be might lose heart, either because they aren't certain their orders would be carried out or because they fear a potential backlash.

Even if said powers dared try a military solution, is it reasonable to expect the U.S. Army to occupy, pacify, and hold some large portion of the interior of the continental United States for an indeterminate period? This is a question both of will and capability.

As to the first, during 2020's woke riots, senior military officers came very close to open insubordination against the commander in chief over the issue of invoking the Insurrection Act and deploying troops to restore order to burning cities. They did so for a seemingly traditional reason: the military's historical reluctance to use force on American soil against American civilians. Granted, the brass is almost uniformly anti-Trump, and the woke riots (on some level at least) served the interests of the ruling class, of which the brass is an integral part. It's therefore conceivable that the generals might be more willing to follow an order to suppress the red countryside differently than one to pacify a blue metro. But would the rank and file? At the very least, the brass's barely concealed disobedience in 2020 set a precedent that might be hard to overcome.

Regarding capability, the American military is very effective at defeating enemy infantry and armor formations and at finding and destroying terrorist cells. But as its experiences in Afghanistan and Iraq demonstrated, it's much less effective at long-term occupation. And those are backward nations with populations, at the time our wars in each started, of about twenty and twenty-five million. How well would the military fare against its own much more numerous and sophisticated people? Even at twice, or five, or ten times the Army's present size—with all that entails for the federal budget, tax rates, the deficit and debt, to say nothing of troop quality—it's hard to see such an endeavor succeeding for any length of time.

It is thus at least possible to imagine red states and counties effectively carving out something like a millet system for themselves over and against federal opposition. Call it "federalism-or-else." The wiser and cooler among the ruling class might resign themselves to an informal understanding under which federal authority quietly, never explicitly, but unmistakably eases back from red America so long as no part of red America moves toward open rebellion or outright secession.

All this may sound far-fetched, but there are signs that the ruling class takes the possibility very seriously. Why else would they be so hair-trigger sensitive to any whiff of red dissent or disobedience? Why are pro-gun and anti-lockdown protests that take place without a single violent incident or even threat described as actually or potentially "terrorist" while mass looting, arson, and assault are consistently white-washed as "mostly peaceful"? I didn't coin this, but it's certainly apt for the times: leftist violence is speech; rightist speech is violence.

Why, also, has just about every federal agency acquired its own armed force? The non-military federal "army" has grown quite large. It's reasonable to ask whether there's a single bureaucracy left without guns. The Environmental Protection Agency? They're armed up, too. The National Institutes of Health? Them, too. The National Oceanic and Atmospheric Administration? Yeah. The National Zoological Park? You bet. I don't want to bore you with a list; suffice it to say, it takes more work to find an unarmed federal agency than one with its own private force. In 2019, the late Senator Tom Coburn revealed that the total number of armed personnel across all federal agencies had tripled since the mid-1990s and now exceeds two hundred thousand—more than the entire United States Marine Corps. Why do all these bureaucrats need weapons?

Apparently, authorities fear that unless they nip every instance of disaffection in the bud—quickly—civil disobedience may grow beyond limits which they can easily control without using force at a level they're not sure they can maintain.

DEM-LEFT CRACK-UP

The above, however, presumes that the present Dem-left coalition can remain united. It looks pretty strong now, to be sure. But a paradox of politics is that size and power can become disadvantageous. As every wily leader knows, complacency breeds division while fear of an external foe fosters cohesion. Dem-left predominance, should it be achieved, will stress their coalition's fault lines while unifying their smaller and weaker opposition.

To recap, there are only two ways the ruling class can hold its coalition together: generate and distribute enough spoils to keep everyone happy and/or stoke the constituent parts' common resentment of their perceived common enemy.

Each of these tactics has a potential sell-by date. What happens when the spoils dip below some threshold level, when the total amount available for distribution is no longer "enough"? Or if one or more groups don't think they're getting as much as they think they ought to have?

As to the second, once red America is demographically and politically powerless at the national level, the Democratic coalition could go the way of the Greek cities after the capture of Byzantium: no common enemy, no common cause. At that point, what's to keep the constituent groups together? They might conclude that they don't need to be in a single party anymore—especially not one led by upscale boomers.

What would a Democratic crack-up look like? One wants to hope for the best, for the reemergence of a politics based on rational economic, regional, and social interests. But given recent trends, plus the left's half century of incendiary rhetoric, it's safer to predict that the emerging new party system would be frankly and openly racialized. In a moral-political climate in which status is derived from suffering, real or alleged, it's hard to see the various groups agreeing on who has suffered the most and so deserves the top spot. It's much easier to envision one group insisting on its own claim's unassailability and being rejected by the others—not necessarily because the rest completely disagree, but simply because they don't want to resign themselves to permanent junior-partner status.

The result might be a mishmash of competing parties, none of which is able to command an electoral majority—whether the Electoral College survives or not. Are we going to settle every presidential election in the House, and always on a plurality of the vote? I suppose it's possible that a new majority party may emerge, but it's hard to see on what basis, around which issues or interests, it might form, especially given the Great Awokening's repeated hammer blows to the last remaining shreds of any common American identity.

What then? That is to say, what happens if the country becomes completely impossible to govern by means of electoral politics? Two undesirable possibilities that no one wants to think about might follow: (1) a formal attempt to split the country; or (2) an attempt by somone on one side or the other of our current divide to seize total power.

SECESSION

Most will immediately dismiss secession as impossible: it's not 1860, there's no single issue dividing the country, our differences are not as strictly sectional, the state governments aren't unified enough, the feds would never allow it, 1865 settled that forever, and so on.

Certainly, there are very grave obstacles to secession ever being successfully enacted in or by any part of the country. The Big Sort notwithstanding, blues and reds alike are widely scattered across a great deal of territory and still intermixed in many metro areas, especially suburbs. The relatively few places where reds form a clear majority tend to be sparsely populated and remote while the more developed red regions tend to have significant blue populations that won't want to break off from the blue coasts, especially not if doing so means placing themselves under red sovereignty. Blue interests still own or control large, valuable assets all over red America, including land, homes, buildings, factories, and other infrastructure; they will use all their power to prevent the loss of those assets or even one dime of revenue from them. Secession requires organization, which requires communication, which will be all but impossible as tech firms and their government clients censor the message. Reds and blues alike are all but certain to disagree among themselves about something or other, preventing the emergence of a unified movement on either side.

There are also, we are told, too many complicating factors, too many issues to determine and things to divvy up: land, water, contiguity, coastal access, commingled and cross-border assets, natural resources and mineral rights, the currency, the debt, and, of course, the military.

Plus, the federal government would do everything in its power to prevent, or halt, a breakup. As a political matter, no one in charge of a large territory with a big population, robust economy, and vast trove of resources ever wants to let any part of it go. Putin's famous lament that "the collapse of the Soviet Union was the greatest geopolitical disaster of the twentieth century"—still ritually denounced by liberals and conservatives alike—was in one respect nothing more than a restatement of this fact. Losing any part of America would lessen our elites' power and wealth, both at home and abroad, and they know it.

But "this can't work" is a different claim than "this won't be attempted." All kinds of long-term unfeasible projects get started because those who start them don't believe they're unfeasible. And not every endeavor that fails does so because it was unfeasible; human error, malfeasance, and bad luck can play decisive roles.

Even if secession were impossible, that fact alone would not necessarily prevent states, counties, cities, towns, or some combination from trying. Indeed, the overconfident assertion that "secession can never happen" may inadvertently give rise to secessionist sentiment. A ruling class—to say nothing of the ostensible "conservative opposition"—that admits no alternative to current arrangements and can't imagine how anyone else could either is more likely to keep the neoliberal pedal to the floor, causing interest to rise in a thing everywhere asserted to be "impossible." All the while, our elites won't even realize what's happening because they have no idea how flyover people think.

Secession, were it to arise, might begin from the left or the right. It might unfold amicably, or at least nonviolently, or lead to war, or something in between. It might go smoothly or cause considerable uncertainty, even chaos. Examples of all types abound, from the "Velvet Divorce" of Slovakia and the Czech Republic to the dissolution of the USSR, from the breakup of Yugoslavia to the partition of India and our own Civil War. All of which, and more, should be studied for the lessons they teach, although such lessons cannot be our focus here.

How Secession Might Begin from the Left

The most obvious trigger for blue secession would be if some rightist figure were to seize power: stage a coup, refuse to leave office after losing an election, extend his term beyond the constitutional limit, or something along those lines. Even if something like that were attempted, the blues would almost certainly quickly run the usurper out of power: coups are dangerous, difficult, and uncertain, and in the present moment blues control virtually every powerful institution in the country. But if somehow they could not stop a red seizure of power, there's no way the blue states would want to stay in *that* union.

Another possible trigger for blue secession might be another electoral "surprise" like 2016, but more shocking because more unexpected. Especially if the win came solely from the Electoral College, tied to a popular vote loss, a majority of blue America would likely not accept the outcome as legitimate.

Indeed, it's already hard to imagine blue America accepting a Trump win in 2020 on any terms whatsoever. If the election were not able to be overturned—in the courts, through boxes of "found" ballots, or by some other means—that alone might trigger "Calexit," followed by other states. The "state compacts" forged between contiguous groupings of blue states during the coronavirus crisis could form the nuclei.

But whenever it were to happen, should blue America once again find the federal government in the hands of a red president they despise and whose authority they do not recognize, and further find that they can't easily or immediately get rid of him, that could be the spark that causes some to say, "We're out."

How Secession Might Begin from the Right

Suppose, on the other hand, that a blue effort to remove a lawfully elected red president were to succeed. That president's red base would be as little likely to accept his removal as the blues had been to accept his election.

But possible triggers for red secession are numerous, and there's no reason to try to imagine them all. The basic dynamic would be blueto-pians continuing to force their will on red counties and states and getting more and more aggressive as time wears on. Then, at some point, a specific provocation breaks the dam of pent-up red resentment and prompts some to say, "To hell with this, we get nothing out of this marriage anymore; we want a divorce."

From there, some red-state legislatures, and perhaps red-county supervisors in blue states, might pass declarations of independence, cease to enforce many federal edicts, and even defy some of them outright.

Amicable Divorce?

Whichever side went first, would the other let them go? If blues filed the papers, red America's likely reaction would be "good riddance"—like re-education camp inmates watching a warden and his guards suddenly walk off the job. Some might worry about lack of access to the coasts, a relative paucity of deepwater ports, and losing connectivity to the massive wealth and productivity in blue America's richest zones. But I doubt that would be majority sentiment among the reds.

If red America attempted to split off from blue, the logic of the blues' elevated sense of self-worth should lead them to a similar conclusion: Just go, already! If red-staters are as dumb, poor, backward, and useless as the coastal elites like to assert, why should blue America want anything to do with them? Why not self-quarantine?

Yet as much as blue America hates red, I don't think they want to let their errant cousins go. They'd much rather tax, lecture, chastise, punish, and humiliate them. Also, blues intuitively fear that they can't run this thing on their own, that the blue metros are not quite as self-sufficiently independent of the red prairies as their boasting would have one think. On some level, leftism knows that it is parasitic on conservatism—just as vice is parasitic on virtue, incompetence on competence, consumers on producers, and disorder on order—which makes separation frightening to many leftist elites.

Perhaps the deepest reason, though, that blue America won't want to let red go is that the blues are hell-bent on punishing the reds. To the left, letting red America, or any part of it, go without forcing it to answer for its "crimes" would be fundamentally unjust. A bill is due, which must be repaid. Punishment is deserved and must be administered. Which, in practical terms, means redistributing remaining red wealth to blue constituencies.

One hopes, nonetheless, that if things ever were to come to that awful pass, both sides will be wise, calm, and moderate enough not to initiate a conflict. Our differences, while profound, are resolvable without recourse to force, if only those with real power can be coolheaded enough to step back from the brink. If they can't?

War!

The phrase "civil war" conjures up images of ordered lines of bearded, blue-uniformed infantry squaring off against equally orderly armies in gray. Here, finally, the "experts" get one right: while it's possible to imagine one or more state legislatures voting to secede, it's all but impossible to imagine any state or combination of states forming their own regular army to fight the U.S. military.

There are any number of reasons for this. To state only the most important, the older and richer a given society becomes, the less its people want to fight real wars, as opposed to Twitter combat or street theater. The more comfortable and retiring (not to say retired) a population gets, the less it wants to march off to battle, and the fewer young men it has to send. So a replay of Gettysburg is—thank God—almost certainly out.

That doesn't mean, though, that there can't be a conflict or that Washington would necessarily let erring brothers of either persuasion depart in peace. The ruling class knows it would be dangerous to let stand a challenge to its authority. One act of defiance unpunished leads to another and then another and, before you know it, the regime's authority collapses. The more fragile the regime—the falser and phonier its account of itself and of the world—the truer this is. Indeed, one reason the ruling class allowed—encouraged!—the woke riots of 2020 was precisely because they knew that the mayhem didn't challenge their authority but augmented it.

But supposing some states took the fateful step; how could Washington stop them? The most obvious means would be to use the military—at first the National Guard, and then, if those units proved insufficient, the regular Army and other units. D.C.'s hope would be to put down any insurrection swiftly, thereby avoiding protracted conflict and discouraging similar attempts elsewhere.

Two issues would determine the outcome: first, would the U.S. military follow such an order to the best of its ability, and second, how effective would resistance be?

To the first consideration, ordinary human compassion and patriotic attachment to fellow citizens may stay some soldiers' hands. In addition, many point out that since the military's combat troops (as opposed to its technicians and specialists) tend to come disproportionately from the country party, those troops in particular might be reluctant to operate against Americans whose cause they might find sympathetic. As to the second, many also note that red America is very well armed, acclimatised to the outdoors, and home to many current and former soldiers. Also, if and as red enlistments into the military decline, recruiters will increasingly be forced to draw troops from blue populations whose recruits don't tend to volunteer for combat roles. Over time, such a shift could make the military less desirous of performing its core mission, and less good at it. But thinking through these and other contingencies provides no clear answer as to what would happen, or who (if anyone) would win, or at what cost. There are ample reasons supporting any number of hypothetical outcomes. No one, therefore, should feel confident that he has any idea where such a conflict might lead.

One possibility that's easy to envision, however—if for no other reason than that it's been depressingly common throughout history and around the world—is protracted insurgency warfare that leaves few parts of the country unscarred. Does anyone want *that*?

CAESARISM?

One way the United States might remain together with its current territory and population after the collapse or breakdown of neoliberalism is by means of Caesarism. Caesarism is a particular form of one-man rule: halfway, as it were, between monarchy and tyranny. It is monarchical in that a single person rules. It is tyrannical in that there is no appeal; Caesar's word replaces constitutionalism and even, in the final analysis, law.

Yet in the most precise sense, Caesarism is not tyranny, which, strictly understood, is a regime that usurps a legitimate and functioning government. The other, more common, understanding of "tyranny"— cruel and oppressive rule—arises from the strong correlation of the latter with the former: usurpers are more apt than legitimate princes to be cruel and oppressive. Some Caesars are oppressive, but many are not, and cruelty is not inherent to Caesarism.

Caesarism is a form of absolute monarchy, but unlike the classic conception of monarchy, it is not—at least not at first—legitimated by time and tradition. Yet neither, according to the classical framework, is Caesarism wholly illegitimate. Caesars assume responsibility for a government that no longer functions. We may define Caesarism, therefore, as authoritarian one-man rule partially legitimized by necessity.

That necessity is the breakdown of republican, constitutional rule—or, if you want it put bluntly, the corruption of the people. A nation no longer capable of ruling itself must yet be ruled; only dogmatic libertarians look forward to anarchy, and none have yet found a way to make it work.

The benefits of Caesarism to Caesar are obvious; to a nation, perhaps less so. But some who see certain features of Caesarism as advantageous might therefore conclude—however wrongly or mistakenly—that their best option is to work toward such a problematic regime. Those features thus deserve a cursory review.

The first and most fundamental is that Caesarism can hold together a country's existing territory and assets. Breaking up is hard to do, and dangerous when it happens to nations. Smaller countries tend to be weaker, with smaller manpower pools from which to draw their militaries and tax bases with which to fund them. When a big state breaks up into two or more states, especially if the cause is internal enmity, the successors sometimes go at each other's throats. Another possibility is that the territory formerly secured by the now defunct big state suddenly becomes a playground for such meddling. A fractured United States could open up the North American continent to foreign adventurism for the first time in more than two centuries. Whether and how America's historic enemies and current rivals might take advantage are open questions, but it stretches credulity to think that they wouldn't at least salivate at the prospect.

Caesarism also provides continuity and thus stability, or at least the greatest measures of each possible in a post-constitutional situation. Revolutions, regime changes, and breakups are usually messy. One priority of Rome's early Caesars, especially Augustus, was to preserve nearly all Roman forms and institutions so that the average citizen's daily life scarcely changed, and arguably even improved.

That's because Caesarism sometimes, though not always, offers the prospect of avoiding conflict. It may be sad to witness a proud old republic surrender its liberty to the rule of one, but if the alternative is bitter and bloody civil war, it becomes more difficulty to condemn such a transition out of hand. Caesarist wars, when they occur, tend to be dynastic rather than ideological or partisan, and thus briefer and less destructive than protracted civil conflict. The original Caesars had to fight to take (or keep) power, but they mostly fought the professional armies of their rivals. With the notable exception of Sulla's proscriptions, civilians were barely scratched in the Roman shift to Caesarism.

Finally, Caesarism tends to engender calm, especially when it follows a long period of civil strife and enmity. "Calm" is, to be sure, at best an attenuated substitute for true republican concord and common purpose. But when the latter are irretrievably gone, calm is preferable to open acrimony and vituperation. In Rome (other examples could be cited as well), when partisans on both sides understood that politics had ended, in the sense that there was nothing left for factions to contend over because all good things were the grant of Caesar, strife mostly melted away.

One also might point out that Roman civilization peaked under the original Caesars. The late classicist and historian J. Rufus Fears reminds us that under the reign of those Machiavelli called the "five good emperors," technology, affluence, and quality of life for the average Roman citizen rose to levels not enjoyed again until the twentieth century. Nearly all the glories of Roman culture, too, were produced in this period.

Against all this is the loss of liberty, which is stupendous indeed. But Caesarism is never a choice made for its own sake—except by Caesar. When and where Caesarism comes, it arises only because liberty is already gone.

How Caesarism Is Established

How does Caesar come to power? The simplest answer is: however he can; Caesars find a way. But Machiavelli provides a more detailed explanation:

Principality is caused either by the people or by the great, according to which of these sides has the opportunity for it. For when the great see they cannot resist the people, they begin to give reputation to one of themselves, and they make him prince so that they can vent their appetite under his shadow. So too, the people, when they see they cannot resist the great, give reputation to one, and make him prince so as to be defended with his authority.

The "people" are the common people, or multitude, while the "great" are the upper class, whether aristocracy or oligarchy. "Principality" here is a euphemism for one-man rule but—as the context makes clear—asserted or granted rather than inherited. The context also posits a level of conflict between the people and the great which presupposes the breakdown of political rule.

The people and the great are natural adversaries: the latter tend to prey on the former. A monarch tends to take the side of the people against the great, for a king and the surrounding nobles are also natural adversaries: the nobles threaten the king's rule in ways the people can't, and don't aspire to. A monarch teaming up with the people against the nobility is the original, and archetypal, "high-low coalition against the middle."

But applying this analysis to our own situation, we immediately see a difference. In the present, divided America there is not one multitude but two: one blue, the other red. Yet there's only one ruling class, to which the blue multitude is allied. Still, the underlying dynamic remains intelligible within the traditional framework. It's clear, for instance, that the blue upper class behaves toward the red multitude exactly the way that aristocracies always behave toward the common people—haughtily and rapaciously—and that the red multitude has exactly as much affection for the blue nobles as people always have for their alleged "betters."

In our case, the blue coalition has the upper hand; it's in charge and is thus less likely to turn to Caesarism. But were the blue multitude to conclude that the ruling class had become too weak to protect or benefit it, or were the ruling class to become afraid of a "Red Menace," that could change.

Still, it's the reds—under constant rhetorical, political, and, increasingly, physical attack, especially in blue states—who are more likely to turn to a Caesar. The woke riots and their aftermath were seemingly tailor-made to illustrate how such a dynamic builds steam. What happens when enough people conclude that the state either won't protect them or actively sides with those trying to harm them? They "give reputation to one and make him prince so as to be defended with his authority."

That still leaves the question of the formal mechanism. The two most common ways a Caesar comes to power are by military coup and by winning office legally and then refusing to give it up when his term ends, or maneuvering things in such a way that he's begged to stay.

Fortunately, a military coup seems unlikely in America. The chief elements that made them frequent occurrences in the ancient and early modern worlds—the immense prestige and wealth of conquering generals, the long durations of their commands, their ability to secure soldiers' personal loyalty by distributing spoils, a populace accustomed to military rule—don't apply here.

Yet I suppose we must admit the possibility that neoliberal oligarchs, if someday fearful that the electorate may decide it no longer wants to spend trillions on overseas conflict of dubious benefit to the nation, could try to install in power a compliant general or admiral with a loyal following within the military. It might not even be hard to find some four-star willing to go along: the brass's response to the woke riots made clear where their sympathies lie. Whether the thing could be pulled off is another matter.

As for the other mode, the instant you hear someone float the idea of repealing, or even "reforming," the Twenty-Second Amendment, you'll know that Caesarism has moved from theoretical possibility to someone's plan. Lawful repeal through actual constitutional means would be hard—the Constitution is difficult to amend by design—but Caesars don't tend to respect constitutional principle. The objection, which I half expect to hear offered seriously, that "the courts would never allow that!" is therefore irrelevant. The mere possibility of Caesarism presupposes a degeneration of politics well below levels at which laws and courts are obeyed. Caesar's contemptuous reply to the courts would echo Andrew Jackson's: you've made your ruling, now let's see you enforce it.

The other thing to look out for is increasing dynasticism—which is happening even now. In 2016, America was one electoral shock away from seeing four out of five consecutive presidencies held by only two families and had already endured three in succession. I don't have much to say in praise of Barack Obama, but at least his 2008 primary victory prevented it from being a certain four in a row.

Who Gets to Be Caesar?

"Who's in charge?" and "What does he want?" are the questions that define any one-man regime. All Caesars, to a greater or lesser degree, rule for their private good. What differentiates them is, first, whether that's their only motivation; second, if not, what is/are the other(s)?; and third, in what mixture?

The best motive for ruling is to secure the common good. Some Caesars in fact do look after the common good, though never without feathering their nests and rewarding their family and friends. To expect zero personal corruption from a Caesar is ridiculous.

Tyrannical oppression, though, is not necessarily a given. Kleptocrats are common enough throughout history and tend not to embrace brutality for its own sake, though their actions against real and perceived enemies can be hair-trigger.

Ideology is a different story. There were plenty of bad Caesars in the ancient world—some of them even "monsters" in Montesquieu's phrase—but none were ideological. As Jeane Kirkpatrick explained in her landmark 1979 article "Dictatorships and Double Standards," tyrants who act from ideological zeal are crueler than those who abuse power for purely private ends. The former also tend to be destructive of their nations' history, culture, traditions, and accumulated social capital while the latter are not. Since America's present divide is as much ideological and cultural as social and economic, there are sound reasons to fear an ideological Caesar.

Blue Caesar

A blue Caesar would not necessarily be ideological, however. Among blue elites are at least as many entitled technocrats as true-believing Wokerati—think Michael Bloomberg versus Elizabeth Warren.

Life under the former kind might not even be so bad, so long as you never, ever challenged Caesar's power or croaked out a word of dissent. Otherwise, the weed would be dank, the porn free, and—for those self-disciplined enough to avoid such vices and able to make it in banking or tech—the restaurants exquisite and the financial markets robust. Liberated from the necessity of appealing to woke Democratic primary voters, a Bloomberg-like Caesar might even revert to form and enforce the law and clean the streets.

Woke Caesar would be an entirely different matter. Just imagine all the worst, most destructive, irrational, vindictive, and punitive atrocities and absurdities you've witnessed in 2020, double them, then double them again, then add a few heaping layers of state-directed persecution—and you might be halfway there.

The main check against the emergence of blue Caesar (of either flavor) is the fractured nature of the blue coalition. The original Caesar's base all shared, more or less, a similar profile: Latin-speaking Italic peoples who worshiped the same gods and had more or less the same habits and culture.

Not so of "diverse" America. The fundamental obstacle facing any potential blue Caesar is that the leaders of any group to which Caesar does not personally belong will protest the prize going to someone not one of their own. One reason to suppose that elective monarchy—taking turns in office—might have some staying power is that under such a regime, all groups have an incentive to prevent any of the others from installing a Caesar.

Would such divisions be enough to prevent the emergence of a blue Caesar altogether? Perhaps not, if reds ever gained enough strength that blues concluded they had no choice but to turn to a Caesar of their own. Should blues achieve an unassailable electoral majority, the near-term political dynamic could be one of blue acrimony and division. But should the reds—whose coalition is already inherently more unified—appear to be gaining strength, the medium- and longer-term trend might be blue reunification.

Should the blues ever conclude—for whatever reason—that Caesarism were necessary, all the power centers and commanding heights of our society would be on their side (with the possible exceptions of the lower ranks of the military and local law enforcement). A blue Caesar could easily rally the federal bureaucracy, and many state bureaucracies, to his cause in ways that would make the anti-Trump resistance seem like child's play.

Once in power, blue Caesar might find blue divisions irksome, but hardly insurmountable. Polyglot despotism is a political arrangement as old as human civilization. The obvious way to manage such divisions would be to stoke fears of red resurgence and insist that elections and "taking turns" won't avert the danger, and might even increase it. Someone must be granted "emergency powers." Left unsaid, of course, will be that once granted, those powers will never be surrendered. The precise mechanism—formal repeal of presidential term limits or something more brute-force—would hardly matter at that point.

Like any tyrant, Caesar will see, and imagine, threats to his power everywhere. He will not need to be reminded that other elements of the left coalition want him gone, either to return to the "turn-based" system (if such were even possible) or to replace him with one of their own. A blue Caesar of near-perfect "intersectionality"—a disabled black Muslim transsexual with a Hispanic surname, for instance—might be able to stave off this threat for a time, but not forever. And what happens when "xe" dies? Who next gets the curule chair? Over time, this dynamic could destabilize blue Caesarism and precipitate its collapse. On the other hand, a blue Caesar willing to be ruthless against left-wing challengers for the throne might be able to hang in there a good long while.

Red Caesar

Red Caesar faces more headwinds than blue Caesar in coming to power but also has a few distinct advantages.

First, for the foreseeable future at least, a red Caesar's potential base of support will still be the country's largest and best-armed single bloc, with much accumulated wealth, social capital, and expertise at everyday necessities at its disposal. Second, it's well within the realm of possibility that red Caesar could win over the majority of law enforcement to his side. He might also be able to do the same with parts of the military, or at the very least dissuade many soldiers from carrying out the orders of the ruling class.

Third, a red Caesar would face far fewer—perhaps zero—challenges to his rule from within his own side. There might well be a few individuals who believe that they, and not he, deserve to be Caesar. But such squabbles would arise purely from personal ambition and thus be nowhere near as acrimonious as a conflict within the Dem-left coalition over which group deserves what.

In fact, there may arise an incentive among reds to clear the field for a red Caesar. A red America that feels sufficiently imperiled by the leftist coalition might well look to unify behind one man with authority.

But a red Caesar's path to power is murky. In fact, it would seem that he has only two: either a fluke election resulting from a Democratic crack-up or a military coup. Should a rural, red American—especially one from a small and "non-representative" state that doesn't "look like America"—win the presidency while losing the popular vote, the leftist coalition might very well refuse to accept the result. If they do, the new president might then be forced from office, forced to accept secession, or else determine that he must consolidate power; that is, become Caesar.

But how? The mere prospect is so improbable that it would seem a prospective red Caesar would have no chance. He would require many confederates, including significant secret support within the military, the intelligence services, law enforcement agencies, and other parts of the government: officials who could help further his rise, stymie any threats, and spring into open action only when the time was right. Attempting to gain such support would be risky in itself. Gauge wrongly just once, and the whole project would collapse, with dire consequences for all involved.

A red Caesar coming to power through a military coup would seem even less plausible. The American military prides itself on being apolitical and subject to strict civilian control. To the extent that it's no longer either, the officer corps, or at least its upper echelons, clearly and increasingly align with the ruling class. To have any chance at all, it seems that a red Caesar would have to start from a very young age, cultivate friends, and debts, throughout his rise, and build a loyal following. It's hard to see how any of that could be done without being noticed, and stopped, by the ruling class.

Given all these and other obstacles, prospects for red Caesarism seem fanciful, the stuff of cheap political thrillers and big-budget summer blockbusters. At any rate, I see and have seen no evidence whatsoever of anyone mounting any such effort anywhere.

But supposing a red Caesar were somehow to emerge, how might he govern? As evinced in a thousand novels and their television adaptations, from *The Handmaid's Tale* to *The Plot Against America*, the left's greatest fear—which they insist is always just around the corner—is an ideologically right-wing dictatorship that reverses every example of "progress" in American history and then adds some sinister new layers: the revival of slavery or at least Jim Crow, followed by forbidding women to work outside the home and turning them into breeding stock. I'm not aware of a book or film accusing the American right of wishing to build death camps, but there's probably something out there I've missed.

Such paranoia is preposterously unfounded and arises almost entirely from projection. The left pretends to fear being ruled by the right because it knows that its own deepest desire is to rule the right without consent or constraint. By contrast, if most on the right had their way, they'd prefer to disconnect from the left and let them do whatever they want—on their own space, on their own time, on their own dime.

The chances that a red Caesar would come to power with the ideological zeal of some rightest Pol Pot are nil. There would be no upside at all—not for Caesar personally, nor for his state—to practicing systematic discrimination or barbarity against any group. Doing so would carry no social or economic benefits while also risking a serious backlash that might have to be put down by force. To be sure, Caesars aren't afraid to use force if they have to, but they prefer not to, which is why they try to avoid creating the need. As Sollozzo said to Tom Hagen, "I don't like violence. I'm a businessman. Blood is a big expense." Caesars never know exactly where force might lead, but intuit in their bones that its use might at any time precipitate the end of their rule. A red Caesar would in decisive respects face the same challenge as a blue Caesar: holding together a polyglot, multiethnic, religiously pluralistic society. The imperial systems that have managed this successfully over long periods have not done so by means of pointless and gratuitous oppression.

Yet neither have they been liberal societies. All despotisms, even the most benign, are intolerant of challenges to their power. They tend to crush the first whiffs of rebellion. Political prisoners are not uncommon. Censorship—to one degree or another—is the rule. Multicultural empires are not conducive to liberty.

Under Caesar, there might be some limited freedom in the sense of "live and let live," but there is never freedom in the sense of "common deliberation about a common destiny" or "I disapprove of what you say, but I will defend to the death your right to say it." Such freedoms will be in hibernation. The destiny of the country would be in one man's hands. Should he be a good Caesar, he will rule as Xenophon's Simonides urges Hiero the tyrant to rule: to see the country as his estate and the people as his children and friends. But there is always a danger that he, or a successor, will rule despotically; that danger is in the nature of Caesarism. Which is why sensible men have always preferred ordered liberty.

KABOOM! AND THE NEW POLIS?

Let's not spend too much time on this one since there's no way to anticipate or predict every possible external shock. Suffice it to say that if the neoliberal regime is as brittle as it appears to be, then something unforeseen—another, greater pandemic or other natural disaster, an economic collapse, a war, or a mass breakdown of civil order—might bring it suddenly to an end.

Should that push come, perhaps the country would break up not into two or three or four parts, but many. An interesting, if remote, possibility is the reemergence of a long-dead (or dormant?) form of political organization: the *polis* or "city-state," an urban core united with the surrounding countryside.

Whatever happens on the North American continent, and however it happens, unless there's some kind of mass extinction, there are still going to be people here. The fundamental dynamic explained in Aristotle's *Politics*—the natural human activity of cooperating to do things that human beings cannot do, or do well, alone—will still prevail.

The question will be the scale. Americans tend to think in terms of states and counties and cities and towns because those are the arrangements we've become used to over the centuries. But if the game board were reset, those might not be the only possibilities.

History, philosophy, and common sense alike teach that successful societies are some mixture of town and country: land to grow the food and pasture the livestock, a market center to sell the land's fruits and to buy the goods necessary to farm it. Also, all or most of the higher arts and sciences emerge from or become concentrated in towns. The reason for this historical combination is obvious: town and country need each other. The towns, however, need the countryside more than the reverse. A town without countryside cannot feed itself; a countryside without any towns can still trade, just more inefficiently. But the countryside without towns is less likely to inculcate the arts and sciences, and its development will be slow and uncertain. Both town and country are better off if they have one another.

By "urban core" I do not necessarily, or even primarily, mean one of America's large cities. Were the *polis* to reemerge, it would be far more likely to do so in and around small to medium-sized towns closely connected to the surrounding land.

In much of America, the towns and small cities are blue but surrounded by red countryside. This would not seem to bode well for town–country cooperation or the emergence of city-states. So at least initially, a more likely place that city-states might emerge would be in small red towns surrounded by red country. Once cut off from the broader economy, they would have no choice but to support themselves. In such places, the cultural comity between town and country would encourage cooperation and mutual aid. There are blue agricultural regions, too—in Northern California, parts of the Pacific Northwest, and in lefty Iowa, for instance—where blue city-states might emerge.

Blue towns surrounded by red countryside would face more difficulty. There are today basically two kinds of blue towns: successful and depressed. Successful ones include college towns, resorts, places with significant or at least well-funded government installations, and those with one or more successful companies or industries. The depressed ones tend to be former industrial centers hollowed out by outsourcing. Both types would, I believe, have a difficult time sustaining themselves in the event of neoliberal failure: they both depend too decisively on influxes of outside money, the largest portion of which is federal, which in the event of real calamity would entirely cease. The successful blue towns especially depend on maintaining their linkage to the rest of blue America. The formula is: subsidies, government funding and contracts, and investment capital in; graduates, research, reports, and (in some cases) luxury goods out. Were the little blue duchies' linkage to the big blue metros cut or curtailed, they would wither at best. The remaining populations of depressed towns would sink further into penury, with all that that entails.

Defense for any *polis* would be an issue, from three primary threats: (1) domestic crime; (2) polis-versus-polis depredation; and 3) foreign interference.

Against all three, red city-states—which would have lower crime rates and populations that are better armed, more likely to have served in the military, less pacifist, and more willing to engage in the spirited defense of their own—would have an advantage. Despite what the blue left says about gun control and crime, most violent crime not committed in the heat of passion—a man catching his wife in bed with her lover—is urban and gang- or drug-related. Blues would have more to worry about than reds on this score and, if the events of May and June 2020 are any guide, may find themselves unable or unwilling to maintain order.

As for the second issue, an interesting question is whether North America would see something like the return of early Rome, in which rival city-states went on raiding expeditions to steal others' stuff. That's probably unlikely. In antiquity, there was no ideological divide, no broad fault line that grouped the tribes and cities of Italy into reds and blues. In our case, I doubt reds will want to attack reds—certainly not in the early days when everyone will be thinking about survival and most will perceive a clear common threat. I imagine some marauding gangs might pop up; human nature breeds criminals, after all. But it's hard to imagine any reds formally organizing such gangs as state policy. Given, again, the events of May and June 2020, it's easier to imagine such a provocation arising from the blues, but also difficult to imagine the enterprise succeeding for long against determined and oganized red opposition.

The largest defensive imperative would be the prevention of foreign interference—"foreign" here defined as nations not emerging from the breakup of the United States. It's the same problem that would be faced in the event of secession, except graver because the resulting states would all be smaller and weaker. The problem might be solved—to the extent that it could be—by consolidation: blues getting together with blues, and reds with reds. City-states in the ancient world banded together in defensive leagues while retaining their domestic independence. Over time, the continent could see the gradual reemergence of something like a unified red, and even one or more blue, Americas as city-states got together and formed large, contiguous nations roughly coterminous with the nations that some might have tried to form through secession had the unforeseen calamity not come along and forced the issue.

Some who have studied the historic *polis* will no doubt point out that its foundation was common belief in an adherence to divine law, with no distinction made between civil and religious law, or "the state and society," or the public versus the private sphere. How can that possibly be recreated in the modern world?

But just because ancient religion was the foundation of the original *polis*, why must that necessarily mean that a town-plus-country arrangement following some sort of crack-up would be impossible absent a revival of paganism? I'm open to hearing the argument but have trouble imagining what it might be.

In any case, while it may seem fantastical to imagine a serious religious revival in the age of iPhones and internet porn, real calamity makes the unthinkable become the imaginable. God doesn't depart the scene just because we—temporarily—stop paying attention to Him.

TROUGH OF THE CYCLE?

I include the following only because, however we may wish something not to be true, probity demands that we not deceive ourselves into assuming that because we don't *want* it to be true, then it must *not* be true.

The ancient philosophers theorized a kind of second law of thermodynamics for politics that became known as the "cycle of regimes." The basic idea is that, absent external forces, men and hence political regimes, ascend from bad to good and then degenerate from good to bad in an endless cycle. Machiavelli sums it up this way:

> Usually provinces go most of the time, in the changes they make, from order to disorder and then pass again from disorder to order, for worldly things are not allowed by nature to stand still. As soon as they reach their ultimate perfection,

having no further to rise, they must descend; and similarly, once they have descended and through their disorders arrived at the ultimate depth, since they cannot descend further, of necessity they must rise. Thus they are always descending from good to bad and rising from bad to good. For virtue gives birth to quiet, quiet to leisure, leisure to disorder, disorder to ruin; and similarly, from ruin, order is born; from order, virtue; and from virtue, glory and good fortune.

It would be nice if virtue and strength could be maintained indefinitely, but Nature and Nature's God seem to have designed human beings differently. Just as tyrannies give way to aristocracies and republics on the upswing, so do democracies collapse into decadence, anarchy, and back to tyranny on the downswing.

It is hardly unreasonable to view American history through the lens of cycle theory and conclude that we have, thus far, followed the script rather closely. Founded by a monarchy which enables the establishment and early growth of the nation?—check. Monarchy becomes overbearing and tyrannical, provoking a revolution?—check. Early, post-revolutionary government consists of exceptionally prudent elites who mostly govern in the interest of the common good?—check. Eventual emergence of an economic oligarchy that fuels massive wealth inequality?—check. Inevitable popular reaction forces massive expansion of the franchise and further democratization of the state and society?—check. Popular government continues to devolve toward the lowest common denominator and the regime becomes incompetent at what used to be its core functions but effective at providing "bread and circuses"?—check.

As if this were not sobering enough, Machiavelli also posits a similar cycle of "sects," by which he means not just religions (though these are emphatically included) but the entire framework and architecture of a civilization. Many countries, which may over time be ruled by different regimes, will exist within any given sect, which may last thousands of years.

But sects, like regimes, also die, and for the same basic reasons. Their very success makes them overconfident, complacent, and corrupt; the very virtues that propelled them to greatness come to be seen as unnecessary and even to be despised. The descendants of the people who built the machinery lose interest in running it and forget how. The rickety old vessel plods on for a time through sheer inertia, but eventually—with an incompetent crew, centuries of "deferred maintenance," and no fuel—just gives out, sometimes with a bang, more often with a whimper.

The West does not, these days, seem especially healthy, robust, or spirited. Consider the mostly passive, obedient response to the coronavirus shutdowns—a passivity that continued long past when it was plain to all that the initial predictions of a doomsday plague were wrong. Consider also the swift capitulation to every woke demand, no matter how ridiculous or destructive, on the part of nearly every ostensibly "conservative" defender of American and Western civilization, from politicians to intellectuals to think tank presidents.

Those are just the events of this year, and hence merely symptomatic. Then consider the West's unprecedented low birthrates, our unwillingness to defend our borders or even allow that a defense is morally justifiable, and our long stagnation and decadence. But these are all just symptoms, too, results of the metastasized civilizational self-loathing among half the populace and all the elites, fueled by a loss of faith, both in God and in the rational structure of His creation, which undergirds human virtue and morality.

A great deal, though by no means all, of what ails Western man today can be traced directly to the ruling class's deliberate and successful effort to hollow out his communities and industries, make forming families ever more expensive and difficult, and ply him with sedatives, virtual and actual. Questions of culpability aside—we can neither fully blame nor fully excuse Western man for his current state—the causes are here less important that the effects. Perhaps he has hidden reserves of strength, unseen below the discouraging surface. One hopes.

But one must also entertain the possibility that our entire civilizational "sect"—the overarching edifice whose first fruits flowered in the Garden of Eden, whose cornerstones were laid in the walls of Troy—is finally, inevitably, giving out. One hopes not.

Yet even if it is so, there is still hope. The cycle of sects, no less than the cycle of regimes, will eventually, inevitably, restart. As long as there is man, there will be virtue, or the potential for virtue. What appears to be death is only sleep. Necessity will return and spur a reawakening. And then the whole human adventure will begin anew.

CHAPTER EIGHT

What Now?

Naturally, all who are anxious about the fate of the American people and of constitutional government in this country will wish to avoid the possibilities sketched in the previous two chapters. But how?

The solution is not complicated—but will be difficult to implement. It's far easier to know *what* to do than *how* to do it.

REELECT TRUMP!

First and foremost, we need to reelect President Trump. I know that some readers will lament that the Trump administration has been a disappointment. "Where's our wall?" I'd like to have seen more progress by now, too. "Why wasn't he tougher during the riots and their aftermath?" I don't know.

But it does seem clear that a few of the things we thought all along are actually true. The presidency is hard enough to manage with decades of experience in politics and a series of elective offices under your belt. It's that much harder when a president assumes the office not merely from the outside but, politically speaking, from out of nowhere.

It's harder still without a party. Yes, President Trump enjoys the overwhelming loyalty of Republican voters. But his hold on Republican donors, and especially officials, is much more tenuous. He ran against them and won—and most of them will never forgive him. They play nice to his face and undermine him behind his back. That's before we even get to the ones in open rebellion. No other president, Democrat or Republican, has ever come to power facing organized efforts by his own party's middle management to tally lists of people declaring on the record that under no circumstances will they work for him. It's been hard, to say the least, to staff up when a good chunk of the party is dead set against its leader and nearly all the rest spent their careers furthering policies diametrically opposed to those he ran, and won, on.

And that's just President Trump's ostensible own side. Then factor in all his open enemies from the other party and virtually every other power center in our society, plus the steadfast opposition of the so-called "deep state": the very federal bureaucrats whom he was elected to oversee and direct. Viewed from this angle, one may fairly wonder how it's been possible for him to accomplish anything at all.

More fundamentally: where do you think we'd be without him? Even if you're disappointed with less than two hundred miles of wall, remember that leading Democrats not only insist that every single new inch is a moral atrocity, but they want to *tear down sections that already exist*.

Think the trade agenda is progressing too slowly? Well, President Trump already renegotiated two of our worst trade deals. How many new, bad ones do you think a Hillary administration would have signed by now? Trump not tough enough on China for you? A little too much talk about his "good friend" Xi Jinping? I sympathize. But he's still done more than all the last four presidents combined. Have you heard how Joe Biden sucks up to China?

And I know that some will insist that so long as a single American soldier, sailor, airman, or Marine is deployed anywhere in the Middle

East, then Trump has failed—or worse, betrayed them. But in fact, the president has mostly succeeded at the tasks he promised for that region: defeating ISIS, revitalizing our alliances while requiring more from our allies, and prudently disengaging from existing conflicts while not starting any new ones.

All of these trends, changes, policies, and initiatives, and many others, however incomplete, would be reversed in the event of a Trump loss. The ruling class would hail the president's defeat as a historic repudiation of his (allegedly) "racist and xenophobic" vision, as a vindication of every charge and complaint they've made against him and his supporters since day one. Their goal would be to erase the last four years, and the 2016 election, as if they never happened. If think tank conservatives want above all to get into a DeLorean and go back to 1985, the ruling class wants to cram America into a Prius and force us back to 2015. And then resume the trajectory the country had been on back then: the road to woke managerial tyranny.

Whenever I'm asked—mostly by leftist concern trolls who want to write "Former Trump Official Bashes President"—if I have any criticisms of the president, my answer is always the same: there's little wrong with President Trump that more Trump couldn't solve. More populism. More nationalism. More patriotism. More law and order. More full-throated advocacy for the neglected American people, for the working class, for the Rust Belt and rural America, for religious believers and law-abiding gun owners. More defense of free speech against tech and corporate censorship and suppression, more support for his voters when they or their interests are attacked. In short, more adherence to the 2016 agenda.

The only way to get more Trump is, literally, to get more Trump. Which means reelect the president and help him implement his core agenda in a second term.

But that alone will not be enough. Saving America as a unified, self-governing republic is a long-term, possibly generational, project.

RESTORE SOME SEMBLANCE OF AMERICAN UNITY

In 1991, former Kennedy White House aide and longtime teacher, scholar, and public intellectual Arthur Schlesinger Jr. published a slim volume entitled *The Disuniting of America: Reflections on a Multicultural Society*. Precisely because of his impeccable liberal credentials, Schlesinger's brief against multiculturalism, anti-Americanism, and anti-Westernism hit the intellectual world like a thunderbolt. Those being (very) different times, his book was—outside the fever swamps of the universities, and even by some within them—widely praised by left and right alike.

Today it would be denounced as a "racist" right-wing screed. Schlesinger criticized multiculturalists as "very often ethnocentric separatists who see little in the Western heritage other than Western crimes," whose "mood is one of divesting Americans of their sinful European inheritance and seeking redemptive infusions from non-Western cultures." We can't go on this like this and remain a "we," he warned, and urged Americans to (re)unite around our shared language, heritage, history, and interests.

About a decade later, three-term Democratic Colorado governor Richard Lamm gave a short speech, a third-person account of which became one of the earliest known documents to "go viral" online. In the speech, Lamm laid out what he called—tongue firmly in cheek—his "secret plan to destroy America." All of his eight points focused on deliberately fostering disunity: encouraging multiculturalism, multilingualism, dual citizenship, "diversity," the politics of victimization and resentment, and so on.

Every dire trend Schlesinger and Lamm warned about was already happening when they gave their warnings. Each is exponentially truer today. The country was still united enough in 1991, and in 1998 when Schlesinger augmented and republished his book, even in the early 2000s when Lamm spoke, that the two of them at least got favorable hearings. Of course, no one, left or right, heeded or acted on any part of what they had to say. Instead, all the trends they warned about were not merely allowed to continue but deliberately intensified.

And now here we are: in so many ways, more divided than we were in 1860—in so many ways, not even a "we" anymore. "Restoring American unity" in this climate sounds almost comically impossible. How to restore unity after five decades and counting of cold civil war, the rancor of which only seems to intensify month to month?

I have some ideas, which I will get to. But first, let's understand what is meant by "unity." It does not mean a unanimous vote in the Electoral College, such as George Washington won twice. It doesn't mean a return to the bipartisan consensus of World War II and the first decades of the Cold War era. It doesn't even mean anything like the 1972 or 1984 forty-nine-state landslides, which can almost certainly never be repeated.

"Unity" in the American political context—really, for any republic, and one may say for republicanism simply—means a shared set of basic goals and assumptions. It doesn't mean everyone has to agree on everything or even like everyone. Indeed, a unified republic may nonetheless be quite divided in certain respects. Historically the most common division in any republic has been economic, with religion and culture providing the underlying bedrock of unity. Divisions between patricians and plebeians over sharing spoils and offices continually wracked Republican Rome, but the city also remained fundamentally unified, as *Rome*, with both classes speaking the same language, believing in the same gods, adhering to the same morality, and committed to Roman greatness and glory.

To say the least, there does not appear to be any shared interest or bond of unity underneath contemporary America's bitter red–blue divide. One side loves America, the other hates it—or can tolerate it only for what it might someday become, were the left's entire program to be enacted without exception. One faction, or most of it, is religious in the traditional sense; the other invented the god of wokeness, which it worships with Dionysian abandon. One side speaks only English, the other boasts of the literally hundreds of languages now heard in America's blue precincts. One side insists that the ultimate moral imperative is to punish the other—which in turn believes that morality requires fairness and equal justice under the law.

What would partisans of either side cite as something they share in common with the other? The land itself? But they each go to great lengths not to live anywhere near one another. "The economy"? It's been reengineered to benefit one side at the expense of the other. As for the culture—that reliable unifying bond throughout most of history—to ask is to laugh and cry at the same time.

The merest shred of cultural unity would seem so far out of reach as to be scarcely worth trying to attain, at least for the foreseeable future. I don't believe the country can continue indefinitely without any semblance of a common culture, but focusing right now on a near- and medium-term impossibility would be folly. Which leaves us with economics.

Even that's going to be hard enough. How to do you reconcile, much less unify, a fundamentally rural, small-town and small-city manufacturing-agricultural economy with an urban and affluent-suburban finance-information-managerial economy? Especially when the profits of the latter so depend on strip-mining the resources—outsourcing the industries and replacing the labor—of the former?

The seemingly paradoxical answer is that one side needs to achieve and keep—electorally!—the upper hand for a while: specifically, the side that has been getting the short end of the stick for the last generation. Should that happen, its leaders will, of course, and of necessity, use their power to benefit their side—their base—but they must also use it to right the ship, to rebalance and benefit the whole.

THE REPUBLICAN PARTY: REFORM OR REPLACE

We see immediately, however, that no political party representing the interests of the rural, small-town and small-city manufacturing-agricultural population currently exists. The Democrats long ago abandoned "the common man" in favor of their high-low coalition. The Republicans would seem to represent the country party—certainly, they get a lot of their votes from such people—but in practice GOP officeholders and donors are just as if not more likely to side with the interests of the ruling class and "global capital" over those of their own ostensible base.

What's needed, then, is a Trumpist political party focused squarely on "old economy"—rural, manufacturing, and blue collar—interests. Which means, in most if not all cases, a party actively opposed to the program of the ruling class. If the Republican Party can become that, all to the good. If it can't, it should go out of business.

Let's not venerate the GOP just because it's old or because of its many real accomplishments. Political parties have life spans. They can outlive their usefulness. The Federalists—who included such giants as Adams, Hamilton, Jay, and Marshall—helped found the United States and set the new country on a course toward great power, prominence, prosperity, and prestige. Yet the Federalist Party failed to adapt to changing times and so died—and deserved to.

The Republican Party before Trump had similarly outlived its usefulness. For now, largely thanks to Trump, it still lives. Its continued existence hinges on whether it can become unabashedly the party of the ordinary Americans, if it can make its central reason for existence the furtherance of their interests. If it can't, it will deserve to die and will die, and be replaced by a party that does.

Trump's 2016 vision and program remain the right ones—the only ones with any hope of restoring what measure of American unity can be salvaged and of keeping the country going as a republic. For them to be carried out, the president must be followed by a succession, an army, of Trumpists. His base, and America itself, will need a new cadre of populist-nationalist leaders at the federal (of course) but also state and local levels. The party—whether Republican or a successor—needs such people both as a farm team or bench, a cadre from which to recruit future elected and appointed high officeholders, and also to force D.C. to respect states and local communities as serious political power centers in their own rights, to make Washington think twice about being too heavy-handed. "Trumpism" needs a strong state and local political class ready and willing to fight for its core supporters and their interests and to resist ruling-class authoritarianism.

Let's also be clear that saving the Republican Party will require, in no small measure, moving it to the left economically. Note well: *moving it leftward*, not "making it a left-wing party." A Trumpist party—whether Republican or something else—will still be the party of property rights and basic economic freedom, and it will oppose "reparations" and other forms of unjust redistribution and expropriation.

But it will be a party much friendlier to the interests of workers: the party of tight labor markets and rising wages, of reasonable worker safety and environmental regulations, of farsighted government spending on infrastructure, and above all of industrial and trade policies that favor and encourage domestic manufacturing. Republican free-trade, low-tax, no-regulation dogma stopped serving the interests of at least half of Republican voters decades ago. The wing of the party that still sings from that hymnal today is nothing but a controlled-opposition adjunct of the ruling class. Its dogma will have to be smashed.

A major area of continuity between the old and new Republican Parties, however, will be the so-called "social" or "cultural" issues. The party must speak forthrightly for people distrustful, even fearful, of social engineering. The left's rout of the right in the "culture wars" has made Republicans so gun-shy that they can't even seize obvious opportunities such as standing up for female high school athletes who suddenly find themselves losing all their track meets to biological boys.

Much, probably most, of the ground lost in the culture war can't be regained (at least not as long as the current "sect" lasts). There's no going back to 1985, much less 1955. Somewhat paradoxically, though, the left's many cultural victories make the right's task easier today. All the low-hanging fruit has been plucked: every social cause that ordinary Americans can be convinced is a matter of simple fairness has been achieved. What's left are radical fervors that sound to Middle America not merely lunatic but dangerous. Fifty-year-old men asserting a fundamental "right" to change in front of eleven-year-old girls in YWCA locker rooms is not the moral equivalent of ending Jim Crow—and despite the left's caterwauling, few Americans see it that way. What they lack are politicians with the spine to stand up to the nonsense.

In other words, the Republican Party needs to become more like the old Democratic Party—more worker-friendly, more concerned with wage and wealth inequality—but also the opposite of today's Democratic Party: openly nationalistic on economics and trade, stalwartly traditional on morality and culture. If the Republicans can so transform themselves, they have a chance. If they cannot, then the party will have to be destroyed and replaced, or else left to wither in the ruling class's anteroom, its dwindling adherents the last to realize their own irrelevance.

To the extent that the Republican Party is animated by ideas—a laughable assertion today, but one that was true within living memory—it will need an entirely new intellectual class. Establishment conservatism, its institutions and scholars, its think tanks and magazines, its handful of professors at elite universities, are a spent force. Many legacy conservatives are fine people with sound opinions, especially compared to what passes for conventional wisdom today. But they've shown themselves to be unequal to the task before conservatism today. Conservative intellectuals aren't merely waging the last campaign; they're forever fighting the 1980 campaign.

A revitalized Republican Party, or a new party that arises from its ashes, will need intellectuals, scholars, professors, and policy wonks, but ones dedicated to the new agenda: immigration restriction, industrial policy, a trading regime that serves the whole national interest, not merely "the markets" and "the economy," and a foreign policy that's a mixture of confident strength and prudent restraint. And it will need new institutions and journals.

In sum, if the Trump administration can make real progress on the 2016 agenda in its second term and the president can remake the Republican Party and conservative movement in his image and set the stage for a series of strong Trumpist successors, then there's still a chance to save America as a unified, self-governing republic that honors and observes the fundamental charters of our liberties as opposed to a neoliberal finance-tech oligarchy whose absolute rule is disguised by meaningless staged elections.

REALIGNMENT?

The way to do *that* is to build a durable governing coalition: a national majority that can earn, and maintain, the support of roughly 55 percent (or more) of the electorate over a generation at least and win approximately two-thirds of national elections during that period.

Historians and political scientists call such fundamental transformations of the electoral landscape "realignments." The last undisputed realignment began with the Democratic landslide in the 1930 midterm that launched a Democratic ascendancy lasting at least through the New Deal, World War II, and most of the 1960s. Professional analysts of American politics agree that the New Deal coalition broke on the rocks of "the Sixties," chiefly over the issues of crime and the war in Vietnam, and that the 1968 election heralded its end. They don't agree on what to call the era that came next, or even whether there has been a true realignment since.

Republicans and conservatives naturally wish to point to 1968 (the "emerging Republican majority") or 1980 (the "Reagan Revolution") or 1994 (the "Republican Revolution") as turning points leading to a new "party system." Yet only twice during this period did the Republicans hold both Congress and the White House, never for longer than four years, and the great Republican hero Ronald Reagan not even for a day.

Democrats and the left just as naturally prefer to point to 1992 and 2008 as heralding new eras. But their party also controlled an undivided government only twice since 1992, in each instance for only two years. Obama won the presidency in 2008 with the highest share of the popular vote since 1988—and then went on to become the first incumbent to see his share of the vote (both electoral and popular) decline since FDR's precedent-desecrating fourth election in 1944. The year 1988 was also the last time the same party won a third consecutive presidential term. Contrast that with five straight beginning in 1932: *that's* what a realignment looks like.

Rather than a new realignment understood in the old sense, it appears instead that the electorate has lately preferred to turn from one party to the other, and back, to check and correct the hubris and missteps of both. Voters outside each party's die-hard base not only have shown no consistent loyalty to either but have actually preferred divided government.

Yet a lasting political solution to the problems that bedevil us will require another realignment, although not necessarily one entirely along party lines, at least not at first. One of the reasons that neither the Nixon nor the Reagan landslides produced a textbook realignment is because so many of their voters remained otherwise loyal—at the congressional, state, and local levels, as well as in their registration—to the Democratic Party. Indeed, one traditional measure of whether a "realignment" may be said to have taken place is the extent to which voters switch parties. When they don't, it hasn't.

But that needn't necessarily be true in our case, and in fact a "bipartisan realignment" may well prove better-suited to today's challenges. Many of the goals of "Trumpism," broadly understood as populist economic nationalism, should be attractive to many traditional Democratic constituencies. That party was, after all, for more than a century the natural home of both the urban-industrial working class and much of rural America. A forthright appeal to more, and steadier, blue-collar jobs—urban, suburban, and rural—at higher wages, with access to affordable, quality healthcare, should appeal to a sizeable chunk of Democratic voters.

Such a program would naturally alienate some who are today stalwart Republicans. But that's the nature of realignments: lose some in your old coalition, gain some in the new. If you gain more than you lose, the realignment is successful.

The calculus, as I said, is simple. The operation? Less so.

The Republicans are not exactly the "white party"—the spiritual and financial core of the Democratic Party is white—but they are the party that draws the overwhelming majority of its support from white voters. Were the Republican Party to die and be replaced by another, the same way the Republicans themselves replaced the Whigs, the new party would also be overwhelmingly white, and so would face the same demographic challenge.

For a Republican—or post-Republican, or Republican/post-Republican-plus-Democratic-defector*—coalition to emerge, it will have to include a substantial proportion of nonwhite voters. That's just math. As our blue overlords never tire of reminding us, "demographic change" means, or soon will mean, that assembling a national majority is impossible without a "diverse" coalition.

There's probably a short window during which the demographics of the country will make it possible for Republicans to win electoral victories by maximizing their share of the white vote. That is, if any Republicans dared to implement such a strategy, which they absolutely will not. Nothing terrifies a Republican more than the specter of being called "racist," and nothing is more certain than Megaphone denunciations of "Republican racism" should the Republicans even make feints in that direction. Indeed, even when Republicans cravenly pander to groups outside their traditional base, they still get called "racist." The mere fact that Republicans get so many of their votes from whites is, to the ruling class and its minions, sufficient proof of the charge.

Funny thing, too: a core tenet of modern liberalism is supposed to be the sanctity of "one man, one vote." Except, you know, not really. The barely concealed presupposition of denouncing Republicans as "racists" simply because whites vote for them is that all votes are *not* created equal. Votes of color are morally superior to white votes, which are

* Throughout the rest of this chapter, "Republican" always means "Republican and/or a successor party," so as to avoid tiresome repetition of the latter phrase.

inherently tainted. Which is why the left holds any election won by a Republican to be morally, if not (yet) politically, illegitimate.

In any case, even if the Republicans would so dare, which they won't, the move would only avail them for a few cycles. Even if the border wall is completed and legal immigration massively restricted, the demographics of the country already ensure that relying on the white vote alone cannot secure a long-term future for the Republican Party. Sooner rather than later, to remain viable, Republicans will have to win over nonwhite voters in much greater numbers than they do today.

Politically, Republicans would have to walk a very fine line: maximize their white support—especially in the Rust Belt and among those on the lower half of the income and education ladder—while actively campaigning for blue-collar, working- and lower-middle-class black and Hispanic votes, without jeopardizing their base.

Another electoral quandary is how, simultaneously, to appeal to Asian voters. On paper, they should be the real "natural conservatives": religious, family-oriented, meritocratic, successful, wealthy, supportive of law and order. And yet they are integral to the "high" part of the Democratic high-low coalition. To update for our time Milton Himmelfarb's 1968 quip that "Jews earn like Episcopalians and vote like Puerto Ricans," Asian Americans earn like Ashkenazis and vote like Somalis.

That it's possible to win, simultaneously, the votes of technocratic and managerial-class Asians and working-class blacks and Hispanics is demonstrated by the fact that Democrats routinely do it. Could Republicans? Maybe—with the right policies and a better message (more on this below.)

It's hard to see how, for the foreseeable future at least, Republicans could get majority support from such voters. Indeed, even to try, they'd have to push policies that would alienate their base, making the whole effort Pyrrhic before it started. This is the chief reason why the Megaphone constantly concern-trolls Republicans into abandoning both their principles and their base to seek Democratic votes. The fact that you consistently lose with those voters proves that you are bad and also that you are doomed. We're trying to help you! Repudiate everything you've ever stood for and betray your base! That's the only way you can win!

Yeah . . . no. But cutting deep into the Democrats' margin with *their* base would likely be enough to secure Republicans a majority for a generation or two—*if* they could manage to do so without losing their own. The Democrats know this. And it terrifies them.

Which is why the ruling class and its minions will use their complete control of the Megaphone to make winning such votes very, very difficult for Republicans. There is practically no end to the left's motivations for calling anyone to their right "racist," but this fear is perhaps the biggest. Hence, if the Republicans ever seriously mount such an effort, the calumny machine will kick into overdrive. The inherently paradoxical propaganda script is already written: the fact that you don't win votes of color proves that you're racist and bad; the only way to redeem yourselves is to court voters of color; but any voter of color who votes for you is a race traitor.

Heads they shoot us, tails they hang us. This 24/7 hysterical Megaphone propaganda will be hard to overcome. But Republicans will not only have to try; they'll have to succeed.

Some will no doubt object that the Republican "brand" is too sullied in the minds of such voters for this ever to work, and that the problem has only gotten worse under Trump. Certainly the Megaphone's volume and shrillness have reached unprecedented levels under Trump. But that could be because Trump—a media-age celebrity if ever there was one—is so obviously not a "racist" but instead a respecter of fame, wealth, and power regardless of race, and moreover exactly the kind of blingy, emotive, trash-talking "big man" whom working-class men of all races are apt to admire. Trump is, or was, the Republicans' first real threat to attract minority votes since the New Deal, and so the demonization had to be intensified in proportion to the threat. Before the 2020 Cultural Revolution raised vilification levels to an intensity hitherto unknown in American politics, Trump's approval rating with minorities (especially men) was, even with all the hate thrown his way, higher than that of any Republican in at least a generation. Granted, those relatively high approvals hadn't—yet—translated into votes. It remains to be seen if they could. But the mere prospect is a mortal threat to the Democratic coalition.

I expect others to insist that what I here propose is impossible. All I can say in response is that, if they're right, then America's future must and will be one of the possibilities discussed in chapters 6 and 7.

A NEW MESSAGE

For this to work, the Republicans will need a new "message." The one they've been using for the last two decades—essentially a fusion of the 1980 platform with pledges never to stop fighting in the Middle East—not only no longer inspires the party's base, it positively repulses many of them. It has no chance whatsoever of winning over any part of the Democratic coalition.

What might? We'll get into specific policies in the next section. But as to a "message," it must combine the promise of concrete benefits with a sincere appeal to voters' sense of dignity, individuality, and self-worth, and also to feelings of common cause, common citizenship, and patriotism. Something along the lines of:

> We're the party of good jobs and higher wages—for *you*. Yes, we're for economic freedom and (mostly) free markets, but not as ends in themselves, rather because theory and practice alike show that these are the best ways to produce prosperity for all. We're well aware that the pseudo-prosperity of the last few decades has not been shared but has been gobbled up by those at the top, that you and your families have been left behind and even left out.
>
> The animating spirit of our party is to change that, to pursue policies that encourage domestic manufacturing, create jobs, and raise wages. And not just any jobs, not just

paper-pushing and burger-flipping jobs, but jobs making real, tangible things that real people want and need. Jobs that Americans, and especially American men, want to do. That means a shift from a purely information-service-consumer economy to a more balanced economy that respects and honors manufacturing. It means moving away from relying almost completely on imports in favor of making things at home, and a return to selling some of what we make overseas. It means no more dumb trade giveaways or tax and regulatory policies that favor bankers and techies while shafting everyone else. It means protecting American industries and jobs when and where beneficial to American workers.

We're also the party committed to ensuring that your hard-earned wage gains won't be wiped out by rising health-care costs. We're not going to do that by forcing a government takeover of the system, which would make everything worse for everyone but the superrich, who could always afford to buy the best care (assuming high quality care could survive a complete government takeover). We're instead going to use government power to make the private market more affordable for routine doctor visits and ordinary care and to create a public backstop to ensure that, in cases of injury or disease, no person or family need worry about how to pay their medical bills.

We're the party of real "meritocracy," not the phony kind the ruling class dangles to trick you into thinking our system is fair to you and yours. We're the party that will neither create nor tolerate any impediments whatsoever in the way of your or your children's rise. Help will be provided where it's needed, but fairly and impartially. We will never pit race against race, group against group, citizen against citizen.

We're the party of military strength and foreign policy restraint—the party that will protect our country's interests while minding our own business. America's days as the world's arbiter-intervener of first resort must and will end. As a commercial republic whose prosperity depends in part on buying and selling overseas, America must be able to project strength abroad. But we will do so only where and when we must to protect our interests, which we will define strictly and narrowly.

Finally, we're the party of the common man and woman, the ordinary Joe and Jane, the average American—the party of family, faith, and our shared, cherished American way of life. We're the party that will defend our common ideas of decency, morality, and citizenship. We're the party that stands in favor of you living and worshiping the way you always have, the way your sacred scripture says and your ancestors taught you. We stand against silly, destructive fads cooked up on university campuses and in big cities to alter and degrade your way of life—and to insult and belittle you in the process.

We're for "progress," but the real kind: progress in shared wealth and new technologies that benefit all, not just a small elite; progress in building up the dignity and honor of you and your families; progress in the strength and greatness of our shared country; progress toward a future in which America's central institutions and power centers care about you and fight for you.

I know that's much too long for a political "message" in the age of sound bites. I leave it to the consultants, pollsters, and focus-group jockeys to carve a workable set of one-liners out of the above material. I am, however, confident that a message based on these themes is the only one that stands a chance at building a majority coalition around Republican or center-right issues capable of uniting the middle- and working-class of all races and capable of beating the hard left at the ballot box.

A NEW PLATFORM

This is not a policy book, and I am not a wonk. Those seeking camera-ready, magic-bullet "solutions" for all our problems will long since have thrown this volume against the wall in anger. But I can, and will, sketch the outlines of a platform that would serve the country, further Republican electoral prospects, and advance the interests of all (with the possible exception of the upper reaches of the blue nobility). Experts in each of the following subjects will have to do the hard work of translating it all into policy. Indeed, many—though as yet far too few—already are. And no doubt they all have ideas of their own. I make no claim to prophecy or infallibility. I assert only that, broadly speaking, this is the direction we need to go.

Immigration

First and foremost is real immigration reform—and not "reform" in the Washington sense: amnesty plus more legal immigration and work visas. Populist-nationalist reform means deep reductions in immigration.

The one question about immigration into the United States (or Europe, for that matter) that is never asked—never *allowed* to be asked—is: how much is enough? Taking into consideration the actual features, assets, and attributes of the existing country—its people, the land, our resources, the infrastructure—what is the optimal population of the United States?

Three hundred and thirty million is a lot. The country certainly *feels* crowded—especially in the coastal and metro areas, where nearly all immigrants settle. Yet we're still taking in around a million and a half a year—though, to repeat, given lax border controls, even factoring in the heroic efforts of the Trump administration, nobody really knows the exact number. Do we *need* that many every year? Even half that many? A tenth?

Consider also the catastrophic effects of the coronavirus shutdown on employment. At the time of this writing, the official unemployment figure stands at nearly 15 percent, the highest since the Great Depression nearly a century ago. And yet America is still taking in immigrants—legally, illegally, and even through visa programs specifically designed to fill American jobs with foreigners. There may be a "rational" explanation for that, in that greedy elites acting in their own narrow, selfish interests are behaving "rationally" from their own perspective. But in the larger sense, there's nothing whatsoever public-spirited, patriotic, or rational about it. Keeping the floodgates open in a time of mass unemployment is the surest possible sign that our country is controlled by a hostile elite or has gone insane. Or both.

The first, last, and only question that should determine America's immigration policy is: how much immigration, chosen on which bases, best serves the current interests of the current American citizenry? That's it. Not what's best for "the economy," or this or that industry, or what we somehow "owe" the rest of the world: America is neither an "economy" nor a refugee camp. We're a country, with our own particular citizen body and interests. Serious countries enact polices to serve those interests. Oligarchies enact policies to further partial, private interests. Joke countries make policy based on sentiment, schmaltz, and cant. When it comes to immigration (and much else), the United States today is a combination of the latter two.

My own view is that America right now does not need any immigration at all. There should be a pause, at least until the country returns to full employment following our economic recovery from the shutdown disaster. When that happens, the question can be revisited. My own view, once again, is that an even longer pause is warranted to help stabilize our society, reduce tribalism, restart a process of real assimilation, make elections less zero-sum and more animated by policies and ideas, and encourage (or force) big business to come to terms with labor on a more equal footing rather than immediately revert to the cynical practice of importing more scabs to undercut wages.

As a practical matter, this means, first, finishing the wall—a real wall, not some "virtual wall" that senators, lobbyists, and party hacks can support because they're confident it won't work. America needs a real wall that really keeps trespassers out. Enforce the border. Enact, and enforce, real workplace sanctions. Businesses caught hiring people who don't have the legal right to work in the United States should be hit with serious civil and even criminal penalties.

End birthright citizenship immediately. As I have argued extensively elsewhere and won't belabor here, there is no constitutional requirement to grant automatic citizenship to anyone born on American soil. The clause "subject to the jurisdiction" in the Fourteenth Amendment was included specifically to exclude from citizenship the children of noncitizens (or at least nonlegal permanent residents)—that is, children whose parents are not "subject to the jurisdiction" of the United States because they are citizens of, and owe allegiance to, a foreign power.

While we're at it, let's end the idiotic and self-contradictory practice of "dual citizenship." No person can simultaneously be loyal to more than one sovereign state at a time. That's a logical and practical impossibility—but one that carries real benefits for the elites who are overwhelmingly dual citizenship's beneficiaries. What oligarch doesn't want more places to hide money, an extra passport or two for getting around travel restrictions, and, if necessary, ready access to a bolt-hole? But these escape routes only serve to further disconnect our elites from their country and make them more mercenary. Dual citizenship does nothing for America itself or its citizenry. In a sane country, only one passport per citizen is allowed. If you have more than one, either give the others back to their issuers or surrender your American one—and leave. No exceptions.

The dumbest and least defensible immigration programs should be ended immediately. These include above all the idiotic diversity lottery that awards the precious right to live and work in America to people literally at random, and "family reunification," or "chain migration," which doesn't even make a pretense of benefiting "the economy."

As immigration patriots seek a full moratorium, they should, if possible, work with those willing to make our immigration system choosier, or more "merit-based" as present terminology has it. "Merit-based" reform is no panacea: it still entails importing workers we don't need, especially in a time of sky-high unemployment, to take jobs that Americans might otherwise fill. It also fortifies our present, predatory elite even as it drains other nations of elites their societies need. But it's better than choosing at random. Criteria for "merit" should include education and skills, low likelihood of utilizing public assistance, enthusiasm for republican government, and eagerness for assimilation.

Infrastructure

Our infrastructure is a shambles and has been crumbling for decades. Fixing it would carry numerous benefits, including improved quality of life and shortened travel times. It would pump money into economically depressed regions, employ thousands and possibly millions of blue-collar workers, and improve the transportation networks that are the arteries of the economy.

Just making the average American's travel experience—whether by road, rail, air, or water—less insulting, inconvenient, and undignified, and also faster, cleaner, safer, and more pleasant, could do wonders for national morale and would constitute an everyday, unmistakable, physical reminder that America is indeed being made "great again."

A special emphasis on alleviating commute times and their attendant annoyances and indignities should be a priority and would also provide many benefits: less time wasted, more time with families, increased productivity, lower carbon emissions, and less stress on the environment. This is an issue that affects millions, literally right where they live, one that's not abstract, but real and in their faces every day. It's also an issue that haunts the middle class, who more often than not must navigate a painful trade-off between two quality-of-life priorities: live near a job in substandard housing, often amidst high crime and crummy schools, or live far from work and endure a long, expensive, unpleasant, and possibly dangerous odyssey twice a day, five days a week. A party that took on this problem with seriousness of purpose could accomplish great things for the country—and win votes in the process.

I know that some will object, "But the debt!" I sympathize. I don't expect the following rejoinder to convince any committed green-eyeshade Republican, but the rest of you should consider: We're already in debt up to our ears. Our entire economy and standard of living are fueled by and dependent on debt. The debt and the entitlement programs that fuel it are problems that will eventually have to be solved.

But there's no way to solve it now, at least not politically. (Should the U.S. economy or the dollar crash, the problem would be "solved" for us—though not in a way most of us would want!) Getting a handle on the debt through the political process will require supermajority popular support. Financial austerity—especially measures that disproportionally affect the hinterland—can't be rammed through on a party-line vote if America is to survive as a united country. One way not to get such support would be to tell people who've endured falling wages and deteriorating quality of life for more than a generation that, sorry, it's time for even more sacrifice—in this case for some abstraction known as "the bond market." And if it appears that Wall Street is making even more money off these necessary "structural reforms" while you fall even further behind, well, sorry again, but "the economy" demands it.

Only creditors and ideologues are going to vote for that. Trying to impose it over the vigorous objections of Middle America might provoke a revolution. If, on the other hand, more debt-fueled spending could produce a generation of broadly shared prosperity, then it's at least conceivable that political support could be gradually built up for addressing the debt. Everyone shares the burden, nobody gets the shaft, the country goes into the dentist's chair strong and emerges from the root canal even stronger. At the very least, the upper and lower teeth suffer equally.

There's no other way. If our politics continue as they are, then we have no chance of ever getting a handle on the debt. If we insist that the debt be our priority now, we'll break the country. We've lived in and on debt for a long time. Yes, it's unsustainable over the long term—but what is "long term"? If it's next year or even the next decade, then we're already finished: there's no way we can solve the problem in that short a time. If it's a generation or more, then we have a chance. But to have that chance, we have to create the political conditions for a political consensus to emerge. Which means, in the medium term, more debt on the road to less debt.

Energy and the Environment

We should augment the American energy sector's recent rip-roaring success while vigorously protecting the environment. Our energy industry is not only thriving, it also drives exports, making it one of the country's few economic sectors that favorably affects our international balance of payments. It also employs millions of blue-collar workers—exactly the people Republicans need as the foundation of their new coalition.

Energy is not only a booming sector in its own right; if infrastructure is our economy's circulatory system, energy is its blood. Lots of it will be needed to fuel an American reindustrialization. The trick will be to keep energy prices high enough that America's relatively high-wage, high-extraction-cost sector remains competitive in world markets, but also low enough to ease costs on other businesses, freeing up revenue and capital for research, development, and investment. All that will require careful policy calibration; that is, government intervention. There's no easy answer here, but either market dogmatism or environmentalist extremism would crush the sector.

Not drinking the environmental-cultist Kool-Aid is essential to crafting sound policy. But that doesn't mean environmental concerns should be ignored. One needn't accept every tenet of climate change theology at face value to wish to conserve America's grand and pristine open spaces, rivers, forests, mountain ranges, deserts, and other natural wonders that are the envy of the world. Nor should obvious public goods such as clean water and air quality be sacrificed on the altar of "deregulation." Government regulation all but solved Los Angeles's notorious "smog" crisis. Republicans breathe too.

There is a long, glorious—and popular—tradition of conservation in American politics for Republicans to draw upon, from Teddy Roosevelt to John Muir, Gifford Pinchot, and Aldo Leopold. One priority—which is about as politically uncontroversial and universally popular as any measure could be—should be the preservation and beautification of our national parks. Another should be to revive the anti-littering campaigns of the 1970s and 1980s that were so effective at cleaning up America's public spaces. Make littering once again a shameful act.

Tucker Carlson has been demonized for daring to mention the observable fact that recent immigrants tend to litter a lot more than the native-born. This is but one way that cutting back on immigration would be good for the environment. Another, of far greater magnitude, is that fewer people living in America means less resource consumption and lower carbon emissions. The hair-shirt left insists that those of us already here must give up cars and hamburgers—but they're all for importing the rest of the world's poor, whom they don't dare lecture on how to live after they arrive.

We should also at least consider getting back to nuclear power, which is not only the cleanest but the cheapest way to generate electricity. Its alleged high costs are largely artificial, the result of crippling regulations and endless approval processes. Focus regulations solely and squarely on safety. Lift the Carter-era ban on reprocessing spent fuel rods, which greatly and needlessly multiplies the amount of waste that must be stored.

Industrial and Trade Policy

There's no easy answer to what an American industrial policy should look like—except that we need one. "The market," left to its own devices—or, more accurately, steered by bankers and CEOs—deindustrialized the country with disastrous social and economic consequences. Some of that was going to happen anyway, owing to automation, obsolescence, and increasing competition. But the goal of policy should be to slow that process as much as possible and blunt its impacts on workers, their families, and their communities.

The country will need a seemingly paradoxical, or at least hard-to-balance, combination of deregulation and liberalization in certain areas, coupled with more focused state intervention in others. Red tape that makes it needlessly difficult to start and run businesses, to build and to renovate, should be cut back while preserving sensible rules that protect worker safety and environmental quality. Regulations focused on social engineering, on redressing alleged "group injustice," should all go.

On the other hand, the country needs to get back into research and development in a big way—a push that can only be led by the government. As David Goldman tirelessly reminds us, a truly staggering number of new technologies with vast commercial applications have in the past emerged from defense and space exploration research—all of it publicly funded. Let's do it again. Focus defense research on countering the capabilities of a rising China—not to start a war but, through preparedness, to avoid one. As for space, make a serious plan to return to the moon—and then go on to Mars. Both are already official policy, but everyone knows, or senses, that we aren't serious about either. Get serious.

To get ahead of, and avoid, the "universal basic income" freight train—a key stop on the road to serfdom—Republicans will have to drop their reflexive opposition to government benefits. Thirty years of unbridled neoliberalism—smothering regulation of the old, productive economy coupled with relatively light and easy-to-circumvent regulation of the "information" sectors—has created a massive wage and wealth gap. The government should find ways to narrow the gap that incentivize work. Wage subsidies—which, unlike a universal basic income, don't disincentivize work—should be on the table. Conservatives will howl, but let them: their recent proposals have failed.

And we need a plan for redressing, to the extent possible, America's horrific trade imbalances. Trump has performed a heroic service simply by forever changing the terms of the debate—on trade generally and China specifically. Yet as the president himself well knows, our country still has more to do: more tariffs to enact and more open challenges to Chinese industrial espionage, intellectual property theft, and the like. In short, if there's to be a "trade war," recognize that it was started by others—and win it. We should all take heart from the fact that the ruling class's dire predictions about Trump's thus-far modest tariffs have proved laughably inaccurate. Neither the markets nor the economy crashed—from the shutdown, temporarily, but not from the tariffs! Still, the more the Trump administration (or a successor) tries to do, the more the ruling class will scream. But treat their screams with the same degree of skepticism you would the latest COVID-19 death-prediction model.

Our goal should be to repatriate as much manufacturing as possible, with priorities being food, medicine and its ingredients, medical supplies, and technologies critical to our military and national security. The government could provide financial assistance—low-interest loans, loan guarantees, or outright grants—to incentivize companies to "onshore" their operations to American soil. There should also be "Buy American" mandates—issued in an executive order or, better yet, a law—requiring companies to prioritize American providers in their "supply chains." This all may be "anti-market," but who cares—so long as it's pro-American.

Healthcare

Here again, the government is going to have to be involved. Just as with universal basic income, the single-payer freight train is coming, unless a sensible alternative can be devised that combines market-based incentives and efficiencies with government subsidies and guarantees. The basic contours should be a nationwide public plan that covers major injuries and diseases, supported by a private market for plans that cover routine care and doctors' visits. The private market should be lightly regulated and allow insurers to price by risk—which is, after all, the only way the insurance business can work.

Other guiding principles should be, first, full transparency of costs. No more mystifying medical bills, incomprehensible even to senior partners at Ernst & Young, with terrifyingly gigantic numbers in one column, a comparatively tiny expected payment in another, and no sense whatsoever of how the one translates into the other.

Second, allow insurance plan competition across state lines. The current restrictions benefit (some) insurers at consumers' expense but otherwise make no sense. Third, implement real tort reform. Our current system goes well beyond redressing genuine malpractice and incentivizes huge windfall fees for a handful of lawyers. We all pay for those fees through higher costs. Trial lawyers, I might also point out, are a core constituency and major source of donations for the Democratic Party.

Expand medical school admissions. We need more doctors. Our present "solution" is to keep importing them from abroad, which—and no one seems to care about this—is not exactly great for the countries those doctors leave behind. In any case, there's no reason why we can't train our own. The fact that lots of our talented and ambitious young people still want to be doctors is evidenced by the difficulty of getting into medical school. Find ways to train them that don't dilute quality. If that's yet another thing that simply "cannot be done" in the world's most advanced nation, ask yourself what that says about our future.

Civil Service Reform

For activist government to be successful, it needs to be competent, which means it needs the best people it can get. Which means its current hiring and promotion practices need to be dramatically reformed. We'll have more to say on the imperative of "identity-neutral" public policy and law enforcement below. For now, it's important to understand that getting the best person for a job—*any* job—stands in tension with hiring according to any criteria other than qualifications and merit. If we're going to use government power effectively to help industries and improve people's lives—a goal the left has always said it prioritizes—then the people who work in the government need to be good at what they do. Today, at the left's insistence, we treat the government like a make-work jobs program, not as a capable force for good.

We didn't always. One of the best Progressive Era accomplishments was civil service reform that included strict job qualification criteria and rigorous testing. The problem back then was not entirely the same—the Progressives were trying to clean out unqualified machine hacks—but the effect was similar: too many unqualified or underqualified workers in important government positions.

The sensible Progressive Era reforms were scrapped by Jimmy Carter in the name of, you guessed it, "ending discrimination"—in this case, discrimination between well qualified applicants and everyone else. That reversal should be reversed. Restore a sensible and rigorous civil service selection and advancement process. Make bureaucracy competent again.

The Family

Republicans are supposedly the party of "family values." Married people with kids overwhelmingly vote Republican. Yet it's hard to see what the party has done for such voters in the last generation.

However, it's not hard to come up with ideas to help them: ways to encourage and reward marriage, family, and fertility. Hungary, Israel, and Russia have greatly raised their birthrates with policies ranging from favorable tax treatment to forthright pro-family "messaging" that might also be termed "propaganda." Well, so what? In today's America, all the propaganda runs in the other direction: "find yourself," "treat yourself," prioritize your career, delay marriage, having "too many" kids is selfish and harms the environment, and so on. If it didn't sound so kookily conspiratorial to say so, one might speculate that such propaganda is part of our civilization's deliberate effort to cause its own extinction.

It's worth remembering, too, that all of the economic policies discussed above are essentially pro-family formation, since a steady income is an essential foundation of marriage and family. But other economic questions need to be examined from a pro-family perspective as well, including high housing costs and bad public schools. As to the latter, count me skeptical of the usual conservative gimmicks, such as vouchers—which, in any case, Conservatism Inc. only gets excited about when the effort is framed as helping the poor, not the struggling middle class.

The biggest factor making public schools worse—which is to say, unusable by taxpaying middle-class parents—is the inundation of immigrant students, most of them from non-English-speaking households.

Getting control of that problem will go a long way toward "fixing the schools." Which is just another way of saying that all these issues are inextricably linked.

Law and Order

There is no downside whatsoever—political or otherwise—to Republicans taking a strong stand for law and order. Yes, there's a strong blue constituency for criminal leniency. But polling shows that even majorities of Democrats are not entirely down with "de-funding" or "abolishing" the police. It's reasonable to assume that Democrats and independents whom the Republicans have a chance at winning over don't enjoy being beaten or robbed.

After the 2020 woke riots, the time is especially ripe for a law-and-order message. The Democrats are moving fast on their long-cherished goal of decriminalizing nearly everything and turning the whole country into a kind of national revival of John Lindsay's Times Square. "Make *Taxi Driver* a Documentary Again" should be their 2020 slogan.

The coronavirus kicked that effort into overdrive. Democratic governors and mayors are literally emptying the jails of hardened criminals while arresting dads for taking their daughters to the park and small business owners for cutting hair.

This is insane. This level of suicidal-homicidal leniency can't possibly be popular with the broader public—and certainly not with anyone who might so much as contemplate voting Republican.

Own the issue. Promise to enforce the law. Pledge that real crimes that do real injury and really threaten public safety will be prosecuted and punished. But insist that law enforcement will never be used as a tool to harass decent citizens who simply want to live their lives, raise their families, and make a living.

The Harlan Standard

The single most important—and beneficial—reform that could restore some measure of civic comity to American life and extend the life of the country would be to implement and enforce the "Harlan Standard." The name refers to Justice John Marshall Harlan, whose stirring defense and affirmation of color-blind justice was quoted in chapter 3. The idea is very simple: treat every American the same, equally before the law, regardless of race.

Today's America practices the opposite: a legally and socially enforced caste system, which is not merely unjust but fundamentally unstable. At the very least, the longer it goes on, the more it will have to be perpetuated by oppressive and suppressive measures that carry great human and civilizational costs.

In America, equality is not merely the central claim of our founding document; it's in our political DNA. Hence a caste system here is especially destabilizing and demoralizing: a recipe for dystopia and decline, and possibly crack-up or collapse. What Christopher Caldwell has termed America's "second Constitution"—special privileges and preferential treatment for some, official disfavor for others—is increasingly a cudgel with which one coalition of Americans beats another.

There's a better way. Return to—or establish for the first time—what those Americans who gave majority support to the civil rights revolution of the 1960s thought they were getting: equality before the law and neutral, fair treatment for all citizens.

Can we do that? Supporters and critics alike of American civil rights laws have alleged that those laws either require or inevitably lead to quotas, preferences, and special privileges. But their clear language—for example, "without discrimination or segregation on the ground of race, color, religion, or national origin"—not only does not require unequal treatment but explicitly forbids it!

To be sure, civil rights laws have been cynically and dishonestly interpreted to require such measures. But no matter what special pleaders, busybody bureaucrats, and activist judges say, the texts of the laws themselves are clear.

So let's operate our government and our legal system under the assumption that civil rights laws actually mean what they say. That would mean no quotas, no set-asides, no affirmative action, no "diversity" as an end in itself, no "disparate impact," no special treatment of any kind. One clear exception would be for Indian tribes, whose distinct status has a long and well-grounded constitutional history in those tribes' early recognition by the federal government as quasi-foreign nations.

Another possible exception, of questionable constitutionality but justifiable on moral grounds, would be to continue certain privileges for the descendants of American slaves—say, preferences in admissions to public universities and in government hiring and contracting. But no exceptions: not for African or West Indian immigrants or anyone else. And in every other respect black Americans would be treated exactly the same as all other citizens: no better, no worse.

Achieving lasting civic comity would also require at least a partial restoration of the age-old core American principle of freedom of association. This one is tricky. Complete freedom of association entails the comprehensive freedom of private individuals and institutions to discriminate on any basis whatsoever—including race, sex, ethnicity, religion, and other factors inherent to an individual's personhood and sense of identity.

Yet almost no Americans believe that such wide-open discrimination is fair or just. (At least not when practiced against nonwhites or women. All the blues, and maybe a third of the reds, are perfectly happy to see it practiced against straight white men.) More to the point, that kind of discrimination—allowing, say, restaurants to refuse service or businesses not to hire solely on the basis of race—clearly violates the letter and spirit of civil rights law, which Americans of all races overwhelmingly support.

The remedy is simple: enforce civil rights laws as written—which means requiring a higher standard of proof than "disparate impact." In a rational anti-discrimination regime designed to unify the citizenry, a plaintiff seeking redress would have to establish, with concrete evidence, that he or she personally and intentionally had been denied some benefit, or inflicted with some punishment, solely or largely because of his or her race or sex.

And no more government-forced social experimentation—such as, for instance, the Obama administration's many-tentacled, intrusive effort to reengineer American cities, towns, communities, and neighborhoods along the government's preferred racial and ethnic lines.

We also need to ensure that the fair application of anti-discrimination law protects America's core founding principle of religious liberty. There will inevitably be some tension here: a church, faith-based organization, and even an individual believer "discriminates" when it (he) selects or rejects associates, or grants or denies a service, based on religious conviction. For America to remain American—and just—this must be allowed. Forcing, say, a Bible study group to accept atheists under the rubric of "civil rights" makes a mockery of Bible study, atheism, civil rights, and even the pretense of freedom of association. Yet this kind of bullying is one of the chief ways that civil rights law is routinely used to attack faith and undermine, weaken, and destroy those voluntary associations that Tocqueville shows were the lifeblood of American democracy.

I'm well aware that under such a regime, successful discrimination suits would be rarer than they are today. Good. The current regime wastes a great deal of resources, weakens institutions, and breeds societal resentment and distrust. The less we do that, the better. Also, and not incidentally, to be tarred as a "racist" is the worst epithet one can endure in our society. It's career-ending and often life-destroying—a virtual guarantee of un-personing, of erasure from the social fabric. With consequences so grave, it's incumbent on—a moral duty of—those making the charge (plaintiffs) and those affirming it (judges and juries) to be absolutely certain they're right.

The left will surely howl that under such a system, mass discrimination would return with a vengeance. In their manufactured nightmare, aggressive enforcement of civil rights law is a rickety dam barely holding back the floodwaters of American racism.

But that's preposterous. All indicators—public opinion polls, admissions policies, hiring practices, private behavior, you name it—tell the exact opposite story. There is no widespread American sentiment in any sector of society—and less than zero among the ruling class and its institutions—favoring discrimination against minorities. To the contrary, the American people as a whole vehemently oppose all discrimination, which is why the ruling class must tie itself in knots rationalizing why the discrimination that it most definitely *does* practice is somehow not "discrimination."

Quotas and preferences have never been broadly popular. Indeed, depending on how polling questions are phrased, majorities of blacks sometimes express opposition to such policies. That's why the ruling class must dissemble about how preferences really work and constantly shift the rationale from "temporary remedy" to "diversity as compelling state interest" to "necessary permanent redress for permanent structural racism." Yet despite all this, nine states have banned such practices—six by a vote of the full electorate. Those bans, of course, extend only to state-level hiring, contracting, and university admissions. But the fact that the bans were passed with popular support suggests hope for a future race-blind America. Indeed, even in blue Washington State, voters in 2019 rejected an effort to reimpose preferences, twenty-one years after the practice had been banned.

For a multiethnic republic to work, everyone must feel that he is an equal participant in the enterprise. Some will end up richer and more prominent than others, of course; that's the way of the world. But all must feel that they have an equal chance or that, at the very least, no artificial restraints are placed on their or their children's potential rise. This principle—already enshrined in law—once enforced in practice could have a unifying effect on our fraying republic.

Foreign and Defense Policy

This one really isn't that hard. Maintain the strongest, best-trained, best-equipped, most technologically advanced military in the world—and then don't use it. Treat the military as a whole the way we view the nuclear arsenal: its primary purpose should be to deter, not fight, wars.

It's there if we need it—well-armed, well-trained, and ready—but the animating principle of our foreign policy should be to ensure that we never do.

The United States has a handful of core interests that bear watching. We don't want any aggressive overseas power to gain a foothold in the Western Hemisphere—especially not in North America. At present, China is the only such power capable of even trying, and its leaders are well aware of American sensitivities on this point, which is why their incursions are more subtle. Massive espionage, debasing our corporations, corrupting our universities with cash and flooding them with spies, buying up strategic assets, and the like—all these not only further the basic goal of establishing toeholds throughout our society but can be, and are, defended by well-paid lobbyists and unpaid ideologues. All of it, and more, will have to be creatively checked.

Second, as a commercial republic and (still) the world's leading economic power, America has a core interest in ensuring that the world's two other leading centers of wealth and innovation—Northwest Europe and the Pacific Rim—remain on friendly terms with us and don't fall under the sway of a hostile foreign power. The only country with a realistic prospect of threatening that is, again, China, which is doing a very good job of altering the strategic balance in Asia. Helping our Indo-Pacific allies stay out from under China's thumb while not provoking a war will be a tricky business. One thing seems certain: the pre-Trump policy combination of naval saber-rattling plus obsequious economic and diplomatic concession didn't work. A core challenge for foreign policy going forward will be to get this calculus right.

One thing that might help would be a new relationship with Russia. Rapprochement with Moscow seems almost impossible to imagine after four years of unhinged—and almost entirely false—anti-Russian propaganda. Yet our two countries share a number of common interests on which we could profitably cooperate if the nonsense could be put behind us. Russia is a "threat" to Europe only insofar as Europe's leaders allow themselves to be threatened—for instance, by voluntarily yoking their countries' energy supplies to a pipeline Moscow can turn on and off at will. Russia has neither the ambition nor the ability to conquer Europe. To the contrary, Russia wants desperately to be *part* of Europe—a peripheral part, to be sure, while also retaining its influence in Asia, but an integral part all the same.

Easing tensions and accommodating Russia's desire for a seat at the European, and even Transatlantic, table is possible—if American and European elites give up their fantastical insistence that Russia "democratize" as the prerequisite. It's conceivable that Russia could become more moderate—indeed, compared to its Soviet days, the country has already traveled a great distance in that direction!—but Russia will always be, at least compared to what we think of as "democracy," "authoritarian." And corrupt. And not a little bit gangsterish. I don't want to make a silly moral equivalence claim; however corrupt we are, I prefer to believe that our ruling class doesn't murder journalists. But the by-product of Washington's lectures to Moscow are not improved Russian behavior but worse U.S.–Russia relations.

Russia is part of our civilizational "sect" in ways that China can never be. For a thousand years, Russia has played an integral part in European history, the history of the West. Tchaikovsky, Mussorgsky, and Rimsky-Korsakov, among many others, are constantly played in our concert halls, just as Chekhov, Tolstoy, and Dostoyevsky are still read (by those in the West who still read).

To be sure, there are obstacles to greater cooperation, perhaps the foremost being Russia's seemingly intractable anti-Americanism. I confess I don't know whether that can be overcome. But it's at least possible that were we to stop the pointless demonization, cease the ineffectual moral lectures, accept the inevitability of Russian influence in the regions on its borders, forgo foolish talk of bringing Ukraine and Georgia into NATO, and try in good faith to make real deals that benefit both countries, tensions might ease and new vistas for cooperation open up. At any rate, all of those things are worth doing for their own sake, for our own interests, whether or not they improve relations with Moscow.

If they did, however, the Transatlantic Alliance, along with our alliances in the Anglosphere and in the Indo-Pacific, would be immeasurably strengthened against our one common foe. The West itself might gather renewed strength if the two Western countries among the world's three greatest powers at long last found themselves on the same side. It's probably too much to hope for. But the benefits are so obvious and potentially immense that it's worth a try.

As for the Middle East, America's long-term priority ought to be gradual disentanglement. Our chief interest there—ensuring that oil flows freely out the Strait of Hormuz—will decline in importance if our domestic energy supplies grow. We will always have an interest in preventing a hostile power from seizing oil supplies and using them against us, just as we will always have an interest in preventing religiously or ideologically (or both) motivated states or groups from doing violence to our homeland or people. But those threats can be deterred—and, if necessary, countered—with a much smaller force presence than we maintain in the region today. And perhaps someday soon, given technological advances, without any presence in the region at all.

Closer to home, Mexican drug cartels are the gravest danger we face. These heavily armed gangs kill Americans with guns and drugs, and terrorize large swaths of the Southwest. Some have actually won tactical confrontations with the Mexican military; the Bowery Boys they ain't. It's time to consider using our own military—whose ultimate purpose is after all to protect the lives of American citizens and the territorial integrity of the United States—to defeat or at least beat back these cartels and secure our border against armed, hostile incursion. Increased drone and other surveillance activity could not only help secure the border but serve as a testing ground for emerging technology.

Other than that, we need to ensure that sea lanes and other transportation routes vital to our commerce remain open and unmolested. It's hard to think of any other urgent interests that require massive American diplomatic or military engagement—which means that something like two-thirds of what we do today on the global stage is at best unnecessary and at worst counterproductive.

STRATEGY AND TACTICS

"How are we going to accomplish any of this?" you must be asking, exasperated. I didn't say it would be easy! I didn't even say that I know how. But here are some thoughts.

A top priority must be to attack, relentlessly, the legitimacy of the ruling class—to deprive them of any pretense of legitimacy. They are unpatriotic, hostile to the common good, ignorant and uneducated (despite their endless list of credentials), selfish and venal, corrupt, seditious, foreign-influenced, hypocritical, racist (but the "good" kind), above the law, moralistic and hectoring, anti-constitutional and anti-democratic. Ridicule them. Constantly expose their corruption and hypocrisy.

The fake-news media—the ruling class's Praetorian Guard—must also be attacked, mocked, and discredited every bit as relentlessly. It would be nice if some conservative billionaire, instead of showering cash on the usual failed think tanks and magazines, could step forward and help found something new—say, a new cable channel? (Nothing against Fox, but Tucker Carlson aside, it's never been especially populist and still isn't.)

Speaking of conservative billionaires, the broader culture is far more influential than cable news and think tank policy shops. Why has no one founded a nationalist-populist movie studio or TV network? I'm aware that the barriers to entry are high, but we must admit to ourselves that so long as the culture remains 100 percent our enemy, victory will elude us. Something bold, risky, and improbable will have to be attempted. Who's willing to try?

Assuming we can win a few elections as this new majority coalition is being built, we need to become much less timid about using government power. In particular, heads need to roll in our corrupt "law enforcement" and "intelligence" agencies. If Republicans cannot find it within themselves to use their legitimate powers to punish genuine illegality and abuse of power, they will deserve the ignominious end that would surely follow for them. They should also not shrink from wielding anti-trust and First Amendment law to break up the tech monopolies and force social media companies to allow free speech.

If the ruling class's Praetorian Guard is the media, its Capitoline Hill is the university. A direct assault on your adversary's strongest point is usually ill-advised. A siege has a better chance of success.

Student debt is perhaps the wickedest form of predatory lending practiced in America today. It bloats up rapacious universities, which gorge their endowments and pad their ranks with frivolous and sinister "administrators," while weighing down young people with crippling debts that at best delay family formation and at worst impoverish their entire lives. Student debt exploitation is backed by the full faith and credit of the United States government—and by law impossible to discharge in bankruptcy. Repeal that law. Allow students to get out from under such debt and put the matriculating school, not the taxpayers, on the hook for it. But for undergraduate degrees only. Would-be commissars and cancellation-enforcers dumb enough to go into hock for useless, frivolous, or destructive M.A. and Ph.D.s are on their own.

Government grants are the universities' other main source of income. Much, if not most, of the money goes to "research" that is either pointless or corrosive. Cut off federal funding for all such dreck—basically everything but science, defense, and medicine, perhaps with limited exceptions for true excellence in the humanities and social sciences. In addition, all grants should be made contingent on a series of reforms that guarantee protections for speech and civil rights. For example, no more Title IX show trials for young men accused of sexual assault who are never told their accuser nor allowed to mount a defense. That kind of Kafkaesque oppression stops—or the money does. We should also make government grants contingent on the elimination of race-based admissions policies.

I don't know how to do this, but a way needs to be found to decouple college "education" from the broader job market, that is, to reverse the trend that makes a B.A. degree "entry level" for jobs that do not require a university education. Lots of students who don't need or want to go to college—who don't learn much nor enjoy the experience—go anyway and spend themselves into lifetime penury because they feel they must. Perhaps some patriotic, reformist business owners could get the ball rolling by making a big public show of dropping the B.A. requirement for a number of positions.

I have no idea how do to this one either, but if it can't be done, we're toast: reform primary education to make it patriotic and assimilationist. Our schools used to be good at this. Kids want to believe in and be proud of their country. The anti-American garbage hate propaganda we bathe them in today is not only false and harmful—to them and to the country—it goes against their natural instinct. America has all but "diversified" away any semblance of a common culture, a common American identity. The key to reestablishing one, if such is possible, must be the schools.

While we're "fixing the schools," let's also take on the education establishment's war on boyhood and masculinity. Biological sex is real, an immutable characteristic of nature, and boys are not girls. Every parent of one knows how exasperating boys can be, and we (partially) sympathize with teachers and others who wish they'd calm the hell down. But the solution is not to dope them up or to punish them into becoming other than who they are. It is to sculpt, channel, and refine their natural masculine energy in productive directions. America will not benefit from raising another generation of sissies and beaten dogs. This is another hard one to solve, given that our entire educational establishment is all-in for the feminization of boys. Perhaps a good start would be to launch a network of all-boys schools, focusing on books that teach the manly virtues and appeal to boys' tastes (they love military history), with a strong emphasis on sports and physical competition.

But so long as we're dreaming, we may as well dream big. How about some conservative money for an academy, or network of academies, walled off from contemporary frivolity and filth, that teaches classics and the Great Books in the morning, useful skills such as woodwork and hunting in the afternoons, and mixed martial arts at night? Sort of like a military school, but more "holistic."

As we fight on, we must never give a millimeter to any attack on free speech, gun rights, due process, or any other fundamental, natural, and historic American liberty. We must instead turn every leftist attack on our liberties back on them and counterattack. Force the left onto the defensive whenever and wherever possible. Recognize that attacks on free speech come in two forms: calls to suppress "hate speech" and complaints about "money in politics." See these for what they are. The former is nothing but an attempt to censor any message the left doesn't like—especially ones they think undermine and threaten their power. The latter is just another way to protect their monopoly: "getting money out of politics" doesn't apply to the billions the left pours through the legacy and social media Megaphones. Leftist complaints are just attempts to disarm their enemies.

This should go without saying, but we must defend the Electoral College at all costs. Trump is wrong about this, to his own detriment. Without the Electoral College, he couldn't have won the first time and he'd have no chance the second. Nor will any of us if the left gets their way and eliminates or finds a way to bypass it. A national popular vote is the surest and quickest route to blue tyranny: massive votebanks in the coastal cities overwhelming, and disregarding, the votes of everyone everywhere else. The Electoral College functions exactly as was designed: it forces presidential candidates to get out of their strongholds and pay attention to other regions of the country, and it prevents small states and rural regions from being entirely ignored. It is, quite literally, one of the last bulwarks standing between Middle America and catastrophe.

Attack the kritarchy. Use Congress (to the extent that we control it) not merely to confirm judges but to impeach the most egregiously activist and anti-constitutional judges. Personal misconduct should no longer be the sole standard. Impeachment is a constitutional—and political—remedy for removing officials who abuse their enumerated powers. Judges who legislate from the bench should be forced to explain their rulings to the American people. Actual removals would no doubt be difficult, but a few impeachment trials might do wonders toward deterring the worst excesses of our robed masters.

Aggressively defend the integrity (such as it is) of our voting system. That means playing defense—opposing all efforts by the Democrats to loosen standards, undermine the system's integrity, and make fraud easier—as well as offense: insisting on and fighting for tighter standards to ensure that only legally eligible (and living!) voters participate in our elections, and that each voter votes only once.

The most important thing we need to do is unquestionably the hardest: create, and elevate, a new elite. Here is what Sam Francis proposed in the wake of the failure of Pat Buchanan's first (1992) presidential campaign:

> The main focus of a Middle American Right should be the reclamation of cultural power, the patient elaboration of an alternative culture within but against the regime—within the belly of the beast but indigestible by it. Instead of the uselessness of a Diogenes' search for an honest presidential candidate or a Fabian quest for a career in the bureaucracy, a Middle American Right should begin working in and with schools, churches, clubs, women's groups, youth organizations, civic and professional associations, local government, the military and police forces, and even in the much-dreaded labor unions to create a radicalized Middle American consciousness that can perceive the ways in which exploitation of the middle classes is institutionalized and understand how it can be resisted. Only when this kind of infrastructure of cultural hegemony is developed can a Middle American

Right seek meaningful political power without coalitions with the Left and bargaining with the regime.

Great. How?

One thing's for sure: a new elite is not going to emerge from the Ivy League. My own institution—Hillsdale College—can, and should, play a leading role. But one college can't do it alone. Others will have to take up the charge. It might be time for conservative billionaires to found a new college. Where they'd find good faculty is not an easy question to answer, given the dismal products being cranked out by America's Ph.D. factories. So we might have to found a few graduate schools, too—as Hillsdale College has in fact done, twice. More will be needed.

Nor, necessarily, should we invest all our hopes for a new elite on a new or reformed higher education system. Relying on colleges to produce America's present elite is partly what got us into the present mess. Perhaps we should be looking elsewhere for elites; suggestions welcome.

One last appeal to red-state grandees, and to anyone with a little on the ball dissatisfied with the present elite and the trajectory they've got us on: you already *are* an elite. Start acting like it. Get involved. Run for office. Lead. Your country—your people—need you.

TO THE DORKWADS, TO MAKE MUCH OF TIME

I address my penultimate words to those "principled conservatives" appalled by my many departures from "conservative principle" who might nonetheless be persuadable.

Yes, this book—especially this chapter—contains many blasphemies against 1981's *Mandate for Leadership*. That's not to criticize that volume overmuch. It served its purpose well, in its time. But its time has long since passed.

The challenges of today are mostly, in some cases entirely, different. As such, they require different responses. Talk of tariffs, industrial policy, government-funded research and development, and state-backed

"Buy American" mandates no doubt made your hair stand on end. It's all so very "intrusive" and "anti-market." The government can't be "picking winners"! Use government power to stop social media censorship, propaganda, and monopoly suffocation? But those are private companies! The almighty market has decided! Reform draconian "civil rights" enforcement? That one especially will be hard for the poor conservatives, who pledge eternal loyalty to the Constitution, constitutional principle, and the rule of law but in practice countenance one rank violation after another. I half expect to see a David French column explaining why "all men are created equal" is, when you really think about it, "racist."

But those of you who want to take part in what's coming will have to get over all that. Whether you like it or not, the debate on the right is going in a populist-nationalist direction—as it should. America's foremost economic challenge today is not high marginal tax rates; it's deindustrialization and financialization. Massive and growing wealth gaps actually *are* terrible for individuals, destructive of communities and corrosive to society. Also, if it makes you feel any better, many of those you claim are your heroes, from Hamilton to Lincoln to Reagan, were perfectly fine with tariffs, industrial policy, and the use of government power to improve the lives of ordinary families. They even enacted those things!

The name you have chosen for yourself—"conservative"—presupposes a thing to be conserved. If, in your case, that's Reagan-Gingrich era tax and regulatory dogma, you're a fool. The true object of the true conservative is not any one policy or set of policies. Nor is it "the economy." It is not even, in the American context—here comes a big blasphemy!—the Constitution. Let me repeat that for emphasis: *the Constitution is not the highest thing.* The Constitution is a means—an exalted means, but still a means, not an end. The people are more important than the Constitution, which exists to serve the people and not vice versa.

Few wish more fervently than I for the restoration of American constitutional principle. Yet the only way for that to happen is to strengthen and reenergize the best habits of the American people.

Conservatism has, of late, failed to conserve—or do much of anything for—the American people. It has also, I note with some irony, failed miserably at conserving the one thing it really cares about, namely "the economy," at least outside Manhattan and Palo Alto. But its most miserable failure of all has been what it has allowed to be done to the Constitution, the shredding of which conservatives have either fecklessly opposed or countenanced with rhetorical support along the lines of "The Conservative Case for [Insert Latest Leftist Insanity Here]."

These failures are inextricably intertwined. Our Constitution only "works" if and to the extent that it fits the character and capabilities of the people it nominally governs, and vice versa. It "works" only for a stable country in which everyone has a chance and a stake, a country whose economy is not a private preserve of the privileged.

So, "conservatives": if the Constitution is what you care about most, then you should have been far more concerned with helping the American people remain fit to maintain it and be governed by it. That would have meant first and foremost promoting those institutions, habits, and practices that promote life, health, and virtue. It would have meant protecting the jobs and industries that put food on people's tables, give meaning to their lives, sustain their cities and towns, and support the self-reliance necessary to republicanism. It would have meant defending people's traditions and faith from the hectoring, destructive, vindictive, revolutionary madness of the woke left and, increasingly, of woke capital. It would have meant making a real effort to stem the endless flow of legal immigrants who take American jobs, reduce American wages, overwhelm American schools, and transform American neighborhoods. In short, you should have supported and not opposed the government "picking winners," insofar as those "winners" are ordinary Americans and not a predatory elite or hostile or dependent foreigners.

But you—or most of you—didn't do any of that. Some of you were passive. Some actively helped the other side. And a few clearly relish backstabbing those ostensibly on your side. Indeed, for a few of you—let's call you the John McCain wing of the conservative intellectuals—it's obvious there's nothing in life you enjoy more.

In many respects, I was once like you: a free-trade absolutist, "small government" anti-tax fanatic, and Iraq War supporter. Some of my former positions I think were right for their times but no longer; others I later realized I had gotten wrong even then. The most I can say for myself is that I tried not to dig in like an Imperial Japanese soldier still defending some lonely atoll in 1974. That, and I always knew not merely *what* but *who* I was for.

Those of you who can see past your own errors and join this struggle, I for one welcome to the fight—and promise to keep the "I told you so"s to a minimum. If you can't, you're irrelevant already. The extent to which you can still draw a salary is just further proof of the conservative establishment's moribund uselessness.

ONE LAST MODEST PROPOSAL

A practical way to ease Americans' present discontent and exasperation with each other would be to allow for counties, cities, and towns unhappy with their current state government to join another. There are precedents. The counties that became Maine split from Massachusetts in 1820, and—more famously—those that became West Virginia left Virginia at the onset of the Civil War. Fittingly, at the time of this writing, West Virginia has generously offered to welcome Virginia counties disaffected with rule from newly, aggressively blue Richmond.

So far nothing has come of it. But why shouldn't the move be allowed to proceed if both the welcoming state and the exiting counties want it?

Some objectors will disingenuously point to Lincoln's first inaugural address, the ne plus ultra anti-secession argument. But Lincoln was talking about replacing ballots with bullets in a sovereign state—overturning not merely the outcome of one election but the form of government itself, reverting from deliberative republicanism to force. The peaceful rearrangement of political and administrative boundaries *within* a state is an entirely different act, with far lesser—and less grave—consequences. Indeed, in the latter case the consequences may be entirely salutary: there is ample precedent in history and around the world of countries redrawing internal lines to suit shifts in population and interests.

Just to preempt sophists, I here caution readers that some will try to buffalo you by facilely equating the peculiarly American use of the term "state" for our fifty subordinate regional governments with the broader—and universal—meaning of state as "sovereign and independent country." Lincoln said secession was unlawful, unconstitutional, and immoral—but this hypocrite Anton who claims to be a Lincolnite is endorsing the very practice! The argument is false and will be offered in bad faith. If you wish to waste a moment of your time, which I don't recommend, remind such liars that the anti-secessionist Lincoln not only supported but presided over the division of Virginia. The decisive point is that this proposal is here proffered for precisely Lincolnite reasons: to save the Union and keep the current territory and population of the United States together.

In the Maine and West Virginia cases, new states were formed, an act for which the Constitution requires "the consent of the Legislatures of the States concerned as well as of the Congress." (In the case of Virginia, then in rebellion against the government of the United States, consent to the formation of West Virginia was neither sought nor required.)

The Constitution is, however, silent on the question of transferring a county from one state to another. No doubt should rural Virginia counties seek to join Charleston, Richmond wouldn't like it—all that lost tax revenue! Look how many fewer people to boss around!

But, constitutionally speaking, the state government would have no power to stop it—nor, if we want to speculate along such lines, the means. All it could do is take the issue to federal court, where, admittedly, any outcome is possible regardless of the law, and any outcome favorable to red interests extremely unlikely. There's little question that any blue state capitol could easily join with the federal judiciary—and at some point in the not-distant future, a Democratic administration—to block any such action. Which would be tantamount to admitting the charge leveled in chapter 5, that in New America "democracy" just means blues outvoting reds, effectively nullifying their franchise. The real question, again, is whether wiser, cooler heads would let such peaceful means proceed as a way of improving civic harmony and extending the life of the republic.

The precedent of even one county, in any state, freeing itself of its distant solons would likely inspire many more attempts. Eastern Washington and Oregon joining Idaho, parts of downstate Illinois joining Iowa, Indiana, or Missouri—the possibilities are endless.

Indeed, such a movement may gain such momentum that, for the first time since the admission of Alaska and Hawaii, the country might see the attempted formation and admission of new states. Far-northern California and the southernmost part of Oregon have been trying for years to break away, join together, and form the "State of Jefferson." They haven't gotten anywhere yet, but the mere fact that the movement exists indicates discontent—specifically, the discontent of rural people with their urban masters. Should that discontent grow, the movement might succeed and make Jefferson, and other new states, become reality.

And why not? Fifty may be a nice round number, but there's nothing magical about it. If rearranging the states helps the people within them live happier and get along better, why shouldn't we do it? The flag has been redesigned before.

Both possibilities—redrawing the map among the existing fifty, or breaking parts of them up in ways that yield a new number—raise the inevitable question of the composition of the Senate. Each side will try to gain the advantage—and prevent the other side from doing the same. Any "reform" that gives blues or reds a clear, potentially decades-long lock on control of the Senate or the Electoral College will not only be a nonstarter but would only reinforce the very problem it's ostensibly trying to solve.

But here, too, there's precedent. It became an informal but strictly observed custom after the Missouri Compromise to admit states to the Union only in pairs—one slave, one free—so as to preserve the balance in the Senate. Modern political scientists don't know much, but they do have a very good bead on who votes for whom. It would be easy enough to redraw state lines with senatorial balance in mind—not to guarantee any particular outcome but the opposite: to prevent either side from achieving total dominance.

A similar, and even easier, measure would be to allow counties and incorporated cities to break up, or merge, as they so choose. There's ample precedent for this too—indeed, much more than there is for reorganization at the state level. The purpose would be the same: to allow like to join with like, to govern local matters in their own ways, free of top-down diktats.

Perhaps paradoxically, it is through greater pluralism that we can achieve greater comity. Today, every little thing turns into a bitter red–blue fight. We could live together better if we could give each other a little more space, become a little more willing to leave one another alone.

Similar changes were made in Rome, which prolonged the life span of that state as a free republic by at least two centuries. Here is how Machiavelli describes those reforms:

> Because of the liberality that the Romans practiced in giving citizenship to foreigners, so many new men were born in Rome that they began to have so much share in the votes that the government began to vary, and it departed from the things and from the men with which it was accustomed to go. When Quintus Fabius, who was censor, perceived this, he put all these new men from whom this disorder derived under four tribes, so that by being shut in such small spaces they could not corrupt all Rome. This affair was well understood by Fabius, and he applied a convenient remedy without an

alteration; it was so well received by the citizenry that he deserved to be called Maximus.

A reorganization of state, county, and city lines in America would be an act of statesmanship on the grandest scale since the Civil War, perhaps since the founding itself. For redeeming Roman freedom after its humiliating sack by the Gauls, Marcus Furius Camillus was given the title "Second Founder of Rome." A statesman who reordered America in the manner of Fabius, ensuring us another century or two of greatness, might earn a similar honorific. Are there any among us with the justice, moderation, talent, courage, and wisdom to perform this great act?

Index